THE REAL GUIDE

PERU

REAL GUIDE CREDITS

Series Editor: Mark Ellingham
U.S. Text Editor: Jamie Jensen
Editorial: Martin Dunford, John Fisher, Jack Holland
Production: Susanne Hillen
Typesetting: Greg Ward
Design: Andrew Oliver

Many **thanks** to Betsy Wagenhauser and the South American Explorers' Club, *Expediciones Mayuc* in Cuzco, Peru's best photographer, Carlos Montenegro, and most importantly to my wife Claire and our young children—Tess, Bethan, Maxi Merlin, and baby Teilo.

Published in the United States by Prentice Hall Trade Division, A Division of Simon & Schuster Inc., 15 Columbus Circle, New York, NY 10023.

Typeset in Linotron Univers and Century Old Style.
Printed in the United States by R.R. Donnelley & Sons.
Incidental drawings by Kate Wilkinson.
Illustrations in Part One and Part Three by Ed Briant; Basics illustration by Dilwyn Jenkins;
Contexts illustration by Henry Iles.

Includes index.

Library of Congress Cataloging-in-Publication Data

Jenkins, Dilwyn.
The real guide: Peru / written and researched by Dilwyn Jenkins; with additional research and accounts by Peter Schoonmaker, Mike Paul, Ted Bowden, Duncan Corpe, and Peter Cloudesley;
drawings by Kate Wilkinson; edited by Dilwyn Jenkins with Mark Ellingham and John Fisher.
352p.
Updated ed. of: The rough guide to Peru. 1985.
ISBN 0-13-783796-8 : $12.95
1. Peru—Description and travel—1981—Guidebooks.
I. Dilwyn Jenkins. Rough Guide to Peru. II. Title.
F3409.5.J46 1988
918.504'633—dc20   89-16325
                                                                                      CIP

THE REAL GUIDE

PERU

WRITTEN AND RESEARCHED BY

DILWYN JENKINS

With additional research and accounts by
Peter Schoonmaker, Mike Paul, Ted Bowden,
Duncan Corpe, and Peter Cloudesley

Edited by
DILWYN JENKINS
with Mark Ellingham and John Fisher

PRENTICE HALL ■ NEW YORK

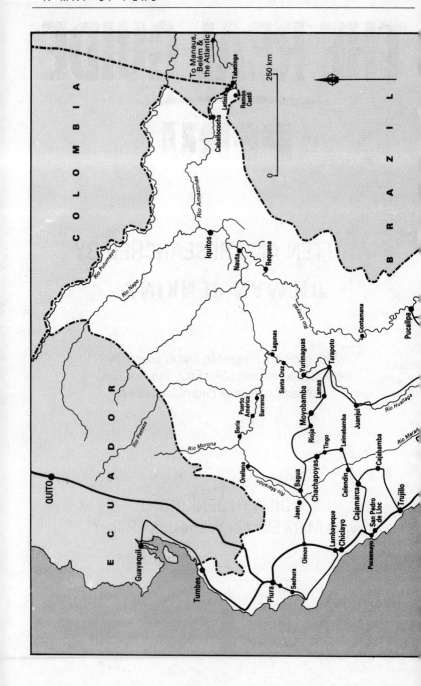

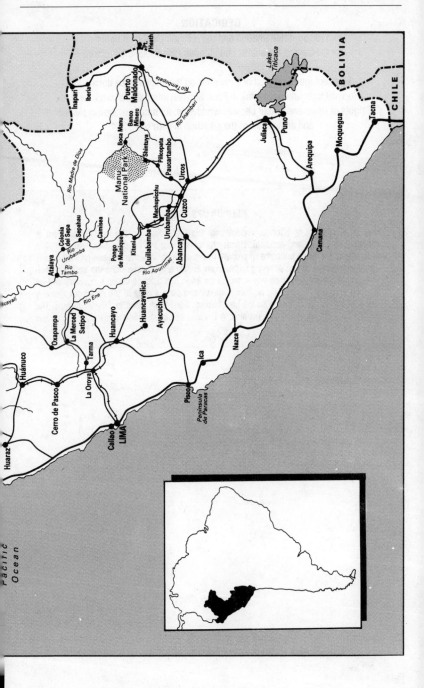

DEDICATION

To self-determination and the recognition of land rights
for the Campa-Ashaninka and all other indigenous tribal groups.

A percentage of the author's royalties on this book will be donated to
Survival International's work in Peru. Survival International work for the
rights of threatened tribal peoples worldwide; for details of their activities
and an account of the situation in Peru see p.324.

HELP US UPDATE

We've gone to a lot of effort to ensure that this first edition of the Real Guide: Peru is completely up-to-date and accurate. Things change so fast in Peru, however, that your help will be invaluable when we come to prepare future editions. Whether you can provide details on a new jungle expedition or hiking route, or are simply able to keep sharp the basic information on places to stay, opening hours and so on, even just a few lines on a postcard will be gratefully received. We'll credit all contributions, and send a copy of the new book (or any other Real Guide, if you prefer) for the best letters. Send them along to: Dilwyn Jenkins, The Real Guides, Prentice Hall Trade Division, A Division of Simon & Schuster Inc., 15 Columbus Circle, New York, NY 10023.

CONTENTS

Introduction viii

INTRODUCTION

P eru—for travelers—is the most varied and exciting of all South American experiences. Most people visualize the country as mountainous, and are aware of the great Inca relics, but the splendor, both of the immense desert coastline and of the vast tracts of tropical rainforest, often comes as a complete surprise. Dividing these contrasting environments, chain after chain of breathtaking peaks—over seven thousand meters high and four hundred kilometers wide in places—ripple the entire length of the nation: **the Andes**. So distinct are the three regions that it is very difficult to generalize about the country. One thing you can say for sure is that for travelers Peru offers a unique opportunity to experience an incredibly wide range of spectacular scenery, and a wealth of human culture.

Racially, too, Peru is diverse. Still very much dominated by the Spanish and *mestizo* descendants of Pizarro, some ten million Peruvians—more than half the population—are nevertheless of pure Indian blood. In the country, native life can have changed little in the last four centuries. But "progress" is gradually transforming Peru—already the cities wear a distinctly Western aspect, and roads and tracks now connect almost every corner of the Republic with the industrial *urbanizaciones* that dominate the few fertile valleys along the coast. Only the Amazon jungle—nearly two-thirds of Peru's landmass but with a mere fraction of its population—remains beyond its reach, and even here lumber companies, cocaine producers, and settlers are taking an increasing toll.

Following the Spanish Conquest in the sixteenth century, the colony of Peru developed by exploiting its Inca treasures, vast mineral deposits, and the essentially slave labour which the colonists extracted from the indigenous people. The Incas and their native allies were unable to realistically resist the mounted and fire-armed conquerors. Achieving "Liberty" from the Spanish crown, Peru became a Republic in traditional South American style on the back of the European Enlightenment and in the shadow of both the French and the American Revolutions. As we enter the 1990s, recent developments in Peru, like the growing power of the terrorist organization *Sendero Luminoso* and the devastating economic crisis, are responsible for what appears to be a new phase in Peruvian politics, ushered in with increasing violence both in Lima and the more remote provinces.

Always an exciting place to visit, and frantic as it sometimes appears on the surface, the laid-back calmness of the Peruvian temperament continues to underlie life even in the cities. Lima may operate at a terrifying pace at times—the traffic, the money-grabbers, the political situation—but there always seems to be time to talk, for a *ceviche*, another drink . . . It's a country where the resourceful traveler can break through barriers of class, race, and language far more easily than most of its inhabitants can. And where the limousines and villas of the elite remain little more than a thin veneer on a nation whose roots lie firmly in its ethnic traditions.

Where To Go And When

With each region offering so many different attractions, it's hard to generalize about which places are best to visit first. **Cuzco** seems the most obvious place to start—a beautiful and bustling colonial city, the ancient heart of the Inca Empire, it's surrounded by some of the most spectacular mountain landscapes and palatial ruins in Peru, and by magnificent hiking country. Yet along **the coast**, too, there are fascinating archeological sites—the bizarre **Nazca Lines** south of Lima, the great adobe city of **Chan Chan** in the north—and a rich crop of sea life, easiest accessible around the **Paracas National Park**. The coastal towns, almost all of them with superb beaches, also offer nightlife and great food. For mountains and long-distance treks there are the stunning glacial lakes, snowy peaks, and little-known ruins of the **northern sierra**, above all around **Huaraz** and **Cajamarca**. If it's wildlife you're into, there's abundance almost everywhere; but **the jungle** provides startling opportunities for close and exotic encounters. From the comfort of tourist lodges in **Iquitos** to the more exciting river excursions around **Puerto Maldonado**, the fauna and flora of the world's largest tropical forest can be experienced first-hand with relative ease.

The attractions of each area are discussed in greater detail in the chapter introductions. Picking the **"best" time to visit** any of them, however, is complicated by the country's physical characteristics. Summer along the **desert coast** more or less fits the expected image of the Southern Hemisphere—extremely hot and sunny from December to March (especially in the north), cooler and with a frequent hazy mist between April and November. But only in the polluted environs of Lima does the coastal winter ever get cold enough to necessitate a sweater: swimming is possible all year round, though the water itself (thanks to the Humboldt Current) is cool to cold at the best of times. To swim or surf for any length of time you'd need to follow local custom and wear a wetsuit. Apart from the occasional shower over Lima it hardly ever rains in the desert. The freak exception, every ten years or so, is when the shift in ocean currents of *El Niño* causes torrential

---

TERRORISM: A WARNING

Terrorism, which has made the world news and worries some potential visitors, is still a real and an increasing problem for Peru. But if you keep away from the danger zones—particularly around Ayacucho and coca growing areas of the jungle—it shouldn't affect you. Even in the risky areas it is rarely aimed at tourists, and you are still more likely to be held on suspicion of being a guerrilla or gunrunner than actually to encounter one.

However, the situation is worsening, and armed robbery is also a growing threat. The author strongly recommends that visitors to Peru register with their embassy on arrival in Lima and check with them which areas are considered too dangerous to risk traveling through. The situation is unpredictable and open to rapid change. Internally, you are safest traveling by air whenever possible.

The U.S. State Department offers advice to travelers on ☎202/647-5225. They are always extremely pessimistic. For a more upbeat view, try the South American Explorers' Club (☎800/274-0568), whose information may also be more recent.

downpours, devastating crops, roads and communities all down the coast. It last broke in 1983.

In the Andes, seasons are more clearly marked, with heavy rains from December to March and a warm, relatively dry period from June to September. Inevitably, though, there are always some sunny weeks in the rainy season and wet ones in the dry. A similar pattern dominates the **jungle,** though rainfall in the *selva* is heavier and more frequent, and it's hot and humid all year round. Ideally, then, the coast should be visited around January while it's hot, and the mountains and jungles are at their best after the rains, from May until September. Since this is hardly likely to be possible there's little point in worrying about it—the country's attractions are invariably enough to override the need for guarantees of good weather.

THE PERUVIAN CLIMATE				
	Sunny Season	Rainy Season	Approx. Temp (°C)	Annual Rainfall
			Jan. July	
Coast	Dec.–March	Rare	18–30 13–20	0.50mm
Andes	May–Sept.	Dec.–March	5–15 0–10	400–1000mm
Jungle	May–Oct.		20–30 20–30	1,000–2000mm

PART ONE

THE

BASICS

GETTING THERE

BY AIR

There's a rather confusing array of flights and fares to Peru from North America; most routes go through Miami, but the prices vary wildly depending on the time of year and from whom you buy. This is one itinerary where careful shopping will really pay off; call as many of the suggested airlines and travel agents as you have patience for. Canadians are habitually shuttled by their travel agents to New York or Miami as a first step; direct tickets out of Canada are almost always astronomically expensive.

If you choose to fly into one South American nation and out of another (U.S. travel agents are very used to such "open-jaw" itineraries in South America and even encourage it to some extent), try to buy all legs of your air journeys before leaving home. Purchasing international air tickets in Peru, for example, runs afoul of a 23% government tax (on top of the usual $10 airport tax). Also, be wary of flying into slightly busier Guayaquil (Ecuador) and covering the last few kilometers to northern Peru by land. Though the flights are slightly cheaper, it usually won't save you any money and can cause a lot of hassle, not least because of the outrageous (and probably illegal) exit taxes, which cost from $20 up.

EAST COAST

The two Peruvian carriers have far and away the most varied and flexible range of offerings if you're buying directly from the **scheduled airlines**. *Aeroperu* (☎800/255-7378) prices for **Miami–Lima** round trip start at $359 for a thirty-day excursion ticket (low season, weekdays only; $459 in high season); for $60 more you'll get a sixty-day stay and one domestic flight within Peru thrown in. A 150-day excursion costs around $500, and a one-year ticket is much the same except for a December blackout. Out of **New York**, the above four daily services are operated in cooperation with *Pan Am* for $500, $600, and $700 respectively. All except the one-year ticket allow you to purchase Peruvian internal flights at $25 apiece—a good value, given the heavy surcharge on tickets purchased within Peru. A simple one-way is available for $250 except during December. *Faucett* (7220 N.W. 36th St. Miami, FL 33126, ☎305/591-0610) has three night services weekly on the Miami–Lima route with prices being much the same though restrictions perhaps a bit more liberal. *Eastern* is generally a poor third with their $359 thirty-day, $500 for longer excursions out of Miami being restricted to the months of January and August–November; they also have a $250 one-way fare.

Among the established **discount/student** operators, *Nouvelles Frontières* often has advantageous prices on the **New York–Lima** line, averaging $310 one way, $530 round-trip, with advertised twice-weekly departures. *CIEE* flies students on the **New York–Guayaquil** route for $400 round-trip, approximately $200 one-way, year round. *STN*'s New York–Guayaquil offerings are virtually identical, but they also advertise **Miami–Guayaquil** for $135 and **Dallas–Guayaquil** at $170, as well as a useful hop from **Panama to Guayaquil** to help overlanders (see below) over the Darien Gap.

WEST COAST

Nonstudents and/or those over 32 should consult the Sunday travel pages of either the *San Francisco Examiner/Chronicle* or the *Los Angeles Times*; **Los Angeles–Lima** and **San Francisco–Lima** round-trips are consistently advertised for $550–600, with one-ways (always something more than half that) available. Possibilities include: *Sunline Express*, 210 Post St., Suite 1004, San Francisco, CA 94108, ☎415/398-2111; *All World Travel Services*, 870 Market St., Suite 705, San Francisco, CA 94102, ☎415/

CIEE IN THE U.S.

Head Office: 205 E. 42nd St., New York, NY 10017; ☎800/223-7401

CALIFORNIA
2511 Channing Way, Berkeley, CA 94704; ☎415/848-8604
UCSD Student Center, B-023, La Jolla, CA 92093; ☎619/452-0630
5500 Atherton St., Suite 212, Long Beach, CA 90815; ☎213/598-3338
1093 Broxton Ave., Los Angeles, CA 90024; ☎213/208-3551
4429 Cass St., San Diego, CA 92109; ☎619/270-6401
312 Sutter St., San Francisco, CA 94108; ☎415/421-3473
919 Irving St., San Francisco, CA 94122; ☎415/566-6222
14515 Ventura Blvd., Suite 250, Sherman Oaks, CA 91403; ☎818/905-5777

GEORGIA
12 Park Place South, Atlanta, GA 30303; ☎404/577-1678

ILLINOIS
29 E. Delaware Place, Chicago, IL 60611; ☎312/951-0585

MASSACHUSETTS
79 South Pleasant St., 2nd Floor, Amherst, MA 01002; ☎413/256-1261

729 Boylston St., Suite 201, Boston, MA 02116; ☎617/266-1926
1384 Massachusetts Ave., Suite 206, Cambridge, MA 02138; ☎617/497-1497

MINNESOTA
1501 University Ave. SE, Room 300, Minneapolis, MN 55414; ☎612/379-2323

NEW YORK
35 W. 8th St., New York, NY 10011; ☎212/254-2525
Student Center, 356 West 34th St., New York, NY 10001; ☎212/661-1450

OREGON
715SW Morrison, Suite 1020, Portland, OR 97205; ☎503/228-1900

RHODE ISLAND
171 Angell St., Suite 212, Providence, RI 02906; ☎401/331-5810

TEXAS
1904 Guadalupe St., Suite 6, Austin, TX 78705; ☎512/472-4931
The Executive Tower, 3300 W. Mockingbird, Suite 101, Dallas,TX 75235; ☎214/350-6166

WASHINGTON
1314 Northeast 43rd St., Suite 210, Seattle, WA 98105; ☎206/632-2448

STN IN THE U.S.

BOSTON
273 Newbury St., Boston, MA 02116; ☎617/266-6014

HONOLULU
1831 S. King St., Suite 202, Honolulu, HI 96826; ☎808/942-7755

LOS ANGELES
920 Westwood Blvd., Los Angeles, CA 90024; ☎213/824-1574
7204 Melrose Ave., Los Angeles, CA 90046; ☎213/934-8722

2500 Wilshire Blvd., Los Angeles, CA 90057; ☎213/380-2184

NEW YORK
17 E. 45th St., Suite 805, New York, NY 10017; ☎212/986-9470;☎ 800/777-0112

SAN DIEGO
6447 El Cajon Blvd., San Diego, CA 92115; ☎619/286-1322

SAN FRANCISCO
166 Geary St., Suite 702, San Francisco, CA 94108; ☎415/391-8407

NOUVELLES FRONTIERES

In the United States
NEW YORK 19 W. 44th St., Suite 1702, New York, NY 10036; ☎212/764-6494
LOS ANGELES 6363 Wilshire Blvd., Suite 200, Los Angeles, CA 90048; ☎213/658-8955
SAN FRANCISCO 209 Post St., Suite 1121, San Francisco, CA 94108; ☎415/781-4480

In Canada
MONTREAL 1130 ouest, bd de Maisonneuve, Montréal, P.Q. H3A 1M8; ☎514/842-1450
QUEBEC 176 Grande Allée Ouest, Québec, P.Q. G1R 2G9; ☎418/525-5255

392-4007; *Le Tourist*, 150 Powell St., Suite 301, San Francisco, CA 94102, ☎415/362-7847; *Costa Azul Travel*, in Los Angeles at ☎213/384-7200 and ☎818/785-8844; *Belton Tours*, 6844 La Tijera Blvd., Los Angeles, CA 90045, ☎213/649-2662 and ☎800/524-2224; *H.I.S. Tours*, 244 1/2 E 1st St., Suite 19, Los Angeles, CA 90012, ☎213/613-0943; and *Camino Real Tours*, in Los Angeles at ☎818/508-5401, ☎800/826-3303 from the rest of California, ☎800/626-5285 from out of state.

Aeroperu has flights out of **Los Angeles to Lima** via Miami, again in conjunction with *Pan Am*, but at $759 for the sixty-dayer these are not competitive; of more potential interest would be a flight on the same terms which included a **stopover** somewhere en route: check out *Varig Brazilian Airlines* (☎800/468-2744) or *Aerolineas Argentinas* (☎800/327-0276).

Among the student/youth establishments, *STN* edges out *CIEE* on the **Los Angeles–Guayaquil** route at $285 one way versus $300-plus; round trip fares at roughly double these amounts are handled but again beware of surcharges as outlined above.

CANADA

The best deals from Canada will generally be routed down through the States to pick up one of the flights discussed above. However *Travel CUTS* does offer direct flights worth checking out: at around CDN$1200–$1400, which will at least undercut the scheduled airlines.

OVERLAND

Though it's possible to travel overland all the way to Peru **from North America**, because of the Darien Gap—a section of Panamanian jungle that's uncrossed by road or trail—you may want to rely on other modes of transportation at least some of the way. Some few hardy souls manage to jeep, hike, or even bicycle through the swampy Darien Gap, but a certain number of would-be expeditioneers have met bad ends at the hands of drug smugglers in this area. If you'd like to attempt a Central American traverse you should keep an ear to the ground about the current military and political situation in this volatile area.

TRAVEL CUTS IN CANADA

Head Office: 187 College St., Toronto, Ontario M5T 1P7; ☎416/979-2406

ALBERTA
1708 12th St. NW, Calgary T2M 3M7; ☎403/282-7687
10424A 118th Ave., Edmonton T6G 0P7; ☎403/471-8054

BRITISH COLUMBIA
Room 326, T.C., Student Rotunda, Simon Fraser University, Burnaby, British Columbia V5A 1S6; ☎604/291-1204
1516 Duranleau St., Granville Island, Vancouver V6H 3S4; ☎604/689-2887
Student Union Building, University of British Columbia, Vancouver V6T 1W5; ☎604/228-6890
Student Union Building, University of Victoria, Victoria V8W 2Y2; ☎604/721-8352

MANITOBA
University Centre, University of Manitoba, Winnipeg R3T 2N2; ☎204/269-9530

NOVA SCOTIA
Student Union Building, Dalhousie University, Halifax B3H 4J2; ☎902/424-2054
6139 South St., Halifax B3H 4J2; ☎902/424-7027

ONTARIO
University Centre, University of Guelph, Guelph N1G 2W1; ☎519/763-1660
Fourth Level Unicentre, Carleton University, Ottawa, K1S5B6; ☎613/238-5493
60 Laurier Ave. E, Ottawa K1N 6N4; ☎613/238-8222
Student Street, Room G27, Laurentian University, Sudbury P3E 2C6; ☎705/673-1401
96 Gerrard St. E, Toronto M5B 1G7; ☎ (416) 977-0441
University Shops Plaza, 170 University Ave. W, Waterloo N2L 3E9; ☎519/886-0400

QUÉBEC (Known as *Voyages CUTS*)
Université McGill, 3480 rue McTavish, Montréal H3A 1X9; ☎514/398-0647
1613 rue St. Denis, Montréal H2X 3K3; ☎514/843-8511
Université Concordia, Edifice Hall, Suite 643, S.G.W. Campus, 1455 bd de Maisonneuve Ouest, Montréal H3G 1M8; ☎514/288-1130
19 rue Ste. Ursule, Québec G1R 4E1; ☎418/692-3971

SASKATCHEWAN
Place Riel Campus Centre, University of Saskatchewan, Saskatoon S7N 0W0; ☎306/343-1601

If cutting your way through the jungle isn't how you want to start off, at some point in Central America you may want to fly to **San Andres Island** and from there to the mainland. San Andres is a useful anomaly on international air routes: it's a bit of Colombian territory in the Caribbean just east of Nicaragua; thus there is a limit to how outrageous the fares to it from the various Central American capitals will be. Every national airline hereabouts serves this route at least daily, and although San Andres is quite remote from Colombian centers—1600km from Cali, for example—the fact that the onward flight is a domestic one again keeps something of a ceiling on fares.

Alternatively you can take a **ferry** or short flight directly from Panama to **Barranquilla** or Cartagena in Colombia. Allow a minimum of a week to overland the final 1800km from the Colombian Caribbean coast to the Peruvian frontier.

There are also two overland routes from other South American countries. **From Brazil**, you can take the amazing boat ride up the Amazon from Manaus to Iquitos—this is a ten-day ride which, if you're prepared for a few discomforts (such as unexciting food), can prove to be a favorably memorable experience. Take a hammock and plenty of reading material. The third main overland route arrives in southern Peru **from Bolivia**. The trip from La Paz across the *altiplano* to Copacabana on Lake Titicaca is by bus or truck; from Copacabana you can continue to Puno in Peru by the ferry or hydrofoil, but most travelers use the cheaper bus services (change at the border), which skirt the southwest shore of the lake en route to Puno.

BY SEA

Though the age of sea travel is virtually over, you can attempt to **work your passage** to somewhere in South America, and make your way from there. Union rules may well exclude you from cargo ships (or banana boats returning to Ecuador), but with a bit of luck you may be able to find work as crew on a **private yacht** sailing in the right direction. Check for advertisements in *Cruising World* or *Yachting* magazine, or hang around marinas in the main Caribbean ports-of-call. You could also try *The Crew List*, published by Marine Data Services, Box 2394, Woodland, CA 95695: it costs $10, and concentrates on the Caribbean, but it's worth a try. Beware of drug smugglers who might want to use you as an innocent-looking, English-speaking front.

PACKAGES

If time is short, or if this is your first visit and the idea of traveling alone seems daunting, then an organized tour might be worth considering. Most are pretty good value for the relative luxury they offer, and all will give the added security of travel in a group, with an experienced courier.

Your local travel agent should be able to recommend one of the more **standard tours**, most of which take in Lima, Cuzco, and Machu Picchu; but these are generally inflexible and relatively unexciting. **Specialist companies** offer more individual and adventurous experiences. Among those worth checking out are: *Cano-Andes Expeditions Inc.*, 310 Madison Ave. (at 42nd St.), New York, NY 10017, ☎212/286-9415 or ☎800/242-5554, who lead all kinds of adventure travel throughout South America, including hiking trips and white-water rafting; *Amazon Tours and Cruises*, 1013 S. Central Ave., Glendale, CA 91204, ☎818/246-4816 or ☎800/243-2791, who specialize in Amazon cruises; and *Vantage Tours*, Box 5774, Greenville, SC 29606, ☎800/826-8268, who organize tours to explore more metaphysical and esoteric aspects of Peru—for example to study *curanderismo*, traditional Peruvian psycho-medicine.

RED TAPE AND VISAS

Anericans and Canadians do not need a visa per se to enter Peru but instead require a tourist card, which is issued at the frontier or on the plane before landing. If you insist, you can get one at a consulate (see box) before setting off, but the staff there will probably tell you to wait until arrival in Peru.

In most cases the cards will be valid for ninety days, although this period can be arbitrarily as short as sixty or even thirty days. In theory, as well as a valid passport, you have to show an outbound ticket (by air or bus) before you'll be given a card, but this is rarely checked and the days of the attendant rackets whereby travelers entering by land were forced to purchase a bogus

Peru–Ecuador bus ticket are probably over. One copy of the tourist card must be kept with your passport at all times.

Should you want to **extend your stay**, there are two basic options. It's simplest to leave the country and get a new tourist card when you come back over the border, since applications for a formal extension entail spending several days going through bureaucratic rigamarole at a *Migraciones* office. These (in Lima and Cuzco) rarely give more than sixty days for a renewal and charge $20; for a second renewal you'll probably get only thirty days.

COSTS AND MONEY

Peru is certainly a very much cheaper place to live than the U.S. or Canada, but how much so will depend very much on where you are and when. As a general rule you should—with care—be able to get by on around $6–$10 a day. If you intend traveling with some comfort, $20 a day should be plenty.

A good **meal** can always be found for under $1, **transportation** is very reasonable, an adequate double **room** $2–$3 a night, and **camping** costs nothing. Expect to pay a little more than usual in the larger towns and cities, and also in the jungle where most food supplies have to be imported by truck from other regions. In the villages and rural towns, on the other hand, things come cheaper—and by roughing it out in the *campo* (fields), and buying food from local villages or the nearest market, you can live well on next to nothing.

In the more popular parts of Peru costs vary considerably with the seasons. Cuzco, for instance, has its best weather from June to August and, crowded with gringos, doubles many of its prices. The same thing happens at fiesta times—although on such occasions you're unlikely to resent it too much. As always, if you're traveling alone you'll end up spending considerably more than you would in a group of two or more people: sharing rooms and food saves considerably. If you have some kind of international **student card**, it's worth taking along for the occasional reduction.

MONEY

For safety's sake the bulk of your money should be carried as **travelers' checks**—preferably of two different types. From time to time rumored forgeries will make one type of check difficult to unload. *American Express* may be the best bet since they have their own offices in Lima and Cuzco, and also offer an efficient *poste restante* service. Large denominations—in notes or travelers' checks—should be avoided; you'll find them hard to change anywhere in South America.

U.S. dollars are far the best currency to carry in Peru—anything else will almost certainly prove a constant annoyance, and even the major European currencies are hard to get rid of outside

Lima. **Inflation** in Peru generally runs at an incredible 150 percent annually, calling for the occasional devaluation such as in 1986 when the currency changed from the *sol* (Spanish for sun) to the *inti* (Quechua for sun), which basically meant a three zero disregard—one *inti* being worth 1000 *sols*. This level of inflation also means that it makes sense to change your money a little at a time: even a week can make a significant difference.

Peruvian currency—the *inti*—can pose the occasional problem for unwary tourists. I./ 1000 notes, the largest in regular circulation, are not very common. You're more likely to come across the I./ 500 (green-and-tan), I./ 100 (beige), the I./ 50 (orange), I./ 10 (blue), and I./ 5 (green). Even as late as 1989 there were still some *sols* notes in circulation—50,000 (also orange = I./50), 10,000 (also blue = I./ 10), and 5000 (also red = I./ 5). Market vendors and even taxi drivers still sometimes refer to I./ 10 as *una libra* or I./ 100 as *diez libras*, a curious linguistic anachronism dating back to the financial influence held by Victorian Britain in Peru. It's particularly hard to change the larger notes in jungle towns, and even in Cuzco and Lima shopkeepers and waiters are often reluctant to accept them; if they do, they'll end up running around trying to find change. It's best to break up any large notes at every opportunity—in large shops, bars, and post offices. If you hang on to the smaller *inti* notes you'll have few difficulties in even the smallest villages.

BANKS—AND THE BLACK MARKET

Banks are open weekdays from 8:45am until 12:15pm (some change to 9:15am–12:45pm in the winter, April to November). The *Banco de la Nación* is the one that officially deals with foreign currency, but most banks seem to deal with dollar travelers' checks, and there is often a shorter line at the *Banco Continental*. The rate of exchange varies daily, and you're invariably better off changing a little at a time. On the other hand, there's an enormous amount of paperwork involved in even the simplest transactions—some places fill out seven copies of each form—and inevitably a good deal of time. You'll always need to show your passport. Peruvian hotels, like the banks, tend to use the "free dollar rate" of exchange which averages some five percent below street prices. For convenience there's a lot to be said for the **Casas de Cambio** which can be found in just about any town on the tourist

circuit. They are open all day, are rarely crowded, and the rate of exchange is often better too.

The very best exchange rates are found on the **black market**. In Peru the difference is never as dramatic as it is in, say, Bolivia, but it is possible to gain between five and fifteen percent over the official rate. "Black market" is a rather nebulous term encompassing any buyer from hotel clerks and waiters to the small men in suits clutching briefcases who constantly attempt to catch tourists' attention while avoiding that of the police. These shadowy characters usually offer the best rates and can be spotted in the commercial or tourist center of any large town—behind the *Hotel Bolivar* in Lima, for example—and at all border crossings.

In 1988–89 there was such a thriving black market in Lima that the central streets thronged with hundreds of money changers competing for business. Symbolic of the state of the economy—and an ideal way of laundering the illicit cocaine trade money—such a situation may not continue through the early 1990s. Theft of signed or unsigned travelers' checks, sometimes under threat of violence, is always a slight risk, particularly in Lima: when changing money on the street in this way, play it safe—and never hand over your checks until given the cash. Going into unfamiliar buildings (with hidden back staircases) "to negotiate" is also *not* advisable. Watch out, too, for forgeries, which are generally pretty crude.

CREDIT CARDS AND EMERGENCY CASH

Credit cards are accepted in the more expensive restaurants and hotels, as well as for car rental. The better known ones (including *American Express*, *Mastercard* , and *VISA*) can also be used with the larger travel companies, but not to pay for bus or train journeys, or at any of the cheaper hotels or restaurants (the bulk of those listed in this book).

It's also worth checking if your bank or credit card company has set up connections with a Peruvian bank: a cash advance on a credit is a handy way of getting **emergency cash** should you need it. Otherwise the quickest method is direct transfer from an account in the U.S. or Canada to an affiliated branch of the better Peruvian banks, like *Banco del Credito*. The money is best transferred and picked up in dollars; if you ask for a telex transfer it can take under five working days.

HEALTH AND INSURANCE

At the moment there are no inoculations required for Peru, but it's a good idea to check with the embassy or a good travel agent before you go. Your doctor will probably advise you to have some anyway: typhoid, cholera, and yellow fever shots are a sensible precaution, as is ensuring that your polio and tetanus boosters are still effective. Gamma globulin against hepatitis is also usually recommended, but if you're traveling long-term you should be aware that the effects are relatively short-lived and you may end up more vulnerable once it's worn off than you were before you had it. You can, of course, get boosters in Peru.

Up-to-date information **in the U.S.** is available from the local Public Health Service or Department of Health. In Los Angeles there's a place for jabs in a hurry—the *Medical Clinic for Immunizations* (7060 Hollywood Blvd.; Mon.–Fri. 1–5pm; ☎213/469-4334).

The illnesses most commonly encountered are **typhoid** or **hepatitis**. **Rabies** does exist but it's a relatively remote possibility. *Soroche* or **altitude sickness** is much more probable, and the best way to prevent it is to eat light meals, drink lots of *coca* tea, and spend as long as possible acclimatizing to high altitudes (over 2500m) before trying anything very strenuous. Anyone who suffers from headaches or nausea should rest; more seriously, a sudden bad cough could be a sign of pulmonary edema and necessitates immediate descent and medical attention—*soroche* can kill. Quite a few people suffer from it on trains crossing high passes; if this happens, don't panic, just rest and stay with the train until it descends. Most trains are equipped with

oxygen bags or cylinders that are brought around by the conductor for anyone in need.

If you intend going into jungle regions, **malaria tablets** (*Maloprim* once a week or *Paludrin* daily) should be taken—starting a few weeks before you arrive and continuing for some time after. Get these or whatever is recommended by your doctor before leaving home.

The only drugs you may need to take with you are **contraceptives** (expensive in Peru), any special or unusual medicines, water purifying tablets, and insect repellents. Another useful money saver is to take **suntan lotion** and sunblock with you to Peru, as they are invariably useful and cost a lot more there. Also, if you wear glasses or contact lenses, take at least one spare set, and lots of any necessary cleaning supplies, with you—it would be a shame to miss enjoying the visual side of the trip!

Doctors, **dentists**, and **hospitals** (detailed for Lima on p.59) are in the phone book; or simply rely on a taxi driver. For **minor ailments** you can buy most drugs in *farmacias* without a prescription. Antibiotics and malaria pills can be bought over the counter (it is however important to know the correct dosage), as can antihistamines (for bite allergies) or medication for an upset stomach (try *Lomotil* or *Streptotriad*).

Peruvian **food** is frequently condemned as a health hazard, though many travelers relish eating almost anything bought from street stalls and haven't suffered frequent or long-lasting problems. To be safe, though, drink bottled **water** and, whenever possible, avoid eating salads. The readily available two-liter plastic bottles of mineral water are an ideal way of coping with the drinking water problem; in backcountry areas sterilizing tablets like *Potable Agua* or liquid iodine are options, if ones that can leave a rather bad taste in the mouth.

Alternative medicines have a popular history going back at least 2000 years in Peru and the traditional practitioners, *herbaleros*, *hueseros*, and *curanderos*, are still commonplace. *Herbaleros* sell curative and magical plants, herbs, and charms in the streets and markets of most towns. They lay out vast arrays of ground roots, liquid tree barks, flowers, leaves, and creams—all with specific medicinal functions and much cheaper than the wrapper-oriented *farmacias*. If told the troublesome symptoms, a *herbalero* will be able to select remedies for most minor (and apparently some major) ailments. *Hueseros* are physiotherapeutic consultants who treat diseases and injuries by bone manipulation (if you can't find them in the phone book ask a taxi driver). *Curanderos* claim magic diagnostic, divinatory, and healing powers and have existed since pre-Inca days. They tend to live on the outskirts of town and hardly ever advertise—so, again, ask a taxi driver. For further information see the *Contexts* section. **Homeopathy** and **Shiatsu** are growing in popularity in Peru (mostly in Lima—again, look in the phone book.

INSURANCE

If you do fall ill, the bills can mount up rapidly, so some form of **travel insurance**—preferably including air evacuation in the event of serious emergency—is essential. Even with insurance most Peruvian clinics will insist on cash up front except in really serious hospital cases, so an emergency stash is again a good idea. Keep all receipts and official papers involved with any claim you're going to want to make.

But before purchasing special **travel insurance**, whether for medical or property mishaps, check that you won't duplicate the coverage of any **existing plans** you may have. For example, **Canadians** are usually covered for medical expenses by their provincial health plans (but may only be reimbursed after the fact). **ISIC** card-holders are entitled to $2000 worth of accident coverage and sixty days ($100 per diem) of hospital in-patient benefits while the card remains valid. University **students** often find that their student health coverage extends for one term beyond the date of last enrollment. Bank and charge **accounts** (particularly *American*

Express) often have certain levels of medical or other insurance included. **Homeowners' or renters'** insurance may cover theft or loss of documents, money, and valuables while overseas, though exact conditions and maximum amounts vary from company to company.

Only after exhausting these possibilities might you want to contact a specialist travel insurance company; your travel agent can usually recommend one. Travel insurance offerings are quite comprehensive, anticipating everything from airline companies going bankrupt to delayed (as well as lost) baggage, by way of sundry illnesses and accidents. **Premiums** vary widely—from the very reasonable ones offered primarily through student/youth agencies (though available to anyone), to ones so expensive that the cost for anything more than two months of coverage will probably equal the cost of the worst possible combination of disasters. Note also that very few insurers will arrange on-the-spot payments in the event of a major expense or loss; you will usually be reimbursed only after going home.

A most important thing to keep in mind—and a source of major disappointment to would-be claimants—is that *none* of the currently available policies insure against **theft** of *anything* while overseas! (Americans have been easy pickings for foreign thieves, and companies were going broke paying robbery/burglary claims.) North American travel policies apply only to items **lost** from, or **damaged** in, the custody of an identifiable, responsible third party, i.e. hotel porter, airline, luggage consignment, etc. Even in these cases you will still have to contact the local police to have a complete **report** made out so that your insurer can process the claim.

INFORMATION AND MAPS

Peru has no official tourist offices abroad. However you can get a range of information from most tour companies (see "*Getting There***") and also, to a limited extent, from Peruvian embassies or consulates. In Peru you'll find some sort of a tourist office in most towns of any size, which can help with information and perhaps free local maps. As often as not, though, these are simply fronts for tour operators, and are only really worth bothering with if you have a specific question—about fiesta dates or local bus timetables for example. In Lima the main branch of**

the official organization, **FOPTUR, is located in an arcade at Belen 1000, near the Plaza San Martin. Even this one is not particularly helpful, though they do have free maps of the city center.**

Maps of Peru fall into four basic categories. A standard **road map** should be available from a good map seller just about anywhere in the world, or in Peru itself from street vendors or *librerías*. **Departmental maps**, covering each *departmento* (Peruvian state) in greater detail, but often badly out of date, should also be fairly widely available. **Topographic maps** (usually 1:100,000) extend over the entire coastal area and most of the mountains: they can be bought in Peru from the *Instituto Geográfico Nacional*, 1190 Av. Aramburu, one block from Avenida Panama in Surquillo (Mon.–Fri. 1:30–3:30pm; ☎45-1939). Aerial photos of some regions are available from the *Servicio Aerofotográfico Nacional*, Las Palmas Air Force base, Chorrillos (Mon.–Fri. 8am–1pm and 1:30–3:45pm; ☎67-1341).

A few **maps for hikers**, in still greater detail, are produced by the *South American Explorers'*

Club, though these cover only the most popular trekking zones. The **South American Explorers' Club** is a nonprofit organization founded in 1977 to support scientific and adventure expeditions, to produce a magazine, and to provide services to travelers. In return for membership ($25) the club offers four copies of the magazine; use of their facilities in Lima (excellent library, detailed members' trip reports, and access to the map collection); a postal address, storage space, discounts on maps, guidebooks, leg pouches, etc.; information on visas, doctors, and dentists; and an "emergency crash pad." The clubhouse in Lima also offers a network of experts available as contacts for specialized information. Apply in Lima at Av. Portugal 146, between Avenidas Bolivia and España (☎31-4488), or by mail to Casilla 3714, Lima 100.

In the **U.S.**, the *South American Explorers' Club* is at 1510 York Street, Denver, Colorado 80218; or Box 18327, Denver, Colorado 80218. You can call them on ☎303/320-0388, or toll free on ☎1-800/274-0568. They'll also offer good advice on the current situation in Peru.

GETTING AROUND

Most Peruvians get around on buses, which are extremely good value and go almost everywhere, though the country's amazing railroads, which connect the major destinations, are often attractions in themselves. Approximate journey times and frequencies of all services can be found in the "Travel Details" section at the end of each chapter, and local peculiarities are also pointed out in the text of the guide.

BUSES

There are several varieties of **bus** in Peru, ranging from the "luxury" *Ormeño* fleets that run along the coast to the beat-up schoolbuses used

on local runs throughout Peru. Services are efficient in that you always arrive some time, if often slowed down by punctures, arguments, and landslides. At least one bus station or stop can be found in the center of any town; buses are the only means of transportation available to most of the population, and run with surprising regularity. Failing this, you can wait for them at the police *control* on the edge of town, or hail one down virtually anywhere. Long-distance bus journeys cost around $1 per hour (i.e., 60 or 70km) on the fast coastal highway and half this on the slower mountain and jungle routes. It's best to buy tickets in advance for intercity rides, making sure you avoid sitting over the jarring wheels.

TRAINS

Peru's **trains** are in themselves one of the country's major attractions—the highest standard gauge tracks anywhere in the world. At least one major train journey should certainly form part of your plans, and the rails felicitously connect many of the major tourist attractions. All are spectacular.

The **Central Railway** climbs and switchbacks its way up from Lima into the mountains as far as Huancayo and Huancavelica. The **Southern**, starting on the south coast at Arequipa, heads inland to Lake Titicaca before curving back towards Cuzco. And from Cuzco a line heads out down the magnificent Urubamba Valley, past **Machu Picchu**, and on into the fringes of the Amazon forest. The trains move slowly and there's ample time to contemplate what's going on outside. On the other hand, you do have to keep one eye on events inside where the carriages—often extremely crowded—are notorious for **petty thefts**. If you want to know something of this less pleasurable side of Peruvian rail travel—and intimate details of being sick on board—read Paul Theroux's *Old Patagonian Express*.

All the major legs (Lima–Huancayo, Arequipa–Puno, and Puno–Cuzco) last about twelve hours, for which you pay around $6. Wherever possible **tickets** should be bought in advance: the day before or very early on the morning you plan to leave.

TAXIS AND *COLECTIVOS*

Taxis can be found anywhere at any time in almost every town. Any car can become a taxi simply by sticking a taxi sign up in the front window; a lot of people, especially in Lima, take advantage of this to supplement their income. Always fix the price in advance since none have functioning meters. In Lima the minimum fare is 75¢, but it's generally much cheaper elsewhere.

Colectivos (shared taxis) are a very useful way of getting around that's peculiar to Peru, connecting all the coastal towns, and many of the larger centers in the mountains. Like the buses, they are usually aging imports from the U.S.—huge old Dodge Coronets with the Virgin Mary dangling from the rearview mirror. The drivers are safe enough, though, and it's certainly a faster form of travel than the bus, if almost twice as expensive. Most *colectivos* manage to squeeze in about six people plus the driver (three in the front and four in the back), and can be found in the center of a town or at major stopping-places along the main roads. If more than one is ready to leave it's worth bargaining a little as the price is often negotiable.

HITCHING

It's very rare that a private car will stop to pick up a traveler (although not impossible; I have had

rides of over 1000km this way), so **hitchhiking** usually means catching a ride with a truckdriver, who will most likely ask for a small payment. With most trucks you won't have to pay before setting off—but there are stories of drivers stopping in the middle of nowhere and demanding higher than usual sums (from gringos and Peruvians alike) before going any farther. Trucks can be flagged down anywhere but there is greater choice around markets, and at police *controls* or gas stations on the outskirts of towns. Trucks travel the roads that buses won't touch, so you may end up having to sit on top of five tons of potatoes or bananas to get where you want to go.

DRIVING

Whether you bring your own four-wheel drive car or rent a motorcycle or moped, **driving** is a good way of getting to places off the beaten track. But it also involves a lot of responsibility. Spare parts, particularly tires, will have to be carried as will a tent, emergency water, and food. The chance of **theft** increases dramatically—the vehicle, your gear, and accessories are all vulnerable when parked. What few traffic signals there are are either completely ignored or used at drivers' "discretion." The pace is fast and roads everywhere are in bad shape: only the Pan American Highway, running down the coast, and a few short stretches inland, are paved. **Mechanics** are generally good and always ingenious—they have to be, due to a lack of spare parts! Also, the 95-octane **gasoline** is much cleaner than the 84, and both are very cheap.

Renting a car is expensive by American standards. The major firms all have offices in the larger towns, and there are one or two Peruvian companies whose charges will generally be lower. In the jungle towns it's usually possible to **rent motorbikes** or **mopeds** by the hour or by the day: it's a good way of getting to know a town or for shooting off into the jungle for a day.

Driving to Peru is not really a practical option—at least not without a major expedition and months of preparation. Political problems in Central America aside, the Pan American Highway has not yet been completed across the **Darien Gap**, which separates Panama from Colombia and is all but impossible to cross except on foot. So you have to ship the vehicle at least part of the way, an expensive and time-consuming business.

PLANES

Some places in the jungle can only sensibly be reached by **plane** and Peru is so vast that the odd flight can save a lot of time. There are two major companies—**Aeroperu** and **Faucett**—which both fly regularly to all the main towns on the coast, in the mountains, and in the jungle. Tickets can be bought from travel agents or the airline offices in every major town. The most popular routes, such as Lima–Cuzco–Lima, are on the expensive side for a tourist (since the 300 percent price hikes in 1988) at around $165 (nationals and residents pay less), and usually need to be booked at least a few days in advance. Others, less busy, also tend to be less expensive. **Grupo Ocho**, the Peruvian Air Force, carry passengers on some of their standard flights. Less regular or reliable, these compensate by being very much cheaper. Check availability at their offices at all the major airports, and don't be too surprised if the promised never materializes.

On all flights it's important to **confirm** your booking two days before departure. Flights are often canceled or delayed, but sometimes they leave earlier than scheduled—especially in the jungle where the weather can be a problem. If a passenger hasn't shown up twenty minutes before the flight, the company can give the seat to someone on the waiting list, so it's best to be on time whether you're booked or merely hopeful. The luggage allowance on all internal flights is 16kg not including hand luggage.

There are also **small planes** (six- and ten-seaters) serving the jungle and certain parts of the coast. For the most part run by local companies, these operate scheduled services between jungle towns at quite reasonable rates. But for an *expresso* service (an air taxi which will take you to any landing strip whenever you want) the price is over $200 per hour and all calculations include the return journey, even though you may just want to be dropped off somewhere.

BOATS

There are no coastal **boat** services in Peru, but in many areas—on Lake Titicaca and especially in the jungle—water is the obvious means of getting around.

From Puno on **Lake Titicaca** you can get to and from Bolivia by ship or hydrofoil. There are also smaller boats which take visitors to the various islands. These aren't expensive and a price can usually be negotiated down at the docks.

In the jungle areas **motorized canoes** come in two basic forms: those with a large outboard motor and those with a Briggs and Stratton *peque-peque* engine. The outboard is faster and more maneuverable, but it costs a lot more to run. Occasionally you can hitch a ride in one of these canoes for nothing, but this may involve waiting around for days or even weeks and, in the end, most people expect some form of payment. More practical is to **rent a canoe** along with its guide/driver for a few days. This means searching around in the port and, from around $35 per day for a *peque-peque* canoe, will invariably come out cheaper than an organized tour, as well as giving you the choice of guide and companions. The more people in the boat, the cheaper it will be individually.

If you're heading downstream it's always possible in the last resort to buy, borrow, or even make a **balsa raft**. Most of the indigenous population still travel this way so it's sometimes possible to hitch a lift, or to buy one of their rafts. Riding with someone who's going your way is probably better since rafting can be dangerous if you don't know the river well. For more details see *Chapter Six*.

ON FOOT

Even if you've no intention of doing any serious hiking, there's a good deal of walking involved in checking out many of the most enjoyable Peruvian attractions. Climbing from Cuzco up to the fortress of Sacsayhuaman, for example, or wandering around at Machu Picchu, involve a lot more than a Sunday afternoon stroll. Bearing in mind the rugged terrain throughout Peru, the absolute minimum footwear is a strong pair of running shoes. Better still is a pair of hiking boots with good ankle support.

Trekking—whether in the desert, the mountains, or the jungle—can be an enormously rewarding experience, but you should go properly equipped and bear in mind a few of the **potential hazards**. Never stray too far without food and something warm and something waterproof to wear. The weather is renowned for its dramatic changeability, especially in **the mountains**, where there is always the additional danger of *soroche* (altitude sickness—see "Health"). In **the jungle** the biggest danger is getting lost. If this happens, the best thing to do is follow a water course down to the main stream, and stick to this until you reach a settlement or get picked up by a passing canoe. If you get caught out in the forest at night, build a leafy shelter and make a fire or try sleeping in a tree.

In the mountains it's often a good idea to rent a **pack animal** to carry your gear. *Llamas* can only carry about 25kg and move slowly; a *burro* (donkey) carries around 80kg, but **a mule** will shift 150kg with relative ease. Mules can be rented from upwards of $3 a day, and they normally come with an *arriero*, a muleteer who'll double as a guide. It is also possible to hire mules or horses for **riding** but this costs a little more. With a guide and beast of burden it's quite simple to reach even the most remote valleys, ruins, and mountain passes, traveling in much the same way as Pizarro and his men over 400 years ago.

ORGANIZED TOURS

There are far too many **travel agents** and **tour operators** in Peru—so much so that their reps are forced to hunt out customers on trains and in the streets—and everything on offer seems expensive when you consider the ease with which you could do it yourself. Nevertheless, organized excursions can be a quick and painless way to see some of the more popular sites, while a prearranged trek can take much of the worry out of camping preparations. Some are positively adventurous—they include:

Explorandes (one of the best)
Bolognesi 159, Moraflores, Lima (☎46-9889)
Calle Procuradores 372, Cuzco (☎22-6671)

Mayuc Expediciones (river running and treks—generally very well priced, friendly, and well organized)
Procuradores 354, Cuzco (postal: Apartado 596, Cuzco; ☎23-2666)

Peruvian Andean Treks (treks, guides, and outfitters)
Av. Pardo 575, Piso 2, Cuzco (☎22-5701)
Percy Tapia, Casilla 3074, Lima 100
Yachay (scientific and cultural treks)
San Martin 453, Barranco, Lima (☎67-0810)
Hirca (educational/adventure travel)
Miguel Dasso 126, Of. 203, San Isidro, Lima (☎22-4487)

SLEEPING

HOTELS

A Peruvian **hotel** is as likely to call itself a *hostal*, a *residencial*, or a *parador* as it is a *hotel*—but in terms of what you'll find inside, these distinctions are almost meaningless. There's no standard or widely used rating system, so the only way to tell whether a place is suitable or not is to walk in and take a look around—the proprietors won't mind this, and you'll soon get used to spotting places with promise. A handy phrase is "*Querria ver un cuarto (con cama matrimonial)*": "I'd like to see a (double) room." The better possibilities—along with hotels in all the cheaper categories—are detailed in the text of the guide.

The cheaper hotels are generally old—sometimes beautifully so, converted from colonial mansions with rooms grouped around a courtyard—and tend to be within a few blocks of a town's central plaza, general market, or bus or train station. In the cheapest, which can be fairly basic with shared rooms and a communal bathroom, you can usually find a bed for between $1 and $4, and occasionally for even less. For a few dollars more you can find a good, clean single or double room with bath, generally for somewhere between $4 and $12. A little **haggling** rarely goes amiss, and if you find one room too pricey, another, perhaps identical, can often be found for less. The phrase for "Do you have a cheaper room?" is "*Tiene un cuarto más barato?*." Savings can invariably be made, too, by sharing rooms—

many have two, three, even four or five beds. A double-bedded room (*con cama matrimonial*) is invariably cheaper than one with two beds (*con dos camas*).

One additional category of hotel, which you'll find in all the larger Peruvian resorts as well as some surprisingly offbeat ones, is the **state hotel**, or *Hotel de Turistas*, often with a swimming pool and invariably among the flashiest places in town. Out of season some of these can be relatively inexpensive (from around $6), and if you like the look of a place it's often worth asking.

CAMPING

Camping is possible almost everywhere in Peru. With a population of around 18 million and a land area twice the size of Texas it's not difficult to find space for a tent. Camping is free since there are only one or two organized campgrounds in the whole country, and it's also the most satisfactory way of seeing Peru: with a tent—or a hammock—it's possible to go all over without worrying if you'll make it to a *hostal*. Some of Peru's most fantastic places are well off the beaten track.

It's usually okay to set up camp in fields or forest beyond the outskirts of settlements, but first ask permission and advice from the nearest farm or house. Apart from a few restricted areas, Peru's enormous sandy coastline is open territory, the real problem not being so much where to camp as how to get there; some of the most stunning areas are very remote. The same can fundamentally be said of both the mountains and the jungle—camp anywhere with local permission, if there are any locals to be found. On the coast it's really too hot to sleep inside, but a tent can be very handy when it rains.

In recent years there have been reports of tourists being attacked for money and belongings while camping in fairly **remote areas**. Personally I've never come across any hostility, nor have I met anyone who has suffered an attack while camping—but it does happen and there have been several reports of trouble along the Inca Trail over recent years. Traveling with someone else is always a good idea, but even on your own there are a couple of basic precautions that you can take: let someone know where you intend to go, be respectful, and try to communicate with any locals you may meet or be camping near.

EATING

As with almost every activity, the style and pattern of eating and drinking varies considerably between the three regions of Peru. Depending on the very different ingredients available locally, food in each area is essentially a *mestizo* creation, combining indigenous Indian cooking with 400 years of European—mostly Spanish—influence. In the past twenty years, with the wave of North American interests in the country, fast food has become commonplace: you'll find *Kentucky Fried Chicken* in Lima and hamburgers are more readily available than guinea pig in any large town. Nevertheless, a wealth of good traditional food remains.

SNACKS AND LIGHT MEALS

For informal eating there's a good variety of traditional **fast foods and snacks** such as *salchipapas* (fries with sliced sausage covered in various sauces), *anticuchos* (a shish kebab made from marinated lamb or beef heart), and *empanadas* (meat- or cheese-filled pies). These are all sold on street corners until late at night. The most popular **sweets** in Peru are made from either *manjar blanco* (sweetened condensed milk) or fresh fruits. Even in the villages you'll find cafés and restaurants which double as bars, staying open all day and serving anything from coffee with bread to steak and fries or lobster.

In general, the **market** is always a good place to head for—you can buy food ready to eat on the spot or to take away and prepare, and the range and prices will be better than in any shop. Most food prices are fixed, but the vendor may throw in an orange, a bit of garlic, or some coriander leaves for good measure. Markets are the best places to stock up for a trek, for a picnic, or if you just want to live cheaply. Smoked meat, which can be sliced up and used like salami, is normally a good buy.

RESTAURANTS

Most larger towns will offer a fair choice of **restaurants** and a varied menu. Among them *chifa* (**Chinese**) places have always featured, and nowadays there are a fair number of **vegetarian** restaurants too. Almost all open early and close late. Usually they will offer a *cena*, or **set menu**, from morning through to lunchtime and another in the evening. Ranging in price from 50¢ to $2, these most commonly consist of three courses: soup, a main dish, and a cup of tea or coffee to follow. Every town, too, seems now to have at least one restaurant that specializes in *pollos a la brasa*—spit-roasted chickens. **Tipping** is normal—rarely more than about 20¢—but in no way obligatory. In the fancier places you may have to pay a **cover charge**—up to $2 if there's some kind of entertainment on offer, around 50¢ in the flashier restaurants in major town centers.

Along **the coast**, not surprisingly, is the specialty. The Humboldt Current keeps the Pacific Ocean off Peru extremely rich in plankton and other microscopic life forms; plankton attracts fish, fish attract bigger fish, which attract fishermen. **Ceviche** is the classic Peruvian seafood dish—depending on what you choose (fish, shrimp, scallops, squid, or a mixture) it will be marinated in lime juice and chili peppers, then served "raw" with corn and sweet potato and onions. *Ceviche*, a Peruvian snack for over 2000 years, can be found along with fried fish and fish soups in most restaurants on the coast for around $1. There are also good **salads** such as *huevos a la rusa* (egg salad), *palta rellena* (stuffed avocado), or straight tomato. *Papas a la Huancaina* is great too, a cold appetizer of potatoes covered in a spicy light cheese sauce.

Mountain food is more basic—a staple of potatoes and rice with the meat stretched as far as it will go. *Lomo saltado*, or diced "prime beef" sautéed with onions and peppers, rice, and a few french fries, is served anywhere at any time. A delicious snack from street vendors and cafés is *papa rellena*, a potato stuffed with vegetables and fried. Trout is also widely available, as are cheese, ham, and egg sandwiches. *Chicha*, a corn beer drunk throughout the *sierra* region and on the coast in rural areas, is very cheap with a pleasantly tangy taste.

In the **jungle** food takes on new proportions. Bananas and plantains figure highly, along with *yuca* (a manioc rather like a yam), rice, and plenty of fish. There is meat as well, mostly chicken supplemented occasionally by game—deer, wild pig, or monkey. Every settlement big enough to get on the map has its bar or café, but in remote areas it's a matter of eating what's available and drinking coffee or bottled drinks if you don't relish the home-made *masato* (manioc beer).

DRINKING

Beers, **wines**, and **spirits** are served in almost every bar, café, or restaurant at any time, but there is a deposit on taking beer bottles out (canned beer was one of the worst inventions to hit Peru this century—some of the finest beaches are littered with empty cans).

Most **Peruvian beer**—except for *cerveza malta* (black malt beer)—is bottled lager, and extremely good. *Cuzqueña* (from Cuzco) is one of the best, but not universally available; you won't find it on the coast in Trujillo, for example, where they drink *Trujillana*. **Soft drinks** range from mineral water through the ubiquitous *Coca Cola* and *Fanta* to home-produced novelties like *Inca Cola* (gold-colored home made taste) and *Cola Inglesa* (red and extremely sweet). **Fruit juices** (*jugos*), most commonly papaya or orange, are prepared fresh in most places, and you can get **coffee** and a wide variety of herb and leaf **teas** almost anywhere.

Peru has been producing **wine** (*vino*) for over 400 years, but with one or two exceptions it is not all that good. Among the better ones are *Vista Alegre* (*tipo familiar*)—not entirely reliable but only around $1 a bottle—and most notably *Tacama Gran Vino Blanco Reserva Especial* for about $3 a bottle. A good Argentinian or Chilean wine will cost about $5.

As for **spirits**, Peru's sole claim to fame is *Pisco*. This is a white grape brandy with a unique, powerful, and very palatable flavor—the closest equivalent elsewhere is probably tequila. Almost anything else is available as an import—Scotch whisky is cheaper here than in the States—but beware of the really cheap imitations which can remove the roof of your mouth with ease.

A LIST OF FOODS AND DISHES

Basics

Arroz	Rice	*pasados*	lightly boiled
Avena	Oats (porridge)	*revueltos*	scrambled
Galletas	Cookies	*Mermelada*	Jam
Harina	Flour	*Miel*	Honey
Huevos	Eggs	*Mostaza*	Mustard
fritos	fried	*Pan (integral)*	Bread (brown)
duros	hard boiled	*Queso*	Cheese

Soup (*sopas*) and appetizers

Caldo	Broth	*Huevos a la rusa*	Egg salad
Caldo de galina	Chicken broth	*Palta*	Avocado
Causa	Mashed potatoes and shrimp	*Palta rellena*	Stuffed avocado
		Papa rellena	Stuffed fried potato
Conchas a la parmesana	Scallops with parmesan	*Sopa a la criolla*	Noodles, vegetables, and meat

Seafood (*mariscos*) and fish (*pescado*)

Calamares	Squid	*Jalea*	Large fish with onion sauce
Camarones	Shrimp	*Langosta*	Lobster
Cangrejo	Crab	*Langostino*	Crayfish
Ceviche	Marinated seafood	*a lo macho*	in spicy shellfish sauce
Chaufa de mariscos	Chinese rice	*Lenguado*	Sole
cojinova		*Paiche*	Large jungle river fish
Corvina	Sea bass	*Tollo*	Small shark
Erizo	Sea urchin	*Zungarro*	Large jungle fish

Meat (*carnes*)

Adobado	Meat/fish in red sauce	*Jamon*	Ham
Aji de galina	Chicken in chili sauce	*Lechon*	Pork
Anticuchos	Shish kebab	*Lomo asado*	Roast beef
Biftek (bistek)	Steak	*Lomo saltado*	Sautéed beef
Cabrito	Goat	*Pachamanca*	Meat and vegetables, roasted over open fire
Carne a lo pobre	Steak, fries, egg, and banana		
Carne de res	Beef	*Parillada*	Grilled meat
Carpulcra	Pork, chicken, and potatoes	*Pato*	Duck
Chicharrones	Deep-fried pork skins	*Pollo (a la brasa)*	Chicken (spit-roasted)
Conejo	Rabbit		
Cordero	Lamb	*Pavo*	Turkey
Cuy	Guinea pig (a traditional dish)	*Tocino*	Bacon
		Venado	Venison
Higado	Liver	*picante de. . .*	spicy dish of . . .

Vegetables (*legumbres*) and Side Dishes

Aji	Chili	Lechuga	Lettuce
Camote	Sweet potato	Papa	Potato
Cebolla	Onion	rellena	stuffed & fried
Choclo	Corn on the cob	Tallarines	Spaghetti noodles
Fideos	Noodles	Tomates	Tomatoes
Frijoles	Beans	Yuca	Manioc (like a yam)
Hongos	Mushrooms	a la Huancaina	in spicy cheese sauce

Sweets (*dulces*)

Barquillo	Ice cream cone	Manjar blanco	Sweetened condensed milk
Flan	Creme caramel	Mazamorra morada	Fruit/maize jello
Helado	Ice cream	Panqueques	Pancakes
Keke	Cake	Picarones	Doughnuts with syrup

Snacks (*bocadillos*)

Castanas	Brazil nuts	Sandwich de butifara	Ham and onion sandwich
Chifles	Fried banana slices		
Empanada	Meat or cheese pie	Sandwich de lechon	Pork salad sandwich
Hamburguesa	Hamburger	Tamale	Stuffed corn-flour roll
Salchipapas	Potatoes, sausage, and sauces	Tortilla	Omelet cum pancake
		Tostados	Toast

DRINKS

Fruit Juices (*jugos*)

Especial	Fruit, milk, sometimes beer	Papaya	Papaya
Fresa	Strawberry	Piña	Pineapple
Higo	Fig	Platano	Banana
Manzana	Apple	Surtido	Mixed
Melon	Melon	Toronja	Grapefruit
Naranja	Orange	Zanahoria	Carrot

Beverages (*bebidas*)

Agua	Water	Limonada	Real lemonade
Agua Mineral	Mineral water	Masato	Fermented manioc beer
Algarrobina	Algarroba-fruit drink		
Cafe	Coffee	Pisco	White grape brandy
Cerveza	Beer	Ponche	Punch
Chicha de jora	Fermented maize beer	Ron	Rum
Chicha morada	Maize soft drink	Te	Tea
Chilcano de pisco	Pisco with lemonade	con leche	with milk
Chop	Draft beer	de anis	aniseed tea
Cuba libre	Rum and coke	de limon	lemon tea
Gaseosa	Soft carbonated drink	hierba luisa	lemon grass tea
Leche	Milk	manzanilla	camomile tea

COMMUNICATIONS—MAIL, PHONES, AND MEDIA

POSTE RESTANTE AND MAIL

The Peruvian postal service is reasonably efficient, if a little irregular. Letters from North America generally take around one or two weeks—occasionally less—and you can have mail sent to you **poste restante** care of any principal post office (*Correo Central*). On the whole the system works quite smoothly. Have letters addressed: YOUR NAME (in capitals), Lista de Correos, Correo Central, CITY. To pick up mail you'll need to take your passport along, and you may need to urge that the files for the initials of all your names (including Ms., Mr., etc.) are checked. Rather quirkily, letters are sometimes filed separately by sex, too—in which case it's worth checking both piles.

An alternative to the official *lista* is to use the **American Express** mail collection service. Their two main offices in Peru are in Lima (*Lima Tours*, Belen 1040, near Plaza San Martin) and in Cuzco, on Avenida El Sol. Officially, *American Express* charges for this service unless you have one of their cards or use their travelers' checks—though they never seem to check.

Outbound letters to the U.S. or Canada should take between ten and fourteen days. **Parcels**, however, are a different matter. They are very vulnerable to being opened en route—in either direction—and expensive souvenirs can't be sure of going beyond the building where you mail them. Likewise, Peruvian postal workers are always happy to "check" incoming parcels which contain cassettes or interesting foods. Don't assume (or even hope) otherwise.

TELEPHONES

With a little patience you can make international phone calls from just about any town in the country. All towns have a **teléfonos** office, which is usually the best place to try. It's impossible to estimate how long this will take—three minutes is quite common, three hours not unknown. All international calls are at present made through the international operator—dial 108. If you want to make a collect call (*al cobro revertido*) you'll need a deposit—$1 at the Lima exchange but often $25 or so elsewhere. Calls within Peru are quite straightforward: just go to any local *teléfonos* office, or in Lima to a phone booth on the street.

MEDIA

For **news** of the outside world, the weekly **Lima Times**, in English, gives summaries of national and world events—slanted towards how it affects industry, culture, and English-speaking expatriates in South America. Published every Friday, it's widely available throughout Lima, and sporadically in Cuzco. The *Times* is useful for listings of events and for its ads. For more serious, in-depth coverage they also produce an economic and political review called the *Andean Report*—recommended if you've any interest in Peruvian (and Andean) developments, and available through their office (Pasaje Los Pinos 156, floor B; ☎47-2552).

If you can read Spanish—which is a lot easier than speaking it—you'll have access to the **Peruvian press**, too. The two most established (and establishment) papers are *El Comercio* and *La Prensa. El Comercio*'s *Seccion C* has the most comprehensive cultural listings of any paper—good for just about everything going. Among the other nationals are *El Expreso*, which devotes vast amounts of space to anti-Communist propaganda; *La Republica*, middle of the road and often sensationalist. One of the better magazines is the liberal *Caretas*, generally offering mildly critical support to whichever government happens to be in power. And finally, if you're really intrigued by the Peruvian political scene, there's a satirical weekly called *Monos y Monedas* ("Monkeys and Moneys").

However, illiteracy is still widespread in Peru and the actual readership of all these papers is very small—traveling around, you'll notice many Peruvians prefer to read comic books. Inevitably, too, they watch a lot of **television**—mostly soccer and soap operas, though TV is also a main source of news. Most programs shown come from Mexico, Brazil, and the U.S., with occasional eccentric selections from elsewhere. There are five main channels—all crammed with ads—and also a cable company, *Channel 27*, which most people seem to pick up quite happily just by tuning in their sets.

If you have a **radio** you can pick up the **BBC World Service** at most hours of the day—frequencies shift around on the 19m, 25m, and 49m short wave bands; for a schedule contact the British Council in Lima. **The Voice of America** is also constantly available on short wave. Alternatively, turn the dials and you'll be confronted by a quite incredible mass of **Peruvian stations**, nearly all of them music and ad based. *Radio Miraflores* (96FM) is one of the best, playing mainly disco and new U.S./British rock, though also with a good jazz program on Sunday evenings and an excellent news summary every morning from 7 to 9am. *Radio Cien* (100FM) has the occasional program in English—there's one on Sunday mornings. Andean music can be found all over the AM dial.

OPENING HOURS

Most stores, services, and tourist sites in Peru stay open all day, from 9am until 5 or 6 in the evening, and many are open on Sunday as well, if for more limited hours. However, during national holidays, Carnival, and the many local fiestas (see following section) everything shuts down: banks, post offices, tourist offices, and museums.

Opening hours for Peru's many **ancient sites** more often than not coincide with daylight—from around 7am to 5 or 6pm daily—for the more important ruins. Smaller sites are rarely fenced off, and are nearly always accessible 24 hours for full-moon strolls. You normally pay a small admission fee to the local guardian—who may then walk round with you, pointing out aspects you'd otherwise miss. Only Machu Picchu, the big tourist attraction of Inca Peru, charges more than a few dollars—and this is one site where you may find it worth presenting an ISIC or FIYTO student card (which generally gets a half-price reduction on admission fees).

MUSEUMS AND CHURCHES

Of the great many **museums** in Peru, some belong to the state, others to institutions, and a few to individuals. Most charge a small admission fee and stay open from 9am to noon in the morning and from 3 to 6pm on weekday afternoons. **Churches**—at their best in Arequipa and around Cuzco—open in the mornings for mass, after which the smaller ones close. The more interesting for tourists, however, tend to stay open all day, or at least from, say, 3 to 6pm. Very occasionally there's an admission charge to churches, and more regularly to monasteries (*monasterios*). Try to be aware of the strength of religious belief in Peru, particularly in the Andes, where churches have a rather heavy, sad atmosphere. You can enter and, quietly, look around in all churches, but in the Andes especially should refrain from taking photographs. People don't like it, which is easy enough to understand.

NATIONAL PARKS

To visit **National Parks**, or nature reserves, there's usually a small charge. Sometimes, as at the *Manu National Park* (near Cuzco), this is a daily rate; at others, like *Paracas Reserve* on the coast, you pay a fixed sum to enter. If the park is in a particularly remote area, permission may also be needed—either from the *National Institute of Culture* or the *Ministry of Agriculture, Flora, and Fauna* (for details check with the *South American Explorers' Club* in Lima or the local tourist office). Keep in mind that the parks and reserves are enormous zones, within which there is hardly any attempt to control or organize nature. Beginning in 1972, the *National System for Conservation Units* (SNCU) has developed a number of parks, reserves, and sanctuaries with the idea of combining conservation, research, and, in some cases, such as the Inca Trail, recreational tourism. The term "park" probably conveys the wrong impression about these huge, virtually untouched areas.

FIESTAS, FESTIVALS, AND PUBLIC HOLIDAYS

Public holidays, Carnival, and the many local fiestas are all big events in Peru, celebrated with an openness and intensity that give them enormous appeal for visitors—despite the fact that most shops and businesses, and many tourist sites, will be closed. The main national holidays take place over Easter, Christmas, and during the month of October, in that order of importance.

Cuzco is a great place to be both for Christian celebrations, and for "Inca" festivals like *Inti Raymi* during June. In October, Lima, and especially its suburb of La Victoria, takes center stage, with processions dedicated to *Our Lord of Miracles*—striking and impressive collective memories of the ever-present earthquake danger, for which many women dress only in purple for the whole month. **Carnival** time (generally late February) is lively almost everywhere in the country, with fiestas held every Sunday—a wholesale license to throw water at everyone and generally go crazy.

In addition to the major regional and national celebrations, nearly every community has its own saint or patron figure to worship at town or **village fiestas**. These local celebrations often mean a great deal more to local people, and can be much more fun. Processions, music, dancing in costumes, eating, and drinking form a natural part of these parties. In some cases the villagers will enact symbolic dramas with Indians dressed up as Spanish colonists, wearing hideous blue-eyed masks with long hairy beards. The *Yawar Fiesta*, for example, involves such feats as capturing a wild condor (representing the Andean

NATIONAL FESTIVALS AND PUBLIC HOLIDAYS

January 1 New Year's Day, public holiday.

February 2 Candlemas

Carnival Wildly celebrated throughout the country immediately prior to Lent, generally at the end of February.

Easter Holy Week (March/April) sees superb processions above all in Cuzco and Ayacucho, the biggest on Good Friday and the eve of Easter Sunday. Easter Saturday is a public holiday.

May 1 May Day, a public holiday, is followed almost immediately by the Fiesta de la Cruz (May 2–3).

June Corpus Christi, in early June, is a much celebrated day, with fascinating processions and feasting in Cuzco.

June 24–30 *Inti Raymi*, Cuzco's main "Inca" festival, traditionally coincides with the solstice, though these days commercialism has largely destroyed the religious nature of the week.

June 29 St. Peter's Day is marked by fiestas in fishing villages along the coast.

July 16 Virgen de Carmen festivals at Pisac and Paucartambo (near Cuzco).

July 28–29 National Independence Day (military and school processions), public holiday.

August 30 Santa Rosa de Lima, public holiday.

October 9 Fall public holiday.

October 18–28 Lord of Miracles festival celebrated with processions: bullfights and other celebrations continue throughout the month in Lima.

November 1–2 All Saints Day, November 1, is a public holiday; the following day, All Souls, is a festive remembrance of dead friends and relatives.

November 5 Festival of Puno, with colorful community dances.

November 12–28 *Pacific Fair* in Lima (biannually, 1990, 1992, etc.).

December 8 Immaculate Conception, public holiday.

December 25 Christmas Day, public holiday.

Indians) and tying it to the back of a village bull (symbol for the Spanish conquerors who brought the bull to Peru). The climax is the inevitable battle, in which the condor usually ends up killing the bull.

Walking up in the hills around towns like Huaraz and Cuzco it's relatively common to stumble into a village that is enjoying a fiesta, and with the explosion of human energy and noise, the bright colors, and the uneasy mixture of pagan and Catholic symbolism, this may prove a highlight of your travels. However, such celebrations are very much local affairs, and while the occasional traveler will almost certainly be welcomed with great warmth, none of these remote communities would want to be invaded by gringos waving cameras and expecting to be feasted for free. Those dates given in the text are therefore only for the more established events, already to some extent on the Peruvian tourist map. If you chance on others, all the better.

In many coastal and mountain *haciendas* (estates), **bullfights** are often held at fiesta times. In a less organized way they happen at many of the village fiestas, too—often with the bull being left to run through the village until it's eventually caught and mutilated by one of the men. This is not just a sad sight—it can be dangerous for you, as an unsuspecting gringo, if you happen to wander into an apparently evacuated village! The Lima bullfights in October, in contrast, are a very serious business; even Hemingway was impressed.

MUSIC AND FILM

It's not possible to talk of a Peruvian national music—or culture—since the country has such a multitude of different forms, each closely bound up in ties of region, history, ethnicity, and often class. In Lima, however, you can come upon a multitude of local sounds, and traveling about the country you're bound to get addicted to at least one. Movies, in contrast, are very much the same Hollywood hits as those in the U.S. and Canada. Tickets are extremely cheap, and most films are shown in the original language (usually but not necessarily English) with Spanish subtitles.

MUSIC

The music people most commonly associate with Peru is **Andean folk**, lively tunes played on instruments such as cane flutes, pan pipes, simple drums, and the *churrango* (a kind of mandolin, with the sound box made from an armadillo's shell). The music is an effective blend of sad songs with plucky singing and whooping; the dances, usually communal, are highly stylized. There are a large number of Andean "folk" groups and as a tourist this is the sort of music that you will come across most often—either in restaurants, folkore clubs (*peñas*), or, the real McCoy, at village festivals.

Peñas—which range from flashy dining clubs to spit-and-sawdust taverns—are also the places to hear **criolla**, or Creole, music. Played on Spanish guitars and percussive *cajones*, this is a thoroughly hybrid, romantic form—based around love ballads, but combining everything from African coastal rhythms to Viennese waltzes. There is also a certain amount of regional variation and each dance comes from a specific area—the *Marinera*, for instance, is traditionally from the north coast.

Chicha music, which developed in Colombia, is faster—the songs full of lyrical insolence and backed by energetic percussion and very twangy electric guitar. Although you hear *chicha* quite a lot in the mountains it really comes from the jungle and the best way to sample it is at a live Saturday night fiesta in one of the larger jungle settlements. Similar in tempo, and the one music that's heard throughout Latin America, is **salsa**, considerably more sophisticated than the others. Like *criolla*, it's best heard in the Lima clubs, many of which, known as *salsadromos*, devote themselves exclusively to the music.

Less expected—but an equally potent cultural force on the Peruvian coast—is **musica negra**, black music with roots in the old slave communities, shipped into the plantations from the sixteenth to the nineteenth centuries by the Spanish. Sometimes linked with social protest, *musica negra* portrays the life and spirit of the communities through songs and dances: in one of the liveliest and most popular dances, the *Alcatraz*, successive pairs of dancers (one male and one female) try to set fire to paper napkins hanging from behind their waists as they twist and turn. It's quite normal for members of the audience to get roped into this number—so be warned!

Musica negra is generally performed in *peñas* on the coast, and occasionally in concert. Keep your eyes open for posters advertising either *Peru Negro* or the *National Folk Ballet* (which specializes in both black and Andean folk dance). There are loads of *musica negra* bands and several dance groups, and an annual **Festival of Black Music and Dance** has just begun in Lima. There are also black songs and dances based on the jingles sung by *pregoneros* (street vendors) who have wandered Lima's streets calling out their wares for well over 100 years: *Tamales! Tamales! Pan dulce! Pan dulce!*

In more recent years there has been increasing interest on the jazz and rock front. Little pure **jazz** reaches Peru but once in a while one of the foreign culture institutions invites an artist to play in Lima. An Afro-jazz group called *Los Chonducos* plays quite regularly and there are a few small groups into the avant-garde (notably Enrique Luna's band). Most of these are formed by wealthy young intellectuals since the market is too small for musicians to make a living.

Much the same can be said for **rock music**, which as a form of musical expression bears almost no relation to Peruvian culture, except as a modern influence on the young rich (those with cosmopolitan contacts) and as a popular influence through the radio stations (mostly stuff like the Beatles, Sting, and Queen). In the late 1980s three Peruvian "new wave" groups have become quite well known in Lima—*Fragil, Toilet Paper,* and *Dr No.*—and they're not bad. For concerts check the newspapers—particularly *El Comercio*—and keep an eye out in Lima for posters, particularly in the streets of Miraflores.

There are also one or two **protest ballad** singer-songwriters who follow in the path of the Cuban Pablo Milanes and the Chilean Victor Jara.

FILM

South America is seen by film distributors as part of the American market, so new films from the U.S. arrive quickly in Lima, where they're shown cheaply and undubbed. European movies are also regularly screened, especially in Lima. Peru itself really started making its own films in the late 1970s, when various producers and directors got together and, with the help of distributors, managed to set up a domestically oriented production industry.

Getting it off the ground required some unusual steps, one of which provided for the obligatory distribution, and guaranteed the showing of all Peruvian-made films for eighteen months after release. What this means is that you'll often see a short (15–20-min.) film before the full-length feature. The bureacracy involved in getting films to the screen has ensured that a lot of them are thematically (and ideologically) unsound as well as often pretty poor technically.

There are, however, two very promising young Peruvian directors, Francisco Lombardi and Chicho Duran, who have both made interesting feature films dealing with important sociological and political issues. Well worth seeing if you get the chance are *Maruja en el Infierno* (Lombardi), *Ojos de Perro* (Duran), and *Malabrigo* (Duran). Lombardi's latest film, *The Mouth of the Wolf,* is an interesting Spanish coproduction attempting, without taking sides, to deal with the brutality and conscience surrounding terrorism in Peru. In recent years a few cinema clubs have sprung up around Lima, giving the public a chance to become a more critical audience and to see less commercially oriented films.

POLICE AND THIEVES

Most of your contact with the police will, with any luck, be at frontiers and controls. Depending on your personal appearance and the prevailing political climate the police at these posts (*Guardia Civil* and *Policia de Investigaciones*) may want to search your luggage; although this seldom happens it can be very thorough.

Occasionally, too, tourists are required to get off buses and register documents at the police controls which regulate the traffic of goods and people from one *Departmento* of Peru to another; these are usually situated on the outskirts of large towns on the main roads but you sometimes come across a control in the middle of nowhere. Always

**stop, and try to be scrupulously polite—
even if it seems that they're trying to make
things difficult for you.**

In general the police rarely bother travelers
but there are certain sore points. The possession
of (let alone trafficking in) either soft or hard
drugs (basically grass or cocaine) is considered
an extremely serious offense in Peru—usually
leading to at least a ten-year jail sentence. There
are many gringos languishing in Peruvian jails,
some of whom have been waiting two years for a
trial—if you have time to visit one of them you
can get details from your respective embassy.
There is no bail on serious charges.

Drugs apart, the police tend to follow the
media in suspecting all gringos of being **political
subversives** and even gun-runners or terrorists;
it's more than a little unwise to carry Maoist or
radical literature. If you find yourself in a tight
spot, don't make a statement before seeing someone from your embassy, and don't say anything
without the services of a reliable translator. It's
not unusual to be given the opportunity to pay a
bribe to the police (or any other official for that
matter) even if you've done absolutely nothing
wrong. You'll have to weigh this situation as it
arises—but remember that in South America
bribery is seen as an age-old custom rather than a
nasty form of corruption, and it can work to the
advantage of both parties, however annoying it
might seem. It's also worth noting that all police
are armed with either a revolver or a submachine
gun and will shoot at anyone who runs.

THIEVES—A WARNING

The biggest problem for travelers in Peru is, without a doubt, **thieves**, for which the country is
beginning to gain perhaps the worst reputation in
South America—on one particular train journey
(Arequipa–Puno at night) it has been estimated
that eighty percent of tourists are robbed.
Countless travelers have urged me to stress the
dangers of pickpockets and robberies in Peru, but
short of recommending a permanent state of
paranoia and constant watchfulness in busy
public situations there is little more a guidebook
can do. The *South American Explorers' Club* (see
above) is one of the best places for a lowdown on
up-to-date thieving practices, some of which
have developed over the years into really elaborate and quite skillful techniques.

Generally speaking, thieves (*ladrones*) work in
teams, in crowded markets, bus depots, and train
stations. One of them will distract your attention
(an old woman falling over in front of you or
someone splattering an ice cream down your
jacket) while another picks your pocket, cuts open
your bag with a razor, or simply runs off with it.
Also, in some of the more popular hotels in the
large cities, especially Lima, bandits masquerad-
ing as policemen break into rooms and steal the
guests' most valuable possessions while holding
the hotel staff at gun point. Objects left on
restaurant floors in busy parts of town, or in
unlocked hotel rooms, are obviously liable to take
a walk. Peruvians and tourists alike have even
had earrings ripped out on the street.

You'd need to hire a full-time security guard or
spend the whole time visibly guarding your
luggage to be even ninety percent sure of not
losing your gear, but a few simple **precautions**
can make life a lot easier. The most important is
to keep your ticket, passport (and tourist card),
money, and travelers' checks on your person at
all times (under your pillow while sleeping and on
your person when washing in communal hotel
bathrooms). Money belts or belt wallets are a
good idea for travelers' checks and tickets, or a
holder for your passport and money can be hung
either under a shirt around the neck, or from a
belt under trousers or skirts. Some people go as
far as lining their bags with chicken wire (called
maya in Peru) to make them knife-proof, and
wrapping wire around camera straps for the
same reason (putting their necks in danger to
save their cameras).

The only certain course is to insure your gear
and cash before you go, take refundable travelers' checks, register your passport at your
embassy in Lima on arrival (this doesn't take
long, and if you can fit it into your schedule can
save days should you lose yours), and keep your
eyes open and aware at all times. If you do get
ripped off, report it to the local police (preferably
the Tourist Police in the larger towns such as
Lima, Arequipa, and Cuzco) and ask them for a
certified *denuncia* —this can take a couple of
days—which will suffice for insurance purposes
when you get home.

Camping can again make your possessions
vulnerable, particularly near towns and on mainstream tourist routes like the *Inca Trail*. The
secret is probably to get on as good terms as
possible with local people; if you become friendly
with someone who allows you to camp nearby
it's very unlikely that anyone else will touch your
gear.

SEXUAL HARASSMENT

So many oppressive limitations are imposed on women's freedom to travel together or alone that any advice or warning seems merely to reinforce the situation. That said, _machismo_ is well ingrained in the Peruvian mentality, particularly in the towns, and the _gringa_ (female foreigner) is almost universally seen as liberated and therefore sexually available.

On the whole, the situations you'll encounter are more annoying than dangerous, with frequent whistling and hissing in the **cities**, sometimes comments or touching on buses or trains. Mostly these are situations you'd deal with routinely at home—as _Limena_ women do here in the capital—but they can, understandably and rightly, seem threatening without a clear understanding of Peruvian Spanish and slang. To avoid getting

caught up in something you can't control, any provocation is best totally ignored. In a public situation, however, any real harassment might best be dealt with very loudly.

In the predominantly Indian, **remote areas** there is less of an overt problem—though this is surprisingly where most physical assaults take place. They are not common, however—you're probably safer hiking in the Andes than in most American cities. Two obvious, but enduring, pieces of advice are to travel with friends (being on your own makes you most vulnerable), and if you're camping, to be quite open about it. As ever, making yourself known to locals gives a kind of acceptance and insurance, and it may even lead to the offer of a room—Peruvians, particularly those in rural areas, can be incredibly kind and hospitable.

DIRECTORY

ADDRESSES are frequently written with just the street name and number: for example, Pizarro 135. Officially, though, they're usually prefixed by _Calle_ or _Jiron_ (street), or _Avenida_. The first digit of any street number (or sometimes the first two digits) represents the block number within the street as a whole. Note too that many of the major streets in Lima have two names—a relic of the military governments of the 1970s.

ARTESANIA Traditional craft goods from most regions of Peru can be found in markets and shops in Lima. Woolen and alpaca products, though, are usually cheaper and often better quality in the _sierra_—particularly in Juliaca and Puno; carved gourds are imported from around Huancayo, while the best places to buy ceramic replicas are Trujilo, Huaraz, and Nazca. Oxfam's _Antisuyo_ shop in Lima is good for jungle crafts.

BARGAINING is generally expected in markets and with taxi drivers (before getting in). It's also sometimes possible to haggle over the price of hotel rooms if you're traveling in a group. Food and shop prices, however, tend to be strictly fixed.

CAMPING EQUIPMENT is difficult to find and relatively expensive. One or two places sell, rent, or buy secondhand gear: the _South American Explorers' Club_ in Lima; the _Hotel Barcelona_ in Huaraz; and a couple of shops and tour/trek agencies in Cuzco, near the Plaza de Armas. It's worth checking the notice boards in the popular gringo hotels and bars for gear that is no longer needed or for people looking for trekking companions. _Camping Gaz_ butane canisters are available from most of the above places and from some _fereterías_ (hardware stores) in the more important tourist resorts.

CONTRACEPTION Condoms (*Profilacticos*) are available from street vendors and some *farmacias*. Rumor has it that these are another example of U.S. rejects being sold to a less discriminating and less well informed market. The pill is also available, officially prescription only but frequently sold over the counter: you're unlikely to be able to match your brand, however, so it's far better to bring a supply. It's worth remembering that if you suffer from moderately severe diarrhea on your trip the pill (or any other drug) may not be in your system long enough to take effect.

CUSTOMS Regulations stipulate that no items of archeological or historical value or interest may be removed from the country. If you try you'll have the goods confiscated at the least, and may find yourself in front of a Peruvian court.

ELECTRIC CURRENT 200 volt/60 cycles AC is the standard except in Arequipa where it is 200 volt/50 cycles. For most standard U.S. appliances you'll need both a transformer and a universal plug adaptor. Even then, don't rely on the supply being too reliable.

EXTRAS you may want to bring include: **film** (expensive in Peru); a **padlock** (additional security in hotel rooms); **glucose tablets** (useful against the milder effects of altitude sickness); **gifts** for kids and adults, particularly if you're hiking (small coins, stamps, pens, pencils, photos, and postcards from home are often appreciated). See also "Health" (pp.9–10).

FEMINIST MOVEMENT Feminism is still relatively new to Peru—and inevitably urban. However, there are two major feminist organizations: *Flora Tristan* (Av. Arenales 601, Lima) and the less radical *Peru Mujer*. The former is allied to the United Left and its basic tenet is "first socialism, then the feminist revolution." There is one feminist magazine, *Mujeres y Sociedad* (Women and Society), produced three or four times a year. For help, literature, or advice try *Flora Tristan*, the *Libreria de la Mujer* bookshop (near the start of Avenida Arenales, Lima), or the *Women's Center* which is run by nuns near the center of Lima (in Quilca just half a block from Avenida Wilson).

GAY LIFE is still pretty much underground but in recent years Lima has seen a liberating advance (in what's still a very *macho* society). Transvestites can now walk the streets in relative freedom from abuse and there are one or two gay clubs. Beyond Lima, however, there is no organized gay life.

INSECTS are more of an irritation than a serious problem, but on the coast, in the jungle, and to a lesser extent in the mountains, the **common fly** is a definite pest. Although it can carry typhoid, there is little one can do; you might spend mealtimes successfully fighting flies from your plate but even in expensive restaurants it's difficult to regulate hygiene in the kitchens. A more obvious problem is the **mosquito**, which in some parts of the lowland jungle carries malaria. Repellents are of limited value—it's better to cover your arms, legs, and feet with a good layer of clothing. Mosquitoes tend to emerge after dark, but the daytime holds even worse biting insects in the jungle regions, among them the **Manta Blanca** (or white blanket), so called because in bad spots they swarm as a blanket of tiny flying insects. They don't hurt when they bite but itch like crazy for a few days after. Antihistamine creams or tablets can reduce the sting or itchiness of most insect bites, but try not to scratch them, and if it gets unbearable ask the locals or go to the nearest *farmacia* for advice. To keep hotel rooms relatively clear, buy some of the spirals of incense-like pyrethrin, available cheaply everywhere.

INSULTS are sometimes hurled at gringos by Peruvians who begrudge the apparent relative wealth and freedom of tourists. Remember, however, that the terms "gringo" or "mister" are not generally meant in an offensive way in Peru.

LAUNDRY can be done in the communal washrooms of most basic hotels; failing this, labor is so cheap that it's no real expense to get your clothes washed by the hotel or in a *lavandeir* (laundry). Things tend to disappear from public washing lines so be careful where you leave clothes drying.

NATURAL DISASTERS Peru has more than its fair share of avalanches, landslides, and earthquakes—and there's not a lot you can do about any of them. If you're naturally wise or cautious you might want to register on arrival with your embassy; they like this, and it does help them in the event of a major quake (or an escalation of the current terrorist activity). Landslides—*huaycos*—devastate the roads and railroads every rainy season, though alternative routes are usually found surprisingly quickly.

PHOTOGRAPHY The light in Peru is very bright with a strong contrast between shade and sun. This can produce a nice effect and generally speaking it's easy to take good pictures. One of the more complex problems is how to take photos of people without upsetting them. You should always talk to a prospective subject first, and ask if s/he minds if you take a quick photo (*un fotito*); most people react favorably to this approach even if all the communication is in sign language. Film is expensive to buy, so take as much as you think you'll need with you. If you can bear the suspense it's best to save getting films developed until you're home—they tend to get badly scratched even in the Lima Kodak laboratory.

PUNCTUALITY is unimportant in Peru except where public transportation is concerned. The bus, train, or plane won't wait a minute. People, however, almost expect friends to be an hour or more late for an appointment (don't arrange to meet a Peruvian on the street—make it a bar or café). Peruvians stipulate that an engagement is *a la hora inglesa* (by English time) if they genuinely want people to arrive within half an hour of the time they fix.

TAMPONS are available—though expensive—at *farmacias*.

TERRORISM is a real problem in Peru these days. You can get up-to-date information on the situation from the *South American Explorers' Club*, but generally speaking there are two main terrorist groups active in Peru—the *Sendero Luminoso* (the Shining Path) and *Tupac Amaru* (MRTA). *Sendero* springs from rural Quechua dissidents while MRTA tends to operate from the larger cities. Neither group is particularly interested in tourists or in gaining the world's attention through publicity. They see themselves as engaged in a battle against the Peruvian political structure. Tourists are not political targets. As the *South American Explorer's Club* puts it, "the visitor, when considering his safety, would be better off concentrating on how to avoid being run over in the crazed Lima traffic." That having been said, tourists have been killed. The Departamento of Apurimac is still a dangerous zone, as is the region and roads around Tingo Maria in the central high jungle and north from here towards the Huallaga valley. Drug trafficking and terrorism are in certain places and at certain times quite difficult to distinguish, and much of the coca-growing area of the eastern Andes/western Amazon is already well beyond the control of the law.

TIME Peru keeps the same hours as New York—Eastern Standard Time.

WATER is usually safe to drink but if you've just arrived in South America it's best to stick to the bottled stuff (*agua mineral*), and in remote areas to ask if it's okay (*es potable?*) before drinking. Occasional outbreaks of water-related hepatitis do occur.

WORK Your only real chance of earning money in Peru is **teaching English** in Lima, or with luck in Arequipa or Cuzco. Given the state of the economy there's little prospect in other fields, though in the more remote parts of the country it may sometimes be possible to find board and lodging in return for a little **building work** or general laboring. This is simply a question of keeping your eyes open and making personal contacts. There is an enormous amount of **bureaucracy** involved if you want to work (or live) officially in Peru. For **biology graduates** there's a chance of free board and lodging if you're willing to work for three months or more as a tour guide in a jungle lodge: for this "Resident Naturalist" scheme contact *Peruvian Safaris S.A.*, Garcilaso de la Vega 1334, Lima (☎31-3047).

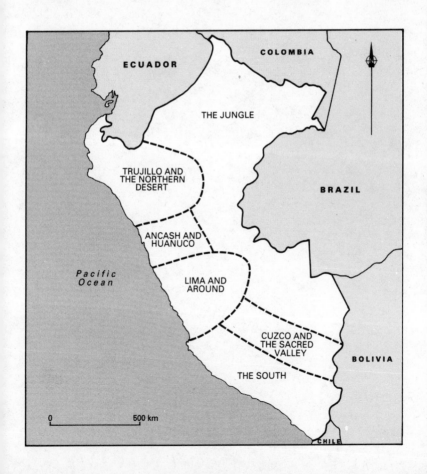

CHAPTER ONE

LIMA AND AROUND

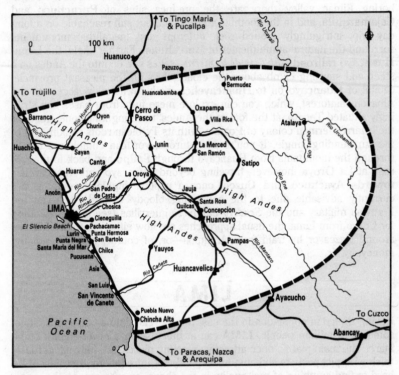

Y ou're almost inevitably going to visit **Lima**—and certainly you can't
fully come to grips with Peru without having seen the capital—but
it's not likely to prove the highlight of your trip. Though long established as the seat of government, and once reputed to be the most
beautiful city of Spanish America, Lima is today a rather daunting, shapeless
sprawl of modern suburbs and *barriadas*—shanty towns that run for miles in
each direction along the Pan American Highway. This is not to say you can't
enjoy it—Limeños are generally very open, and the way of life (with its
incredibly complex status system) is distinctive and compelling—but it's
important not to come here expecting the city to be something it's not. There
is still a certain elegance to its old colonial center, and a string of excellent
and important museums befitting its position as seat of national government,
but Lima is not impressive or exotic, and most of the downtown areas are
blandly Western in style.

As some compensation, the area immediately **around Lima** does offer plenty of reasons to delay your progress on towards Arequipa or Cuzco. Within an hour or so's bus ride south, toward the sheltered bay of **El Silencio**, the coastline is deserted and lined by a series of near-perfect beaches. Above them the imposing fortress-temple complex of **Pachacamac** stands poised above a sandstone cliff at the edge of the ocean. In the neighboring Rimac valley there are the pre-Inca sites of **Puruchuco** and **Cajamarquila**, and in the foothills above Lima, but still reachable on a long day trip, intriguingly eroded rock outcrops and megalithic monuments surround the natural amphitheater of **Marcahuasi**. Farther afield, the **Lima-Huancayo railroad**—*El Tren de la Sierra*—takes you up into the Andes on a steep and startling climb above the clouds through the pleasant provincial capital of **Huancayo** on to **Huancavelica**; both towns allow access to the Amazon rainforest, which you can explore more fully from bases like strikingly situated **Tarma**, at the foot of the Andes' towering limestone crags, or the bizarre German colony of **Pozuzo**, with its Tyrolean roofs peaking out of the surrounding jungle. If you're adventurous, you can complete a circuit through the mountains from Huancayo through **Satipo** and back to the railroad at **La Oroya**; however, traveling beyond Huancayo and Huancavelica **towards Ayachuco and Cuzco**, once a popular highland route, is not currently advisable due to the continuing bloody struggle between the Peruvian military and the *Sendero Luminoso* guerrillas (see p.301). Heading for Cuzco from Lima, the usual approaches are now either up from the coast around Nazca or by train from Arequipa—or, of course, if you've got the money, by air.

LIMA

Having tripled in population in the past twenty years into a boisterous city of some eight million people, **LIMA** can at times seem a never-ending nightmare. The main plazas, once attractive meeting places, are now dangerously thick with pickpockets, exhaust fumes, and, not infrequently, riot police. It's hard to find anything of real quality in the shops, or even among the *ambulantes*, Lima's traditional street sellers who have recently been herded into a small zone along the uninviting Rimac river, which trickles along the city center. Perhaps overriding everything else, it's the **climate** that seems to set the mood: outside the summer months (December to April), a low, heavy mist descends over the arid valley in which the city sits, forming a solid gray blanket from the beaches up as far as Chosica in the foothills of the Andes—a dulling and depressing phenomenon which is undoubtedly made worse by the critical air pollution problems.

The positive side of Lima is more difficult to pin down. On a strictly guidebook level there are the **museums** (the best of which are excellent and should be mandatory before setting off for Machu Picchu or any of the other great Inca ruins of Peru), the Spanish **churches** in the center, and some distinguished **mansions** in the wealthy suburbs of Barranco and Miraflores.

And in their own way, too, there's a powerful atmosphere in the *barriadas*—future hope of Peru's landless peasants.

Personally, staying and working in the city—immersed in its noisy, fast-moving craziness—I've always found my frustrations mellowed by the presence of the sea and the beaches, and by the mix of lifestyles and peoples: from the snappy, sassy Creole style—all big, fast, American cars, cruising the broad main streets—to a ridiculously easygoing, happy-go-lucky attitude that can come like a godsend when you're trying to get through some bureaucratic hassle. And, as anyone who stays here more than a week or so finds, Limeño hospitality and kindness are almost infinite once you've established an initial rapport.

Some History

Even if you don't have the time or the inclination to search out and savor the delights and agonies of Lima, it is possible to get a good feel for the place in only a few days. Out at Ancón, now a popular beach resort just north of Lima, an important **pre-Inca** burial site shows signs of occupation—including pottery, textiles, and the oldest known archer's bow in the entire Americas—going back at least 3000 years. Although certainly one of the most populous valleys, the Rimac area first showed indications of true urbanization around A.D. 1200 with the appearance of a strong, independent culture—the **Cuismancu State**—in many ways parallel to, though not as large as, the contemporary Chimu Empire which bordered it to the north. **Cajamarquilla**, a huge, somewhat crowded, adobe city-complex associated with the Cuismancu, now rests peacefully under the desert sun only a few kilometers beyond Lima's outer suburbs. Dating from the same era, but some 30km south of the modern city, is the **Temple of Pachacamac**. For hundreds of years, until ransacked by the *Conquistadores*, this shrine attracted thousands of pilgrims from all over Peru, the Incas being the last in a series of dominant groups to adopt Pachacamac as one of their own major *huacas*.

When the Spanish first arrived here the valley was dominated by three important **Inca**-controlled urban complexes: **Carabayllo** to the north near Chillón; **Maranga**, now partly destroyed by the Avenida La Marina, between the modern city and the Port of Callao; and **Surco**, now a suburb within the confines of greater Lima but where, until the mid-seventeenth century, you could still see the adobe houses of ancient chiefs lying empty yet painted in a variety of colorful images.

Francisco Pizarro founded **Spanish Lima**, "City of the Kings," in 1535—only two years after the invasion. Evidently recommended by canny mountain Indians as a site for a potential capital (this part of the coast doesn't have a very healthy climate at the best of times), it proved essentially a good choice, offering a natural harbor nearby, a large well-watered river valley, as well as relatively easy access up into the Andes. By the 1550s the town had grown up around a large plaza with wide streets leading through a fine collection of mansions, all elegantly adorned by wooden terraces, and well-stocked shops run by wealthy merchants. Since the very beginning Spanish Lima has been separate and quite different from the more popular Peruvian image: it looks out, away from the Andes and the past, towards the Pacific for contact with the world beyond.

Lima rapidly developed into the capital of a viceroyalty which encompassed not only Peru but also Ecuador, Bolivia, and Chile. The University of San Marcos, founded in 1551, is the oldest on the continent, and Lima housed the headquarters of the Inquisition from 1570 until 1813. It remained the most important, the richest, and—hardly credible today—the most beautiful city in South America until the shockwave of independence radically altered the continental balance of power during the early nineteenth century.

Perhaps the most prosperous era for Lima was the **seventeenth century**. By 1610 its population had reached a manageable 26,000, made up of 40 percent Blacks (mostly slaves), 38 percent Spanish, no more than 8 percent pure Indian, another 8 percent (of unspecified ethnic origin) living under religious orders, and less than 6 percent of mixed blood—now probably the largest proportion of inhabitants. The center of Lima was crowded with shops and stalls selling silks and fancy furniture from as far afield as China. Even these days it's not hard to imagine what Lima must have been like in the seventeenth century. A substantial section of the colonial city is still preserved—many of its streets, set in large regular blocks, are overhung by ornate wooden balconies, and elaborate baroque facades bring some of the older churches to life, regardless of the din and hassle of modern city living. **Rimac**, a suburb just over the river from the Plaza de Armas, and the port area of **Callao**, developed as satellite settlements—initially catering to the very rich though now predominantly "slum" sectors.

The eighteenth century, a period of relative stagnation for Lima, was dramatically punctuated by the tremendous **earthquake** of 1746, which left only twenty houses standing and killed some 5000 residents—nearly ten percent of the population. From 1761 to 1776 Lima and Peru were governed by Viceroy Amat, who, although more renowned for his relationship with the actress *La Perricholi*, is also remembered as the instigator of Lima's **rebirth**. Under him the city lost its cloistered atmosphere, opening out with broad avenues, striking gardens, rococo mansions, and palatial salons. Influenced by the Bourbons, Amat's designs for the city's architecture arrived hand in hand with other transatlantic reverberations of the Enlightenment.

In the nineteenth century Lima expanded still farther to the east and south. The suburbs of **Barrios Altos** and **La Victoria** were poor from the start; above the beaches at **Magdalena**, **Miraflores**, and **Barranco** the wealthy developed new enclaves of their own. These were originally separated from the center by several kilometers of farmland, then still studded with fabulous pre-Inca *huacas* and other adobe ruins.

It was **President Leguia** who revitalized Lima by "cleaning up" the central areas betwen 1919 and 1930. Plaza San Martin's attractive colonnades and the *Gran Hotel Bolivar* were erected, the Presidential Palace was rebuilt, and the city was supplied with its first ever drinking-water and sewage systems. This was the signal for Lima's explosion into the modern era of ridiculously **rapid growth**. The 300,000 inhabitants of 1930 mushroomed into over 3,500,000 by 1975, and the population has more than doubled again in the last fifteen years. Most of this growth is accounted for by massive immigration of peasants from the provinces into the *barriadas* or *pueblos jovenes*—"young towns"—now pressing in on the city along all of its landbound edges.

Today the city is as cosmopolitan as any other in the Third World, its thriving middle classes seeking standards of living comparable to those of the West or better. The majority, however, scrape together meager incomes while being physically, ethnically, and economically considered marginal. The fact that they form the core and very essence of modern Lima is perhaps easier to realize as a visitor.

Arriving and Getting Around

Arriving in Lima, whether by air from another continent or overland from some other region, can be disorienting. At ground level there are few landmarks even to register the direction of the center of town. Laid out across a wide, flat alluvial plain, Lima fans out in long, straight streets from its old colonial heart; one, **Avenida Benavides**, stretches out towards the harbor area around Callao and the airport, while perpendicular to this, another arm, **Avenida Arequipa**, reaches out to **Miraflores** and the old beach resort of **Barranco**. Initially, every place looks the same—dusty shanty settlements surrounding increasingly more permanent constructions as you get closer to the central **Plaza de Armas**.

Coming into Lima **by air** it's possible, on a clear day, to get some perspective on the city. After crossing the high Andes, the flight path follows a narrow, desolate desert strip bordering the Pacific Ocean, its only relief small yellow studs of foothills rising towards the east. As you near the city you can usually make it out, crowded into the mouth of a river valley with low sandy mountains closing in around its outer fringes. On the ground you're thrown, almost unexpectedly, onto the middle of a bustling, very modern airport concourse. The immediate urge, and quite a sensible one, is to get out as quickly as possible. **Taxis** to the center will cost around $5, or $8 to Miraflores. Many of the drivers might start off by asking for $10, but if you're really prepared to haggle and shop around you may get into town on $3. A much cheaper, very efficient alternative is to take the **airport bus** which sells tickets from a little office just beyond Customs; for a flat rate (around $1) this will take you to a hotel of your choice anywhere in Lima.

If you're **arriving overland**, the chances are you'll end up in the older, more central areas of town, around Parque Universitario, the *Hotel Sheraton*, or La Victoria. Whichever of these, it's unwise to wander off looking lost or bemused by a new and exciting environment—thieves abound at bus and train terminals. If you're not confident of finding your way out of the crowds, the best move is probably to hail the first **taxi** you see, name a hotel, and fix a price.

Getting to know Lima and **finding your way around** takes some time. In the old center, the obvious points of reference are the **Plaza de Armas** and the more modern **Plaza San Martin**—separated by some five blocks of the

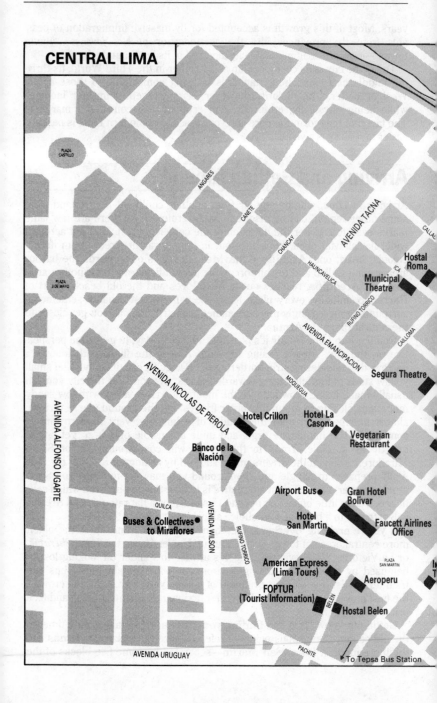

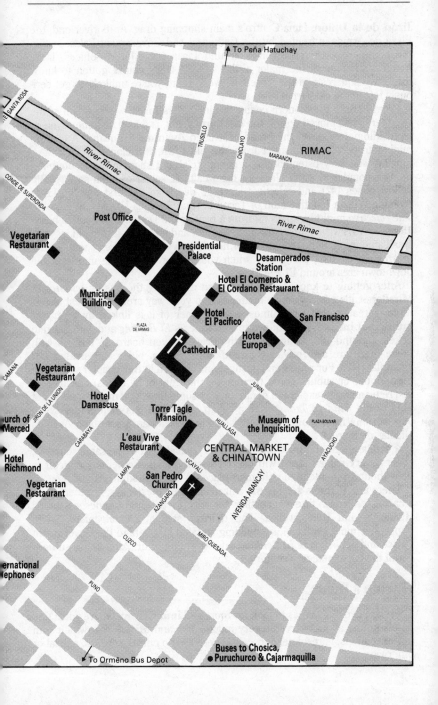

↑ To Peña Hatuchay

River Rimac

TRUJILLO

CHICLAYO

MARANON

RIMAC

CONDE DE SUPERONDA

River Rimac

Post Office

Vegetarian Restaurant

Presidential Palace

Desamperados Station

Hotel El Comercio & El Cordano Restaurant

Municipal Building

Hotel El Pacifico

San Francisco

PLAZA DE ARMAS

Cathedral

Hotel Europa

CAMANA

Vegetarian Restaurant

JIRON DE LA UNION

JUNIN

Hotel Damascus

Torre Tagle Mansion

HUALLAGA

Museum of the Inquisition

PLAZA BOLIVAR

urch of Merced

CARABAYA

L'eau Vive Restaurant

CENTRAL MARKET & CHINATOWN

AYACUCHO

Hotel Richmond

UCAYALI

LAMPA

San Pedro Church

AVENIDA ABANCAY

Vegetarian Restaurant

AZANGARO

MIRO QUESADA

CUZCO

ernational ephones

PUNO

↙ To Orméno Bus Depot

Buses to Chosica, ● Puruchurco & Cajarmaquilla

Jirón de la Unión, Lima Centro's main shopping drag. At its river end, the Plaza de Armas is fronted by the Cathedral and Government Palace, while the commercial center revolves around Plaza San Martin—offices, large hotels, and some of the major airline offices. Once you've gotten to know these two squares and the streets between them you're unlikely to get seriously lost in the old part of town.

From here to the modern center of Lima, **Miraflores**, where much of the commerce has moved during the last thirty years, is a haul of some seven or eight kilometers down the broad, tree-lined **Avenida Arequipa**. A cliff-top mini-metropolis, very distinct from the old town, Miraflores is slick, fast-moving, and very ostentatious—a commercial and shopping zone doubling up as a popular meeting place for the wealthier sector of Lima society. Big yellow buses (#2) and *colectivos* leave all day from the first few blocks of Avenida Wilson (continuation of Tacna beyond Avenida Nicolas de Pierola). The *colectivo* might be anything from a beat-up old Dodge Coronet to a plush 15-seater VW; wave it down from any corner, and if it stops just get in, pay the small amount of money the driver or his chum will ask for, then shout *"baja a la proxima esquina, por favor!"* when you're approaching the unmistakable downtown area around **El Pacifico**.

After getting to know Lima Centro and mastering the bus or *colectivo* to Miraflores, it's a fairly simple matter to find your way around the rest of this huge, spread-eagled city. Almost every corner of it is linked by a regular **municipal bus service**, known to everyone as *El Bussing* and with flat rate tickets (around 10¢) bought from the driver as you board. In tandem with these there are also privately owned **microbuses**, older and smaller but again flat rates. For routes and destinations covered in this chapter you'll find the number or suburb name (written on the front of all buses) specified; if you're planning to explore in depth, or stay some time, you might want to get hold of the *Guía de Transportes*, a cheap, up-to-date bus map guide, which you can buy from most of the stalls around Plaza San Martin and Avenida Nicolas de Pierola.

A similar guide, **Lima: Guía de Calles** (available from the same sources), covers every named street with an index and a map—something difficult to do without if you intend to visit many places in and around the capital.

There are no trams serving the citizens of Lima these days, but there is an amazing **railroad line** connecting the city to the high Andes as far as Huancayo and Huancavelica. The railroad station, *Desamperados*, is an impressive nineteenth-century building situated just behind the Government Palace and opposite the *El Cordano* café, an eating or drinking house straight out of the late nineteenth century.

Finding a Room

There are two main areas to look for rooms—**Lima Centro**, where you'll find hotels in just about every category imaginable, and **Miraflores**, which with few exceptions, is resolutely upscale. There are no **campgrounds**, official or otherwise.

Lima Centro

Most travelers **on a tight budget** seem to end up in one of three traditional gringo dives around *Desamperados* train station. The *Hotel Europa* (☎27-3351), always one of the best of these, opposite San Francisco church at Jirón Ancash 376, has been substantially renovated and improved but is still reasonably priced. The others—*El Commercio* and *Hotel Pacifico*—are cheap (from around $1) but leave a lot to be desired; both are situated opposite the right-hand side of the Government Palace in Carabaya. An unnamed hotel at Nicolas de Pierola 730, on the first floor, is a little more expensive but offers hot water, a common room, and the relative peace and quiet of a twelve bed *hostal* in the center of a busy city. More impressive looking, though seldom offering hot water, is the *Hotel Richmond*, an old mansion with plenty of rooms for around $1, in a very central location at Jr. Union 706. Also within a few blocks of the Plaza de Armas are the *Hostal Machu Picchu* (Cailloma 231), basic but good value, and the easygoing *San Sebastian* (Jr. Ica 712). For somewhat better facilities you might also try the *Hostal Belen*, again well situated, at Belen 1049, just below the Plaza San Martin. The *Hotel Damascus* (Ucayali 199), just one block away from the Plaza de Armas, is well priced and safe for around $4 single.

Slightly upscale, the *Hostal Roma* is a very pleasant place to stay, with communal or private bathrooms and a luggage storage service (Jr. Ica 326; ☎27-7576—from around $7 single). Or, at about the same price there's the very pleasant *Hotel la Casona* (Moquegua 289; ☎27-6273/74/75), excellent value if you can afford it, the once extremely elegant rooms set around an inviting colonial courtyard, with a handy restaurant opening onto it; the hotel has a good laundry service too. Care should be taken with luggage and hand-bags on arrival, or when having a bite at the patio tables, since the courtyard is open to the street and this *is* central Lima. Up the ladder, but not into the $70 to $120 range of the *Gran Bolivar, Sheraton, Crillon,* and *Miraflores Cesar* hotels, one of the only options for relative luxury in central Lima is the *Hotel San Martin* (Nicolas de Pierola 887; ☎285337)—under $35 for a double room on the Plaza San Martin (above Parilladas San Martin).

Miraflores and the Suburbs

There are no cheap places to stay in **Miraflores**, though the **youth hostel** (*Albergue Juvenil International*, Av. Casimiro Ulloa 328; ☎46-5488) is quite reasonable at $4 or $5 and you don't have to be a member. It's within a ten- or fifteen-minute walk of downtown Miraflores and, although the beds are communal bunks, it does have the advantage of kitchen facilities and a swimming pool (not always open). Most other places in Miraflores are nearer the top of the range: the *Pensión Alemana* (Av. Arequipa 4704; ☎45092) offers superb accommodation, excellent service, and is on the main *colectivo*/bus route connecting Miraflores with Lima Centro. The *Residencial Inn* (General Borgoño 280; ☎471704) also comes well recommended and favorably priced at around $12 per person. *Hotel La Alameda* (Jose Pardo 930; $20 per person) is clean and comfortable and well positioned in Miraflores. There are scores of more expensive hotels in this area, but if you don't mind going slightly farther afield into the lovely cliff-top suburb of Barranco, more or less next to

Miraflores, you might want to stay from around $10 at the *Hostal Barranco* (Malecon Osma 104; ☎67-1753), towards the ocean just beyond the municipal park.

If you intend on staying in Lima for some length of time, it's often worth checking the ads in *El Commercio* or the *Lima Times* for the addresses of **private householders** willing to rent out rooms, by the week or longer, to gringos passing through.

Lima Centro: The Old City

Since its foundation, Lima has spread steadily out from the Plaza de Armas—virtually all of the Río Rimac's alluvial soils have now been built on and even the sand dunes beyond are rapidly filling up with migrant settlers. When Pizarro arrived here he found a valley dominated by some four hundred temples and palaces, most of them pre-Inca, well spread out to either side of the river; the natives were apparently peaceful, living mostly by cultivating gardens, fishing from the ocean, or catching freshwater crayfish. As usual, Pizarro's choice for the site of this new Spanish town was related as much to politics as it was to geography: he founded Lima next to the Rimac on the site of an existing palace belonging to *Tauri Chusko*, the local chief who had little choice but to give up his residence and move away.

The Plaza de Armas

Today in the **Plaza de Armas**—or "armed plaza" (*Plaza Armada*) as the early Conquistadores preferred to call it—not a sign remains of Indian heritage. Standing on the site of Tauri Chusko's palace is the relatively modern Government Palace, the Cathedral occupies the site of an Inca temple once dedicated to the Puma deity, while the Municipal Building lies on what was originally an Inca envoy's mansion. The **Presidential Palace** was Pizarro's house long before the present edifice was ever conceived of. It was here that he spent the last few years of his life and was eventually assassinated in 1541. Its ground might even be considered somewhat "sacred" since as he died, his jugular severed by an assassin's rapier, he fell to the floor, drew a cross, then kissed it. What you can see today, however, was completed in 1938. It's a clean, almost impressive building, though nothing special. Between 12:30 and 1pm you can usually witness the **changing of the guards**—not a particularly wonderful spectacle but immediately afterwards there are **guided tours** of the Palaces (starting from the visitor's side entrance in Jr. Union).

Less than 50m away, the **Cathedral**, squat and austere, was modeled on that of Jaén in Spain. Like Jaén, it has three aisles following the Renaissance design adopted by Francisco Becerra. When Becerra died in 1605, however, it was still far from completion. The towers weren't finished for another forty years and, in 1746, the ultimate frustration arrived in the guise of a devastating earthquake. The "modern" building, essentially a reconstruction of Becerra's design, is primarily of interest for its **Museum of Religious Art and Treasures** (daily 10am–1pm and 2–5pm; small charge) and, in the first chapel on the right, some human remains thought to be **Pizarro's body** (quite fitting since he placed the first stone shortly before his death). Although gloomy, the interior retains some of its appealing Churriguerresque—highly elaborate baroque—decor. The stalls are superb and, even more impressive, the choir was exquisitely carved in the early seventeenth century by a Catalan artist. The Archbishop's Palace next door was rebuilt as recently as 1924.

Directly across the square, the **Municipal Building** (Mon.–Fri. 9am–1pm; free) is a typical example of a half-hearted twentieth-century attempt at something neocolonial. Brilliant white on the outside, its most memorable features are permanent groups of heavily armed guards and the odd armored car waiting conspicuously for some kind of action. Inside, the **Pinacoteca Museum** houses a selection of Peruvian paintings, notably those of Ignacio Merino from the nineteenth century. In the library (*la biblioteca*) you can also see the city's Act of Foundation and Declaration of Independence.

Between the Municipal Building and the post office, set back from one corner of the main square, is the church and monastery of **Santo Domingo** (daily 9am–1pm and 4–8pm; monastery closes at 5:30pm; small charge). Completed in 1549, Santo Domingo was presented by the pope, a century or so later, with an alabaster statue of Santa Rosa de Lima. Rosa's tomb, and that of San Martin de Porres, are its great attractions—and much revered. Otherwise it's not of great interest nor architectural merit, although it is one of the oldest religious structures in Lima, built on a site granted to the Dominicans by Pizarro in 1535.

East of the Plaza de Armas

Ancash leads away from the Presidential Palace and Desamperados train station towards one of Lima's most attractive churches, **San Francisco** (daily 10am–12pm and 3–6pm). A large seventeenth-century construction with an engaging stone facade, San Francisco's vaults and columns are elaborately decorated with *mudéjar* (Moorish-style) plaster relief. It's a majestic building which has withstood well the passage of time and devastation of successive tremors. Guided tours are offered (at 1pm and 5pm) of the monastery and its **catacombs**, both of which are worth a visit. Discovered only in 1951, the vast crypts contain the skulls and bones of some 70,000 persons. Opposite San Francisco, at Ancash 390, is **La Casa Pilatos** (Mon.–Fri. 11am–1:30pm), now the home of the *Instituto Nacional de Cultura* and one of several well-restored colonial mansions in Lima. Quite a simple building, and no competition for Torre Tagle (see below), it nevertheless has an attractive courtyard with an unusual stone staircase leading up from the middle of the patio.

A couple of blocks away, the **Museum of the Inquisition** (Junin 548) faces out onto Plaza Bolivar near the Congress building. Behind a facade of "Greek" classical columns, the museum (Mon.–Fri. 9am–7pm, Sat. 9am–3pm; free) contains the original tribunal room with a beautifully carved mahogany ceiling. Underneath are dungeons and torture chambers with a few life-sized human models to show what it was really like. From 1570 until 1820 this was the headquarters of the Inquisition for the whole of Spanish-dominated America. The few blocks behind the Museum of the Inquisition and Avenida Abancay are devoted to the **central market** and **Chinatown**. Perhaps one of

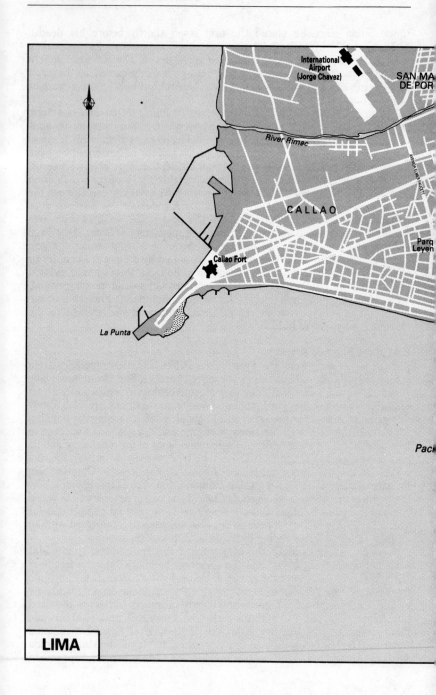

International
Airport
(Jorge Chavez)

SAN MA
DE POR

River Rimac

CALLAO

Parq
Leyen

Callao Fort

La Punta

Pac

LIMA

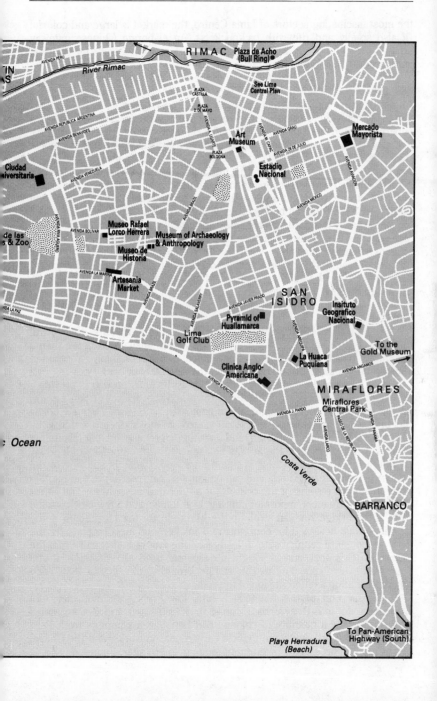

the most fascinating sectors of Lima Centro, the market is large and colorful (if also smelly and rife with pickpockets). An elaborate Chinese gateway crosses over one of the main streets, a perfect reference point for the best and cheapest *chifa* restaurants.

Torre Tagle Palace, pride and joy of the old city, can be found at Ucayali 363, between Chinatown and the Plaza de Armas. Now the home of Peru's Ministry for Foreign Relations and consequently recognizable by the security forces with machine guns on the roof and top veranda, Torre Tagle is a superb mansion built in the 1730s and beautifully maintained. It is embellished with a decorative facade and two wooden balconies—typical of Lima in that one is larger than the other. The porch and patio are distinctly Andalucian, although some of the intricate wood carvings on pillars and across ceilings display a visionary native influence; the *azulejos*, or tiling, also shows a strong fusion of styles—this time a combination of Moorish and Limeño tastes. In the left-hand corner of the patio you can see a set of scales like those used to weigh merchandise during colonial times, and the house also contains a magnificent sixteenth-century carriage complete with mobile toilet. Originally, mansions such as Torre Tagle served as refuges for outlaws, the authorities being unable to enter without written and stamped permission. Now the building is occupied by the Foreign Ministry, and afternoons are the best time to visit.

Rimac

It's a short walk north from the Plaza de Armas to the **Puente de Piedra**, the stone bridge which arches over the Río Rimac—usually no more than a miserable trickle—behind the Government Palace. Initially a wooden construction, today's bridge was built in the seventeenth century, using egg whites to improve the consistency of its mortar. Its function was to provide a permanent link between the center of town and the district of San Lazaro, known these days as **Rimac**, or, more popularly, as *Bajo El Puente* ("below the bridge"). This zone was first populated in the sixteenth century by African slaves, newly imported and awaiting purchase by big plantation owners; a few years later Rimac was beleaguered with outbreaks of leprosy. Although these days its status is much improved, Rimac is still one of the most run-down areas of Lima and can be quite an aggressive place at night—unfortunate since some of the best *peñas* are located down here. The **Plaza de Acho**, Lima's most important bullring, is in Rimac, and a few blocks to the right of the bridge you can stroll up the **Alameda de los Descalzos**, a fine tree-lined walk designed for courtship and an afternoon meeting place for the early seventeenth-century elite. It leads past the foot of a distinctive hill, the Cerro San Cristobal, and although in desperate need of renovation, it still possesses twelve appealing marble statues brought from Italy in 1856, each one representing a different sign of the zodiac.

At the far end of the Alameda a fine, low Franciscan monastery, **El Convento de los Descalzos** (Mon.–Sat. 9:30am–1pm and 3–6pm; small charge), houses a quantity of colonial and Republican paintings from Peru and Ecuador. A little museum depicts early monastic works, and the Chapel of El Carmen possesses a beautiful baroque gold-leaf altar. Founded in 1592, the monastery was situated in a then secluded spot beyond the town, protected from earthquakes by the Cerro San Cristobal. The Convento offers half-hour **tours** for under 50¢.

South of the Plaza de Armas

The largest area of old Lima is the stretch **between the Plaza de Armas and Plaza San Martin.** Worth a quick look here is the church of **San Augustin** (daily 8:30am–noon and 3:30–5:30pm) on the corner of Ica and Camana. Severely damaged by earthquake activity, only the small side chapel can be visited nowadays but it has a glorious facade, one of the most complicated examples of Churrigueresque inspiration in Peru. Close by, at Jirón Unión 224, is the **Casa Aliaga**, an unusual mansion renowned as the oldest in South America—and occupied by the same family since 1535. You can arrange to visit through a tour company (try *Lima Tours* on Belen). It's one of the most elaborate mansions in the country, with sumptuous reception rooms full of Louis XIV mirrors, furniture, and doors. Around the corner, at Camana 459, the **Casa de Riva-Aguero** (Mon.–Fri. 5–8pm; free) is more conducive to unorganized visiting. A typical colonial house, its patio has been laid out as an interesting **folk-art museum**.

Perhaps the most noticed of all religious buildings in Lima is the **Church of La Merced** (daily 7am–noon and 4–8pm), just two blocks from the Plaza de Armas along the busy commercial street of Jr. Unión. Built on the site where the first Latin mass in Lima was celebrated, the original church was demolished in 1628 to make way for the present building. Its most elegant feature, a beautiful colonial facade, has been adapted and rebuilt several times—as have the broad columns of the nave to protect the church against tremors. But by far the most lasting impression is made by the **Cross of the Venerable Padre Urraca**, whose miraculous silver staff is smothered by hundreds of kisses every hour and witness to the fervent prayers of a constantly shifting congregation. If you've just arrived in Lima a few minutes by this cross will give you an insight into the depth of Peruvian belief in miraculous power. The attached **cloisters** (daily 8am–noon and 3–6pm) are less spectacular though they do have a historical curiosity: it was here that the Patriots of Independence declared the Virgin of La Merced their military Marshal.

More Churches

Of the other churches worth visiting in Lima Centro, San Pedro and Jesus Maria are the most central. **San Pedro** (daily 7am–1pm and 6–8:30pm), near the Torre Tagle on the corner of Azangaro and Ucayali, was built by the Jesuits and occupied by them until their expulsion in 1767. Richly decorated and dripping with art treasures, it's a typical colonial temple. **Jesus María** (daily 7am–1pm and 3–7pm) is down towards Plaza San Martin at the corner of Camana and Moquegua; the home of Capuchin nuns from Madrid in the early eighteenth century, its sparkling baroque gilt altars and pulpits are quite outstanding.

Two more interesting sanctuaries can be found on the edge of old Lima, along the Avenida Tacna. The **Sanctuary of Santa Rosa de Lima** (daily

9:30am–1pm and 3:30–6:30pm) is named in honor of the first saint created in the Americas. The construction of Avenida Tacna took away a section of the already small seventeenth-century church, and what remains is fairly plain, but in the patio next door you can see the saint's **hermitage**, a small adobe cell, and, just off this, a fascinating **Ethnographic Museum**. At the junction of Tacna and Huancavelica, the church of **Las Nazarenas** (daily 7am–noon and 4–8pm) is again small and outwardly undistinguished but it has an interesting history. After the severe 1655 earthquake, a mural of the crucifixion, painted by an Angolan slave on the wall of his hut, was apparently the only object left standing in the district. Its survival was deemed a miracle—the cause of popular processions ever since—and it is on this site that the church was founded. The widespread and popular processions for the Lord of Miracles, to save Lima from another earthquake, take place every October (18th, 19th, 28th, and also 1st of November), based around a silver litter which carries the original mural. Purple is the color of the procession and many women in Lima wear it for the entire month.

Parks and Gardens

In many ways more typically Limeño, and more expressive of the city's contemporary personality than its churches, are the **parks and gardens.** The most central of them is **Parque Universitario**, just a few short blocks east of the Plaza San Martin. This was the site of South America's first university, San Marcos, and although it's no longer even an important annex for the university, it's worth a look if only to check out the small **archeological museum**. The park itself is the base for numerous *colectivo* companies and street hawkers, and almost permanently engulfed in crowds of cars and rushing pedestrians. Farther out, the **Parque de la Exposición**, situated between Paseo Colón and Avenida 28 de Julio beneath the towering *Hotel Sheraton*, is much larger. Created for the International Exhibition of 1868, the park has long been neglected and seems mainly to attract courting couples who have nowhere else to go in the evenings or on Sundays. To the north lies the shady **Parque Neptuno**, with a small **Museum of Italian Art** within its boundaries. Nearby, the former International Exhibition Palace houses the **National Museum of Art** (Paseo Colón 124; daily 9am–7pm; small charge), with interesting small collections covering art and crafts from pre-Columbian times through colonial to modern. Film shows and lectures are also offered on some weekday evenings (for details check posters at the museums or listings in *El Commercio*).

Finally, some eight blocks west of the Plaza San Martin, on the site of an old gate dividing Lima from the road to Callao, **Plaza Dos de Mayo** still greets visitors (now from the airport) as they enter the city. Built to commemorate the repulse of the Spanish fleet in 1866 (Spain's last attempt to regain a foothold in South America), it's probably one of the most air-polluted spots in Lima. It's markedly busier and dirtier and an altogether unfriendlier environment for a foreign visitor than Plaza San Martin. That said, there's usually a great street market on the far side of this plaza, with some fascinating bargains to be found.

Downtown Lima: Miraflores and Around

As far as the city's modern inhabitants are concerned, **MIRAFLORES** alone is downtown Lima. To its east is **San Isidro**, a very plush suburb with a golf-course surrounded by sky-scraping apartment buildings and ultramodern shopping complexes, and many square kilometers of extraordinarily stylish houses. To its south begins the oceanside suburb of **Barranco**, one of the oldest parts of the city and now one of its most attractive above the steep sandy cliffs of the **Costa Verde**. The center of the city's action and nightlife, though, is Miraflores, its streets lined with street cafés and the capital's flashiest shops. Until you've experienced it, it's hard to grasp what modern Lima is really about.

Although still connected to Lima Centro by the long-established Avenida Arequipa, another highway—Paseo de La República (or more familiarly *El Zanjón*, "the ditch")—now provides **Miraflores** with an alternative approach. Coming out here on the yellow #2 bus, get off at *El Haiti* café/bar at the stop just before Miraflores central park. A good place to make for first, from where you can get some bearings on the whole downtown area, is the **Huaca Puquiana**, a vast pre-Inca adobe mound which continues to dwarf all but a handful of skyscrapers. It's just a two-minute walk from the Avenida Arequipa, to the right as you come from Lima Centro at block 44. One of a large number of *huacas*—sacred places—and palaces that formerly stretched across this part of the valley, little is known about the Puquiana, though it seems likely that it was originally named after a pre-Inca chief of the area. It was partially excavated in the late 1980s, and there are rumors that during the next few years it may be landscaped or even flattened completely. Interestingly, it has a hollow core running through its cross-section and is thought to have been originally constructed in the shape of an enormous frog, symbol of the rain god, who evidently spoke to priests through a tube connected to the cavern at its heart. It may well have been the mysteriously unknown oracle after which the Rimac (meaning "he who speaks") valley was named; a curious document from 1560 affirms that the "devil" spoke at this mound.

From the top of the *huaca* you can see over the office buildings and across the flat roofs of multicolored houses in downtown Miraflores. Its central area focuses on the small, almost triangular **Parque Miraflores** at the end of the Avenida Arequipa. Flashy cafés and bars surround the park, where, during the day, the streets are crowded with busy shoppers, flower-sellers and young men washing other people's big cars. In the park, particularly on Sundays, there are artists selling their canvasses—some are good, most are aimed purely at a tourist market. From the end of Avenida Arequipa, **Larco** and **Diagonal** both fan out along the park en route to the ocean less than 2km away. Miraflores has one important mansion open to the public—the **Casa de Ricardo Palma** (Mon.–Fri. 10am–12:30pm and 2–7pm) at General Suarez 189. Palma, probably Peru's greatest historian, lived here for most of his life.

Barranco and the Coast

Barranco, a much quieter place than Miraflores, is easily reached on a bus or *colectivo* along Diagonal. Overlooking the ocean, and scattered with old mansions and fascinating smaller homes, this was the capital's seaside resort in the last century and is now a kind of Limeño Greenwich Village, with young artists and intellectuals taking over many of the older properties. There's little specific to "see," though you might at some stage wander over to take a look at the cliff-top remains of a funicular railway, which used to carry aristocratic families from their summer resort straight down to the beach; also there's a really pleasant municipal park, a fine place to while away an afternoon. Within a block of the funicular, an impressive white church sits on the cliff with gardens to the front, and an old wooden bridge crosses over a gully filled with attractive and exotic dwellings.

Down beside the pounding rollers the **Costa Verde**, so named because of vegetation clinging to the steep sandy cliffs, majestically marks the edge of a continent. A bumpy road follows the shore from an exclusive yacht club and the Chorrillos fishermen's wharf, along past both Barranco and Miraflores, almost to the suburb of Magdelena. The sea is cold and not too clean—and there's nothing here really, other than sand, pebbles, a couple of beach clubs, a few restaurants, and a resident surfing crowd—but downtown Lima would seem sparse without it and swimming in the surf is as good a way as any to extend a day mulling about Barranco and Miraflores. As everywhere in Lima, however, keep a sharp eye on your clothes and valuables.

San Isidro

Unless you're shopping, looking for a sauna, trying to find a disco, or visiting someone, there are few good reasons to stop off in **San Isidro**. One, though, might be to take a stroll through the Bosque El Olivar, just 150m west of block 34 of the Avenida Arequipa. A charming grove first planted in 1560, it's now rather depleted in olive trees but you will find the old press and mill-stone as well as a stage where concerts and cultural events are often held. A few blocks away, at Avenida El Rosario, there is also an impressive recon-structed adobe *huaca*, **Huayamarca** (Nicolas de Rivera 201). Like Puquiana, this dates from pre-Inca days and now stands neatly surrounded by wealthy suburbs. The ruins have their own site museum (Tues.–Sun. 9–11:30am and 3–5:30pm) containing funerary masks and art work found in the *huaca*—including textiles oddly reminiscent of Scottish tartans. Again, San Isidro has one colonial mansion worth checking out: the **Casa de la Tradición** (Mon.–Fri. 2:30–5pm; small charge) at Av. Salaverry 3032. A rather elegant old house, this has a private collection of artifacts and pictures covering the history of Lima.

Callao and La Punta

Stuck out on a narrow, boot-shaped peninsula, Callao and La Punta ("The Point") form a natural annex to Lima, one that looks out towards the ocean and worldwide communication. Originally quite separate, they were founded in 1537, and were destined to become Peru's principal treasure-fleet port before eventually being engulfed by Lima's other suburbs in the course of the twentieth century.

Still the country's main commercial harbor, and one of the most modern ports in South America, **Callao** lies about 14km west of Lima Centro (easily reached on bus #25 from Plaza San Martin, which runs all the way there—and beyond, past the fort, to La Punta). It's none too alluring a place—indeed its suburbs, being slum zones infamous for prostitution and gang-land assassins, are considered virtually "no-go" areas for the city's middle classes—but if you're unworried by such associations, you will find some of the best *ceviche* restaurants anywhere in the continent.

Farther along, away from the heavier quarters and dominating the entire peninsula, is the great **Castle of Real Felipe**. Built after the devastating earthquake of 1764, which washed ships ashore and killed nearly the entire population of Callao, this is a superb example of the military architecture of its age, designed in the shape of a pentagon. Although built too late to protect the Spanish treasure fleets from European pirates like Francis Drake, it was to play a critical role in the battles for independence. Its fire-power repulsed both Admiral Brown (1816) and Lord Cochrane (1818), though many Royalists starved to death here when it was besieged by the Patriots in 1821, just prior to its surrender. The fort's grandeur is marred only by a number of storehouses, built during the late nineteenth century when it was used as a customhouse. Inside, the **Military Museum** (Tues.–Thurs. 9am–noon and 3–5pm, weekends 2–5:30pm; free) houses a fairly complete collection of eighteenth- and nineteenth-century arms and various rooms dedicated to Peruvian war heroes.

Out at the end of the peninsula, what was once the fashionable beach resort of **La Punta** is now overshadowed by the Naval College and Yacht Club. Many of its old mansions, however, still remain, some of them very elegant, others extravagant monstrosities. Right at the very point an attractive promenade offers glorious views and sunsets over the Pacific, while at the back of the strand there are some excellent restaurants serving traditional local food (many of these are difficult to find, being in what look like private houses—probably best to ask someone to point one out).

Lima's Museums

Not surprisingly, given Peru's rich history, Lima abounds in museums, most of them fascinating, and a few, like Larco Herrera and Amano, specializing in specific categories of art or culture. Their scattered locations throughout the city, however, make it difficult to visit more than three or four without it turning into a full-time occupation. At the most brutally selective don't miss either the Gold Museum or the Archeological and Anthropological Museum, both of them fairly tricky to find in their respective suburbs but well worth the effort or a taxi fare.

Gold Museum (*Museo Miguel Mujica Gallo*; Av. de Molina 100; daily noon–7pm; $5, $1.50 with student card). Isolated way out of town in the well-to-do suburb of Monterrico, Lima's Gold Museum, owned by the high-society Mujica family, is a must. On the ground level it boasts a vast display of **arms and uniforms,** many of them incredible antiques which help bring to life some of Peru's bloodier history. But it's the safe-room downstairs that contains the real gems. Divided into several sections, these basements are literally crammed with treasures and beautiful craft goods from **pre-Columbian** times. Most of the **gold and silver jewelry** is in the metalwork rooms, but more fascinating perhaps are the pre-Inca weapons and wooden staffs, or the amazing Nazca yellow-feathered poncho designed for a noble's child or child high-priest. One thing that generally causes a stir, too, is a skull enclosing a full set of pink quartz teeth—in the corner on the right as you enter the main room from the stairs.

There are **buses** from Lima Centro that go to Monterrico but they are hard to locate and generally very crowded when you do. It's simpler to catch a *colectivo* from Miraflores or Lima Centro along the Avenida Arequipa to block 48, then switch to Avenida Angamos to take #72 microbus (yellow and red) as far as Monterrico's *Centro Commercial* shopping center at the very end of Angamos. From here the Gold Museum (a Fort Knox type building set back in the shade of tall trees) is a short walk of three blocks up Avenida Primavera, two to the right along Santa Elena. A **taxi** from the center or Miraflores shouldn't cost more than $2 to $3 one way.

Archeological and Anthropological Museum (Plaza Bolivar, corner of San Martín and Antonio Pola; daily 10am–6pm; small charge; ☎63-5070). Although much of the Archeological and Anthropological Museum's immense collection has been rotting in storage for decades, the selection on display must still be the most complete and varied exhibition of pre-Inca artifacts anywhere. It also gives a detailed and accurate perspective on Peru's prehistory, a vision that comes as a surprise if you'd previously thought of Peru simply in terms of Incas and *Conquistadores*.

Divided into a number of galleries set around two colonial-style courtyards, the exhibits begin with the evolution and population of America: the earliest Peruvian pieces are stone tools some 8000 years old. One of the finest rooms is that showing carved **Chavin stones** such as the magnificent *Estela Raymondi*, a diorite block intricately carved with feline, serpent, and falcon features, or the *Tello Obelisk*, a masterpiece in granite. The *Manos Cruzados*, or "Crossed Hands" stone from **Kotosh,** is also on display, evidence of a mysterious cult some 5000 years old. The **Paracas room** is rich in amazing weavings and replete with excellent examples of deformed heads and trepanated skulls; one shows postoperative growth; in another of the cases sits a male mummy, "frozen" at the age of 30 to 35 and with fingernails still visible, the fixed sideways glance from his misshapen head enough to send shivers down your spine. The **Nazca room**, stuffed full of incredible ceramics, is divided according to what each pot represents—marine life, agriculture, flora, wildlife, trophy-heads, mythology, sexual and everyday life. The **Mochica** and **Chimu rooms** are also well stocked; there's one entirely devoted to music and dance, containing remarkable ceramics depicting musicians, even birds playing the drums; and, lastly, a room devoted to the **Inca**—a useful initial overview with impressive models of the main ruins like Machu Picchu and Tambo Colorado.

The Archeological and Anthropological Museum, and the National Museum of History described below, are both in the suburb of Pueblo Libre on the Plaza Bolivar; to get here take microbus #41 (white and blue) from the corner of Cuzco and Carabaya in Lima Centro. **A new site** has been chosen for the museum beside the Parque de las Leyendas, fittingly next to the *Huaca Cruz Blanca* (once the heart of the Maranga culture). Estimated to cost around $40 million, with half of the money coming from the Inter-American Development Bank, this was President Belaunde's brainchild but was shelved for twelve years following the Military Revolution in 1968. Since some 15,000 archeological pieces are confiscated at Lima airport every year, a larger museum has long been needed—it *might* conceivably be open by the mid-1990s.

National Museum of History (*Museu Nacional de la República*; Mon.–Fri. 9am–6pm; small charge; ☎63-2009). Next door to the Archeological and Anthropological Museum, the National Museum of History is laid out in a nineteenth-century house, with dazzling antique clothing, extravagant furnishings, and other period pieces complemented by early Republican paintings. The liberators San Martin and Bolivar both made their homes here for a while.

Museo Rafael Larco Herrera (Bolivar 1515, Pueblo Libre; Mon.–Sat. 9am–1pm and 3–6pm, Sun. 9am–1pm; $4, $1.50 with student card; ☎61-1312). Undoubtedly the city's most unusual museum, the Museo Herrera contains over 400,000 excellently preserved ceramics, many of them Chiclin or Mochica pottery from around Trujillo. Its outstanding collection, however, is an intriguing selection of **pre-Inca erotic art**. This place could easily combine with a visit to the Archeological and Anthropological Museum. Take either bus #23 (from Avenida Abancay) or micro #37 (green) from Avenida Nicolas de Pierola. There are also buses here from Avenida Emancipación in the center.

Mochica Drinking Vessel

Amano Museum (Calle Retiro 160, Miraflores; hours by appointment; ☎41-2909; free). A close rival to the above, the Amano Museum has a fabulous exhibition of **Chancay weavings**, as well as bountiful **ceramics**. A private museum open weekdays only, it's reached by *colectivo* or bus along Avenida Arequipa, then a walk or bus ride down Angamos Oeste; or take microbus #13 (red and cream) from Avenida Tacna down to Santa Cruz. Calle Retiro is off block 11 of Angamos Oeste.

Museum of Natural History (Avenida Arenales, block 12; Mon.–Fri. 8am–6pm, Sat. 9am–12 noon). Little visited though quite fascinating, its main attraction, a "sun fish," is one of only three known examples in the world. Take microbus #13 (red and cream) from Avenida Tacna.

National Museum of Peruvian Culture (Av. Alfonso Ugarte 650; Mon.–Sat. 10am–7pm; small charge). For material artifacts like carved gourds, costumes, and ceramics from most corners of Peruvian history, this is the best place. It's easy enough to find, near Plaza 2 de Mayo.

Museum of Contemporary Peruvian Folk Art (Saco Oliveros 163, off the third block of Avenida Arequipa; Tue.–Fri. 2:30–7pm, Sat. 8:30am–12 noon; donations welcome). Along the same lines as the above, though concentrating more on modern pottery, and well worth a look.

Peruvian Health Sciences Museum (Junin 270; Mon.–Sat. 9am–5pm; $1). An interesting collection despite the dreadful name, covering pre-Conquest medical, sexual, and magico-medical activities. Within two blocks of the Plaza de Armas.

Philatelic Museum (Central Post Office, off the Plaza de Armas; Mon.–Fri. 8:30am–1:30pm and 2–4pm, Sat. 8am–1:30pm, Sun. 8am–12 noon; free). Near the Presidential Palace, the Philatelic Museum possesses a myriad of antique stamps as well as displays on the Inca postal system. Stamp trading here among dealers on the last Sunday of every month.

Numismatic Museum (Cuzco 245, on the second floor of the *Banco Wiese*; Mon.–Fri. 9am–1pm; free). For coin enthusiasts; on a similar note and just a short stroll away from the above.

Bullfight Museum (Plaza de Acho, Hualgayoc 332, Rimac; Mon.–Fri. 9am–1pm and 3–6pm, weekends 9am–1pm). Lima's biggest bullring houses some original Goya engravings, several interesting paintings, and a few relics of bullfighting contests.

Museum of Italian Art (Paseo Colón 125; Tue.–Fri. 9am–7pm, Mon., Sat., and Sun. 11am–5pm; free). Located inside an unusual Renaissance building on the second block of the Paseo de la República (next to the *Hotel Sheraton*), the Museum of Italian Art exhibits **contemporary Peruvian art** as well as reproductions of the Italian masters.

Museum of the Inquisition (Junin 548); **Pinacoteca Museum** (in the Municipal Building); **National Museum of Art** (Paseo Colon 125); and the **Military Museum** (Callao fort) have already been detailed in the text, see pp.41, 46, and 49. The Military Museum can be combined with a visit to the **Naval Museum** on Avenida Jorge Chavez, off Plaza Grau in Callao (Mon., Fri., and Sat. 9am–12:30pm and 3–5:30pm; free).

The Zoo (*Parque de las Leyendas*, between Lima Centro and Callao; Tue.–Sun. 9am–5pm; nominal charge). In a relatively deserted spot on the sacred site of the ancient Maranga culture, the park and zoo are laid out, very roughly, according to the three regions of Peru—*costa, sierra,* and *selva*—though there's little attempt to create the appropriate habitats. It's nothing special, just animals in cages—condors and pumas, even penguins, elephants, and other non-native exotica—but the park makes a fine place for a picnic, and there are good *artesania* stalls just outside, particularly hot on cases of magnificent dead insects. It's some way out, but the yellow bus #48 goes directly there from the Plaza de Armas.

Nightlife and Entertainment

For listings of music, film, and theater events—indeed everything detailed below—much the best source is the daily *El Comercio*, whose *Seccion C* is usually pretty comprehensive. In English, a much less complete selection is printed in the *Lima Times*.

Music

All forms of **Peruvian music** can be found at their best in Lima, and as a modern city it also has an interesting range of clubs and discos. As far as the **live scene** goes, the great variety of traditional and hybrid sounds is one of the most enduring reasons for staying in, and returning to, the capital. As usual, things are at their liveliest on Friday and Saturday nights, particularly among the folk group *peñas* and the burgeoning *salsadromos*.

Among the peñas—some of which only open on weekends—the surest bet for authentic **Andean folk music**, and one of the cheapest, is *Peña Hatuchay*, just over the bridge into Rimac at Trujillo 228; *Peña Wifala*, though smaller and more tourist oriented, is also quite good—at Cailloma 633, off Nicolas de Pierola. If you're into pure **musica negra**—excellent coastal "roots" music —*La Valentina*, on Avenida Iquitos (La Victoria district), is the most popular; like the peñas it usually gets going around 10pm, though you can often find things just as lively at 5 o' clock the following morning. **Creole music,** lying somewhere between Andean folk and *musica negra* and incorporating a lot of Spanish influence, is generally pretty good at *La Palizada*, a large peña at Av. Ejercito 800 in Miraflores (☎41-0552).

Lima is also an excellent place for **salsa music**, and there are *salsadromos* scattered around many of the suburbs—*Sarava* in Surquillo; *Bertoloto* in Magdalena; *La Maquina de Sabor* in Balconcillo; and the *Havana Club* in Miraflores. There's also a good disco-salsa group called the *Hermanos Silva*

Band, well worth keeping an eye open for. Virtually everywhere in Lima that has live music also serves **food;** many places—such as Hatuchay—include the price of a meal on the entrance ticket.

A welcome recent addition to the night scene was the creation of *La Estación de Barranco* (Pedro de Osma 112) near the municipal park in Barranco. This is a lively, if expensive, nightspot where you get to see, hear, and dance to all kinds of Latin American sounds. Check the paper for listings on weekends. Other relatively young nightspots in Barranco to check out if you've the time and money, include *El Buho Pub*, a *criolla* joint at Sucre 315 (next to *El Otro Sitio*); *Karamanduka*, another *criolla* place, Sanchez Carrion 135 (☎47-3237); and *La Casona de Barranco*, modern jazz at Grau 329.

Bars and Discos

Of the numerous **discos** in Lima, many have a members only policy, though if you can provide proof of tourist status (a passport for instance) you usually have no problem getting in. Most of them are in **San Isidro:** *Up and Down*, a new wave, rock, and reggae joint in Augusto Tamayo (opposite *Sears*); the English-run *Percy's Bar*, more of a drinking place than a dance spot, also in Augusto Tamayo; *Mediterraneo*, a trendy, new wave, rock, and disco dive, opposite the *Camino Real* Shopping Center; *La Manzana*, mostly disco, at Miguel Dasso 143; *Ebony Sicodelico* at Las Magnolias 841. In **Miraflores,** *La Miel* at Jose Pardo 120 (underneath the *Indianapolis* Restaurant) is the most central, popular with sailors and touring sports teams. It plays lots of disco, a little salsa, and often levies a heavy cover charge. Just over the road, above El Pacifico cinema, another disco—*Arizona Colt*—blasts rock and disco onto a rather dimly lit dance floor.

For less stereotyped evenings out there are a few **bars** in Miraflores, mostly done up like English pubs—*The Brenchley Arms* pub (Atahualpa 174, Miraflores) which serves English food by an English dart board in as English an environment as you could expect to find within a block of *El Pacifico*. *Sergeant Peppers* (San Martin, off Larco) and the *Lion's Club* (Madrid 338, on the Plaza Bolognesi) are also good, each sometimes offering live music; drinks, however, are expensive. *Satchmos* (La Paz 538, Miraflores) makes a refreshing change from all the others.

Film and Theater

Moviegoing is an important part of life in Lima and there are clusters of **movie theaters** all around the Plaza San Martin, Jiron Union, and Avenida Nicolas de Pierola in Lima Centro, and on the fringes of the park in Miraflores—notably *El Pacifico* by the Haiti Café, and *Romeo y Julietta* at the ocean end of the park. The *Cine Roma*, which often shows quality films from all over the world, can be found off block 8 of the Avenida Arequipa. For any film that might attract relatively large crowds, it's advisable to buy tickets in advance; alternatively, be prepared to purchase them on the "black market" at inflated prices—lines are often long and large blocks of seats are regularly bought up by scalpers. For background information on the Peruvian film industry, see p.23.

Though it's not always so accessible, Lima also has a **theater** circuit and in addition to regular outlets, short performances sometimes take place in theater bars. The country's major prestige companies, however, are the **National Ballet Company** and the **National Symphony**, both based seasonally at the *Teatro Municipal* in downtown Lima. There are frequent performances too by international musicians and companies—often sponsored by the foreign cultural organizations. The **British Council** are quite active in this line—and surprisingly imaginative—and they also show British-made films at their building on the Avenida Arequipa.

Bullfights and Sport

Bullfighting has been a popular pastime among a relatively small, wealthy elite from the Spanish Conquest to the present day, despite 160 years of independence from Spain. Pizarro himself brought out the first *lidia* bull for fighting in Lima, and there is a great tradition between the controlling families of Peru—the same families who breed bulls on their *haciendas*—to hold fights in Lima during during the months of October and November. They invite some of the world's best bullfighters from Spain, Mexico, and Venezuela, offering them up to $25,000 for an afternoon's sport at the prestigious **Plaza de Acho** in Rimac. To get tickets, if you feel the need to observe such a spectacle, you'll do best to buy them in advance from the ticket office (block 2 of Huancavelica) or, failing that, on the door an hour or so before the fights (usually on Saturday and Sunday afternoons —particularly during October).

If you're in Lima for April, an interesting day trip would be to visit the National Concourse for **Pacing Horses** (*Caballos de Paso*) out in the tourist recreation center at Pachacamac on the Pan American South (usually between the 23rd and 29th). Lima's high society is always there in full force, an attraction in itself, regardless of the horse and rider displays.

Peruvian **soccer** is also centered in Lima, home of all the most successful teams. *El Comercio* will again have details of matches: teams worth seeing include *Alianza* and *Sporting Cristal* (who both play at Estadio Alianza, Alejandro Vilanueva), *Universitario* (based at the University), and *Sport Boys*, who play at the Estadio Telano Cabajo in Callao.

Eating and Drinking

Among South American capitals, Lima has one of the widest variety of **restaurants** and an equally broad range of prices. Regardless of class or status, virtually everyone eats out regularly, and although it's considered no big deal, it usually ends up as an evening's entertainment in itself. Restaurants of every type and size, from expensive hotel dining rooms to tiny set-meal street stalls, seem to crowd every corner of the city. There are no "not-to-be-missed" places, since it's ultimately a matter of taste, though there are plenty worth recommending.

Lima Centro

In and around **Lima Centro** the choice is almost limitless. *El Cordano* is rich in style, very cheap, has a fast waiter service, and is also something of a traditional drinking dive—watch out for con artists after your travelers' checks or wallet (Ancash 207, opposite Desamperados train station, behind the Government Palace). In the *Hotel Crillon* (Avenida Nicolas de Pierola), the *Sky Room* has good fixed-price meals and offers an excellent view across the city—rather plush and quite expensive though. *L'Eau Vive* (Ucayali 370; ☎27-5612), opposite Torre Tagle Palace, is very reasonably priced and an interesting experience in itself, serving superb French food cooked by nuns; set menu for lunch and evening meals (8:15–11pm), closing after a chorus of Ave Maria. The *Restaurant Campari* is a nice place to chat over a drink or snack and is very central, only 100m from Plaza San Martin at Apurimac 286. More or less opposite the modern Hotel Crillon, *Chalet Suisse* serves pretty reasonable international food (Av. Nicolas de Pierola 560).

There are several **vegetarian restaurants** in central Lima. Among the best are: the *Asoc. Naturista* on Ucayali 133; *La Naturaleza* at Camana 489; *La Natural* (near the corner of Moquegua and Torrico), which has a co-op shop and restaurant around an attractive patio, serving very cheap lunches and excellent fare all day (8am–8:30pm); *El Giraso* (Camana 327), which takes great care to serve quality food; or for really inexpensive meals you could try the stalls and snack-sellers in the central market.

The area around the central market is also the best place for **Chinese food**, or *chifa*, one of Lima's finest specialties. Besides the many places here you might try *El Dorado*, a sky-scraping *chifa* restaurant—with panorama views at Av. Arequipa 2450 (☎22-1080).

Miraflores

Miraflores has even more to offer, even if it is nearly all on the expensive side. One place hard to beat for breakfasts, afternoon snacks, or just take-out cakes and breads is *La Tiendacita Blanca*, Larco 111, in the very heart of Miraflores. Along the park, on Diagonal, there are several places to choose from: the *Haiti* is okay for drinks and soups, and is Lima's number one meeting place—the service tends to be slow and unfriendly though; the *Roxy*, farther down the street, is hard to beat for pasta but is more introvert, formal, and expensive; or *La Pizzeria* is a good bet for a pie. Across the park towards Larco through Diez Canseco, there's the excellent lunchtime restaurant *El Parquecito*, almost hidden down a commercial arcade opposite the *Sala de Exposicion de la Municipalidad de Miraflores* (one of Lima's best and fastest changing modern art galleries). There are also plenty of restaurants-cum-bars on Larco—*Manolo's* probably being the most popular—which become more reasonably priced as you approach the ocean. Along Schell, the road going away from the park below *Roxy* and at right angles to Diagonal, there are a few places worth checking out; *La Colina* (no. 727) offers local dishes at very good rates and doesn't mind you sitting around for a few drinks if you're not hungry; *Govinda* and *Bircher Berner*, at Schell 670 and 598 respectively, have **vegetarian** specialties; and a couple of doors beyond *La Colina* there's an excellent *cevicheria*. Ardent meat eaters will find the *parilladas* of *La*

Tranquera (Jose Pardo block 2) and *El Rancho* (Av. Benavides 2650) hard to beat.

French and **Italian** cuisine is easy to find in Lima these days. Among the best are *La Trattoria* (Manuel Bonilla 106; ☎46-7002), *Los Faisanes* (La Paz 610; ☎44-1280), and *El Carlin* (La Paz 646; ☎44-4134), all in Miraflores.

A few restaurants in **San Isidro** are worth a mention: *Jose Antonia* (Monteagudo 21) has live entertainment and serves typical Peruvian dishes; and *La Barca*, on the corner of Avenida Ejercito and Avenida Salaverry, produces some of the best seafood around.

Barranco and the Costa Verde

Barranco has a good collection of cheaper restaurants (geared more to the locals than tourists), most of them spreading out from the municipal park. Possibly the best *cevicheria* serving fresh seafood at lunchtime can be found here (Panamericana del Sur 270). Another excellent spot, but quite pricey and much more of an evening location, is *El Otro Sitio* (Calle Sucre 315; ☎67-8972) with a wide range of typical dishes in the pleasant surroundings of a colonial house: excellent *criolla* cooking.

Below Barranco, along the **Costa Verde**, you'll also find shacks cooking *anticuchos* and seafood; for some bizarre reason, many of these hire transvestites to wave in customers as they drive past along the coastal road. Much more upscale are two very plush beachside restaurants: the *Costa Verde*, which includes turtle on its menu; and the relatively new (1983) *Rosa Nautica* (☎47-0057), which cost over one million dollars to set up. Calling itself a tourist restaurant it's constructed on a platform over the sea and at night surfers ride curling waves under spotlights. Expect to pay about $25 per person for all this.

If you're prepared to go a bit farther out you'll find a place which hardly ever sees a gringo, *Latin Brothers* restaurant in the **suburb of Lince** (Av. Jose Leal 1277-81; ☎71-0260). Specializing in enormous communal platters of delicious seafoods, Latin Brothers is a large "spit-and-sawdust" eating house whose image is represented on the walls in hallucinogenic paintings of the great salsa artists. Loud salsa music often accompanies the meals. El Señorio de Surco (Tacna 276 in the suburb of Surco) offers some of the city's best *criolla* food at lunchtime. For either of these, take a taxi.

Listings

Airlines Offices are nearly all on the Plaza San Martin or along Avenida Nicolas de Pierola in Lima Centro. Some of the main airlines in Lima include: *Aeroperu*, Plaza San Martin (☎31-7626/domestic, ☎32-2995/international) in Lima and Pardo 601 (☎47-8900) in Miraflores; *Air France*, Juan de Arona 830, San Isidro (☎70-4870); *British Airways*, Larco 101, Miraflores (☎47-7219); *Air Canada*, Paseo de la República 138 (☎31-9293); *Eastern*, Juan de Arona 830, San Isidro (☎42-8555); *Faucett*, Plaza San Martin (☎33-6564); *KLM*, Jose Pardo 805, Miraflores (☎43-1818); *Lufthansa*, Centro Camino Real, Torre de Pilar, 8th floor, San Isidro (☎42-4455); and *VIASA*, Jose Pardo 805, Miraflores (☎47-8666).

Airport buses Regularly from outside their office on Camana, near the corner with Nicolas de Pierola and behind the Hotel Bolivar. *Transhotel* also connects the airport with every hotel or zone of Lima. Contact them at the airport (they have a kiosk at the international end; ☎51-8011) or in Miraflores at Ricardo Palma 780 (☎46-9872).

American Express (Mon.–Fri. 9am–4pm) Mail service and travelers' checks, from the main branch inside *Lima Tours* at Belen 1040 (☎27-6624), near the Plaza San Martin.

Banks *Banco de la Nacion*, just off Nicolas de Pierola, usually has the quickest service. The *Banco de Credito* (Jr. Lampa 399) offers good rates on travelers' checks—and is generally open 9–11:30am, weekdays.

Beaches Costa Verde has the nearest beaches, though Herra Dura (out on the point beyond Barranco and Chorrillos) is much cleaner and more pleasant for swimming. Ancón to the north and El Silencio to the south (both about 30km away) are the most fashionable. More details in the following section.

Black market cash Peruvian currency can be bought with travelers' checks or cash from guys hanging around behind the *Hotel Bolivar* or in some of the smaller hostels. Many of them are fast operators out to get as much of your money as they can; check their arithmetic then recount their notes carefully before handing yours over. Safest black market way is to exchange your money in the *Casa de Cambios* on Ocoña.

Books A few shops on Nicolas de Pierola stock English books (try the one at 689) and *The Book Exchange*, just around the corner at Ocoña 211, sells or swaps second-hand paperbacks. The *South American Explorers' Club* (see *Basics*) operates a free book exchange among members. The *ABC Bookstores* at Colmena 689 (Lima Centro) and in the *Todos* shopping complex, San Isidro, are well supplied with all kinds of works in English, including books on Peru. On the Jirón Unión the *Librería Ayza* usually has some interesting books and maps, while in Miraflores the *Libreria El Pacifico* generally has a wide range of books and magazines for English readers.

Buses Most bus terminals and offices are between the *Hotel Sheraton* and Parque Universitario, or in the district of La Victoria along Avenida 28 de Julio and Prolongación Huanuco. For a complete list see Lima's yellow pages telephone guide. Among them are: *Morales Moralitos* (Av. Grau 141; ☎28-6252); *Tepsa* (with daily buses to Tumbes and Cajamarcas; Av. Paseo de la República 129 opposite the *Hotel Sheraton*; ☎28-79995); *Leon de Huanuco* (Av. 28 de Julio, La Victoria 1520; ☎32-90880); *Ormeño* (Carlos Zavala 145, near Parque Universitario; ☎27-5679); *Condor de Chavin* (for Huaraz and Chavin only; Montevideo 1039; ☎28-8122); *Cruz del Sur* (daily to Cuzco and Arequipa Av. Grau 141; ☎27-7366); and *Hidalgo* (for Huancayo and Tarma; Bolivar 1535; ☎24-0522).

Camping gear Try the *South American Explorers' Club* (Av. Portugal 146; ☎31-4480—English spoken) or failing that buy or rent equipment in Huaraz or Cuzco.

Car rental Expensive but available through: *Budget* (La Paz 522, Miraflores; ☎45-4685); *Hertz* (Jr. Ocoña 262, Lima; ☎28-6330); *National* (Av. España 449, Lima; ☎23-2526); *Dollar* (Mexico 333, Lima; ☎72-5565); *ABC* (Av. Tacna 542, Lima; ☎33-5922); and *Avis* (Sheraton Hotel; ☎32-7245).

Casas de Cambio Mostly along Nicolas de Pierola and Ocoña between the Plaza San Martin and Plaza 2 de Mayo.

Cock-fighting Traditional Spanish-American bloodlust—still enacted on weekends in the *Coliseo de Gallos*, Sandia 150.

Crafts Shopping for *artesanía* is best in the markets on blocks 3 and 10 of Avenida La Marina in Pueblo Libre, or in the new (and cheaper) Co-operative Regional Artesan market along Avenida Javier Prado Este; jungle artifacts are excellently selected and sold by *Antisuyo* in Miraflores (Jr. Tacna 460; Mon.–Fri. 9am–7:30pm, Sat. 10:30am–6:30pm ☎47-2557), while *La Gringa* (La Paz 522) in Miraflores is also one of the better all-round *artesanía* shops.

Dentists and doctors Ask your embassy for a list of addresses of English-speaking practitioners.

Embassies CANADA—Calle Libertad 130, Miraflores (☎44-4015); US—Grimaldo del Soilar 346, Miraflores (☎44-3621) and an embassy office at Av. Garcilaso de la Vega 1400 (☎28-6000). Embassies of other South American countries include BOLIVIA—Los Castanos 235, San Isidro (☎22-8231); BRAZIL—Commandante Espinar 181, Miraflores (☎45-2421); CHILE—Javier Prado Oeste 790, San Isidro (☎40-7965); ECUADOR—Las Palmeras 356, San Isidro (☎22-8138).

Emergencies The tourist police can be contacted at Salaverry 1156, Jesus Maria or phone ☎23-7225 or ☎24-6571. If you can travel safely don't wait for an ambulance—get a taxi straight to the hospital address that they give you. For an ambulance phone ☎40-0200 (San Cristobal, Av. Arequipa 2485, Lince).

Health food Best places are the *Natural Co-op* on Monquegua (near corner with Torrico) and *El Girasol* at Camana 327 (not far from the Plaza de Armas).

Hiking information Look in at the *South American Explorers' Club*, Av. Portugal 146 (☎31-4480), for advice, trail maps, and helpful tips. For **mountain climbing** the *Club Alpino Peruano* (Las Begonias 630, San Isidro) is helpful. See also "trekking" below.

Hospitals The following are all well equipped: *Clinica Anglo Americana* (Avenida Salazar, San Isodro; ☎40-3570); *Clinica Internacional* (Washington 1475; ☎28-8060); and *Clinica San Borja* (Av. del Aire 333, San Borja; ☎41-3141). All have emergency departments which you can use as an "outpatient" or you can ask for house-calls by telephoning.

Inmigración The main offices for any visa enquiries or renewals is on block 11 of 28 de Julio/500 Paseo de la República, at the Lima end of the Paseo de la Republica. Get there by 8:30am to be near the front of the line.

International telephones Calls can be made both nationally and internationally from *Entelperu*'s offices in Colmena 878, just off the Plaza San Martin. Dial 108 for international calls from any phone.

Krishna consciousness The Lima headquarters for this movement, also known as the *Vedic Cultural Circle*, is at Jr. Junin 415.

Laundry Many hotels will do this quite cheaply, though there are also numerous *lavanderías* in most central, downtown, and suburban areas.

Opticians Good shop on Schell in Miraflores, near corner with Larco. Dr. W.A. Morgan—Optometrist—is good for glasses and contact lenses, offices at General Cordova 185, no. 101, and the Plaza San Martin 937 (☎27-9852).

Phones All Lima call boxes are operated by *rins*, tokens which you can buy in many corner shops or on the street in Lima Centro. Most *bodegas* also have a phone for public use; this usually costs little more than the price of the rin.

Photography For gear, accessories, or fast developing there are only a few good places, all of them expensive: the co-op on Avenida Galvez (off Avenida Grau, near the *Sheraton*); a small shop (one-hour rapid developing service) on 28 de Julio, in Miraflores (near the corner with Larco); and *Hartmans* of Diagonal, Miraflores. Kodak's laboratories will develop Ektachrome but not Kodachrome (Avenida Arriola, just off Javier Prado Este in La Victoria). **Camera repairs** are skillfully done by a little Japanese shop near the *Cine Romeo y Julietta* in Miraflores.

Post office There are three post offices worth knowing about in Lima. Two are in the center: one (the city's main office) is next to the Presidential Palace near the Plaza de Armas, the other opposite the *Hotel Crillon* on Avenida Nicolas de Pierola nearer the Plaza San Martin. The third is in Miraflores, one block from the corner of Angamos and Petit Thouars.

Post restante Letters are kept for up to three months in the Central Post Office (left side of the Presidential Palace on Plaza des Armas). See *Basics* for details.

South American Explorers' Club (Av. Portugal 146; ☎31-4480) welcomes nonmembers for a cup of tea and a half-hour perusal of their facilities in Lima. They also sell used camping equipment and operate a book exchange for members. Membership offers many advantages (see *Basics*).

Tipping Around 10% is usual if the service is OK.

Tourist office *Foptur*, the official tourist information body, are in the plush arcade at Belén 1066, near the Plaza San Martin (Mon.–Sat. 9am–7pm; ☎32-3559). The state chain of *Hotel de Turistas* is run by *Enturperu* from offices on Av. Javier Prado Oeste 1358 (Mon.–Fri. 10am–7pm and Sat. 9am–1pm).

Trains The **Lima to Huancayo** train—*El Tren de la Sierra*—leaves daily (except Sun.) at 7:40am (best to buy tickets the day before) arriving Chosica (859m/54km) at 8:27am, the high pass at Ticlio (4758m/171km) around midday, the La Oroya mines (3726m/222km) by 1:40pm, Jauja (3359m/301km) at 3:39pm and Huancayo (3261m/346km) around 4:30pm. From **Huancayo to Lima** the train leaves on the same days at 7am, arriving Lima around 4:30pm. Trains **between Huancayo and Huancavelica** leave Mon. to Sat. at 7:30am in both directions, arriving approximately 2pm. Another service connects **La Oroya with Cerro de Pasco** (also a possible overland route to Huanuco)—leaving La Oroya most days at 1:30pm, arriving Cerro de Pasco about 5:15pm. The return trip leaves at 6:30am arriving 9.35am.

Tr........................s station, to the back of the Government
Pal....................t an hour prior to departure (opens 6am).

Tra...................s tour operators, most of these are in the
cent...................*ma Tours* (Belen 1040, near Plaza San
Mart...................mana 868; and *Hada Tours* with several
office...................1411), Av. La Paz 380, in Miraflores (☎44-
4888),...................and Las Begonias 706 (☎42-3695).

Trekk...................est are *Explorandes*, Bolognesi 159,
Miraflo...................*ones Mayuc*, Conquistadores 199, San
Isidro. ....ra Blanca, around the Cuzco area and
along th...................

Turkish...................vailable most days and evenings from:
Windsor, ...; *Pizarro*, Jr. Union 284, Lima; and *Jose
Pardo*, Av. ....

AROUND LIMA

Stretching ....th directions, the **Pan American
Highway** ru...................h of Peru, with Lima more or less
exactly at its ....metimes very arid coastline immediately north an...................of the capital are of minor interest to most travelers,
though there are some **glorious beaches**, one very impressive ruin—at
Pachacamac—and pretty much infinite potential for beach camping.

The foothills above Lima contain a few places of interest, not least the
animistic rock outcrops of **Marcahuasi**, a long day-trip out from the city.
Lima is also the starting point for one of the most marvelous train journeys in
the world, climbing up into the Andes and on into the rainforests of the upper
Amazon basin on *El Tren de la Sierra*, which leaves daily for the mountain
towns of **Huancayo** and **Huancavelica**, and gives access to the little-visited
backcountry villages in the surrounding jungle.

Lima's Southern Beaches ... and Pachacamac

Most of the better **beaches** within easy reach of Lima are to the south—
beginning about 30km out at the hulking pre-Inca ruins of Pachacamac, a
sacred citadel which still dominates this stretch of coastline. The site can
easily be combined with a day at one or other of the beaches—and it's little
problem to get out there from the capital. **Microbuses** leaves regularly for
Pachacamac from Plaza Santa Catalina and around the Parque Universitario
on Calles Montevideo and Inambari in Lima Centro, and there are also
frequent departures for the village-resort of PUCUSANA (65km from Lima),
passing Pachacamac and three excellent beaches along the way.

Pachacamac

PACHACAMAC (daily 9am–5pm) is by far the most interesting of the Rimac Valley's ancient sites—and a group of ruins you'll probably want to make time for even if you're about to head out to Cuzco and Machu Picchu. There's a small entry charge for the citadel, which includes admission to the site museum, well worth looking around on the way in. It takes a good two hours to wander around the whole extent of the ruins.

Pachacamac means (more or less) "the Earth's Creator": it was certainly occupied by A.D. 500 and probably for a long time before that. When other *huacas* were being constructed in the lower Rimac valley, Pachacamac was already a temple-citadel and center for mass pilgrimages. The god-image of Pachacamac evidently expressed his/her anger through tremors and earthquakes, and was an oracle used for important matters affecting the State: the health of the ruler, the outcome of a war, etc. Later it became one of the most famous shrines in the Inca Empire, with Pachacamac himself worshiped along with the sun. The Incas built their Sun Temple on the crest of the hill above Pachacamac's own sacred precinct. In 1533, Francisco Pizarro sent his brother Hernando to seize Pachacamac's treasure; it ended as a disappointing trip, its only prize the incredible wooden idol on show today in the site museum. This wooden representation of Pachacamac may well have been the oracle itself: it was kept hidden inside a labyrinth and behind guarded doors—only the high priests could communicate with it face to face. When Hernando Pizarro and his troops arrived they had to pass through many doors to arrive at the main idol site, which was raised up on a "snail shaped" (or spiralling) platform, with the wooden carving stuck into the earth inside a dark room closed to the world by a bejeweled curtain.

Entering **the ruins** today, after passing the restored sectors which include the **Temple of the Moon** and the **Convent of the Sun Virgins** (or *mamaconas*), you can see the **Sun Temple** directly ahead. Constructed on the top level of a series of "pyramidical" platforms, it was built tightly onto the hill with plastered adobe bricks, its walls originally painted in gloriously bright colors. Below this is the **main plaza**, once covered with a thatched roof supported on stilts, and thought to have been the area where pilgrims assembled in adoration. The rest of the ruins, visible though barely distinguishable, were dwellings, storehouses, and palaces. From the very top of the Sun Temple there's a magnificent view out beyond the modern highway to the beach (Playa San Pedro) and across the sea to a sizable, uplifted island. Standing in the ruins, this island—clearly geologically related to the Pachacamac mound—appears like a huge whale approaching shore.

Farther South, Toward Pisco

Beyond Pachacamac lie some of Lima's most attractive beaches. Closest of these—just a couple of kilometers outside Pachacamac—is **PLAYA SAN PEDRO**, a seemingly endless and usually deserted strip of sand. Constantly pounded by rollers, however, it can be quite dangerous for swimming. Much more sheltered, and more popular, is the beautiful bay of **EL SILENCIO**,

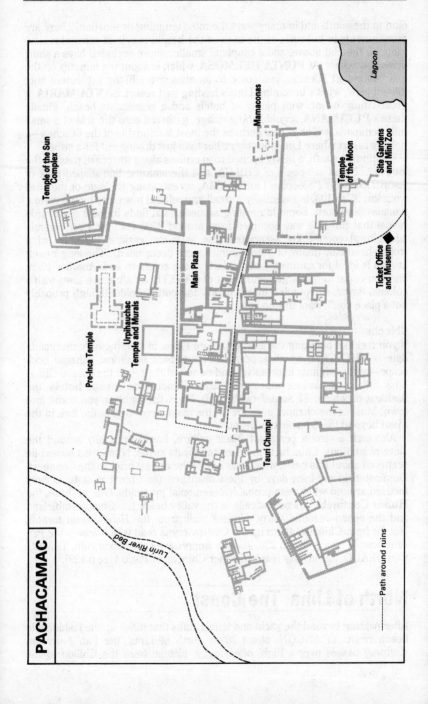

PACHACAMAC

Lagoon

Temple of the Sun
Complex

Mamaconas

Temple
of the Moon

Site Gardens
and Mini Zoo

Main Plaza

Pre-Inca Temple

Urpihauchac
Temple and Murals

Ticket Office
and Museum ◆

Tauri Chumpi

Lurin River Bed

- - - Path around ruins

6km to the south and in many ways the most tempting destination. There are refreshments in hut-cafés at the back of the beach, excellent seafood restaurants on the cliff above, and a couple of smaller, more secluded bays a short drive downcoast. At **PUNTA HERMOSA**, which is about ten minutes on the bus beyond El Silencio, you come to an attractive cliff-top settlement and, down below, what's becoming Lima's leading surf resort, **SANTA MARIA**, a great family haunt, with plenty of hotels and a reasonable beach. Finally there's **PUCUSANA**, an old fishing village, gathered onto the side of a small hilly peninsula, which is now perhaps the most fashionable of the beaches—a holiday resort where Limeños stay rather than just driving out for a swim.

Continuing south, a newly opened road cruises along the coast, passing the long beach and salt-pools of CHILCA, and the amazing lion-shaped rock of **León Dormido** ("Sleeping Lion"). **ASIA**, spread along the side of the road from km 95 to 103, is essentially a small agricultural town, producing cotton, bananas, and corn. Some interesting archeological finds in local graveyards reveal that this site was occupied from around 2500 B.C. by a pre-ceramic agricultural community associated also with the earliest examples of a trophy-head cult (many of the mummies were decapitated). The long **beach** at Asia is ideal for camping—particularly at the southern end. Another 40km and you come to the larger settlement of CAÑETE, an attractive town with a colonial flavor, surrounded by marigolds and cotton fields, though probably not a place you'll want to stop in.

Chincha

If you feel like breaking the journey before Pisco, in fact, the only real candidate is **CHINCHA**, which appears after a stretch of almost Saharan landscape—and a mightily impressive sand dune—at the top of the coastal cliff. A busy little town, selling wines and *piscos*, Chincha has several **hotels**, the flashiest of which, *El Sausal* (with pool), is on the right as you come into town. Most of the cheaper ones are on the main street (left at the fork in the road) beyond the *Ormeño* bus depot.

Although a strong center of Black culture, based originally around the slave plantations, Chincha is more visited for its **ruins**. Numerous *huacas* lie scattered about this oasis, which was one of the richest prior to the Conquest. Dominated in pre-Inca days by the Cuismancu (or Chincha) state, activity focused around what were probably ceremonial pyramids. One of these, the **Huaca Centinela**, sits majestically in the valley below the Chincha tableland and the ocean—around thirty minutes' walk from the *Hotel Sausal* turnoff. Not far from Chincha, 40km up the Castrovireyna road which leaves the Pan American Highway at km 230, another impressive Cuismancu ruin, TAMBO COLORADO, lies in easy reach of either Chincha or Pisco (see p.129).

North of Lima: The Coast

After passing beyond the yacht and tennis clubs that make up the fashionable beach resort of ANCÓN, about 30km north of Lima, the Pan American Highway passes over a high, often foggy, plateau from the Chillon to the

Chancay valley. This fog zone, still covered by sparse vegetation, was a relatively fertile *lomas* area (a place where plants grow from moisture in the air rather than rainwater or irrigation) in Pre-Inca days. Evidence of winter camps from 5000 years ago has been found here and it's an exciting spot to explore for anyone interested in a unique habitat. Beyond CHANCAY (by-passing the market town of HUARAL) the road continues through stark desert, broken only by more *lomas* at LACHAY (km 105). A little farther, however, at km 133, a track turns off onto a small peninsula making for the secluded bay of **EL PARAISO**—a magical beach perfect for **camping**, swimming, and scuba.

Crossing more bleak sands, the Pan American Highway comes next to **HUACHA**, an unusual place with some interesting colonial architecture and a ruined church in the upper part of town. From here to BARRANCA and the maze-like ruins of the Fortress of Paramonga (see p.172) only the town and port of SUPE break the monotonous beauty of desert and ocean.

Foothill Ruins: Puruchuco and Cajarmaquilla

Puruchuco and Cajarmarquilla, the most impressive sites around Lima after Pachacamac, are typical of ruins all over Peru, and easily enough reached to make a good introduction to the country's archeology. Both lie near the beginning of the "Central Highway," the road that climbs up behind Lima towards CHOSICA, LA OROYA, and the Andes. To get out to Puruchuco (signposted at km 11 of the highway) you can take bus #200, #202, or #204 from the Nicolas de Pierola terminal; Cajamarquilla, 6km farther, is served by bus #202d, either from Pierola or by picking it up on the highway by Puruchuco.

An 800-year-old, pre-Inca settlement, **PURUCHUCO** (daily 9am–5pm) comprises a labyrinthine villa and a small but interesting site museum containing a complete collection of artifacts and attire found at the site (all of which bears a remarkable similarity to what Amazon Indian communities still use today). The adobe structure was apparently rebuilt and adapted by the Incas shortly before the Spanish arrival. It's a fascinating ruin, superbly restored in a way which vividly captures what life was probably like before the Conquest. Very close by in the Parque Fernando Carozi (ask the site guard for directions) two other ruins—**Huaquerones** and **Catalina Huaca**—are being restored, and at **Chivateros** there's a quarry apparently dating back some 12,000 years.

The **CAJAMARQUILLA** bus (#202d) actually goes to a refinery, so ask the driver to drop you off shortly after leaving the main road, then ask for directions—the **ruins** (daily 9am–5pm) are well hidden next to an old hacienda. First occupied in the Huari Era (A.D. 600–1000), Cajamarquilla flourished under the **Cuismancu culture**, a city-building state contemporary with the better known Chimu in northern Peru. It was an enclosed city containing thousands of small complex dwellings clustered around a higher section, probably nobles' quarters, and numerous small plazas. The site was apparently abandoned before the Incas arrived in 1470, possibly after being devastated by an earthquake. Pottery found here in the 1960s by a group of Italian archeologists suggests habitation over 1300 years ago.

Marcahuasi

MARCAHUASI, one of Peru's lesser-known marvels and something of a mystical enigma, can be reached in one day from Lima and makes an amazing weekend camping jaunt. The main attractions are the incredible rock formations which, particularly by moonlight, take on weird shapes—llamas, human faces, turtles, even a hippopotamus. There's also a large clearing known locally as the amphitheater. The nearest facilities to this high altitude site (just over 4000m) are in the village of SAN PEDRO DE CASTA about two or three hard walking hours down the mountain, so it's best to arrive well prepared!

There are no direct buses from Lima to San Pedro, but if you take a bus (from block 15 of Nicolas de Pierola, one block beyond the Parque Universitario) or train to CHOSICA, you can pick up buses and trucks to Marcahuasi from *Parque Echinique*. The buses—*Empresa Santa Maria*—usually have signs saying *San Pedro de Cajas* or *Marcahuasi*, but for trucks it's a matter of asking all drivers where they're bound. Heaviest traffic tends to be on Saturdays. If your bus or truck terminates at LAS CRUCES, don't worry, it's only half an hour's walk farther to San Pedro, and another three hours to Marcahuasi itself.

In San Pedro you'll find almost everything you need around the main plaza. There's an *Albergue* with some sixteen beds, the *Hostal Communal* (which is really intended for large groups of up to sixty people), and the *Hotel Huayrona* which, despite its name, is actually the schoolteachers' residence. *Tienda Natches*, which doubles up as tourist information center when the official tourist office is closed, also offers cheap floor space to travelers. When it is open, the tourist office can arrange accommodation and even mules for the uphill climb (bags and/or people). If you happen to be in Marcahuasi on the 28th, 29th, and 30th of July, expect to get wrapped up in an incredible village festival that involves two days of ceremony, music, dance, and festivities in the amphitheater on the mountain.

Into the Andes: El Tren de la Sierra

The **train journey** from Lima up into the Andes is one of *the* great highlights of Peruvian travel—spectacular in itself (the construction alone is incredible) and for many travelers their first sight of llamas and of Peru's indigenous Indian mountain world. With the train inching its way to a pass some 4800m above sea level—at times literally zig-zagging its way forwards, backwards, forwards again, up the steepest slopes—it's also likely to be your first experience of altitude sickness, *soroche*, and you may well need to take a breath from the bags of oxygen brought up and down the carriage at this point by the guard. If you're worried about altitude sickness, or can't face returning this way, the *colectivo* services between Lima and Huancayo (*Comité* #12 from Montivideo 733) or Tarma (*Comité* #1 from Renovación 399) are a lot quicker. Otherwise, the train leaves the Desamparedos station (watch for pickpockets here) every day except Sunday at around 7:40am, rolling into Huancayo officially at 4:30pm, but generally at least an hour later; tickets are on sale from 6am but are best bought the day before.

It usually takes around six hours to reach LA OROYA, nearly all this time high in the Andes as the factories and cloudy skies of Lima are swiftly left behind. At Oroya there's a connection—at 2:30pm—for CERRO DE PASCO, a possible approach to HUANUCO (see below), but most travelers stay on the train for the ride to HUANCAYO. Passing through the astonishing **Javja Valley**, this is the most beautiful scenery of the trip, striped by fabulous colored furls of mountain. Even Paul Theroux—who didn't much care for Peru, and still less for this trip ("no railroad journey on earth can be so aptly described as going on *ad nauseam*")—was impressed. Arrival at HUANCAYO, however, can certainly be a relief. Going on to HUANUCO your best bet is to move sharply and catch the bus connection at the end of the rail route at CERRO DE PASCO—it's only another three to four hours, which by this stage makes little difference.

Neither **LA OROYA** nor **CERRO DE PASCO** are particularly inviting places, bleak little mining towns separated by 130km or so of rather desolate landscape, and fiercely cold at night. If you break the journey this way it's best to do it in Cerro, which has a slightly wider selection of **hotels**: the *El Viajeno* by the plaza, *Los Angeles* in the market area, and *Gran Hotel Cerro de Pasco* on Avenida Angamos in the suburb of San Juan. Trains **returning to Lima** from CERRO leave at 6am for the considerably quicker downhill trek.

Building the Railroad: Some History

For President Balta of Peru and many of his contemporaries in 1868, the iron fingers of a railroad, "if attached to the hand of Lima would instantly squeeze out all the wealth of the Andes, and the whistle of the locomotives would awaken the Indian race from its centuries-old lethargy." Consequently, when the American railroad entrepreneur **Henry Meiggs** (aptly called the "Yankee Pizarro") arrived on the scene it was instantly decided that the coastal guano deposits would be sold off to finance a new railroad, one which faced technical problems (i.e., the Andes) never prevously encountered by engineers. With timber from Oregon and the labor of thousands of Chinese workers (basis of Peru's present Chinese communities), Meiggs at last reached La Oroya via 61 bridges, 65 tunnels, and the startling 4800m pass. An extraordinary feat of engineering, it nevertheless bound Peru more closely to the New York and London banking worlds than to its own hinterland and peasant population.

Huancayo and Huancavelica

Although relatively close together, these two towns offer highly contrasting visions of life in the central Peruvian Andes. **Huancayo**, at 3261m, is a large commercial city, thriving on agricultural produce, while **Huancavelica**, higher at 3680m, is a remote colonial town with a sad history revolving around its mercury mines. Both fascinating in their own ways, and with a distinct culture represented in colorful rustic costumes and dances like the *Chunguinada* or *Huaylas*, both are also strategic points on the traditional (though no longer practicable, due to the ongoing civil unrest) highland route to Cuzco. As well as the railroad and *colectivo* **connections**, a bus—taking about nine hours—runs from Lima to Huancayo (*Etusca*, Prolongación Huanuco 1439–1441, La Victoria). The *colectivo Comité 12* (Calle Montevideo 736 in Lima and Loreto 425 in Huancayo) does the trip in about seven hours. Trains are scheduled to leave Huancayo for Huancavelica daily at 7am and 1:30pm (less than $2 first class, 4–6 hr.).

Huancayo

HUANCAYO is now capital of the Junin Department, and an important market center dealing in vast quantities of wheat. It's a very old settlement, however, and the cereal and textile potential of the region has long been exploited. Back in the 1460s the native *Huanca* tribe was conquered by the Inca Pachacuti's forces during his period of Imperial expansion; occupied by the Spanish since 1537, it was on the map economically, though remaining little more than a staging point. It was the railroad, reaching Huancayo in 1909, that truly transformed it into a city. Being relatively modern , the town has very little of architectural or historical merit, though it's a lively place and it does have an extremely active market, or *feria* (best on Sunday). This sells the usual fruit and vegetables, and also has a good selection of woolen and alpaca clothes and blankets, superb San Pedro de Cajas weavings, and some silver jewelry.

There are several reasonable **hotels** in Huancayo, including the *Hotel Kiya* (bed, hot showers, and towel for about $4) and the *Turistas* (also quite reasonably priced; Jr. Ancash 72; ☎23-1072) on the Plaza de Armas, and the *Huancayo* and *Primavera* on Giraldez, just around the corner from the station. Excellent **bed and breakfast** is available at very low prices at Jr. Galena 169, in the district of Millo-tingo (☎23-3786). **Calle Real** is the main street, a wide commercial drag housing the *Banco de la Nacion*, the **tourist office,** and *Huancayo Tours* (check with them for flights to Lima; Calle Real 543; ☎23-3751/23-6470).

It's possible to eat and drink well in any one of the **restaurants** around the Plaza de la Constitución, the renamed Plaza de Armas: *Olímpico*, at Av. Giráldez 199, is especially recommended. And although you should rest for a day or two to acclimatize if you've come straight up from the coast, there is plenty of **nightlife**. Local music and dance is performed most Sundays at 3pm in the *Coliseo* on Calle Real, and there are some good Creole and folklore peñas—*Dale "U"* (corner of Calle Ayacucho and Huancavelica), *Algarrobo* (13 de Noviembre, Libertad), and *Cajon* (Calle Real—open every night). Every May, Huancayo erupts into the splendid **Fiesta de las Cruces**.

The **post office** can be found on the Plaza de Huanamarca by the *Hotel de Turistas*. It's best to change travelers' checks and U.S. cash into *intis* in Lima rather than be subject to the slightly lower rates of Huancayo, but if you need to change money here, try the *Casas de Cambio* on Calle Real.

Out from Huancayo

Using Huancayo as a base you can make a number of enjoyable excursions into the Jauja valley. The **Convent of Santa Rosa de Ocopa** (Wed.–Mon.

10am–noon and 3–5pm; 65 ¢), about forty minutes or 30km out of town, is easily reached by taking a microbus from the Church of Immaculate Conception (or the Lima train—7am daily, except Sunday) to CONCEPCION, where another bus covers the last 5km to the monastery. Founded in 1724, and taking some twenty years to build, this was the center of the Franciscan mission into the Amazon—until their work was disrupted and finally halted by the Wars of Independence, after which their mission villages in the jungle disintegrated and most of the natives returned to the forest. The **cloisters** are more interesting than the church, though both are set in a pleasant and peaceful environment, and there's an excellent **library** with chronicles from the sixteenth century onwards, plus a **Museum of Natural History and Ethnology** containing lots of stuffed animals and native artifacts from the jungle. There's also a guesthouse, which costs $2.50 a night. A trip out here can be conveniently combined with a visit to the nearby village of SAN JERONIMO, well known for its Wednesday market of fine silver jewelry; a 45-minute walk from San Jerónimo brings you to HUAYLAS, where high quality **woolen goods** are cheaper than elsewhere, because you buy directly from the maker. For the energetic, **bicycles** can be hired for this trip (or any other) from *Huancayo Tours* (Calle Real 543).

There are a number of other worthwhile trips from Huancayo, all of which are served by buses from the market. Forty kilometers out from Huancayo is **JAUJA**, a little colonial town which was the capital of Peru before the founding of Lima—a past reflected in its generally unspoiled architecture, surrounded by some gorgeous countryside; buses leave from Huancayo market. And, near the pueblo of HUARI stand the **Huari-Huilca ruins**, the sacred complex of the Huanca tribe which dominated this region for over two hundred years before the arrival of the Incas. The distinct style the ruins display went unrecognized until 1964 when local villagers rediscovered the site under their fields. At the site is a small museum showing collections of ceramic fragments, bones, and stone weapons.

Many people come up to Huancayo simply to buy the crafted carved **gourds** which are a specialty of two local villages, COCHAS CHICAS and COCHAS GRANDES (half an hour by frequent bus from the Church of Immaculate Conception in Huancayo's main plaza). In these villages you can buy straight from cooperatives or the individual artisan. Strangely, Cochas Grandes is the smaller of the two and you have to ask around to find the gourds here, but there are some good ones. Expect to pay anything from $1 up to $100 for the finer ones, and if you are ordering some to be made, expect to pay half the money in advance.

The *Hidalgo* company, at the time of writing, continues to run a **bus to Cuzco**—a two-day journey via AYACUCHO, every Monday, Wednesday, and Friday, leaving Huancayo at 7am. This is an incredible route—and a historically fascinating region—but for the moment the area between HUANCAVELICA and AYACUCHO is extremely **dangerous** for gringos to enter with any degree of confidence: accelerating guerrilla activity makes it unsafe to pass through even on a bus. If you're still interested, see the Cuzco chapter, p.78 for more details.

Huancavelica

From Huancayo, a three and a half hour train ride up through beautiful countryside ends at **HUANCAVELICA**, a surprisingly pure Indian town in spite of a long colonial history and a fairly impressive array of Spanish-style architecture. The weight of its past, however, lies heavily on its shoulders. After mercury deposits were discovered here in 1563, the town began producing ore for the silver mines of Peru—replacing expensive imports previously used in the mining process. In just over a hundred years so many Indian laborers had died of mercury poisoning that the pits could hardly keep going: after the generations of locals bound to serve by the *mitayo* system of virtual slavery had been literally used up and thrown away, the salaries required to attract new workers made many of the mines unprofitable. Today the ore is taken by truck to Pisco on the coast, but many mines have been closed and local people are somewhat discontented, made restless by the continuing struggles between the *Sendero Luminoso* guerrillas and the Peruvian military.

If you do come here—and it's possible to complete a circuit down to the coast via Pisco, a spectacular twelve-hour journey over amazingly high terrain—you'll probably not stay for long. The cheaper **hotels** are pretty nasty, though the *Turistas* is quite reasonable value. Huancavelica's main sights, around the main **Plaza de Armas**, are the **cathedral**, with its fine altar, and a handful of **churches**. Two of them—San Francisco and Santo Domingo—are connected to the cathedral by an underground passage. These apart, there's not a lot of interest. If you're here on Sunday you'll hit the **market;** if you like walking at this altitude there are natural **hot springs** on the hill north of the river, and a **weaving co-op** 4km out at TOTORAL.

The bus from Huancavelica to **Pisco** is operated by *Oropesa* and leaves at 6am; make sure it's going the whole way though—sometimes it turns around midway at SANTA INES, a cold hamlet on top of the *Puna*. For Lima, via Huancayo, an *Empresa Huancavelica* bus leaves daily at 5pm. The train back to Huancayo leaves at 7am.

Tarma and the High Jungle

The region around **Tarma**, east of the railroad junction at La Oroya, is one of Peru's most beautiful corners, the mountains stretching down from high craggy limestone outcrops into steep canyons forged by Amazon tributaries powering their way down to the Atlantic. By far the nicest mountain town in this part of Peru, Tarma sits on the edge of the Andes almost within touching distance of the Amazon forest—a good alternative goal from Huancayo, making a satisfyingly adventurous high jungle circuit. The other major towns here, La Merced and San Ramon, are less attractive but good places to take a break in some degree of comfort before setting off for **Pozuzo** or **Satipo**, two of the most interesting of Peruvian jungle towns.

Tarma

TARMA itself is a pretty colonial town, making a good living from its traditional textile and leather industries and from growing flowers for export and for its own celebratory use. Its greatest claim to fame came during Juan Santos Atahualpa's rebellion in the 1740s and 1750s; taking refuge in the surrounding mountains he defied Spanish troops for more than a decade, though peace returned to the region in 1756 when Juan Santos and his allies mysteriously disappeared. Today it's a quiet place, disturbed only by the flow of trucks climbing up towards the jungle foothills, and the town's famous Easter Sunday procession from the main plaza, when the streets are covered in carpets of dazzling flowers.

For **rooms**, the *Hotel Turistas* (as you come into town from Lima) is reasonable at $10 to $15 single, but much more so are the *Hotel Galaxia*, on the plaza, and *Hotel America*, opposite the market. **Tourist information** is available from *Turismo Tarama* (Huaraz 537; ☎2286) and the **post office** is on Callao within two blocks of the plaza. Most of the bus and *colectivo* offices are clustered on Calloa and Castilla near the gas station (close to the *Hotel de Turistas*).

A practical day's outing—though better appreciated if you camp over-night—takes you to the rural village of PALCAMAYO (1½ hr. by bus). From here it's an hour's climb to the **Caves of Huagapo**, the country's deepest explored caves, accessible for over 1km with flashlight and waterproof cloth-ing. If you've got a car at your disposal, or plenty of time, craftspeople in the beautiful village of SAN PEDRO DE CAJAS, within hitching distance of the caves, produce superb quality weavings. Coincidentally (or not) the village lies in a valley neatly divided into patchwork field-systems—an exact model of the local textile style. From here you can either take a bus or hitch back to Tarma.

San Ramon and La Merced

San Ramon and **La Merced** (80–88 *slow* km from Tarma), known jointly as CHANCHAMAYO after the valley in which they sit, mark the real beginning of the jungle. Both are well served by **buses** operated by *Etusca* and *Los Andes*—runs which continue on to SATIPO, or in the other direction back towards Lima. (Tarma is also connected to Lima by **colectivos**, which leave the capital at *Comité No. 1*, Renovacion 399, La Victoria.) Well-established settler towns, they are separated by only 8km of road, some 2500m below Tarma under the strong sun of the high jungle. Getting there from La Oroya the road winds down in ridiculously precipitous curves, keeping tight to the sides of the **Rio Palca canyon**, at present used for generating hydroelectric power. Originally a forest zone inhabited only by Campa-Ashaninka Indians, this century has seen much of the best land cleared by invading missionaries, rubber and lumber companies, and, more recently, waves of settlers from the Jauja valley.

The smaller of the two towns, **SAN RAMON** is probably the more pleasant place to break your journey. Its cheap **hotels**, *Chachapoyas* and *Selva*, are both reasonable though there are better places (including private bungalows with hot running water at *El Refugio*), and if you're feeling extravagant or in a hurry there are six- and ten-seater planes to the jungle towns of Satipo and Pucallpa. **LA MERCED** (hotels *Christina*, *Mercedes*, or the cheaper *Hostal Santa Rosa*), on the other hand, is quite a lot busier with a market and plenty of good restaurants thriving around the main plaza. Both places are on the river and surrounded by exciting hiking country and are linked with each other—and at least daily with Oxapampa/Pozuzo and Satipo—by a stream of trucks and buses.

Oxapampa and Pozuzo

Some 78km by good road north of La Merced, **OXAPAMPA** is a small settlement dependent for its survival on lumber and coffee, though most of the forest immediately around the town has been cleared for cattle grazing. The indigenous **Amuesha Indians**, disgruntled at being pushed off their land so that the trees could be taken away and cows put out to grass, are battling hard on local, national, and international levels for their land rights. Strongly influenced in architecture, blood, and temperament by the nearby Germanic settlement of Pozuzo, this is actually quite a pleasant frontier town in its own way. There's a fair **hotel**—the *Bolivar*.

POZUZO, a weird combination of European rusticism and native Peruvian culture, is all that's left of a unique eighteenth-century project to open up the Amazon using European peasants as settlers. Some 80km down the valley from Oxapampa, along a very rough road that crosses over two dozen rivers and streams, its wooded chalets with sloping Tyrolean roofs have endured ever since the first Austrian and German colonists arrived in the 1850s. As part of this grand plan to establish settlements deep in the jungle—brainchild of President Ramon Castilla's economic adviser, a German aristocrat—eighty families left Europe in 1857; seven emigrants died at sea and six more were killed by an avalanche, causing another fifty to turn back only 35km from here. Amazingly, many of the town's present inhabitants still speak German, eat *schitellsuppe*, and dance the polka. Well worth the ride, Pozuzo is an unusual and friendly place (try the *Hostal Tyrol* or *Hotel Maldonado*). **Trucks** for Pozuzo leave irregularly from opposite the *Hotel Bolivar* in Oxapampa.

Satipo

SATIPO, accessible by daily *Los Andes* bus from La Merced, is a real jungle town. Developing around rubber extraction some eighty years ago, it now serves as the economic and social center for a widely scattered population of over 40,000 colonists—offering them tools, food supplies, medical facilities, banks, and even a cinema. It's also the most southern large town on the jungle-bound *Carretera Marginal*. Above all else it's a town where otherwise isolated settlers go to get "civilized," as they say. The **Campa-Ashaninka Indians**, indigenous to the area, have either taken up plots of land and begun to "compete" with colonists, or moved into one of the ever-shrinking zones just out of permanent contact with the rest of Peru. Unmistakable in their reddish-brown or cream *cushma* robes as they walk through town or sit in the square, the more traditional natives are very proud of their culture.

An ideal town in which to get kitted out for a jungle expedition, or merely to sample the delights of the *selva* for a day or two, Satipo is about eight hours' drive down a bumpy road from La Merced (frequent buses and *colectivos*). It possesses an interesting **market**, an **airstrip** (two commercial airlines —*SASA* and *Aguila*—fly to San Ramon, Pucallpa, and Atalaya), and is in the middle of a beautiful landscape—a fascinating walk is to follow the path from the other side of the suspension bridge to one of the plantations beyond the town. Farther afield, local *colectivos* go to the end of the *Carretera Marginal* into relatively freshly settled areas such as that around San Martin de Pangoa—a frontier settlement that is frequently attacked by armed bandits or terrorists who live on coca plantations in the forest (hence the sandbags lined up outside the police stations). The *Hotel Majestic*, on the plaza, is the best place to stay in town (deliciously cool rooms), though the *Hostal Palmero* works out cheaper and there are others around the market area and along the airport road.

As an alternative to retracing your steps back via LA MERCED and SAN RAMON, there's a breathtaking **direct road to Huancayo** (*Los Andes* bus, 12 hr.). For the really adventurous, a **flight to Atalaya**, a small settlement on the Ucayali river in deep jungle, could turn out to be an exciting excursion (again, though, this is dangerous territory these days, rife with illicit drug cultivation and smuggling and controlled by armed bands). It's sometimes possible to find a boat going downstream from here to PUCALLPA (2–5 days; be sure it's not a coke boat!).

travel details

Buses and *Colectivos*
From Lima Regular connections to just about anywhere in Peru, including, among towns detailed in this chapter, Barrranca (3–4 hr.), Chincha (3–4 hr.), Huancayo (10–12 hr.), and Tarma (5–7 hr.). For frequency of service and journey times for destinations in other chapters, see their respective listing and travel details.

From Huancayo Huancavelica (daily; 4–5 hr.); Tarma (daily; 4 hr.); Huanuco/Pucallpa (daily; 10–12 hr./20 hr. or more); Cuzco (no longer practicable; see p.69).

Huancavelica–Pisco (daily; 12 hr.)

Tarma–La Merced (daily; 2–4 hr.)

From La Merced Satipo (daily; 8 hr.); Oxapampa/Pozuzo (more or less daily; 6 hr./14 hr.)

Trains
From Lima La Oroya/Huancayo (daily except Sundays; 6 hr./9–14 hr.)

Huancayo–Huancavelica (daily except Sundays; 6–8 hr.)

La Oroya–Cerro de Pasco (daily connection with Lima train; 4½ hr.)

Boats
Atalaya–Pucallpa (occasional boats; 2–5 days)

Flights
From Lima Numerous international connections (see p.57 for location of airline offices). Domestic flights several times daily to Cuzco (1 hr.); twice daily to Arequipa (1¼ hr.) and Tacna (2½ hr.); daily to Juliaca (for Puno; 2 hr.), Trujillo/Chiclayo (45 min./1 hr. 40 min.), Piura (1¼ hr.), Iquitos (1½ hr.), Pucallpa (1 hr.), Tingo Maria (40 mins.), and Huanuco (25 min.); 5 a week to Yurimagus (2 hr.), and Rioja/Maoyabamba (1½ hr.); 4 a week to Tarapoto (1 hr.).

From San Ramon Satipo and Pucallpa (several times a week).

From Satipo Atalaya and Pucallpa (several times a week).

CHAPTER TWO

CUZCO AND THE SACRED VALLEY

T he mountainous region around Cuzco is the most fascinating part of Peru and the focus of interest for all travelers, South American and gringo alike. **Cuzco** itself is the prime destination, a Spanish city built on the sumptuous remains of Inca temples and palaces and as rich in human life and activity today as it must have been at the height of the Empire. Despite the floods of tourists it remains a welcoming place, with an attractive dose of home comforts and a rare opportunity for close encounters with native Quechua Indians, who make up most of the quarter of a million population.

Once you've acclimatized—and the altitude here, averaging 3500m, is something which does have to be treated with respect—there are dozens of enticing destinations within easy reach. For most people the **Sacred Valley** of the Urubamba river is the obvious first choice, with the magical site of **Machu Picchu** as its ultimate goal and hordes of other ruins—**Pisac** and **Ollantaytambo** in particular—amid glorious Andean panoramas on the way.

Around Cuzco, too, is some of the finest **trekking** country in Peru: not just the **Inca Trail** to Machu Picchu but hundreds of less well known, unbeaten paths into the mountains. And heading farther afield you can begin to penetrate the jungle, either by staying on the train beyond the Sacred Valley to QUILLABAMBA, (see p.269) or forging northeast by truck to **Paucartambo**, on the edge of the vast rainforest of **Manu National Park**. To the south lie more Inca and pre-Inca sites, at **Tipón** and **Pikillacta**, which are nearly as spectacular yet far less visited, while continuing beyond them the **train journey** south to Puno and Lake Titicaca is as dramatic as any you could hope to find. To the west, between Cuzco and Lima, the region around **Ayacucho**, once the main highland route in and out of Cuzco, is now more or less off-limits due to the terrorist activities of the *Sendero Luminoso* guerrillas.

CUZCO

"Navel of the world" for the Incas, **CUZCO** still captivates the hearts and imaginations of all who pass through. A busy little city enclosed between high hills, Cuzco is of great interest both for its substantial Inca ruins and for its many churches and monasteries of Catholic Spain. Visually dominated in

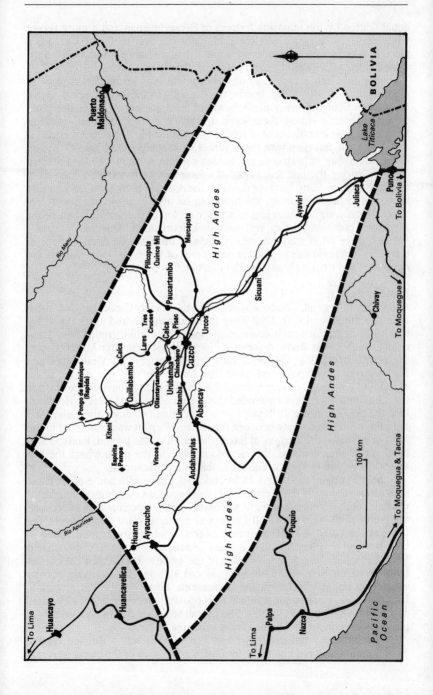

equal degree by the imposing fortress of Sacsayhuaman and a more recent white-stone Christ figure, stretching his arms out over the town, Cuzco is a place to take in slowly, wandering about the numerous sites and museums, sampling the active nightlife, and gradually absorbing its living history.

During Inca times Cuzco, as imperial capital, was an important place of pilgrimage, and still today hundreds—even thousands—of tourists arrive daily, often filling up every plane, bus, and train. It's not an expensive place by any standards—many visitors end up staying quite some time—fulfilling to some degree its often-quoted role as the "Katmandu of South America." A true haven for travelers with its wealth of reasonably priced hotels, relaxed cafes, fascinating little streets, and hidden corners, Cuzco is the kind of town to savor during the last few weeks of a long trip, or to use as a base from which to explore Peru. Looking down on the red-tiled roofs from the amazing viewpoint of Sacsayhuaman, the town can be held in perspective, a deceptively peaceful sight, snuggling in a valley on top of the world. Down below the streets constantly throng with townsfolk, tourists, and Quechua Indians—the last, more often than not, selling crafts in the Plaza de Armas or one of the many *artesania* markets. Only **one word of warning**—pick-pockets are numerous and extremely skillful. But don't let that put you off.

Some History...

According to legend, Cuzco was founded by Manco Capac and his sister Mama Occlo around A.D. 1200. Over the next two hundred years the valley was home to the Inca tribe, one of many localized warlike groups then dominating the Peruvian sierra. A series of chiefs led the tribe after Manco Capac, the eighth one being Viracocha Inca, but it wasn't until Viracocha's son Pachacuti assumed power in 1438 that Cuzco became the center of an expanding empire. Pachacuti pushed the frontier of Inca territory outward at the same time as he masterminded the design of imperial Cuzco. He canalized the Saphi and the Tullumayo, two rivers that ran down the valley, and built the center of the city between them: Cuzco's plan was conceived in the form of a puma—the fortress of **Sacsayhuaman** as the jagged, tooth-packed head and **Pumacchupan**, the sacred cat's tail, at the point where the two rivers merge, just below the Temple of the Sun, **Koricancha**.

In building their capital the Incas endowed Cuzco with some of its finest structures—the walls and foundations of all important buildings were of hard volcanic rock, streets ran straight and narrow with stone channels to drain off the heavy rains—but above all Cuzco was a sacred place whose heart, the heart of the puma, was **Huacapata**, a ceremonial square approximating in both size and position the modern Plaza de Armas. Four main roads radiated from the square, one to each corner of the empire. Pachacuti's palace was built on one corner of Huacapata (you can still see the perfectly regular courses of andesite stone in the *Restaurante Roma*), while his grandson, Huayna Capac, situated his palace in the opposite corner, next to the cloisters of the Temple of the Sun Virgins. The overall achievement was remarkable, a planned city without rival at the center of a huge empire.

By the time the Spanish arrived in Peru, Cuzco was a thriving capital. Nobles and conquered chieftains lived within the body of the puma, servants and artisans on the outskirts, while subjects from all over the empire made regular official pilgrimages. Of all the Inca rulers only Atahualpa, the last, never actually resided in Cuzco—and even he was on his way there when the Conquistadors captured him at Cajamarca. In his place, **Pizarro** eventually reached the native capital on November 15, 1533. The Spaniards were astonished—the city's beauty surpassed anything they had seen before in the New World—but as usual they lost no time in plundering its fantastic wealth of gold and booty.

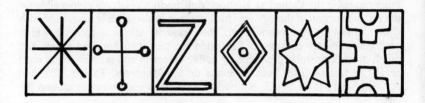

Designs abstracted from an Inca emperor's tunic

The Spanish city, divided up among 88 of Pizarro's men who chose to remain as settlers, was officially founded in 1534. Manco Inca was set up as a puppet ruler, governing from a new palace on the hill just below Sacsayhuaman. Within a year power struggles between the colonists—two of whom were Pizarro's sons—had reached the point of open violence, though serious trouble was averted when their main rival, Almagro, departed to head an expedition to Chile. With him out of the way, Juan and Gonzalo Pizarro were free to abuse the Inca and his subjects, which eventually provoked Manco to open resistance. In 1536 he fled to Yucay, in the Sacred Valley, to gather forces for the Great Rebellion.

Within days the two hundred Spanish defenders, with only eighty horses, were surrounded in Cuzco by over 100,000 rebel Inca warriors. On May 6 Manco's men attacked, setting fires among the dry thatched roofs and laying siege to the city for the following week. Finally, the Spaniards, still besieged in Huacapata, led a desperate attempt on horseback to break out, riding up to counterattack the Inca base in Sacsayhuaman. Incredibly, the following day they defeated the native stronghold, putting some 1500 warriors to the sword as they took the fortress.

Cuzco never again came under such serious native threat, but its battles were far from over. By the end of the rains the following year the small Spanish stronghold was still awaiting reinforcements: Pizarro's men were on their way up from the coast, while Almagro, returning from Chile, was at Urcos, only 35km to the south. Unsure of his loyalties and the cause of the Inca insurrection, Almagro tried to befriend Manco but the Emperor, unable to put his trust in any Spaniard, chose to retreat into a remote mountain refuge at **Vilcabamba**—now called Espiritu Pampa, deep in the jungle northeast of Cuzco. Almagro immediately seized Cuzco for himself and defeated the Pizarrist force arriving from Lima. For a few months the city became the center of the Almagrist rebels until Francisco Pizarro himself arrived on the scene, defeated the rebel force on the edge of town and had Almagro garrotted in the main plaza. The rebel Incas, meanwhile, held out in Vilcabamba until 1572, when the Spanish colonial Viceroy, Toledo, captured Tupac Aymaru—one of Manco's sons who had succeeded as Emperor—and beheaded him in the Plaza de Armas.

From then on the city was left in relative peace, ravaged only by the great earthquake of 1650. After this dramatic tremor, remarkably illustrated on a huge canvas in the Cathedral, **Bishop Mollinedo** was largely responsible for the reconstruction of the city, and his influence is also closely associated with Cuzco's most creative years of art. The *Cuzqueño* school of painting, which emerges from his patronage, flourished for next two hundred years, and much of its finer work, produced by native Quechua and *mestizo* artists such as Diego Quispe Tito, Juan Espinosa de los Monteros, Fabian Ruiz, and Antonio Sinchi Roca, is still exhibited in museums and churches around the city.

Arrival

Most people arrive in Cuzco either by air from Lima or by train from the south, via Arequipa and Puno, but unless you're really pressed for time there's little advantage in flying. The bus (or *colectivo)* ride down the south coast to AREQUIPA (18 hours), then by train to PUNO and Lake Titicaca (10–12 hours) before continuing north through the stunning Vilcanota valley for the final 10–12 hour stage, is an exciting and quite stunning journey with a great deal of interest along the way and extreme ranges of climate and topography (see p.167 for details).

Alternatively, and slightly faster, there are **direct buses** from Lima which take around 30–50 hours to reach Cuzco, either via Pisco and Ayacucho or through Nazca and Abancay. These are rough overland journeys passing through extravagantly steep mountain scenery and over extremely high passes—magnificent and often thrilling routes. But with the guerrilla activity in the area around Ayacucho and, to some extent, Abancay (which both routes pass through), they are also potentially dangerous. Buses are occasionally stopped by "terrorists" or more often hassled by police looking for guerrillas and gun-runners.

The other traditional route, by train from Lima to Huancayo and across the Andes from there by bus or truck to Cuzco, is probably even more dangerous. It passes directly through this terror-struck and politically explosive area, and although it used to be *the* route for the hardened traveler, few will attempt it now. A section on **Ayacucho** and the Lima to Cuzco route is included at the end of this chapter.

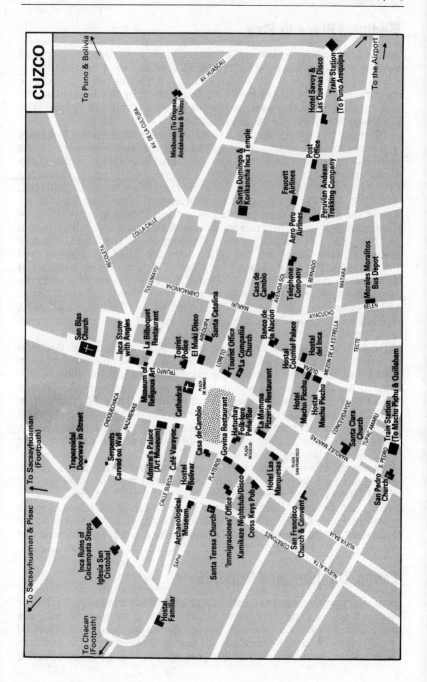

Finding a Place to Stay

Small enough not to get lost in, Cuzco is still sufficiently large to cater to all needs and to keep you busy for as long as you like—most travelers stay at least a week. It's a good idea to check out a few **hostels** before deciding on the right one for you: if you're initially knocked out by the altitude take the first you find, dump your gear, and go out for a coca tea (*maté de coca*). You can always search out a better place later on.

There are two very inexpensive, clean, safe and central hostels that come well recommended in Cuzco: the *Hostal Suecia* (Calle Suecia) which has small shared dormitories with an average of four beds each; and the nearby *Hostal Huaynapata* (Huaynapata 369). However, every regular visitor has their favorite hotel in Cuzco and mine is the *Hostal Familiar* (Calle Saphi 661; ☎23-9353). Only 2½ blocks uphill towards Sacsayhuaman from the Plaza de Armas, the Familiar is reasonably priced at about $2.50 single, has private or communal showers, its own cafe with a notice board for travelers' information and messages, and a laundry service. There are many other slightly cheaper places between here and the plaza, particularly along Plateros and Procuradores. The *Hotel Caceres* (first block of Plateros) is very popular and quite safe at around $1.50 a night. One of the very cheapest in town is the *Hostal Bolivar*; turn left at the top end of Procuradores and you'll find it tucked away in a corner, behind the ancient walls of Pachacuti's palace. A typically basic gringo's hotel, it has earned a reputation for drugs and consequently gets raided now and then by the police.

Downhill from the Plaza de Armas there are plenty more, though they tend to be on the expensive side. The *Hostal Machu Picchu*, however, isn't overpriced and, set around a picturesque courtyard, is a pleasant place to stay (just off Avenida Sol at Quera 274). Virtually next door, the *Hostal Colonial Palace* is upscale but good value. Over the road, at Quera 251, the modern *Hostal del Inca* (☎2009) costs up to $7 per night in the high season (July and August), less at other times. Another option, surprisingly cheap and friendly, is the *Hostal Tipón*, slightly away from the town center on Calle Tecte but handy for most bus and all train terminals.

Nearer the Plaza de Armas there is the *Hotel Loreto* (Calle Loreto 115) at around $7 single, or, just up from the Plaza Regocijo, the superb and similarly priced *Hostal Los Marqueses* (Garcilaso 252) and the *Hotel Garcilaso* (opposite. . . not the other *Hotel Garcilaso* farther up the street, which is much more expensive, though excellent, at about $14 single). If you're after luxury in Cuzco it is hard to beat the *Hotel Conquistador* (from $20 per person), just down Avenida Arequipa from the tourist police and opposite *El Muki* disco.

Eating, Drinking, and Nightlife

Generally speaking, **food** in Cuzco is very good, if not quite as interesting or as varied as it is along the coast or in Lima. Most of the more central cafes and restaurants accommodate all tastes, offering anything from a toasted cheese sandwich or a hamburger to the best in Creole dishes. The best area for restaurants and bars is **Procuradores alley**, a true gringo dive leading off Portal de Panes on the Plaza de Armas. Down here, where you can get virtually anything at most times of day or night, there's a pizza parlor, vegetarian restaurant, and several cheapish cocktail bars. Most places stay open from early in the morning until around midnight, when those hungry for other action disappear into one of the numerous late-night **bars** or nightclubs. Apart from Lima, no other Peruvian town has as varied a **nightlife** as Cuzco and, importantly, each place is within staggering distance of another one.

Food

There are plenty of places for **breakfast** and **lunch**. Among these, *Le Paris* (on the corner of Calle Media and the Plaza de Armas) is cheap and friendly with background pop and rock; the *Allyu* cafe, beside the cathedral, is a more tranquil place, a favorite meeting spot which plays perpetual classical music; there's also the bohemian *Varayoc*, on Plaza Regocijo, which serves good coffee, has a notice board, and offers an interesting rack full of magazines.

To sample the **local food** there are two obvious choices: you can eat from the stalls at the **central market** (near the San Pedro railroad station) where there's an endless selection of good, very cheap meals; or you can try one of the many *quintas* , which specialize in foods like *chicharrones*, guinea pig, and spicy Creole dishes. Ordinarily, being open-air places, *quintas* only serve at lunch times—one favorite is the *Quinta Eulalia* (Choquechaca 384; ☎2421), unusually central with a very lively atmosphere and a good jukebox well supplied with *chicha* music.

If you want to feel like you're still at home, there are several **pizza** houses in Cuzco, two of the best being around Plaza Regocijo (of these *La Mamma Pizzeria* has the tastiest food, the most room, and excellent service, but expect to pay higher than the usual Cusquenian prices). The first two blocks of Plateros coming from the plaza boast a number of quite reasonable **cafes**, though one of the best and cheapest is the Japanese vegetarian restaurant on the right hand side.

For **vegetarians**, there are a couple of other excellent places: *Govinda*, a Hindu eatery with cheap set meals just off the main plaza at Calle Espaderos 128, or *Pura Vida*, attached to the "Community of Sun—a universal fraternity," in the pleasant colonial courtyard of the *Hostal Marqueses* at Garcilaso 256.

For **evening meals**, or simply more substantial food, the list could be almost infinite. There are several places—like the *Restaurant Roma, Chef Victor,* and the *Chifa Los Angeles*—right on the Plaza de Armas. Probably the most trendy place to dine out these days is the French-run *La Bilboquet* (Herraje 171a) which serves superb crepes; you can also sample their wide range of drinks in the downstairs bar if you're not that hungry.

Nightlife: Bars and Clubs

As far as **nightlife** goes, there are roughly speaking three scenes: *peñas* for Peruvian music; discos for international jiving; and bars for serious drinking. Of the peñas, *Q'Hatuchay* , on the Plaza de Armas at Portal Confituria 233, is the liveliest and most popular. Just around the corner, on Plaza Regocijo, music and food can be found most evenings at *El Truco*, a relatively expensive but good Creole *peña*. The best of Cuzco's discos is undoubtedly *Las Quenas* (in the basement of the Hotel Savoy, below the post office on Avenida del Sol) which stays open until at least 3am most nights. If you tire of this there is the cave-like *El Muki* (Santa Catalina Angosta 114, opposite the *Hotel Conquistadores* near the cathedral on Arequipa). To watch folkdancing to mountain music, try the *Centro Quosqo* (Av. del Sol 604; ☎3708) which has performances most evenings between 6:30 and 8pm.

For **heavy drinking** into the early hours the in place at present is *Kamikasi*, a largish alternative club/disco tucked away in the northeast corner of Plaza Regocijo. Here the entertainment ranges from live mime and political poetry to loud rock music. The English-run **pub**—*The Cross Keys*—located on San Juan de Dios, just up from Plaza Regocijo, was closed in 1988. Its owner, Barry Walker, is one of the best ornithological guides in Peru (particularly for Manu and other jungle regions), and many people (locals and visitors alike) will be pleased if and when the pub either reopens at the same place or new premises are found for it.

The City: Orientation

Cuzco's ancient and modern center, the **Plaza de Armas**, is the obvious place to get your bearings—uphill towards the ruined fortress of Sacsayhuaman, and with the cathedral squat and unmistakable along one side. Behind is the Church of La Compañía, smaller than the cathedral but with an equally impressive pair of belfries, and next door to it the glass-fronted **tourist office**. Wherever you are in Cuzco it's always possible to find your way back to the Plaza de Armas simply by locating the ruins of Sacsayhuaman or, at night, the illuminated white **Christ figure** which stands beside it on the steep horizon.

Back on ground level there are a few other points of reference that ease orientation. From the bottom corner of the plaza, near La Compañía, two streets lead off at 90° angles to each other—**Mantas**, leading uphill to the **central market** and **San Pedro railroad station** (for Machu Picchu and Quillabamba), and the wider **Avenida del Sol** going straight down towards Koricancha, the **Avenida del Sol train station** (for Puno and the south), and the airport. Both railroad stations, and most of the **bus terminals** (scattered all over town, see p.96), are within walking distance of the center. From the **airport**, 6km out, you'll need to use a taxi or the very cheap local bus service.

Each of the zones outlined below is within easy walking distance of the Plaza de Armas and can be covered in a couple of hours, allowing extra time for real historical enthusiasm or browsing in the bars and shopping en route. Notice, as you wander around Cuzco, how many of the important Spanish buildings have been constructed on top of Inca palaces and temples, often incorporating the exquisitely constructed walls and doorways into the lower parts of churches and colonial structures. The closer you are to the Plaza de Armas, ancient Huacapata, the more obvious this is.

HISTORIC BUILDINGS AND MUSEUMS

To get into most of Cuzco's museums, churches, and mansions—and many of the nearby sites in the Inca's Garden and Sacred Valley—you'll need a **general entrance ticket:** available from the tourist office on the Plaza de Armas (Portal Belen 115) for $10 (half price for students). **Opening hours** for most of these buildings are daily from 9am until 5:30pm (except Sunday), usually closing for lunch between noon and 2:30pm.

Around the Plaza de Armas

The **Church of La Compañía de Jesus**, erected after the earthquake of 1650 and closed for restoration after the 1986 tremor, spreads its Latin cross formation over the foundations of *amara cancha* — originally Huayna Capac's Palace of the Serpents. Cool and dark, with a grand gold-leaf altarpiece, high vaulting, and numerous paintings of the Cuzco School, its most impressive features are the two majestic towers of its main facade, a superb example of Spanish Colonial baroque design. To the right, the **Lourdes Chapel**, restored in 1894, is used mostly as an exhibition center for local crafts, while the early Jesuit **University building** alongside often has traditional dance performances or film shows in the evening (check with the tourist office). On the other side of La Compañía, also covering the ancient space chosen by Huayna Capac, is the **House of the Inquisition**, a large hall today relatively harmlessly occupied by the **tourist office**.

Separating La Compañía from the *Acclahuasi*, or Temple of the Sun Virgins, **Callejón Loreto** shows off the sturdily intricate Inca masonry of both. Today the Acclahuasi block is taken up by shops along the plaza, and the **Convent of Santa Catalina** down Arequipa. Santa Catalina exhibits an impressive Renaissance altarpiece, some exceptional Cuzqueño paintings, and unusual Moorish balconies.

The **Cathedral** (most days 10am–noon and 3–6pm) sits squarely on the foundations of the Inca Viracocha's palace. Its massive lines look fortress-like in comparison with the delicate form of La Compañía. Also constructed, beginning in 1560, in the shape of a Latin cross, the three-aisled nave is supported by only fourteen massive pillars. After entering through the Triunfo Chapel with its finely carved granite altar, you'll see an exceptionally carved Plateresque pulpit, and a neoclassical high altar made entirely of fine embossed silver. In the sacristy there's a painting of the crucifixion attributed to Van Dyck, but the huge canvas depicting the terrible 1650 earthquake, high on the right as you enter Triunfo Chapel, is by far the most fascinating of the cathedral treasures. Ten smaller chapels surround the nave, with the Chapel of the Immaculate Conception, and the Chapel of *El Señor de los Temblores* ("The Lord of Earthquakes") worthy of special attention. However, and much more powerful than anything you can see, the cathedral's magic lies in its mingling of history and legend. Local myth claims an Indian chief lies imprisoned in the right-hand tower, awaiting the day when he can restore the glory of the Inca Empire. Here too hangs the huge and miraculous gold-and-bronze bell of Maria Angola, named for a freed African slave girl. And on the massive main doors of the cathedral native craftsmen have left their own pagan adornment—a puma's head.

To the left of the cathedral, and slightly uphill, Cuzco's most stunning colonial mansion, **El Palacio del Almirante** ("The Admiral's Palace"), looks down onto the Plaza de Armas. Again constructed on Inca foundations—this time the Waypar stronghold where the Spanish conquerors were besieged by Manco's forces in 1536—it now houses the University's **Regional Historical Museum**. The mansion is particularly noteworthy for its simple but well-executed Plateresque facade, surmounted by two imposing Spanish coats-of-arms, but the museum itself is less spectacular. The main exhibition rooms, some with period furniture, face onto an aristocratic patio on two levels, and house a multitude of paintings from the Cuzco School. Most are rather dull religious adorations, but room 5 is worth checking out to see the rapid intrusion of canons, gunpowder, and violence during the eighteenth century; while by room 10 the eighteenth- and nineteenth-century Cuzco-*mestizo* works display much bolder composition and use of color. The museum deserves a quick visit, if only because it's included on the Cuzco entrance ticket.

The remaining two sides of the Plaza de Armas are mostly taken up by shops and restaurants. Of these blocks, only one—Portal de Panes—had any significant Inca building before the Conquest. This was Pachacuti's palace whose magnificent walls are now best appreciated from inside the *Restaurant Roma* on the corner.

Koricancha

The supreme example of Cuzco's combination of Inca stonework underlying colonial buildings is just a short walk from the Plaza de Armas, two blocks down Avenida del Sol, where the church of **Santo Domingo** rises from the walls of the Temple of the Sun—*Koricancha*. The uninspiring baroque decoration of the seventeenth-century church makes a poor contrast to the superbly crafted Inca masonry—in fact, much of the church has been gutted to reveal the extent and quality of the temple complex. The tightly interlocking blocks of polished andesite abut the street as straight and solid as ever, but before the Conquistadores set their gold-hungry eyes on it, the temple must have been a breathtaking sight indeed.

The complex (there's a scale model of it on the upper floor of Santo Domingo) consisted of four small sanctuaries and a larger temple set around a courtyard, the whole enclosed within a circular cornice of gold (*Koricancha* means "golden enclosure"). Inner walls, too, were hung with sheets of beaten gold, and in the great Temple of the Sun there stood a revered sun-disk—*Punchau*—made of solid gold and far larger than a man. Punchau had two companions in the temple, a golden image of *Viracocha* on the right and another representing *Illapa*, god of thunder, to the left. Below the temple, towards the tail of Cuzco's puma, was a garden in which everything was made from gold or silver and encrusted with precious jewels, from llamas and shepherds to the tiniest details of clumps of earth and weeds, even snails and butterflies. Not surprisingly, none of this survived the arrival of the Spanish.

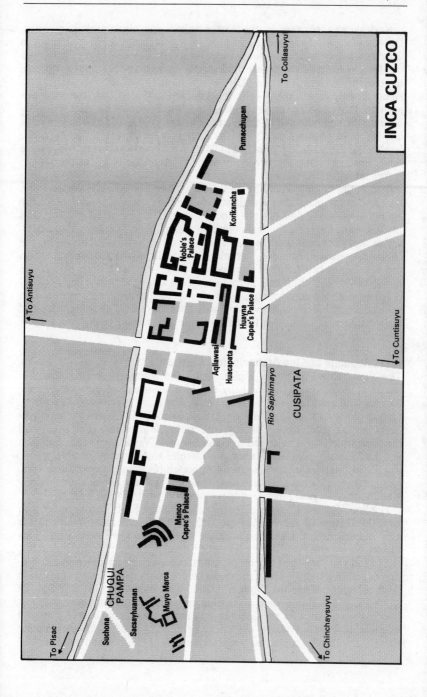

INCA CUZCO

To Collasuyu

Pumacchupan

Korikancha

Noble's Palace

Huayna Capac's Palace

To Antisuyu

Aqllawasi

Huacapata

To Cuntisuyu

Rio Saphimayo

CUSIPATA

Manco Capac's Palace

CHUQUI PAMPA

Suchona

Muyo Marca

Sacsayhuaman

To Pisac

To Chinchaysuyu

Koricancha's position in the Cuzco valley was also carefully planned. Dozens of *ceques* (power lines, in many ways similar to ley-lines, though in Cuzco they appear to have been related to imperial geneology) radiate from the temple towards more than 350 sacred *huacas*, special stones, springs, tombs, and ancient quarries. Also, every summer solstice, the sun's rays shine directly into a niche—the **tabernacle**—in which only the Inca was permitted to sit. Still prominent today, the tabernacle must have been incredible with the sun reflected off the plates of beaten gold, studded with emeralds and turquoise. Mummies of dead Inca rulers were seated in niches at eye level along the walls, the principal idols from every conquered province were held "hostage" here, and every emperor married his wives in the temple before taking up the throne.

The entire temple complex was also an intricate celestial observatory. Along with the main temple dedicated to the Sun, there were others for the adoration of lesser deities—the Moon, Venus, Thunder and Lightning, and the Rainbow. Entering the main enclosure from Santo Domingo, the sanctuary of the Moon and Stars is the large one on the right, while those for the climatic potencies (Thunder, Lightning, and the Rainbow) are smaller and on the left. Some two hundred *Mamaconas* ("Sun Virgins") were part of the divine household, their sole purpose to serve *Inti*—the Sun. They not only prepared his food and clothing, but were expected to ask favors from *Inti* on the emperor's behalf, and give him sexual satisfaction by sleeping, "covered with blankets of iridescent feathers of rare Amazonian birds," on a stone bench next to his statue.

Plaza Regocijo and the Archeological Museum

The **Plaza Regocijo**, today a pleasant garden square sheltering around a statue of Bolognesi, was originally the Inca *Cusipata*, an area cleared for dancing and festivities immediately beside the more ceremonial *huacapata*. Only a block west of the Plaza de Armas, Regocijo is fronted by an attractively arched Municipal Building, the *Hotel de Turistas,* and a colonial mansion which once belonged to Garcilaso de la Vega, the prolific half-Inca and half-Spanish poet and author, who wrote, among many notable works, *The Royal Commentaries of the Incas.* Although his house is now the government archives, it's possible to explore inside or just take a look at the impressive doorway—a neat mixture of Inca stonework with Spanish building.

Leading off from the other side of Regocijo, along Santa Teresa Street, you pass the **House of the Pumas** (no. 385). Not as grand as it sounds, this is now a small cafe: the six pumas above its entrance were carved into Inca blocks during the Spanish rebuilding of Cuzco. Turn right at the end of this street and you pass the **Church of Santa Teresa** (with an interesting collection of paintings on the life of the saint) before crossing Plateros to the Cuzco **Archeological Museum** (Mon.–Fri. 8am–1pm and 3–6pm; $1.50), at Calle Tigre 165. Housed in a colonial mansion, the museum may not have the most impressive collection of pre-Columbian artifacts, but it is the best in town and worth checking out above all for some superb wooden *keros*—drinking vessels graphically painted with representations of the Inca and "transitional" eras.

The **ceramics** are generally of poor quality—you'll find better on the desks of executives in the National Institute of Culture—but there is a fascinating pottery monkey whose head was evidently filled with *chicha* beer so that it would "urinate" into a long snaking channel, enabling initiated Inca priests to divine the future. The section on **carved stones** is of special interest for its turquoise miniatures, and for what are presented as Inca architects' scale models, possibly prototypes for Sacsayhuaman and Pisac. There's also a collection of Inca **weapons**—essentially mace-heads and boleros—and upstairs lurks the inevitable mummy room including a number of trepanated **skulls**.

Plaza San Francisco
Ten minutes' walk south along Calle Mantas from the Plaza de Armas, then left along Calle San Bernardo, the church and monastery of **La Merced** sits peacefully amid the street bustle of one of Cuzco's more interesting quarters. Rebuilt after the 1650 earthquake in a rich combination of baroque and Renaissance architecture, the church has a beautiful star-studded ceiling, a finely carved chair, and, like many Peruvian temples, a huge silver cross—an idol adored and kissed by a constantly shuffling crowd. Its real fame, though, comes from an incredible 1720s monstrance crafted by Juan de Olmos, a Spanish jewelsmith, using over 600 pearls, more than 1500 diamonds, and upwards of 22kg of solid gold; it stands over 1m high. The monastery also possesses a fine collection of paintings, particularly in the cloisters and vestry.

The **Plaza San Francisco**, another block south, fronts the simply deco-rated church and convent from which it takes its name. Inside, two large cloisters boast some of the better colonial paintings by local masters such as Diego Quispe Tito and Marcos Zapata, and an exceptional candelabra made out of human bones. The square is perhaps better known for its *papas relle-nas*, delicious stuffed potatoes sold from stalls by Quechua women.

Passing under a crumbling archway from here you come to the **Church of Santa Clara**. Built around a single nave, it's small inside, decorated with a gold-laminated altar and a few canvases. The outside walls, however, show more interesting details: finely cut Inca blocks support the upper, cruder stonework, and four andesite columns, much cracked over the centuries, complete the doorway. The belfry is so time-worn that weeds and wildflowers have taken permanent root. Just up the street, in the busy market area next to the railroad station for Machu Picchu, stands another colonial church—**San Pedro**, whose steps are normally crowded with colorful Quechua market traders. Relatively austere, with only a single nave, its main claim to fame is that somewhere among the stones of its twin towers are ancient blocks dragged here from the small Inca fort of Picchu.

The Religious Art Museum and San Blas
The **Religious Art Museum** (Mon.–Sat. 9am–noon and 3–6pm, Sun. 3–6pm only), one block uphill on the Triunfo side of the cathedral, stands on the impressive foundations of *hatun rumiyoc*, the palace of the sixth emperor, Inca Roca. A superb mansion, until recently the Archbishop's residence, the

museum now houses a valuable collection of paintings well displayed in period rooms. The most interesting exhibit—a large painting of the Last Supper—seems nothing special until you notice that Christ is partaking not of bread, but of the body of a guinea pig. This unique work was painted in the seventeenth century by an anonymous artist who also appears to be responsible for several other canvases; one of these, of San Sebastian, shows Inca nobles present at the saint's martyrdom.

Beside the museum, up the narrow Calle Hatun Rumiyoc, every visitor to Cuzco seems to spend at least a few minutes trying to find the celebrated **Inca stone with twelve angles**. Made even more famous by its popular representation on *Cuzqueña* beer bottles, it's one of the very best examples of Inca stonework. This twelve-cornered block fits perfectly into the lower wall of the Inca Roca's old imperial residence, but it's often hidden behind Quechua women selling crafts who've placed themselves strategically in front of it.

Another one-and-a-half blocks from here the tiny **Chapel of San Blas**, located appropriately in the *Barrio de los Artesanos*, has an unbelievably intricate pulpit. Carved from a solid block of cedar wood in a complicated *churrigueresque* style, it takes long, staring study to unravel the intricate detail: cherubim, a sun-disk, faces, and bunches of grapes all believed to have been carved in the seventeenth century by the native craftsman Tomas Tuyro Tupa.

Returning to the main square via Plaza Nazarenas you can pass by two more historic buildings. The sixteenth-century seminary and chapel of **San Antonio Abad** (closed for renovation into a hotel) was originally a religious school before becoming a university in the seventeenth century. Virtually next door is the **Nazarenas Convent**, converted by OPESCO (the body reponsible for restoring tourist sites) into their own offices. There were nuns here until the 1950 earthquake damaged it so badly that they had to leave. You can still look around, though, and its central courtyard has been sensitively rebuilt.

Sacsayhuaman and the Inca's Garden

The megalithic fortress of **Sacsayhuaman**, which overlooks the Plaza de Armas and dominates the whole of Cuzco, is the closest and most impressive of several sacred sites scattered around the Cuzco hills, collectively known as the **Inca's Garden**. Within easy walking distance beyond are the great *huaca* of **Kenko** and less visited **Salapunco**—the Cave of the Pumas. A few kilometers farther, to what almost certainly formed the outer limits of the estate, you come to the small castle of **Puca Pucara** and the stunning imperial baths of **Tambo Machay**.

It makes an ideal day's walking—once you've acclimatized to the altitude—but you'll need to purchase a general **Cuzco tourist ticket** (see above) to visit Sacsayhuaman and any of the other sites in the Inca's Garden. It's often a good idea to devote a whole day to Sacsayhuaman, leaving the other sites until just before you leave Cuzco, when you'll probably feel more energetic and adjusted to the rarefied air. Or, if you'd rather start from the top and work your way downhill, it's possible to take one of the regular *Morales Moralitos* buses going to Pisac (from Belen 451), or the more frequent minibus from the corner of Avenida Collasuyo and Calle Ejercito (just out of town along Recoleta), asking to be dropped off at Tambo Machay, the highest of all the Inca's Garden sites; from here it's about a two-hour walk back into the center of Cuzco.

Sacsayhuaman

Although it looks relatively close to central Cuzco, it's actually quite a steep forty-minute climb up to the ruins of Sacsayhuaman. The easiest route from the Plaza de Armas is along Calle Suecia, uphill from the cathedral side, taking the first right (up a few steps) and turning almost immediately left up a narrow cobbled street, aptly named Resbalosa ("slippery") to the Church of San Cristobal. This attractive adobe structure stands next to the even more impressive ruined walls of *Kolkampata*—palace of expansionist emperor Manco Capac. From Kolkampata follow the road a few hundred yards to the point where it bends around on itself; here you'll find a well-worn path and crude stairway which takes you right up to the heart of the fortress.

SACSAYHUAMAN, as the head of Cuzco's ethereal puma, points its fierce-looking teeth away from the city. Protected by such a steep approach from the town, the defensive walls were only needed on one side. The three massive, parallel walls zigzag together for some 600m, bounding what was originally a "spiritual distillation" of the ancient city below, with many sectors named after areas of imperial Cuzco. There's not much of the inner fortress left, but the enormous ramparts still stand 20m high, quite unperturbed by past battles, earthquakes, and the passage of time. The strength of the massive, mortarless stonework—one block weighs over 300 tons—is matched by the brilliance of its design: the zigzags, casting shadows in the afternoon sun, not only look like jagged cat's teeth, but also expose the flanks of any attackers trying to clamber up.

In Inca times, the inner fort was covered in buildings, a maze of tiny streets dominated by three major towers. Two of these—*Salla Marca* and *Paunca Marca*—had rectangular bases about 20m long; the other, **Muyu Marca**, whose foundations can still be clearly seen, was round with three concentric circles of wall, the outer one roughly 24m in diameter. Standing over 30m tall, Muyu Marca was an imperial residence with apparently lavish inner chambers and a constant supply of fresh water carried up through subterranean channels. The other two towers were essentially warriors' barracks, and all three were painted in vivid colors, had thatched roofs, and were interconnected by underground passages: in its entirety, the inner fortress could have housed as many as ten thousand people under siege. At the rear of this sector, looking directly down into Cuzco and the valley, was a **Temple of the Sun**, reckoned by some to be *the* most important Inca shrine.

In front of the main defensive walls, a flat expanse of grassy ground—the esplanade—divides the fortress from a large outcrop of volcanic diorite. Intricately carved in places, and scarred with deep glacial striations, this rock, called the **Rodadero** (or sliding place), was the site of an Inca throne. Originally there was a stone parapet surrounding this important *huaca*, and it's thought that the emperor would have sat here to oversee cermonial gatherings at fiesta times, when there would be processions, wrestling matches, and running competitions. On the far side was another cleared space, the sacred spring of **Calispucyo**, where ceremonies to initiate young boys into manhood were held.

It was the energetic Emperor Pachacuti who began work on Sacsayhuaman. The chronicler Cieza de León, writing in the 1550s, thought that some 20,000 men had been involved in its construction: 4000 cutting blocks from quarries; 6000 dragging them on rollers to the site; and another 10,000 working on finishing and fitting them into position. According to legend, some 3000 lives were lost while dragging one huge stone!

Various types of rock were used in the fortress, including massive diorite blocks from nearby for the outer walls, Yucay limestone from over 15km away for the foundations, and dark andesite, some of it from over 35km distant, for the inner buildings and towers. With only natural fiber ropes, stone hammers, and bronze chisels, it must have been an enormous task. First, boulders were split by boring holes with stone or cane rods and wet sand; next, wooden wedges were inserted into these holes and saturated to crack the rocks into more manageable sizes; the blocks were then apparently shifted into place with levers. Despite the near century of creative work, though, it took only a few years for the Conquistadors to dismantle most of the inner structures, treating the place as a quarry for the building of Spanish Cuzco.

Very little is known about the site's history previous to the arrival of the Spanish, and the fateful battle of 1536, when the Spanish wiped out the Incas. Juan Pizarro, Francisco's younger brother, was killed as he charged the main gate in the surprise assault, and a leading Inca nobleman, armed with a Spanish sword and shield, caused havoc by repulsing every enemy who tried to scale Muyu Marca, the last tower left in Inca hands. Having sworn to fight to the death, he leapt from the top when defeat seemed inevitable, rather than accept humiliation and dishonor. After the battle the esplanade was covered in native corpses, food for vultures and inspiration for the Cuzco Coat of Arms which, since 1540, has been bordered by eight condors "in memory of the fact that when the castle was taken these birds descended to eat the natives who had died in it."

Today the only dramatic event that seems to take place at Sacsayhuaman is the colorful—if overly commercialized—**Inti Raymi festival** every June 24. Generally packed by thousands of townsfolk and tourists, it is an attempt both to rekindle the vitality of Inca heritage and to make a few more bucks.

The Inca's Garden: Kenko, Salapunco, and Chacan

An easy twenty-minute walk from Sacsayhuaman brings you to the large limestone outcrop of **KENKO**, another important Inca *huaca*. This great stone, carved with a complex pattern of steps, seats, geometric reliefs, and puma designs, illustrates the critical role of the **Rock Cult** in the realm of Inca

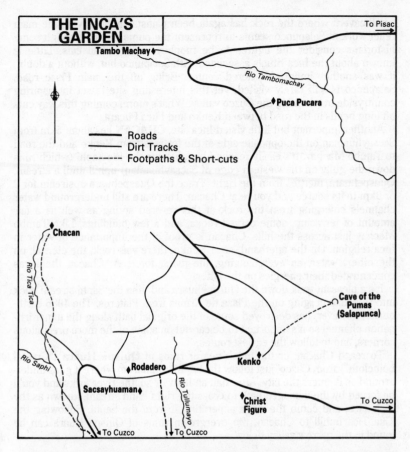

THE INCA'S GARDEN

To Pisac

Tambo Machay

Rio Tambomachay

Puca Pucara

—— Roads
—— Dirt Tracks
----- Footpaths & Short-cuts

Chacan

Rio Tica Tica

Cave of the
Pumas
(Salapunca)

Rio Saphi

Kenko

Rodadero

Rio Tullumayo

Sacsayhuaman

Christ
Figure

To Cuzco

To Cuzco

To Cuzco

cosmological beliefs. Worship in pre-Columbian Peru, from at least the Chavin Era (1000 B.C.), returned again and again to the reverence of large (and sometimes small) rocky outcrops, as if they possessed some hidden life-forc, a power belonging to the spiritual dimension.

At the top end of the *huaca*, the Incas constructed a circular amphitheater containing nineteen vaulted niches (probably seats) facing in towards the impressive limestone. Llama's blood or *chicha* beer may well have been poured in at the top of some of the prominent zigzagging channels that run down the *huaca*—the speed and routes of the liquid, in conjunction with the patterns of the rock, giving the answers to the priests' supplications. Models of similar divinatory channels can be seen in Cuzco's Museum of Archeology and Anthropology, but only on site is it possible to appreciate fully the power of this great oracle.

Another short stroll, slightly uphill and through a few fields from Kenko, leads to **SALAPUNCO**—the fascinating Cave of the Pumas. Essentially a small cavern where the rock has again been painstakingly carved, the main relief work at Salapunco seems to represent the puma motif, although some historians consider the figures to be monkeys rather than cats. Little is known about the Inca rituals associated with Salapunco but, without a doubt, it was another important sacred center. Being off the main Pisac road, Salapunco is still rarely visited, yet this interesting site is set in inspiring countryside overlooking the Cuzco valley. What's more, coming this way cuts off long bends in the road between Kenko and Puca Pucara.

Another important but little visted Inca site, **CHACAN** lies about 5km from Sacsayhuaman on the opposite side of the fortress from Kenko and the road to Tambo Machay. It's easily reached by following the Río Saphi (which runs down the gully on the western edge of Sacsayhuaman) uphill until a stream, Quespehuara, merges from the right. Trace the Quespehuara upstream for 2 or 3km to its source and you're at Chacan. There are still underground water channels emerging from the rock at this revered spring as well as a fair amount of terracing, some carved rocks, and a few buildings. Like Tambo Machay just across the hills, Chacan is proof of the importance of water in Inca religion. On the one hand, as at Kenko, there was rock, the eternal; on the other, water, an everchanging, life-giving force. At Chacan the Incas concentrated their energies on the latter.

It's a pleasant walk down the Quespehuara and then the Saphi stream back into Cuzco, emerging on the Plaza de Armas from Plateros. The 1986 earthquake, however, has destroyed some of the original path along the upper irrigation channel so it's important to be careful on some of the more precipitous corners, and to follow the easiest routes.

To reach Chacan, or the much nearer ruins of **Quispe Huara** ("Crystal Loincloth") from Cuzco, just follow the Saphi uphill from where it goes underground as it enters the city. After half an hour or so, the river forks and you'll be forced by the damaged path to cross the right hand stream, known as the Tica Tica, and climb the ridge seperating it from the Saphi. Following the Tica Tica uphill to Chacan, the overgrown ruins of Quispe Huara can be found in the narrow valley below.

Puca Pucara and Tambo Machay

Although a relatively small fort, **PUCA PUCARA** ("Red Fort") is impressively situated: overlooking the Cuzco valley and on the road separating the ancient capital from the Sacred Valley. At most an hour's cross-country walk, uphill from Sacsayhuaman (or up to 2 hours keeping to the curvaceous main road), this zone of the Inca's Garden is dotted with cut rocks. Many were perhaps worked to obtain stones for building, but overall they must be seen as part of the carefully planned Emperor's estate. If Cuzco and its environs could be seen as sacred ground, then the Inca's claim for ideological supremacy over neighboring territories would be all the more strong.

Although in many ways reminiscent of a small European castle, it is generally thought to have been more a hunting lodge for the emperor—on the outer edge of his gardens—than a genuine defensive position. Although well protected on three sides it could have contained only a relatively small garrison, and in any case Sacsayhuaman was far better equipped to secure Cuzco's rear. Puca Pucara may, however, have served also as a guard post controlling the flow of people and produce between Cuzco and the Sacred Valley, which lies just beyond the mountains to the northeast. Its semicircle of protective wall is topped by a commanding esplanade, while on the lower levels there are a number of stone-walled chambers; you can still make out the ducts that distributed fresh water from a nearby spring.

TAMBO MACHAY, less than fifteen minutes' walk away along a sign-posted track that leads off the main road just beyond Puca Pucara, is one of the more impressive Inca baths. Conveniently situated at a spring near the Inca's hunting lodge, its main construction lies in a sheltered, grotto-like gully where some superb Inca masonry again emphasizes the Inca fascination with and adoration of water.

The ruins basically consist of three-tiered platforms. The top one holds four trapezoidal that which were probably used as seats; on the next level, underground water emerges directly from a hole at the base of the stone-work, and from here cascades down to the bottom platform, creating a cold shower just about high enough for an Inca to stand under. On this platform the spring water splits into two channels, both pouring the last meter down to ground level. Clearly a site for ritual bathing, the quality of the stonework suggests that its use was restricted to the higher nobility, who perhaps used the baths only on ceremonial occasions.

The spring itself is about 1km farther up the gully; its water diverted through underground channels to the bathing area. Follow the stream up and you'll come to a cave (in Quechua, *machay* means cave) where it emerges: here too there is quality stonework embellished with relief carving. Evidently an aqueduct once connected this water source with Puca Pucaca, which can also be seen poking its head over the horizon from here. Not only important as a water supply for the Cuzco valley, Tambo Machay must have also been a favorite site in the Inca's Garden—a place the Emperor could visit regularly to rest, bathe, and worship.

Listings

American Express has an office in Cuzco (Av. del Sol 567) that can be used as a mail collection point (Mon.–Fri. 3–5pm only); you can't, however, replace stolen travelers' checks here—you have to go to Lima for that. Their postal address is *American Express*, c/o *Lima Tours*, Casilla 531, Cuzco.

Books The best bookshop for English-language books—new and second-hand—is *Librería Studium*, on Mesón de la Estrella 144. For anyone planning to hang around for more than a week or so, the most thorough guide to Cuzco and its surrounds is *Exploring Cuzco* by Peter Frost—on sale all over town.

Buses Bus offices are scattered all over Cuzco, but here are a few of the main ones: *Ormeño* for Lima via Abancay (Portal de Carnes, on the north corner of the Plaza de Armas for tickets, the depot on Avenida Huascar for bus departures; ☎228712); *Hidalgo* for Lima via Ayacucho and Pisco (Cuichipunco 299; ☎23061); *Transturin* for Puno and La Paz (Portal de Panes 109—over Restaurant Roma; ☎222332); *San Cristobal* for Juliaca, Arequipa, and Lima (Av. Huascar 120; ☎3184); *Morales Moralitos* for Lima via Nazca, the Sacred Valley, and Puno (Belen 451; ☎5035).

Camping equipment is generally quite easy to get hold of in Cuzco. Several adventure travel outfitters rent equipment from offices on Procuradores and a couple around the Plaza de Armas: it's worth checking the available equipment and comparing prices before doing a deal with any particular office. You'll need to leave a deposit (travelers' checks will do). Alternatively, travelers often advertise for hiking companions for set hikes (like the Inca Trail) on notice boards—try the *Hostal Familiar* on Saphi , the *Hostal Suecia* on Calle Suecia, or the tourist office on the plaza.

Cinemas There are two: the *Cine Garcilaso* (Union 117) and the *Cine Ollanta* (Meloc 417).

Dentist Teeth can get very sensitive at high altitudes, so if you have any sign of trouble it's well worth getting it seen to before going anywhere vaguely remote—try the office at Quera 253.

Fiestas Cuzco's principal annual fiestas begin in April with the traditional Holy Week processions, followed by those of Corpus Christi, usually in early June. Corpus Christi is Cuzco's big holiday, when there are amazing processions and during which the silver carriage and gold monstrance are taken out of the cathedral as are all the images of the patron saints of the bordering towns, parishes, and even economic associations. Corpus is also the great block party of Cuzco, a time when the Avenida del Sol becomes a food market and the entire town meet to eat and drink together. June 16–22 there's an excellent folklore festival of Raqchi at Sicuani south of Cuzco; and June 24, at Sacsayhuaman, is the main day of *Inti Raymi*, now an internationally appreciated revival of the Inca Sun Festival. More exciting and less commercialized is the Virgin of Carmen fiesta at Paucartambo, on July 16. Later in the year, All Saints' Day, November 1, is celebrated with religious processions and music in the streets, as, of course, is Christmas. The best is the *Santuranticuy Fiesta* on December 24 when, in typical Andean fashion, religious images, idols, and certain toys are sold in the Plaza de Armas. The toys, it seems, represent the aspirations of those who buy them—meaningful gifts for the gods.

Flights *AeroPeru* (Av. de Sol 600, same side and block as the post office; ☎233051) flies to Lima (8am and 11am), Puerto Maldonado (9am), and Arequipa (11am) every day if all goes well. *Faucett* (office at Av. de Sol 567; ☎233151) has the same prices though a slightly sparser schedule—flying to Lima (8:20am and 10:20am), Puerto Maldonado on Tues., Thurs., and Sat. (at 8:15am) and to Arequipa four days a week (also at 8:15am). It's vital to reconfirm any normal booking 24 hours before the flight. *Grupo Ocho de la Fuerza Aérea*—the military airline—has one flight a week to Lima and Puerto Maldonado in a Buffalo aircraft. Their schedule is inevitably erratic and there's a long waiting list, but this is amply made up for by the prices (50 percent cheaper than commercial airlines). The only *Grupo Ocho* office is at the airport.

Herbal medicines are available from Sr. Elaez, a pracitioner who lives just below Koricancha in Calle Arrayan. You can also find herb stalls around the central market.

Hospital Cuzco's Regional Hospital is on Avenida de la Cultura (☎223691, or 2486 for emergencies).

Inmigración For any problems with passports/visas, the immigration offices are at Calle Santa Teresa 364.

Laundry Cuzco is a good place for laundering clothes. Among the quickest *lavanderías* are the ones at Procuradores 354 and Suecia 328.

Manu National Park, one of the Amazon's few protected areas, is also the closest jungle zone to Cuzco. Up–to–date information on access is available from the Park Office (*CENFOR*) at Quera 235 (☎233632/233653).

Maps For maps of local hikes, particularly the Inca Trail, try any of the main equipment hire or trekking companies on the plaza or up Procuradores.

Money changing The *Banco de La Nación* is on Av. del Sol (☎3488); *Casas de cambio* with more flexible hours can be found by the *El Dorado Hotel* on Avenida del Sol and in the alley off the Plaza de Armas between Procuradores and Plateros. One of the best rates, though, usually comes from the laundry in the little courtyard off Procuradores (on the right beside Mayuc's office at Procuradoes 354).

Poste Restante The main post office in Cuzco, on block 8 of Avenida del Sol, will hold mail for up to three months. You'll need your passport as ID when picking it up.

Sauna A good sauna, spiced with pungent herbs, is open to the public in the *Hostal Colonial* (Av. Matara 288).

Shopping For ponchos and other *artesania*, try the shop on the corner of Tupac Aymaru and Santa Clara, a small market on the corner of Quera and San Andres, another little market on block 5 of Avenida del Sol, or the arcade at Triunfo 372. For *f*resh foods the central market is best, while for canned foods try the Chinese supermarket on the first block of Avenida del Sol.

Taxis It's generally easiest to pick up a taxi on the Plaza de Armas. They are quite cheap in Cuzco (e.g., one way up to Sacsayhuaman for around $3).

Tourist police have offices on the Cathedral side of the Plaza de Armas near the *Restaurant Tumi* and *Hotel Conquistador* on Arequipa, and are helpful if you get ripped off or have any other problems—even getting lost. Open 24 hours.

Tourist information The main tourist office is on the Plaza de Armas (Portal Belen 115; ☎237364; Mon.–Fri. 8:30am–5:30pm and Sat. 8:30am–12:30pm). Travelers' notice board for messages and ad-hoc groups for the Inca Trail.

Tours For local tours in and around Cuzco it's hard to beat *Inca City Tours* (Portal Nuevo 246). Others include *CBS Tours* (Ayacucho 171; ☎223410); *Dasatour* (Plateros 373; ☎223341); and *Condor Travel* (Heladeros 164; ☎225921). Or, if you're able to share costs with fellow travelers, it's quite simple to organize trips as far away as Pisac and even Ollantaytambo in taxis or minibuses (it's a matter of bargaining with the driver/owners who usually hang around the plaza in their vehicles).

Trains For **Machu Picchu** the San Pedro railroad station is at the top of Calle Santa Clara, opposite the main market. Every day there are two local trains (5:30am and 2pm—both stopping at Ollantaytambo and going on to Quillabamba), two tourist trains (7am and 8am), and a night train (10:15pm—also going to Quillabamba). Local trains have special ($1 flat rate extra), first, and second class seats, while the tourist train is relatively plush throughout. You can get tickets for either just before boarding but, to avoid hassles with your gear in crowds, it's much safer to buy them the day before. Ticket office for the tourist train is open Mon.–Fri. 6am–8:30am, 10–11am, and 3–5pm, Sat., Sun., and holidays noon–2:30pm; for the local train, Mon.–Fri. 9am–noon and 4–5pm, Sat. 5–6am and 12–2:30pm. For **Puno, Arequipa,** and the south, the railroad station is at the bottom of Avenida del Sol. Trains leave every day except Sunday, at 8am—arriving Puno around 6pm and Arequipa at 6am the following morning. Essentially first and second class ($4.50 and $3.50 to Puno, $8 or $6 to Arequipa) the trains also have a buffet wagon for an extra 50 cents. Again, you can buy tickets either just before leaving or in advance (ticket office is open Mon.–Sat. 9:30–11am and 3–5pm; Sun. 8–10am).

Trekking There are several companies now running treks, Inca Trail hikes with porters, even white-water rafting expeditions. *Expediciones Mayuc* (Procuradores 354; ☎232666) is certainly one of the best companies for all the standard treks and, in recent years, some more unusual ones too, including trips to the jungles of Manu (8 days), the Tambopata river (13 days), and the Macaw Colpa (5 days). From about $20 a day *Mayuc* also offer horseriding and canoeing trips. *Explorandes* (Procuradores 372 and Urb. Magisterio N-17; ☎226599) has a very good reputation and regularly work with several foreign "outward bound" trekking groups—they do the Inca trail with cooks, guides, tents, food, and porters, charging $300 for five days. *Rio Bravo SA* specializes in river-rafting trips (Portal Carnes 236); and Tom Hendrickson's *Peruvian Andean Treks* (Av. Pardo 575; ☎225701) are always fun, very reasonable, and well organized. Others include *Hirca Ventures* (Garcilaso 230; ☎223292) and *Tambo Treks* (San Juan de Dios 236; ☎233350).

Trucks are the easiest, cheapest, and sometimes the only way to reach a lot of places around Cuzco. For Chinchero, Mollepata, and Limatambo, trucks (and minibuses) leave Calle Arcopata every morning until around 8am (10am for Chinchero's Sunday market). For Paucartambo, Tres Cruces, and Shintuya, trucks leave Avenida Huascar on Mon., Wed., and Fri., usually before lunch. For Ocongate, trucks leave daily from the small cobbled parking zone opposite Koricancha (any time of day).

U.S. Consulate A representative agency is at *Instituto de Cultura Peruana Norte Americana* (Av. Tullumayo 125; ☎224117).

THE SACRED VALLEY

The **Sacred Valley**, *Vilcamayo* to the Incas, traces its winding, astonishingly beautiful course to the northwest of Cuzco. Known today as the Urubamba—Valley of the Spiders—it's still easy to see why the Incas considered this a special place. In the upper sector, the stupendous ruins of **Pisac** dominate the broad alluvial valley floor: less than an hour by bus from Cuzco, this is a site often compared to Machu Picchu in its towering elegance. Farther downstream, beyond the ancient villages of CALCA, YUCAY, and URUBAMBA, **Ollantaytambo** is a magnificent little town overwhelmed by a great temple-fortress that clings to the sheer cliffs across the river valley. Beyond here, the valley twists below **Machu Picchu** itself, the most famous ruin in South America and a place that—no matter how jaded you are, and however commercial it may at times seem—can never be a disappointment.

The classic way to arrive at Machu Picchu is to do the three- to five-day hike along the stirring **Inca Trail**. If you're not into walking, the **train** trip from Cuzco or Ollantaytambo is a quicker, if equally breathtaking journey. Beyond Ollantaytambo the valley closes in around the tracks, the river begins to race, and the route becomes too tortuous for any road to follow.

By road you can follow the Sacred Valley only as far as Ollantaytambo, from where it cuts across the hills to CHAULLAY, just beyond Machu Picchu. A regular and very cheap **bus** service as far as Ollantaytambo is run by *Morales Moralitos* (Belen 451, Cuzco; ☎5035) every two hours from 6am until 4pm. Still more frequent, slightly faster, and perhaps more interesting, is the cooperative minibus service which picks passengers up from the corner of Avenida Collasuyo and Calle Ejercito, a short walk down Recoleta from the heart of Cuzco.

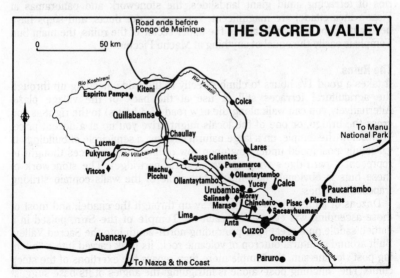

If, after Machu Picchu, you're tempted to explore farther afield, the evening train continues to **Chaullay** from where you can set out for the remote ruins of **Vilcabamba**—*Vitcos* and *Espiritu Pampa*—the legendery refuge of the last rebel Incas, set in superb hiking country. Final destination of this train is the jungle town of **Quillabamba** (see p.269), the only Amazon town in Peru that can be reached by train.

Pisac and Ollantaytambo

Standing guard over the open end of the Sacred Valley, Pisac and Ollantaytambo are among the most evocative ruins in Peru. Pisac, only 30km from Cuzco, can be visited easily in a morning, maybe checking out the market on the main square (Thurs. and Sun.) before taking a *colectivo* on to Ollantaytambo by lunchtime. Ollantaytambo itself is a charming place to spend some time, perhaps taking a tent and trekking off up one of the Urubamba's minor tributaries, or joining up with the Inca Trail for Machu Picchu. For either of the main sites here you'll need a Cuzco **general entrance ticket**, which can be purchased at the sites themselves.

Pisac

A vital Inca road once snaked its way up the canyon that enters the Urubamba valley at **PISAC**. The citadel (daily 9am–5pm), at the entrance to this gorge, now in ruins, controlled a route which connected the Inca Empire with Paucartambo, on the borders of the "savage" eastern jungles. Set high above a valley floor patchworked by patterned fields and rimmed by centuries of terracing amid giant landslides, the stonework and panoramas at Pisac's Inca citadel are magnificent. Terraces, water ducts, and steps have been cut out of solid rock, and in the upper sector of the ruins, the main Sun Temple is easily the equal of anything at Machu Picchu.

The Ruins

It takes a good 1½ hours to climb directly to the ruins, heading up through the agricultural terraces still in use at the back of the village plaza. Alternatively you can walk along the new road (2–4 hours) to the right as you cross the bridge, or one of the locals might drive you up at a decent price. Way below the temple, on a large natural balcony, a semicircle of buildings is gracefully positioned under row upon row of fine stone terraces thought to represent a partridge's wing (*pisac* meaning partridge). The stonework of these huts is obviously post-Incaic, but some of the walls contain striking trapezoidal niches.

Dozens of paths crisscross their way up through the citadel, and most of those ascending will eventually reach the **Temple of the Sun**, poised in a flattish saddle on a great spur protruding north–south into the Sacred Valley. Built around a natural outcrop of volcanic rock, its peak carved into a "hitching post" for the sun, the temple more than repays the exertions of the steep climb. The "hitching post" alone is intriguing: the angles of its base suggest that it may have been used for keeping track of important stars, perhaps after they had been lost on cloudy nights, or for calculating the changing seasons with the accuracy so critical to the smooth running of the Inca Empire.

Above the temple lie still more ruins, mostly unexcavated, and among the even higher crevices and rocky overhangs several ancient burial sites are hidden. One of the most amazing features of the citadel is that it must have channeled water from a much wider area of this upper mountain to irrigate so extensive a spread of agricultural land.

Practicalities

Back down in the **village** there are markets in the plaza on Thursday and Sunday mornings. Tourism notwithstanding, it's still possible to pick up the occasional bargain here and this is also the best place to buy some of the attractive, locally handpainted ceramic beads. For lunch or a snack, try the excellent *Samana Wasi* **restaurant** on the corner of the square, with a pleasant little courtyard out the back. If you want a **place to stay**, there's the cheapish *Hotel Pisac* on the plaza, the *Hotel Roma* near the bridge, and a more expensive *Albergue Turistica* just out of town along the road towards the ruins. **Rooms** are often rented at ridiculously low prices by villagers, or you can **camp** almost anywhere if you ask permission first. The only month when it may be difficult to find accommodation is September when the village is generally full of pilgrims making their way to the nearby Sanctuary of Huanca.

Onward to Ollantaytambo

Of the three towns between Pisac and Ollantaytambo, only **Urubamba** offers much of interest to travelers. CALCA, just outside Pisac on the main road, has popular thermal baths within an hour's walk of the modern settlement, and was a place favored by the Incas for the fertility of its soil, sitting as it still does under the hanging glaciers of Mount Sahuasiray. YUCAY, a smaller village just before you get to Urubamba, is worth a quick look to appreciate the finely dressed stone walls of a ruined Inca palace probably once the country home of Sayri Tupac, though also associated with an Inca princess or *Nusta*.

Urubamba

URUBAMBA itself, though well endowed with tourist comforts, has little in the way of historic interest. If you're after a hotel with swimming pool try the expensive *Hotel de Turistas*. If, on the other hand, you simply want to use Urubamba as a base for visiting the site of Moray or some fascinating, still functioning, Inca salt pans, the *Hotel Urubamba* is a lot cheaper.

Moray, an amazing Inca farm, lies about 6km north of Maras village on the other side of the river, within easy striking distance from Urubamba. The ruins, probably of an Inca agricultural experimental center, are deep, bowl-like depressions in the earth, the largest comprising seven concentric circular stone terraces, facing inward and diminishing in radius like a multilayered roulette wheel.

The **salt pans of Salinas**, still in use after more than four hundred years, are situated only a short distance from the village of Tarabamba, 6km along the road from Urubamba to Ollantaytambo. Cross the river by the footbridge in the village, turn left to follow a stream up beside the graveyard, and you'll soon stumble across these Inca salt-gathering terraces, set gracefully against an imposing mountain backdrop.

The eastern side of the valley is formed by the Cordillera Urubamaba, a range of snowcapped peaks dominated by summits of Chicon and Veronica. Many of the ravines can be hiked: on the trek up from the town of Urubamba you'll have stupendous views of Chicon, and following the stream up behind YUCAY takes you to the village and nevada of San Juan. Also, there's a lake within hiking distance high up in the mountains to the south, between Yucay and Calca at Huallabamaba.

Ollantaytambo

On the approach to **OLLANTAYTAMBO** from Urubamba, the river runs smoothly between a series of fine Inca terraces that gradually diminish in size as the slopes get steeper and more rocky until, just before the town, the railroad tracks reappear and the road climbs a small hill into the ancient plaza. A very traditional little place—and one of the few surviving examples of an Inca grid system—it's an agreeable town to stay in for a few days, particularly during the *Ollantay Raymi Fiesta* (generally on the Sunday after Cuzco's *Inti Raymi*—the last Sunday in June) or during Christmas when the locals wear flowers and decorative grasses in their hats.

Ollantaytambo is an excellent spot to begin **trekking** into the hills, either following the Patacancha up to remote, very traditional villages, or by walking (or catching the train) 20km along the south bank of the river down to km 88 for the start of the Inca Trail to Machu Picchu. Beyond Ollantaytambo the Sacred Valley becomes a subtropical, raging river course, surrounded by towering mountains and dominated by the snowcapped peak of Salcantay.

The Inca Fortress of Ollantay

In the immediate vicinity of the town, the main attraction is the majestic fortress of **Ollantay**, just across the Río Patacancha. Legend has it that Ollantay was a rebel Inca general who took arms against Pachacutec over the affections of the Lord Inca's daughter—the Nusta Cusi Collyu. As protection for the strategic entrance to the lower Urubamba valley, and an alternative gateway into the Amazon via the Pantiacalla pass, this was the only Inca stronghold ever to have resisted persistent Spanish attacks. Brought into the empire by Pachacuti after fierce battles with the locals, it remained a prize Inca possession until the rebel Inca Manco retreated to Vilcabamba in 1537.

Manco and his die-hard force had withdrawn to Ollantaytambo after the unsuccessful siege of Cuzco in 1536-37, with Hernando Pizarro in hot pursuit. Some seventy horsemen, thirty foot-soldiers, and a large contingent of native forces trooped down the Sacred Valley to approach the palatial fortress, stuck out on a river cliff at the lower edge of Patacancha canyon. They arrived to find that not only had the Incas diverted the Patacancha stream to make the valley below the fortress impassable, but they had also joined forces with neighboring jungle tribes to form an army so great in number that they supposedly overflowed the valley sides. After several desperate attempts to storm the fortress, Pizarro and his men uncharacteristically slunk away under cover of darkness, leaving much of their equipment behind.

Climbing up through the fortress today, the solid stone terraces, jammed tight against the natural contours of the cliff, remain frighteningly impressive. Above them, huge red granite blocks mark the unfinished sun temple near the top, where, according to legend, the internal organs of mummified Incas were buried. From this upper level a dangerous path leads around the cliff towards a large sector of agricultural terracing which follows the Patacancha uphill, while at the bottom you can still make out the shape of a large Inca plaza through which stone aqueducts carried the ancient water supply.

Practicalities

In Ollantaytambo there are several **hotels** to choose from, including an inexpensive rustic place set around a courtyard, a block and a half up the first street on the right, as you enter the plaza on the road from Urubamba. The *Hostal Miranda* and the *Parador Turistico* are very reasonable, popular, clean, and safe. Overnight lodging at reasonable rates is also available at the *Cafe Alcazar*, with the added advantage of varied food and good *pisco*. Down near the train station, the *Albergue*, run by North Americans, is no longer a hostel as such but often offers the chance to go on organized treks to unusual places. For a decent **meal** both the *Alcazar* and *Parador Turistico* are usually excellent.

The Inca Trail

Although indisputably a very fine hike, the **INCA TRAIL** is just one of a multitude of paths across remote areas of the Andes. What it does offer, though, and what makes it so popular, is a fabulous treasure at the end— **Machu Picchu**.

It's important to choose your season for hiking the Inca Trail. Between June and September it's usually a pretty cosmopolitan stretch of mountainside, with gringos from all over the globe converging on Machu Picchu the hard way. From October through until April, in the rainy season, it's much less crowded and there's a more abundant fresh water supply, but of course it can get very wet. That leaves May as the best month, with everything exceptionally verdant and yet with superb clear views and fine weather to add a touch of springtime. According to local tradition, and it seems to work, around full moon is the perfect time to hike the Inca Trail.

As far as **preparations** go, the most important thing is to acclimatize, preferably allowing at least three days in Cuzco if you've flown straight from sea level. Even basic equipment like a tent, sleeping bag, and backpack can usually be rented in Cuzco, where you should also pick up a good map (see p.95). Apart from these you should take at least four days' food (and some-

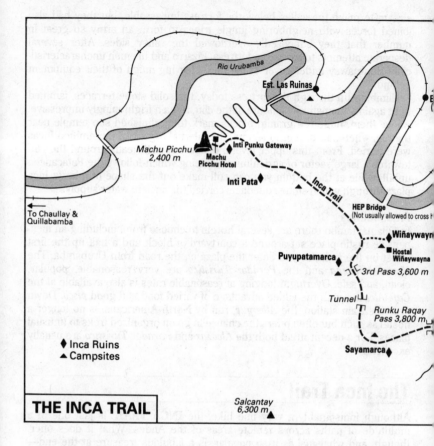

Rio Urubamba

Est. Las Ruinas

Inti Punku Gateway

Machu Picchu
2,400 m

Machu
Picchu Hotel

Inti Pata

← To Chaullay &
Quillabamba

Inca Trail

HEP Bridge
(Not usually allowed to cross H

Wiñaywayn

Hostal
Wiñaywayna

Puyupatamarca

3rd Pass 3,600 m

Tunnel

Runku Raqay
Pass 3,800 m

Sayamarca

♦ Inca Ruins
▲ Campsites

THE INCA TRAIL

Salcantay
6,300 m

thing to boil water or cook on, unless you can cope with cold foods) and iodine or other water sterilizer. **Porters** for the Inca Trail, not always the embarrassing luxury you might think, charge less than $10 a day (less if you find one at Huayllabamba to take you as far as the first pass) and are usually arranged through trekking agencies in Cuzco. So many people are walking this route every year that toilets have now been built and hikers are strongly urged to take all their trash away with them—there's no room for burying any more tin cans!

If you can only allocate three days to the walk, you'll be pushing it the whole way. It *can* be hiked in two to three days but it's a gruelling walk unless you're in Iron Man shape and used to rugged terrain. It's far more pleasant to spend five or six days, taking in everything as you go along. Those trekkers who mean to do it in two-and-a-half days should give themselves a head start by catching the afternoon train and striking up the Cusichaca valley as far as possible on the evening before.

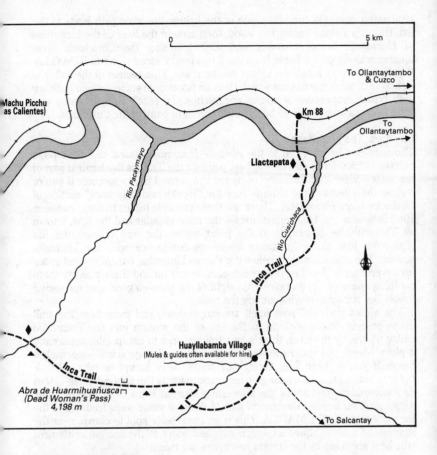

Day One: Setting Off

The trailhead is at km 88 along the train route from Cuzco, at a barely noticeable stop announced almost clandestinely by the train guard. Have your gear ready to throw off the steps, since the train pulls up only for a few brief seconds and you'll have to fight your way past sacks of grain, flapping chickens, men wearing woollen hats and ponchos, and women in voluminous skirts with babies wrapped tightly to their backs in multicolored shawls.

From the station a footbridge (where you pay the $10 fee—$5 for students—which includes admission to Machu Picchu) crosses the

---

A WORD OF WARNING

There are increasing reports of theft, muggings, and even a murder on the Inca Trail so it is clearly a good idea to hike with a group of friends and keep a good eye on your gear the whole time. It is such a popular route, though, that it's sometimes hard to get away from other hikers anyway.

Urubamba river. On the other side of the bridge the main path leads to the left, through a small eucalyptus wood, then around the base of the Inca ruins of *Llactapata* before crossing and then following the Cusichaca River upstream along its left bank. It's a good two hours' steep climb to HUAYLLA-BAMBA, the only inhabited village on the route. This section of the valley is rich in Inca terracing among which rises an occasional ancient stone building with typical trapezodial windows and niches. To reach Huayllabamba you have to cross a well-marked bridge onto the right bank of the Cusichaca.

Day Two: The First Pass

The next five hours or so to the *Abra de Huarmihuanusca*, **the first pass** (4200m/13,500 feet!) and the highest point on the Trail, is the hardest part of the walk—leave this (or some of it) for the second day, especially if you're feeling the effects of the altitude (see the "Health and Insurance" section of *Basics* for more on *soroche*). There are three possible places to camp between Huayllabmaba and Huarmihuanusca—the most popular and the first, known as Three White Stones, is at the point where the trail crosses the Río Huayruro, just half a kilometer above its confluence with the Llullucha stream. The next camp, just below the Pampa Llullucha, has toilets and space for several tents. Another twenty minutes farther up and there's plenty more camping space on the pampa within sight of the pass—a good spot for seeing rabbit-like *viscachas* playing among the rocks.

The views from the pass itself are stupendous, and from here the trail drops steeply down, sticking to the left of the stream into the Pacamayo valley where, by the river, there's an attractive spot to **camp** (also apparently a place where you can expect to see playful—and vegetarian—**spectacled bears** if you're there long enough or simply very lucky) or take a break before continuing up a winding, tiring track towards the **second pass**—*Abra de Runkuracay*—just above the interesting circular ruins of the same name. About an hour beyond the second pass, a flight of stone steps leads up to the Inca ruins of **SAYCA MARCA**. This is an impressive spot to **camp**, near the remains of a stone aqueduct which supplied water to the ancient settlement (the best spots are by the stream just below the ruins).

Day Three: Wiñay Wayna

Continuing, make your way gently down into increasingly dense cloud forest where delicate orchids and other exotic flora begin to appear among the trees. By the **third pass** (which, compared to the previous two, has very little incline) you're following a fine, smoothly worn flagstone path where at one point an astonishing tunnel, carved through solid rock by the Incas, takes you beyond an otherwise impossible climb. The trail winds down to the impressive ruin of **Puyupatamarca**—"Town Above the Clouds"—where there are five small stone baths and in the wet season constant fresh running water. There are places to **camp** actually on the pass (i.e., above the ruins), commanding stunning views across the Urubamba valley and, in the other direction, towards the snowcaps of *Salcantay* ("Wild Mountain")—this is probably one of the most magical camps on the trail (given good weather), and it's not unusual to see deer feeding here.

It's a two- or three-hour, very rough descent along a non-Inca track to the next ruin, a citadel almost as impressive as Machu Picchu, **WIÑAY WAYNA**—"Forever Young"—another place with fresh water. These days there's an official *Trekker Hotel* ($3 a bed; $1 floor space) and restaurant too—nothing splendid, but with a welcome supply of cool drinks. A well-marked trail from here takes a right fork for about two more hours through sumptuous vegetated slopes to INTIPUNKU, for your first sight of Machu Picchu: a mind-blowing moment however exhausted you might be. Aim to get to Machu Picchu well before the 10:30am arrival of the tourist train hordes, if possible making it to the "hitching post" of the sun before dawn, for the unforgettable experience of a sunrise that will quickly put the long hike through the pre-dawn gloom well behind you—bring a flashlight if you plan to try it.

Short Alternative Inca Trek

A short alternative to doing the entire Inca Trail is to leave Machu Picchu on foot via Intipunku and retrace the last section of the Inca Trail as far as Wiñay Wayna—an easy, two-hour stroll. This is one of the more beautiful sections of the Trail and the Wiñay Wayna ruins are some of the most spectacular. Here you can spend several hours exploring the ruins, and then return via the same route to sleep at the *Machu Picchu Hotel* or in Aguas Calientes. A more relaxing trip would be to spend the night at the *Trekker Hotel* at Wiñay Wayna, returning to appreciate Machu Picchu very early the next day, carrying a day pack and some food and water. If you don't mind a three- or four-hour uphill climb, and you're equipped with a tent, you could even retrace the trail back as far as Puyupatamarca and spend the night there before returning to Machu Picchu.

Machu Picchu

Probably the most dramatic and enchanting of Inca citadels, constructed from white granite in an extravagantly terraced saddle between two prominent peaks, **MACHU PICCHU** (daily 6:30am–5pm; $10; $5 students) defies description. Set against a vast and scenic backdrop of dark green forested mountains that spike magnificently up from the deep valleys of the Urubamba and its tributaries, the distant glacial summits are dwarfed only by a huge sky.

Getting There

Virtually every tourist and traveler in South America tries to wind up here sometime, at the very least on a **day trip** from Cuzco. This is easy enough to do, either taking the 5:30am local train (arriving Machu Picchu at 9:35am) and returning at 3:50pm (getting back to Cuzco around 8pm), or the 2pm local train (spending the night at Machu Picchu Pueblo/Aguas Calientes and visiting the ruins early next morning). Technically tourists are no longer allowed to buy local train tickets to Machu Picchu—they're supposed to pay for the deluxe and very expensive tourist train (see below for details).

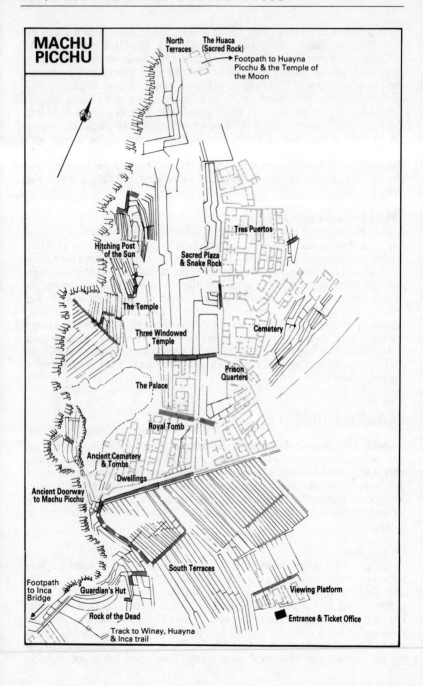

MACHU PICCHU

North Terraces

The Huaca (Sacred Rock)

Footpath to Huayna Picchu & the Temple of the Moon

Tres Puertos

Hitching Post of the Sun

Sacred Plaza & Snake Rock

The Temple

Three Windowed Temple

Cemetery

The Palace

Prison Quarters

Royal Tomb

Ancient Cemetery & Tombs

Dwellings

Ancient Doorway to Machu Picchu

South Terraces

Footpath to Inca Bridge

Guardian's Hut

Viewing Platform

Rock of the Dead

Entrance & Ticket Office

Track to Winay, Huayna & Inca trail

However, by buying a ticket to somewhere beyond Machu Picchu—say Chaullay or Quillabamba—it is still possible to get there for little more than $1 (people start lining up for tickets at 7:30am, but the ticket office is only open 9am–noon and 4–5pm, so you have to buy the day before if you want to get the early train). If you do take the local train be aware that it has a traditional reputation for backpack and pickpocket robberies.

The **tourist train**, on the other hand, runs quite differently. There are two groups of tickets sold each day. Group 1 leaves Cuzco at 7am going direct by rail to Machu Picchu, returning at 2:30pm as far as Ollantaytambo by train, then on to Cuzco by bus. Group 2 leave Cuzco by bus for Ollantaytambo at 8am, then on to Machu Picchu by train, returning at 5pm direct to Cuzco by rail. For about $50 most tour agencies will arrange such an excursion, with seats reserved on the train, lunch at the Machu Picchu *Hotel de Turistas*, and a guided walk around the ruins.

Near PUENTE RUINAS, the railroad station for Machu Picchu itself, there's a small **site museum** (Tues.–Sun. 10:30am–3:30pm) and **buses** heading on up the road over the river to the ruins themselves (up to ruins 7am–3pm and back down 1–5pm; $2 per person round-trip). If you walk it'll take between one-and-a-half and three hours depending on whether you take the very steep direct path or follow the paved road. Once you've made it up via an apparently infinite series of treacherous hairpins, you arrive at the *Hotel de Turistas* where there's a restaurant (even more expensive than the hotel itself), a luggage consignment, toilets, shop, and the **ticket office** for the site.

From the Machu Picchu railroad station there are usually two local trains a day in each direction: to Cuzco at 8:20am and 4pm; to Quillabamba at 9:30am (not on Sun.) and 6:30pm.

Finding a Place to Stay

Machu Picchu is infinitely more stimulating before the tourist train arrives in the morning, or after it has gone in the afternoon, so rather than rushing from Cuzco in a day, or exhausting yourself along the three-day Inca Trail, spend a night at the *Trekker Hotel* (at Wiñay Wayna), two hour's walk from the ruins, or head for the tiny settlement around the railroad station at **AGUAS CALIENTES** (now known as Machu Picchu Pueblo) where there are several **places to stay** overnight and a good selection of bars and restaurants. The *Hotel Machu Picchu* (beside the platform on the left-hand side of the train) is cheap and not a bad place to stay, or you could try the larger and slightly upscale *Hostal Los Caminantes* over on the other side of the tracks. *Gringo Bill's (Bar y Grill)*—also known as the *Hostal Q'oni*—is an excellent value at $2 single, with hot water, English spoken, and a fantastic jungle of rooms added on in any available space. Larger and also quite a good deal is the modern *Youth Hostel* farther up towards the hot springs.

In **peak season** (June–Sept.) there can be a lot of competition for lodgings, with large groups of travelers turning up and taking over entire hotels: by arriving on an earlier train you'll have a much better choice. Wherever you stay, and particularly if you end up **camping**, you'll soon realize that you're nearly in the jungle: flies and other buzzing insects are everywhere, the climate is distinctly muggy in comparison to Cuzco, and the vegetation is semitropical forest. At the back of the settlement there are some excellent communal **thermal baths**—*aguas calientes*—an excellent revitalizer after a day's tramping around the ruins.

Some History

For years the site of Machu Picchu lay forgotten, except by local Indians and settlers, until it was "discovered" by the North American explorer **Hiram Bingham**, who, on July 24, 1911, accompanied by a local settler who knew of some ruins, came upon a previously unheard of Inca citadel which was to become the most famous ruin in South America. In Bingham's reconstruction of the Incas' past, Machu Picchu fell into place as *Vilcabamba*, the site of the last refuge from the invader Spanish Conquistadors. Not until another American expedition surveyed the ruins around Machu Picchu in the 1940s did serious doubts begin to arise over this assignation, and more recently the site of the Inca's final stronghold has been shown to be Espiritu Pampa, beyond Quillabamba in the Amazon jungle (see p.110).

Meanwhile, Machu Picchu began to be reconsidered for what it is, perhaps the best preserved of a whole series of agricultural centers which served Cuzco in its prime. The city was probably conceived and maybe even partly built in the fifteenth century by the Emperor Pachacuti, the first to expand the empire beyond the Sacred Valley towards the forested gold-lands. With crop fertility, mountains, and nature so sacred to the Incas, such an important agricultural center as Machu Picchu became would easily have merited the site's fine stonework and temple precincts. Even if Machu Picchu has lost its original claim to fame, none of its characteristic mystique has gone.

The Ruins

Though it would take a lot to detract from the incredible beauty and unsurpassed location of Machu Picchu, the authorities seem to be trying their best to do just that: **the ruins** are oversupervised and very expensive —double-check the entrance fees in Cuzco before arriving here. After any of the other, less well known Inca ruins, Machu Picchu seems quite constricted, and it can be hard to let your mind wander back to imagine the place in its heyday when you're constantly assaulted by signs telling you where to go and what to do; even the "hitching post" of the sun has been roped off, and it's generally difficult to explore without a guard either blowing his whistle at you or shouting across the terraces if you deviate from one of the main pathways. If you arrive from the Inca Trail (or anywhere else) with a heavy **backpack**, the guards— recognizable by their plastic hardhats—will immediately order you to take your gear down to the ticket entrance below, when all you feel like doing is relaxing and absorbing the spellbinding atmosphere. Don't be put off, however, for in the end the experience of Machu Picchu will more than overwhelm any minor irritations.

There's little point giving a zone-by-zone account of the ruins; you simply have to wander around with a guide, a map, or alone to absorb its provocative grandeur. Though in fact more than 1000m lower than Cuzco, Machu Picchu seems much higher, constructed on dizzying slopes overlooking a U-curve in the Urubamba river. Over a hundred flights of steep stone steps interconnect its palaces, temples, storehouses, and terraces, and the outstanding views command not only the valley below in both directions but also extend to the snowy peaks around *Salcatay*. Wherever you stand in the ruins spectacular terraces can be seen slicing across ridiculously steep cliffs, transforming mountain into suspended garden.

Perhaps the most enthralling sector of the ruins is that above the **Sacred Plaza** where you can find the Temple of the Sun, the Temple of the Three Windows, and **Intihuatana**: the famous "hitching post" of the sun. An amazing carved rock in a tower like position overlooking the Sacred Plaza, the Urubamba and the living *huaca* of *Huayna Picchu*, Intihuatana's base is said to have been cut to represent a map of the Inca Empire. Its main purpose, however, was as a clock for telling the time of year, indicating important celestial movements and predicting the solstices.

The prominent peak of **Huayna Picchu**—"Young Height"—is easily scaled by anyone reasonably energetic (record for this climb is about 22 minutes). From the summit, whence there's an awe-inspiring panorama, another little trail leads down to a **Temple of the Moon** hidden in a grotto hanging magically above the Urubamba river.

Beyond Machu Picchu: Into the Jungle

Until recently, the area along the Urubamba river onwards from Machu Picchu was a quiet, yet relatively accessible, corner of the Peruvian wilderness; as the train descends along the valley floor, jungle vegetation thickens and the air gets steadily warmer and more humid. For the moment, however, the region is a restricted zone and allegedly a hideout for *Sendero Luminoso* terrorists, and with the army swooping the area in helicopters it's become very dangerous to wander around casually: nobody should enter the area without first obtaining written permission from the National Institute of Culture (in San Bernando, two blocks from Cuzco's Plaza de Armas)—which is virtually impossible to get. You can, however, pass through the restricted zone on the train, staying on until the end of the line at QUILLABAMBA (see p.269), a jungle outpost near the Inca ruins of **Espiritu Pampa** that's also the starting point for thrilling whitewater trips along the Urubamba and into the Amazon jungle.

The area that's most definitely off-limits, around the village of **Pukyura** in the Vilcabamba river valley, has, appropriately enough, a long history of guerrilla fighting and a tradition of willful anti-authoritarian independence. Chosen by Manco Inca as the base for his rebel state in the sixteenth century, it was also the political base for land reformer and Trotskyist revolutionary Hugo Blanc in the early 1960s. The only reason travelers might come here, should the current political situation quiet down, would be to see the ruins at **Vitcos**, the legendary site of Incaic blood sacrifices, on a hill overlooking the troubled area.

"Vilcabamba": The Ruins at Vitcos and Espiritu Pampa

In 1911, after discovering Machu Picchu (which he thought was the site of the legendary last stand of the Incas, **Vilcabamba**—where Tupac Aymaru lived in hiding until the Spanish captured him in the 1570s), Hiram Bingham set out down the Urubamba to CHAULLAY, now a stop on the Cuzco–Quillabamba railroad line, then up the Vilcabamba valley to the village of Pukyura where he expected to find more Inca ruins. What he found—**VITCOS**—(known locally as *Rosapata)*—was, and is, a relatively small but clearly palatial ruin, based around a trapezoidal plaza spread across a flat-topped spur.

Down below the ruins, Bingham was shown a spring flowing from beneath a vast white granite boulder intricately carved in typical Inca style and surrounded by the remains of an impressive Inca temple. This white rock *huaca—Chuquipalta—*15m long and 8m high, was proof that he really had found Vitcos, for it was clearly the great Inca oracle where blood sacrifices and other "pagan" rituals had, according to the chronicles, so infuriated two Spanish priests (guests at the rebel Incas' refuge) that they exorcized the rock and set its temple sanctuary on fire.

Within two weeks Bingham had followed a trail from Pukyura down into the jungle zone as far as the *Condevidayoc* plantation, near some more "undiscovered" ruins at **ESPIRITU PAMPA**—"Plain of the Spirits," near today's QUILLABAMBA. After briefly exploring some of the outer ruins at Espiritu Pampa, Bingham decided they must have been built by Manco Inca's followers; they were certainly post-Conquest Inca constructions since many roofs were Spanish tiled. Believing that he had already discovered the Inca's "last refuge" in Machu Picchu, Bingham paid little attention to the discoveries. Consequently, and in view of its being accessible only by mule trail, Espiritu Pampa remained covered in thick jungle vegetation.

Only in 1964 was serious exploration first undertaken, by Gene Savoy: he found a massive ruined complex with over 60 main buildings and some 300 houses along with temples, plazas, wells, and a main street. Clearly this was the largest Inca refuge in the Vilcabamba area, and Savoy rapidly became convinced of its identity as the true site of the last Inca stronghold. More conclusive evidence has since been provided by the English geographer and historian John Hemming who, using the chronicles as evidence, was able to match descriptions of Vilcabamba, its climate and altitude, precisely with those of Espiritu Pampa.

The sites of Vitcos and Espirtu Pampa, set in amazing and highly contrasted scenery, will hopefully soon reopen as superb potential hiking country for the outward-bound traveler. The village of **PUKYURA**, below Vitcos, is easily reached in six hours by truck from Chaullay station on the Cuzco-Quillabamba line. It used to be possible to camp at Pukyura and arrange for an *arriero* (muleteer) to take you over the two- or three-day trail to Espiritu Pampa for around $5 a mule per day, but given the circumstances as they stand, no one is likely to get beyond the police control at Pukyura. If you're still seriously interested in visiting this region, you should check on the prevailing situation with the National Institute of Culture in Cuzco before attempting what may well prove a wasted journey.

OTHER TRIPS FROM CUZCO

Cuzco is easily the most exciting region in Peru, but all too many visitors overlook the area's less well known attractions. Quite rightly, most people choose to spend at least three days in the immediate vicinity of the city, and nearly everyone visits Machu Picchu and the other sites in the Sacred Valley—at least another two or three days gone. But there are an infinite number of villages and sites left to stimulate the energetic traveler with more than a week to spend.

Chinchero, an old colonial settlement resting on Inca foundations and boasting a spectacular market, is only two hours' drive west, overlooking the Sacred Valley. To the east, towards the jungle, is the fiesta village of **Paucartambo**, while nearby **Tres Cruces** offers (at the right time of year) perhaps the most incredible sunrise and maybe one of the greatest panoramas in the world—from the high Andes, east across the lowland Amazon basin. To the south are the superb **ruins** of Tipón, Pikillacta, Rumicolca, and Raqchi, the rustic and legendary village of **Urcos,** as well as an admirable trekking base at **Sicuani**. And even if you aren't bothered about seeing Lake Titicaca, the **rail journey south to Puno**, which starts off through here, is one of the most soul-stirring train rides imaginable. One last trip, the highland route beteen Cuzco and Lima passing through **Ayacucho**, passes right through the worst of the fighting in the ongoing battles between the government and the *Sendero Luminoso* guerrillas.

Chinchero

The best time to visit **CHINCHERO**—"The Village of the Rainbow" which sits high above Cuzco—is on September 8 for the lively traditional fiesta; failing that, on any Sunday morning you'll catch the **weekly market**, much less tourist oriented than the Thursday one at Pisac and with an interesting selection of local craft goods. **Trucks** leave Cuzco from Calle Arcopata early every morning, until as late as 10am on Sunday. The hour-long ride takes you up above the Cuzco valley to the *Pampa de Anta*, a huge lake during the Quaternary period but now relatively dry pastureland, which on a clear day seems surrounded by snowcapped *nevadas*. Plans are afoot to build a new Cuzco airport here, one that will take international traffic and, no doubt, eventually damage the many ruins within a wide radius of the city.

The village itself lies on a high *mesa* (3762m above sea level), off to the right of the main road, overlooking the Sacred Valley of the Incas, with the *Cordillera Vilcabamba* and the snowcapped peak of *Salcantay* (over 6000m) dominating the horizon to the west. It's a small, mud-built place where the women, who crowd the plaza during the Sunday morning market, still go about their business in traditional dress. You'll need a Cuzco **general entrance ticket** (which can be bought in the village) to gain access to the church and ruins around the plaza, and if you want to spend the night there's a choice of only two places—the *Hotel Inca* or the *Albergue Chincheros*—though it is possible to **camp** beyond the village.

Raised above the square, an adobe colonial church dating from the early seventeenth century has been built on top of the foundations of an Inca temple or palace, perhaps once belonging to the Emperor Tupac Yupanqui who particularly favored Chincheros as an out-of-town resort. It was he who had most of the stylish aqueducts and terraces around Chincheros built—some of them still in use today. Inside the church there are a few interesting frescoes and paintings, some of which are attributed to the celebrated local artist Mateo Cuihuanito. One side of the plaza is bounded by a superb wall, somewhat reminiscent of Sacsayhuaman's ramparts, though nowhere near as massive. Some ten classical Inca trapezoidal niches order the surface of the wall.

Close to the village, around the terraced areas you can see carved rocks, while within a short walk you'll find the **Lake of Piuray**. A more interesting, but much longer walk, of about four or five hours, takes you down to the town and river of URUBAMBA (see p.99) in the Sacred Valley, and a good place to connect with the train line to Machu Picchu or back into Cuzco.

Paucartambo and Tres Cruces

Northeast of Cuzco, **PAUCARTAMBO**—"The Village of the Flowers"—guards a major entrance to the jungle zone of Manu. Trucks—leaving Cuzco on Monday, Wednesday, and Friday only from Avenida Huascar—take around four hours to get there. Beyond, following the Kosnipata valley, the road continues through cloudy tropical mountain regions to the mission of SHINTUYA on the edge of the Manu National Park (see p.266). *Kosnipata*—its name means "Valley of Smoke"—allegedly enchants anyone who drinks from its waters at Paucartambo, drawing them to return again and again. But even without such magic Paucartambo regularly attracts visitors by the thousand during the month of July, when it's transformed from a peaceful colonial village into one huge mass of frenzied, costumed dancers.

The Fiesta de la Virgen de Carmen

Eternally spring-like because of its proximity to the tropical forest, Paucartambo spends the first six months of every year preparing for the **Fiesta de la Virgen de Carmen**. Usually taking place in mid-July (actual dates from tourist office in Cuzco), this energetic, almost hypnotic ritual continues for three full days. Many themes recur during the dances, but particularly memorable is one in which the dancers, wearing outlandish, brightly colored costumes with grotesque blue-eyed masks, act out a parody of white man's powers. Malaria tends to be a central theme, since it's basically a post-Conquest problem: the participants portray an old man suffering its terrible agonies until a Western medic appears on the scene, with the inevitable hypodermic in his hand. When he manages to save the old man—a rare occurrence—it is usually due to an obvious and dramatic muddling of the prescriptions by his dancing medical assistants; the old man is cured by Andean fate rather than medical science.

Anyone who gets it together to go to Paucartambo for the fiesta will have a fascinating few days. If you can't make this, there are some ruined *chullpa* burial towers at Machu Cruz, only one hour's walk away. At any time it's best to take a tent with you to Paucartambo because **places to stay** are difficult, though not impossible, to find.

Tres Cruces

Sunrise at **TRES CRUCES**, in the months of May and June, is in its own way as magnificent a spectacle as the Paucartambo festival. A site of pilgrimage since pre-Inca days, Tres Cruces is situated on the last mountain ridge before the eastern edge of the immense Amazon forest: at any time the view (at night an enormous star-studded jewel, by day a twisting jungle river system) is a marvel. Yet when the sun rises it's a spectacle beyond words: multicolored, with multiple suns, an incredible light show which goes on for hours. To get there from Paucartambo it's about 25km down the road towards Shintuya, then left for another 15km. **Transportation** to Tres Cruces, however, is a problem except during May and June, and the only **accommodation** there is an empty house which has been used as a visitors' shelter.

South from Cuzco: Tipón, Urcos, and Sicuani

The first 150km of the road (and railroad) south from Cuzco towards Lake Titicaca passes through the beautiful valleys of Huatanay and Vilcanota, whence the legendary founders of the Inca Empire are said to have emerged. A region outstanding for its natural beauty and rich in magnificent archeological sites, it's easily accessible from Cuzco and offers endless possibilities for exploration or random wandering. With only one (slow) **train** a day in either direction—between Cuzco and PUNO—it makes more sense to take one of the frequent **buses** or minibuses along the route, stopping off when and where you like. *Transportes San Cristobal* (Av. Huascar 120; ☎3184) runs nine buses daily (6am–5:30pm) all the way from Cuzco to Sicuani, while there's a faster and much more frequent minibus service along the road as far as Urcos which you can pick up from block 1 of Avenida Huascar in Cuzco, or anywhere en route. Although the whole area is ideal for **camping** and **trekking**, only Urcos and Sicuani are large enough to accommodate overnight lodgers.

Tipón

Leaving Cuzco by road, after about 5km you pass through the little *pueblo* of SAN SEBASTIAN. Originally a small, separate village, it's now become a virtual suburb of the city. Nevertheless, it has a tidy little **church**, ornamented with baroque stonework and apparently built on the site of a chapel erected by the Pizarros in memory of their victory over Almagro. The next village of any special interest is picturesque **OROPESA**, traditionally a town of bakers, whose adobe church, with a uniquely attractive three-tiered belfry—with cacti growing out of it—is also notable for an intricately carved pulpit. And although it's only a small village, with no cafes as such, you can usually pick up some bread and a bottle of beer or a can of drink from one of the tiny shops.

Much more interesting than the town, though, is the ruined Inca citadel of **TIPÓN**, a stiff uphill walk from here. Both in setting and architectural design, Tipón is one of the most impressive Inca sites. Rarely visited, and with a guard who seems to be permanently on vacation, it's essentially open all the time and free. From Oropesa, the simplest way to reach the ruins is by backtracking down the main Cuzco road some 2km to a sign-posted track. Follow this up through a small village, once based around the now crumbling and deserted *hacienda Quispicanchi*, and continue along the gully straight ahead. Once on the trail above the village, it's about an hour's climb to the first ruins.

The Temples and Aqueducts

Well hidden in a natural shelf high above the Huatanay valley, the lower sector of the Tipón **ruins** is a stunning sight: a series of neat agricultural terraces, watered by stone-lined channels, all astonishingly preserved and many still in use. Imposing order on nature's "chaos," the superb stone terracing seems as much a symbol of the Incas' domination over a subservient labor pool as it does an attempt to increase crop yield.

At the back of the lower ruins water flows from a stone-faced "mouth" around a spring—probably an aqueduct subterraneously diverted from above. The entire complex is designed around this spring higher up, reached by a path from the last terrace. Another sector of the ruins contains a reservoir and temple block centered around a large exploded volcanic rock—presumably some kind of *huaca*. Although the stonework in the temple seems cruder than that of the agricultural terracing, its location is amazing; by contrast the construction of the reservoir is of necessity very fine—originally built to hold nine hundred cubic meters of water which was gradually dispersed along stone channels to the Inca "farm" directly below.

Coming off the back of the reservoir, a large tapering stone aqueduct crosses a small gully before continuing uphill, about half-an-hour's walk, to a vast zone of unexcavated terraces and dwellings. Beyond these, over the lip of the hill, you come to another level of the upper valley literally covered in Inca terracing, dwellings, and large stone storehouses. Equivalent in size to the lower ruins, these are still used by locals who've built their own houses among the ruins. So impressive is the terracing at Tipón that some archeologists believe it was an Inca experimental agricultural center, much like Moray (see p.99), as well as a citadel.

With no village or habitation in sight, and fresh running water, it's a breath-taking place to **camp** and you feel you could explore for weeks. More ruins probably exist even higher up, though if you're only here for a day there's a splendid stroll back down to the main road following a path through the locals' huts in the upper sector (i.e., above the reservoir) over to the other side of the *quebrada* and following it down the hillside opposite Tipón. This route offers an excellent perspective on the ruins, as well as vistas towards Cuzco in the north and over the Huatanay/Vilcanota valleys to the south.

Pikillacta and Rumicolca

About 7km south of Oropesa, the neighboring pre-Inca ruins of Pikillacta and Rumicola can be seen right alongside the road. After passing the Paucartambo turnoff, near the ruins of an ancient storehouse and the small red-roofed pueblo of HUACARPAY, the road climbs to a ledge overlooking a wide alluvial plain and Lucre lake (now a weekend resort for Cuzco's work-ers). At this point the road traces the margin of a stone wall defending the pre-Inca settlement of Pikillacta.

Spread over an area of at least fifty hectares, **PIKILLACTA**—"The Place of the Flea"—was built by the Huari culture around A.D. 800, before the rise of the Incas. Its unique, geometrically designed terraces surround a group of bulky two-storied constructions: apparently these were entered by ladders reaching up to doorways set well off the ground in the first story—very unusual in ancient Peru. Many of the walls are built of small cut stones joined with mud mortar, and among the most interesting finds here were several round turquoise statuettes. These days the city is clearly in ruins but it seems evident still that much of the site was taken up by barrack-like quarters. When the Incas arrived they modified the site to suit their own purpose, possibly even building the aqueduct that once connected Pikillacta with the ruined gateway that straddles a narrow pass by the road, just fifteen minutes' walk farther south.

This massive defensive passage, **RUMICOLCA**, was also initially constructed by the Huari people and served as a southern entrance and barrier of their empire. Later it became an Inca checkpoint, regulating the flow of people and goods into the Cuzco Valley: no one was permitted to enter or leave Cuzco via Rumicolca between sunset and sunrise. The Incas improved on the rather crude Huari stonework of the original gateway, using regular blocks of polished andesite from a local quarry. The gateway still stands, rearing up to twelve solid meters above the ground, and is one of the most impressive of all Inca constructions.

Andahuaylillas and Huaro

About halfway between Rumicolca and Urcos, the insignificant villages of Andahuaylillas and Huaro hide deceptively interesting colonial churches. In **ANDAHUAYLILLAS**, the adobe-towered church sits raised above an attractive plaza, just ten minutes' walk from the roadside restaurant where buses and minibuses stop to drop off and pick up passengers. Built in the early seventeenth century on the site of an Inca temple, it's a magnificent example of provincial colonial art. Huge Cuzqueño canvases decorate the upper walls, while below are some unusual murals, slightly faded over the centuries: the ceiling, painted with Spanish flower designs, contrasts strikingly with a great baroque altar and an organ alive with cherubs and angels. The village itself is a tranquil and proudly preserved haven, its plaza fronted by colonial houses, one with an Inca doorway.

South, the road leaves the Huatanay river behind and enters the Vilcanota valley. **HUARO** is a very different place, crouched at the foot of a steep bend in the road, with a much smaller church whose interior is completely covered with colorful murals. Out in the fields beyond the village, climbing towards Urcos, you can see how boulders have been gathered together in mounds, clearing the ground for the simple ox-pulled plows which are still used here.

Urcos and Viracocha's Huaca

Climbing over the hill from Huaro, the road descends to cruise past **Lake Urcos** before reaching the town which shares its name. According to legend, the Inca Huascar threw his heavy gold chain into these waters after learning that strange bearded aliens—Pizarro and his motley crew—had arrived in Peru. Between lake and town, a simple chapel now stands poised at the top of a small hillock: if you find it open there are several excellent Cuzqueño paintings inside.

URCOS itself rests on the valley floor surrounded by weirdly sculpted hills. One of these, known locally as Viracocha, is said to have been climbed by the creator-god, Viracocha: from the summit he ordered beings to emerge from the hill, thus creating the town's first inhabitants. In tribute, an ornate *huaca* was constructed with a bench of gold to house a statue to the god. This local shrine probably stemmed from pre-Inca days, and it was here that the eighth Inca emperor received a divinatory vision in which the god Viracocha appeared to him to announce that "great good fortune awaited him and his descendants." In this way he obtained his imperial name, Viracocha-Inca, and supposedly the first inspiration to plan permanent expansion into non-Inca territory, though it was his son, Pachacuti, who carried the empire to its greatest heights.

Back in town, an inordinate number of huge old trees give shade to the Indians selling bread, soups, oranges, and vegetables around the plaza, which is particularly packed for the traditional Sunday market. On one side of the square there's an old church; on the other, low adobe buildings splattered with fervent graffiti supporting the United Left. It's not really a tourist town, but the occasional traveler is made welcome: in the back streets you can stop off at one of the *tiendas* for a glass of *chicha* beer (those selling *chicha* advertise by sticking out a pole with a blob of red plastic on the end) and some friendly conversation, and you can usually **find a room** either on the plaza (at F. Belaunde 150—ask in the shop) or on the street coming into town (J. Arica 316). There are a couple of good **places to eat** fronting the square, and this is one of the few places in the world where you can buy good *quinoa* soup—which is supposed to be excellent for skin problems. Electricity lasts until midnight only—so take some candles or a flashlight if you're a late-nighter.

The Temple of Raqchi and Sicuani

Between Urcos and Sicuani the road passes CHECACUPE village, site of a church with a startling sixteenth-century mural and the turnoff for the textile-weaving center of PIRUCARTI. The road and railroad rejoin after about 30km, and the imposing ruin of the **Temple of Raqchi**—once again dedicated to Viracocha—looms above, drawing most passersby to make another detour. Situated close to the village of SAN PEDRO DE CACHA (4km), the temple was evidently built to appease Viracocha after he had caused the nearby volcano of Quimsa Chata to spew out fiery boulders in a rage of anger, and even now massive volcanic boulders and ancient lava flows scar the landscape in constant reminder. With its adobe walls still standing over 12m high on top of polished stone foundations, and the site scattered with numerous other buildings and plazas, Raqchi exudes a strong feeling of animistic ritual. Barracks, cylindrical warehouses, a palace, baths, and the usual aqueducts can also be identified, clearly showing that this was an important religious center. Today the only ritual left is the annual **Raqchi Festival** (normally June 16–22), one of the most dramatic and least commercialized native fiestas in the Cuzco region.

SICUANI, nearly 150km from Cuzco, is quite a thriving agricultural and market town, not entirely typical of the settlements in the Vilcanota valley. Its busy Sunday market is renowned for cheap and excellent woollen artifacts, which you may also be offered on the train if you pass through between Puno and Cuzco. One thing to do here is to visit the nearby **hot springs** of **Uyumiri**: although not a particularly exciting place in itself—daunting looking with too many tin roofs and an austere atmosphere—the people are surprisingly friendly and it's an excellent base for trekking into snowcapped mountain terrain, being close to the vast Nevada Vilcanota mountain range which separates the Titicaca Basin from the Cuzco valley. **Camping** is really the best way of seeing this part of Peru, but if you haven't got a tent there are several **hotels** in town, including the basic *Hotel Raqchi* and the plusher *Hotel de Turistas*.

The train journey south from Cuzco continues on to PUNO and Lake Titicaca—which in reverse order is one of the more popular routes into the Cuzco region. Beyond Sicuani the Vilcanota valley begins to close in around the railroad as the tracks climb La Raya Pass (4300m), before dropping down into the desolate *pampa* that covers much of inland southern Peru. You might well feel compelled to leave the train at the pass and head off toward the horizon or into the surrounding mountains, as this is your last chance to do so before Puno and the arid south, all of which are described in the next chapter.

From Cuzco to Lima: Ayacucho and the Guerrilla War

The fact that Ayacucho—the troubled Andean *departmento* lying between Lima and Cuzco—is included in this travel guide does not in any way mean that the political upheaval and violence that has racked the area for the past ten years has abated. On the contrary, most people would claim that the clandestine war between the Maoist *Sendero Luminoso* guerrillas and the military police has, if anything, gotten worse. That said, there are still plenty of travelers making it to Ayacucho either overland by bus from Lima or Cuzco, or by air. The airport has been taken over by the military and it is obvious from the army's massive and clearly long-term presence that this is still considered a war zone. The ordinary people of Ayacucho, the ones who continue to suffer from the political strife, are actually among the friendliest in the Peruvian Andes and the local tourist office is naturally eager to attract more visitors. For a detailed outline of the politics and recent history behind Ayacucho and *Sendero Luminoso* see the *Contexts* section at the end of this book.

Most people who visit the region's capital city, **Ayacucho**, do so only in passing on the road connecting Lima with Cuzco via the Pisco valley; the ongoing civil strife has certainly discouraged extended visits to what was once one of the most popular Andean cities, renowned for its twenty fine **churches**, the exquisite **crafts** skills of its people, and its rambunctious **fiestas**. Apart from the city of Ayacucho itself the only other major town on route is **Abancay**, a large market center with little to offer the traveler apart from a roof for the night (try the *Gran Hotel*) and transportation out by truck or bus.

It often takes at least two days to travel from Cuzco to Lima and so Ayacucho, with its interesting architecture and superb *artesania,* is, in some ways, an obvious pit stop. There is another road from Cuzco which leaves Abancay for the coast and Lima via the Nazca valley, bypassing Ayacucho completely—a slightly faster route between Cuzco and Lima that, nevertheless, can easily take two or three days even in the dry season. On either route, there's one place that merits a stop between Abancay and Cuzco. Near the village of **Carahuasi**, there's a beautifully carved ancient stone known as *Sahuite*—a graphic representation of an Inca village.

The City of Ayacucho

Roughly halfway between Cuzco and Lima, the city of **AYACUCHO** sits almost 3000m high in the Andes in one of the most archeologically important valleys in Peru, with evidence from nearby caves at Pikimachay strongly suggesting that the region has been occupied for over 20,000 years. Ayacucho was the initial center of the *Huari* culture which emerged in the region around A.D. 700, spreading its powerful and evocative religious symbolism throughout most of Peru over the next three or four hundred years, and later became a major Inca administrative center. The original

Spanish site for the city at Huamanguilla was abandoned in favor of the present location and, known then as the city of *San Juan de la Frontera*, Ayacucho was officially founded in 1540.

The bloody **Battle of Ayacucho**, which took place near here on the *Pampa de Quinoa* in 1824, finally released Peru from the shackles of its one-way links with Spain. Although most of Peru had already declared its independence and proclaimed the Republic, the last Royalists were holding out in Ayacucho. The armies met early in December, when Viceroy Jose de la Serna attacked Sucre's Republican force in three columns. The pro-Spanish soldiers, were, however, unable to hold off the Republican forces, who swept through the very heart of the Royalists and captured the viceroy with relative ease.

A radical university town with a long tradition, today Ayacucho is most famous for the outbreaks of violence from both terrorists and the Peruvian armed forces. The exact figure isn't known but something like 7000 people have disappeared (presumed dead) in this region over the last nine years. Entire villages have been massacred and hundreds of young students have evidently been liquidated while the army, the media, and the *Sendero* disagree on who is responsible.

As a gringo (or anything else for that matter), there are a few things to keep in mind while you're here: it's obviously unwise to get into political discussions in this town; always **walk, don't run**, no matter how much of a hurry you're in; and finally, carry your passport at all times and stop at any army checkpoints. Armed **soldiers**, more than anywhere else in Peru, must be treated with respect: they are, in the main, trigger-happy young men, some of them nervous and touchy. Don't try and stick a camera in their faces and if they ask you to do something, it is advisable to do it. However, most people on the streets of Ayacucho, although quiet and reserved, are helpful, friendly, and kind. Very little English is spoken; in fact, Quechua is the city's first language.

Some Practical Details

The **hotels** in Ayacucho are rarely full these days so there's generally plenty of choice. The *Hotel Samary* (two blocks east of the central plaza) is certainly one of the better budget places, though *La Colmena* (by *Alamo Rest* on Cuzco and within half a block from the Plaza de Armas) and the *Hostal Santa Rosa* (again, only half a block away from the plaza but this time on Calle Lima) are very good deals too. If in doubt, *La Colmena* has the added luxury of a very beautiful courtyard full of flowers, while *Santa Rosa* offers hot water. The best in town, as usual, is the *Hotel de Turistas* (one block from the plaza on Calle 9 de Deciembre), but they don't get many *turistas* these days. Most of the clientele here are on business of one kind or another.

Food and **nightlife** are both surprisingly good in Ayacucho. The basic restaurant *Los Portales* on the Plaza de Armas is very popular though not as good as *Alamo* (Cuzco, by the *Hotel La Colmena*). Also on the Plaza de Armas, the *San Augustin Cafe Turistico* serves good food and wonderful lemon meringue pie. The *Restaurant Tradicional* (San Martin 406) is excellent value and the *Restaurant La Fortaleza* (Calle Lima, across from the *Hotel*

Santa Rosa) has the best coffee in town. If you're after **live music** in the evenings, Ayacucho has a few good *peñas: Arco Blanco* (Jr. Asamblea 280); *Los Portales* (Portal Union 33); and *La Casona* (Jr. Bellido 463). *La Tuna* (Portal Union 23) and *La Estrella* (Jr. Dos de Mayo 148) are the only **discoteques** in Ayacucho.

The **tourist office** (Asamblea 138; Mon.–Fri. 7:30am–4pm), on the Plaza de Armas, has a helpful staff (Rudy Oswaldo speaks English and French) able and willing to help arrange trips in the area. There's also *Ayacucho Tours* around the corner from the *Banco de La Nacion* on San Martin, just one block from the Plaza de Armas. The **post office** is two blocks away from the plaza on Asamblea.

The Sights: Churches, Mansions, and Museums

Ayacucho, despite the often threatening presence of so many anxious soldiers on its streets, is still an attractive and unperturbed colonial city, with dozens of splendid churches and mansions packed together in dense blocks around the central Plaza de Armas. The **cathedral**, which is the focus of nightly, candle-lit processions during Easter week, was built between 1612 and 1671 by the Bishop Don Cristobal de Castilla y Zamora, and has a fine, three-aisled nave culminating in a stunning baroque wooden and gold-leaf altarpiece. The **Casona Jauregui** (block 2 of Dos de Mayo), a lovely seventeenth-century mansion built by Don Cayetano Ruiz de Ochon, is another major attraction; it has a superb patio and balcony with a shield displaying a two-headed eagle. Farther out, the **Museum of Archeology and Anthropology** (Avenida Independencia; ☎91-2056) is full of fascinating local finds dating from several millenia ago, and there are also a couple of quite interesting art galleries: the *Casona Vivanco* (Jr. 28 de Julio 518) and the *Popular Art Gallery* (Jr. Asamblea 138).

Artesanía: Rugs, Retablos, and Stone Carving

For many visitors, more interesting than museums or old houses is the thriving **craft industry** in Ayacucho. The city used to be *the* place in Peru for woven rugs and retables, those finely worked little wooden boxes containing intricate three-dimensional religious scenes made mainly from papier-mâché. You can still find these objects in the city but, with the drastic fall in local tourist demand over the last decade, most of them are exported direct and the artisans now seem to expect much better prices than they used to. Some of the cheaper *retablos*—but still very good—are made by Cesar Urbano (Av. Peru 308–318, La Libertad). Among the best **shops** for buying or just looking are *Artesanias Helme* (Portal Unión 49) and *Pokra* (Jr. Dos de Mayo 128). If you've got the time to spare, however, it certainly pays both financially and in terms of satisfying interest and curiosity to visit some of the actual craft workshops and buy from the artisans themselves. Most of the **workshops** are found in the *barrio* of **Santa Ana**, just uphill from the Plaza de Armas.

For **rugs**, check out Edwin Sulca—probably the most famous weaver here—who lives opposite the church on the Plaza Santa Ana. His rugs go from around $100 (almost double this in Lima's shops). Many of his latest designs graphically depict the horrors of the present political situation around Ayacucho. Another excellent weaver—Gerado Fernandez Palomino—lives at Jiron Paris 600, also in Santa Ana.

As far as **retables** go, the Jimenez family, in the same *barrio*, make some of the best. Their most simple work is not all that expensive, but if you want to buy one of their more complicated modern pieces illustrating the military/terrorist situation it could cost as much as $300 (they can take three months to complete).

Alabaster stone carvings—known in Peru as **Huamanga stone carvings**—are another specialty of Ayacucho (Huamanga being the old name for the city). It's probably worth asking at the tourist office for the names of some stone carvers but evidently Benjamin Pizarro Lozana (Jr. Unsch 278, Barrio Belen) is one of the best. The craft co-op *Ahuaccllacta* (Huanca Solar 130) is also worth checking out.

The Easter Fiesta: Semana Santa

If you can be in Ayacucho for *Semana Santa*, the Holy Week beginning the Friday before Easter, there are fabulous processions and pageants every day for over a week. But beware of the beautiful procession of the *Virgen Dolores* (Our Lady of Sorrows) which takes place the Friday before Palm Sunday: pebbles are fired at the crowd (particularly at children and gringos) by expert slingers so that even onlookers are taking on the pain of *La Madre de Dios*, and so reducing Her suffering. According to Betsy Wagenhauser, of the South American Explorers' Club in Lima, who experienced this procession in March 1988—"it hurts" !

Around Ayacucho

Around Ayacucho there are a few interesting places which it is still alright to visit, but it's a good idea to check with the tourist office beforehand. The political situation is always changing and certain villages might become more sensitive even before this sentence reaches the printers. The cave of **Pikimachay**, where archeologists have found human and, apparently, some gigantic animal remains, is only 24km away. The ancient city of **Huari**, sometimes written "Wari," is only about 20km from Ayacucho on the road to Huancayo. Some historians have claimed that this site used to house some 50,000 people just over 1000 years ago, and there's a museum displaying skulls and stone weapons found here in the 1960s.

About 26km from Ayacucho the sleepy village of **QUINUA** is just a short bus ride away through acres of *tuna cacti*, which is abundantly farmed here for both its delicious fruit (prickly pear) and the red dye (cochineal) extracted from the *cochamilla*—larvae that thrive at the base of the cactus leaves. Apparently sitting on the site of the nineteenth-century Battle of Ayacucho, marked by an obelisk, the village's most characteristic feature is the small, highly ornate ceramic models of churches placed on many of the roofs. There are some artisans working in the settlement: at *San Pedro Ceramics* (at the foot of the hill leading to the obelisk) it's often possible to see the functioning workshop processes. Mamerto Sanchez has a workshop on Jirón Sucre.

travel details

Buses

From Cuzco Several departures a day for Lima (via Nazca or Pisco; 30–50 hr.); Arequipa (20 hr.); Juliaca/Puno (10/11hr.); Abancay (10 hr.); and Ayacucho (24 hr.). To La Paz every Sunday (24hr). **Local routes** are all detailed in the text.

Trucks to Puerto Maldonado (48–60 hr.) leave every other day

Trains

From Cuzco to Juliaca/Puno (10/11 hr.) and Arequipa (22 hr.) leave once a day at 8am, except Sunday.

From Cuzco to Machu Picchu (4 hr.) and Quilllabamba (8 hr.), four times a day. A combination **tourist train/bus** between Cuzco and Machu Picchu makes two 2–hr. round-trips a day.

Flights

Several planes a day **from Cuzco** to Lima, Arequipa, and Puerto Maldonado (see *Listings* for Cuzco on p94). To La Paz every Tues. and Sat. with Lloyd Aereo Boliviano (Av. Sol 348; ☎22-2990).

CHAPTER THREE

THE SOUTH

The South has been populated as long as anywhere in Peru—for at least 9000 years in some places—but up until this century no one had any idea that this arid region had given rise to a number of unique cultures whose enigmatic remains, particularly along the coast, show signs of a considerably sophisticated and highly advanced civilization. With the discovery and subsequent study, beginning in 1901, of ancient sites throughout the coastal zone, it now seems clear that this was home to at least three major **cultures:** the **Paracas** (500 B.C.–A.D. 400), the influential **Nazca** (A.D. 500–800), and finally, contemporaneous with the Chimu of northern Peru and the Cuismancu around Lima, the **Ica Culture**, or **Chincha Empire**, overrun by and absorbed into Pachacutec's mushrooming Inca Empire around the beginning of the fifteenth century.

The three main towns along the coast, **Pisco, Ica,** and **Nazca**, all preserve important and intriguing sites from the three cultures. **The Nazca Lines**, a perplexing network of perfectly straight lines and giant figures etched over almost five hundred square kilometers of bleak *pampa*, are just one of southern Peru's many enduring and mysterious archeological features, all of which are worth stopping for on a journey most travelers make in a couple of quick bursts down the Pan American Highway south from Lima. And if you have any interest in wildlife, Pisco and Nazca offer three of the most outstanding reserves in the country—the **Ballestas Islands** and **Paracas National Park** (outside Pisco), and the rare vicuña reserve of **Pampa Galeras** (in the Andes above Nazca).

Arequipa, second city of Peru and an all-day journey from Lima, reflects a different and altogether more dramatic environment than the coast in between, poised at the edge of the Andes against an extraordinary backdrop of volcanic peaks. The major center of the south, Arequipa is an enjoyable place to rest up for a while, distinguished for its architecture (including the magnificent **Santa Catalina Monastery**) and for several spectacular, if tough-going, excursions into the surrounding countryside. It's also the last good place to stop before continuing on south to the Chilean border.

Heading inland, you'll probably want to spend less time in the region around **Lake Titicaca** and its main town and port of **Puno**—a sad, austere section with a cold climate and incredibly rarefied air. It is impressive in its own way, though: quite unique to South America and an interesting route to travel, allowing you to make the trip from Arequipa to Cuzco or head on into Bolivia.

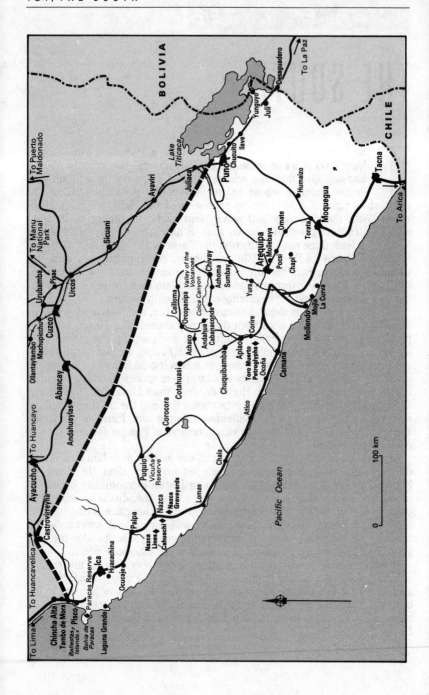

ALONG THE COAST

The coastal area between Lima, the capital, and Arequipa, Peru's second-largest city, contains enough ancient ruins and unusual landscapes—including some of the best assortments of wildlife in South America—to tempt almost any traveler off the Pan American Highway, the four-lane highway that runs the length of Peru. Around **Pisco**, 200km south of Lima, the unspoiled coastline is one of the best places in the world for birdwatching, while the desert plains around **Nazca** are indelibly marked by gigantic, alien-looking figures scratched into the brown earth over 2000 years ago. And in the cooler hills above you can search out herds of the soft-wooled vicuña or see real pink flamigoes in their natural Andean habitat at stunning **Lake Parincochas**.

Transportation is not usually a problem in this area; however, it can get very hot here, and food and water are sometimes hard to come by outside the larger towns.

Pisco and Around

Only three hours by bus from Lima, **Pisco** is an obvious and rewarding stop en route south to Nazca and Arequipa. Although of little interest in itself, it makes a pleasant base—and provides access to the **Paracas Nature Reserve**, the wildlife of the **Ballestas Islands**, and the well-preserved Inca coastal outpost of **Tambo Colorado**. Just off the Pan American Highway, it is also a crossroads for going up into the Andes: you can take roads from here to Huancavelica and Huancayo, as well as to Ayachuco and Cuzco.

Arrival and Getting Around

Getting to Pisco from Lima is simple by road—there are frequent buses (*Ormeño* is the best operator) and *colectivos* (Comite 3, Montevideo 561;☎281423). If you're heading for the **Paracas Reserve** the best way is to catch a bus from the Pisco market. Most of the buses only go as far as the waterfront at San Andres (it is possible to hitch from here), but there are normally at least two buses per hour which go as far as the *Paracas Hotel*.

To leave Pisco for Lima, Cuzco, and most other destinations, catch *colectivos* from the Plaza de Armas. For Lima (3–4 hours), Nazca (3–4 hours), Arequipa (14 hours), or Ayacucho (12 hours) the best **bus** company is undoubtedly *Ormeño* (one block east of the plaza), while for Huancavelica (14 hours) it's *Oropesa* on Calle Commercial.

The Town

Presumably because of its ease of access, the Spanish considered making **PISCO** their coastal capital before eventually deciding on Lima. The town still possesses a few fine colonial showpieces, clustered about the **Plaza de Armas** with its statue of liberator San Martín poised in the shade of ancient ficus trees. The mansion where he actually stayed on his arrival in Peru can still be seen—a block out towards the **bus station** and now adapted as the local social club. Another impressive building, unusual in its Moorish style, is the **Municipal Palace**, and if you're wandering around there are a couple of elegant churches nearby, among them the heavy baroque **Compañía** with its superb carved pulpit.

The town's focus of activity is the **plaza** and adjoining Jirón Comercio; every evening the square is crowded with people walking and talking, stopping to buy *tejas* (small sweets made from pecans) from street vendors. **Hotels** are mostly reasonable, even the plusher-looking *Hotel Embassy* on Jirón Comercio; *Hostal Pisco* (San Francisco 115; ☎2018) on the plaza is more basic, though very friendly, and with its own restaurant; *Hostal Callao* (Callao 163) cheaper still but very rudimentary. **Nightlife** revolves around relaxing in the plaza or eating and drinking in one of the many restaurants and bars: on the main square an excellent corner *chifa* serves good *pisco* (local grape brandy) and almost next door the *Restaurante As de Oro* will prepare you excellent local seafoods (it's worth checking or ordering in advance to make sure they've got the fresh fish you like), while on the same side as *Hostal Pisco*, *Las Vegas* offers traditional dishes. Going down towards the *Hotel Embassy*, another café, *Restaurant Flamengo*, prepares very fresh fish and chips. The town **disco** is on block 2 of Callao. Plenty of hotels and boat-trip companies change cash dollars, but only the **Banco de la Nación** (on the main street towards San Andres) takes travelers' checks.

The Ballestas Islands, San Andres, and El Balneario

Often called the Guano Islands, because every inch is covered in bird droppings, the very rocks of the **Ballestas Islands**, which lie off the coast due west from Pisco, seem to be alive and moving with a mass of flapping, noisy pelicans, penguins, terns, boobies, and Guanay cormorants. The waters around them are equally full of life, sometimes almost black with the shiny dark bodies of seals and sea lions. An excellent day trip from Pisco, the islands are served by two companies that run combined bus and boat tours— each similarly priced (around $5–$6), leaving early in the morning and returning towards midday. Tickets are best bought the day before—from the *Hotel Pisco* or the office at Jr. Comercio 128—and you'll be picked up around 6:30am, from the plaza in front of the *Hotel Pisco*.

The buses run south along the shoreline past the old fishing port of **SAN ANDRES**, where you can watch the fishermen bringing in their catch; on the way back they stop so you can buy fresh *ceviche* or local turtle steaks. Turtles are a favorite local food and are known as the meat with seven flavors—some parts of the creature taste of fish, others of chicken, another of beef, and so on. Warm turtle blood, too, is still occasionally drunk here, reputedly a cure for bronchial problems.

El Balneario

At the far end of San Andres the road passes by the big Pisco Air Force Base before reaching **EL BALNEARIO**, a resort for wealthy Limeñans, whose large bungalows line the beach. If you want to stay out here it is possible to **camp** on the sand, though the Paracas Reserve (see below) is really a much nicer place to be. The *Hostería Paracas* (Avenida Los Libertadores) is comfortable but not cheap, and there is an expensive *Hotel de Turistas* with a pool next door (Ribera del Mar.; ☎2220).

El Balneario also serves as a base for the Ballestas boat-trip people. You climb off a small jetty surrounded by pelicans into a wooden launch and chug out across the sea for the next 3½ or so hours, circling one or two of the islands and returning past the famous "Paracas Trident"—a huge cactus-shaped figure drawn in the sandstone cliffs (see below).

From El Balneario you have two alternatives for onward travel. You can go back in the bus to Pisco (get the driver to drop you off for lunch in San Andres) or, more exciting, hitch a few kilometers farther south along the bay road, well beyond the fish-processing factories and the obelisk commemorating San Martin's landing, into the Paracas Nature Reserve.

Paracas Nature Reserve and Lagunillas

A peninsula of even greater "natural" interest than the Ballestas Islands, the **Paracas Nature Reserve**, a 15km bus journey from Pisco, has added attractions in its superb and quite deserted beach where you can **camp** for days without seeing anything except the lizards and birdlife, and maybe a couple of fishing boats. It really is a magical sort of place, devoid of vegetation yet full of energy and life. Schools of dolphins play in the waves offshore, condors frequently scour the peninsula for potential food, and lizards scrabble across the hot sands. If you go, plan to stay a few days, and take food, water, and a sun hat—facilities are almost nonexistent.

The entrance to the reserve is marked these days by a barrier-gate, just off the Pan American Highway, where the wardens collect a small fee from visitors, a charge that allows you to stay in the park for up to a week. Not far from the barrier is a small archeological museum, and the **park office** (with natural history exhibits) where maps are sometimes available. The **museum**, the first landmark as you make your way up a gentle slope into the very bleak and arid peninsular zone, is well worth a look. Restored in 1983, its exhibits include a wide range of Paracas culture artifacts—mummies, ceramics, funerary cloths, and a reconstructed dwelling.

Paracas Flying Figure

Right next to the museum is the oldest discovered site in the region, the **Necropolis of Cabeza Largas**, dating from over 5000 years ago and once containing as many as sixty mummies in one of its graves. Most were wrapped in vicuña skins or rush matting, and buried along with personal objects like shell beads, bone necklaces, lances, net bags, and cactus-spine needles. A little farther on, near the beach where you can often see dozens of tall and graceful pink flamingos, there are more remains—the Disco Verde, a Chavin-related settlement.

The Paracas Trident

Another 2km or so on past the museum you come to a fork in the main road: the paved part continues straight on, parallel to the shore, terminating after 20km at PUNTA PEJERREY, the modern port for Pisco, and full of fish canneries. There's nothing of interest here—but shortly before the port a sandy side road leads away from the sea and around the hills on the outer edge of the peninsula.

This trail, which is occasionally signposted and barely passable by car, takes you 13km across the hot desert to **the Trident**, a massive, 50m candelabra carved into the hillside. No one knows its function or its creator, though writer Eric Von Daniken speculates it was a sign for extra-terrestrial spacecraft, pointing the way (inaccurately as it happens) towards the mysterious Nazca lines that are inland to the southeast; others suggest it was constructed as a navigational aid for eighteenth-century pirates. Somehow it seems more likely that it was a kind of pre-Inca ritual object, perhaps representing a cactus or tree of life. Perhaps High Priests during the Paracas or Nazca eras worshiped the setting sun from this spot.

Lagunillas and Some Fine Beaches

Unless you want to see the Trident figure (which is more impressive from the sea in any case), instead of heading on toward Punta Pejeery, it's a better idea to take the dusty sand trail which cuts off to the left of the main road, towards the tiny and likable port of Lagunillas some 6km away. **LAGUNILLAS**, a fishing hamlet with a few huts serving *conchitas* (scallops) and other seafood, is really the point on Paracas to make for—a strange, very beautiful part of the peninsula, so flat that if the sea rose just another meter the whole place would be submerged. Pelicans and sea lions hang around the bobbing boats waiting for a fisherman to accidently drop a slippery fish, and little trucks regularly arrive to carry the catch back into Pisco.

From Lagunillas the rest of the Paracas Reserve is at your feet. Nearby are the glorious **beaches** of **La Mina** and **Yumajque**, where you can often **camp** for days without seeing anyone, and a track goes off 5km north to a longer sandy beach, **Arquillo;** on the cliffs beyond there's a viewing platform (*Mirador de los Lobos*) above a large colony of sea lions. Another path leads north from here, straight across the peninsula to the Trident and on to Punta Pejerrey.

South around the bay from Lagunillas, turning right across the sandy hills rather than heading back to the museum, it's about 4km to the spectacular **cathedral cave** (*La Catedral*), down on a pebbly beach. Bats line its high

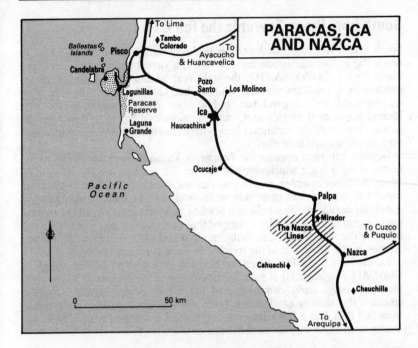

vaulted ceilings and huge waves pound the rocky inner walls. This trail continues to the fishing village of LAGUNA GRANDE, from where it's possible to track back inland to Ocucaje on the Pan American Highway between Ica and Nazca. There's usually enough traffic to hitch a ride.

Tambo Colorado

Some 48km inland from Pisco, the Inca ruins of **TAMBO COLORADO** are easily enough reached: the road to HUANCAVELICA (see p.70) runs straight through the site, and you can take the *Oropesa* bus, which leaves from Jirón Comercio at 10am each morning. The ruins are around twenty minutes beyond the village of HUMAY.

Originally a fortified administrative center, Tambo Colorado was probably built by the Chincha before its adaptation and use as an Inca coastal outpost. Its position at the base of steep foothills in the Río Pisco valley was perfect for controlling the flow of people and produce along the ancient road down from the Andes. You can still see dwellings, offices, storehouses, and row upon row of barracks and outer walls, some of them retaining traces of colored paints. The rains have taken their toll, but even so this is considered one of the best preserved adobe ruins in Peru—roofless, but otherwise virtually intact. Though in an odd way reminiscent of a fort from some low-budget Western, it is nonetheless a classic example of a preplanned adobe complex, everything in its place and nothing out of order—autocratic by intention, oppressive in function, and rather stiff in style.

South from Pisco Towards the Ica Oasis

South from Pisco, the Pan American Highway sweeps some 70km inland to reach the fertile wine-producing Ica Valley, a virtual oasis in this stretch of bleak desert. **POZO SANTO**, the only real landmark en route, is distinguished by a small towered and whitewashed chapel, built on the site of an underground well. Legend has it that when *Padre Guatemala*, the friar Ramon Rojas, died on this spot, water miraculously began to flow from the sands. Now there's a restaurant here where *colectivo* drivers sometimes stop for a snack, though little else.

Beyond, the road crosses the *Pampa de Villacuri*. An hour's hike to the north, along a track which starts at the km 280 marker, are the ruins of an adobe **fortress** complex, where you can see dwellings, a plaza, a 40m-long outer wall, and ancient manmade wells—still used by local peasants to irrigate their cornfields. Seashells and brightly colored plumes from the tropical forest found in the graves here suggest that there was an important trade link between the ancients on this southern coast and the tribes from the eastern jungles on the other side of the formidable Andean mountain range.

Farther down the Pan American Highway, the pretty roadside village of GUADALUPE (km 293) signals the beginning of the Ica oasis. To the right there's a large, dark, conical-shaped hill, *Cerro Prieto*, behind which, in amongst the shifting sand dunes, there are even more **ruins**, these dating from 500 B.C. Just a few kilometers on, beyond a string of wine *bodegas* and shanty-town suburbs, you reach the center of Ica itself.

Ica

An attractive old city, **ICA** is famous throughout Peru for its wine and *pisco* production. Its very foundation (in 1563) went hand in hand with the introduction of grapevines to South America, and for most Peruvian visitors it is the *bodegas* or wineries that are the town's biggest draw. For foreign travelers they're likely to be at least equalled by the **Museo Regional**, whose superb collections of pre-Colombian ceramics and Paracas, Ica, and Nazca culture artifacts would alone make Ica worth an excursion.

Sleeping, Eating, and Drinking

There are plenty of **hotels** in Ica, though they can fill up over fiesta weekends. Even so it's usually possible to find some kind of room here, or alternatively at nearby **Huacachina** (see below). In Ica the *Hotel Colon* on the main Plaza de Armas is one of the best—if not quite as comfortable as it should be—for the price (about $2 single); its restaurant, looking out onto the plaza, offers cheap and varied set meals. The less pricey *Hostal del Valle* (San Marin 159—around the corner from Iglesia San Francisco) is a quiet place with a pretty courtyard, a garden-aviary, and its own basic restaurant. More upscale is the *Hotel de Turistas* (Avenida Los Maestros: ☎233320) with a swimming pool, on the way to Huacachina, or the *Hotel Las Dunas* (at km 300 as you enter Ica from Lima; ☎231031).

Not surprisingly, Ica **wines** are very much a part of the town's life and it's quite customary here for passersby to pop into a *bodega* and knock back a quick glass of neat *pisco* before carrying on about their daily business. Probably the best places to do likewise are *La Vina* on the Plaza de Armas, or a cheaper shop on the left half a block along Calle Lima from the square. Another place where you can sometimes get a drink, and meriting a visit anyway by virtue of the fascinating *artesanía* that it sells, is the *Feria de Pinchos* on Av. Municipalidad 344.

Among **restaurants** my own favorite is the *Mogambo* (just off the plaza, up Tacna) where they dish up an exquisite *aji de gallina* and sometimes the local specialty, *la carapulchra*. The Mogambo has a strong Iqueñan atmosphere and frequently adds spice to appetite by blasting out invigorating salsa music while you eat. On Sunday lunchtime it's also worth checking out the restaurant in the *Hotel de Turistas* near the stadium, en route to Huacachina, where they offer an amazing "all you can eat" spread for a few dollars per person. Or at any time you can get fresh *empanadas* from the bakery on the Plaza de Armas—ideal for a snack or light lunch.

Some Practical Details

Free maps of Ica and the region are usually available at the **tourist information office**, near the main square (Jiron Cajamarca 179; **☎**2173). The **post office** is on Calle Callao, two blocks north of the plaza beside the *Hotel Colon*, and there's a **Casa de Cambio** (9am–6pm daily) on Av. Municipalidad 263, less than a block from the square, much faster than the **Banco de La Nacion**, which is opposite the tall, mushroom-shaped tower on Avenida Matias Manzanilla, some eight blocks west of the plaza towards the Picasso Stadium and *Hotel de Turistas*.

Colectivos for Lima, Pisco, and Nazca leave from the Plaza de Armas all day long. **Buses** to Lima, Nazca, Arequipa, and Cuzco also run at least daily, operated by four diferent companies—*Ormeño* (the best, on Lambayeque, three blocks from the plaza), *Roggero*, *Morales*, and *Tepsa*.

Fiestas

There are several important **fiestas** during the Ica year. Probably the most enjoyable period is in March, after the grape harvest has been brought in, when there are open-air concerts, fairs, artisan markets, cockfighting, and *caballo de paso* meetings. Over the *Semana de Ica* (mid-June, climaxing on the 17th) there are more festivities, and again in September for the *Semana Turistica*. As in Lima, October is the main month for religious ceremonies and public processions.

The Town

Ica's colonial heart—the inevitable **Plaza de Armas**—remains its modern center, adapted with the intrusion of an obelisk and fountains. Within a few blocks are most of the important churches, rarely of great architectural merit but considerably revered within the region. The **cathedral**, just off the plaza, contains Padre Guatemala's tomb—said to give immense good fortune if touched on New Year's Day. On the main street around the corner, Calle Municipalidad, is the perhaps grander **San Francisco**, whose stained-glass windows dazzle against the strong Ican sunlight; to the south of the plaza (down Calle Lima, then left along Ayabaca) is a third major church, **El Sanctuario de Luren**. This, housing the *Imagen del Señor*, patron saint of the town, is something of a national shrine, and the center of pilgrimage on the third Sundays of March and October.

The Museo Regional

The **Museo Regional** (Mon.–Sat. 8am–6pm, Sun. 8am–noon), one of the best archeological museums in Peru, is a little way out from the center on the Prolongación Ayabaca. To get there take bus #17 from the plaza, or walk six blocks down Avenida San Martin from the church to San Franciso, then another six blocks right along Ayabaca; either way you can't miss the concrete museum building stuck out on its own in the middle of barren desert parkland.

Certainly the most striking and possibly the most important of the museum's collections is its display of **Paracas textiles**, the majority of them discovered at Cerro Colorado in the Paracas Peninsula by Julio Tello in 1927. Enigmatic in their apparent coding of colors and patterns, these funeral cloths (exhibit 217 is an outstanding example) consist of blank rectangles alternating with elaborately woven ones—repetitious and identical except in their multidirectional shifts of color and position.

The textiles are displayed in the first room to the right off the main lobby, which has a fairly gruesome display of **mummies**, **trepanned skulls**, **grave artifacts**, and **trophy heads**. It seems very likely that the taking of trophy heads in this region was related to specific religious beliefs—as it was until quite recently among the head-hunting Jivaro of the Amazon Basin. The earliest of these skulls, presumably hunted and collected by the victor in battle, come from the Asia Valley (north of Ica) and date from around 2000 B.C.

The museum's main room is almost entirely devoted to pre-Columbian **ceramics**, possibly the finest collection outside of Lima. On the left as you enter are spectacular Paracas urns—one particularly outstanding with an owl and serpent design painted on one side, a human face with arms, legs, and a navel on the other. There is some exquisite Nazca pottery, too, undoubtedly the most colorful and abstractly imaginative designs found on any ancient Peruvian ceramics. The last wall is devoted mainly to artifacts from the Ica-Chincha culture, which seems to have been specifically marked by a decline in importance of the feline god, and in a move towards urbanization. My favorite piece is the beautiful **feather cape**, its multicolored plumes in almost perfect condition.

Displayed also in the main room are several **quipus**, ancient calculators using bundles of knotted strings as mnemonic devices. According to the historian Alden Mason these numerical records followed a decimal system very much like our own—a simple knot representing "one," digits from two to nine denoted by longer knots in which the cord was wound or looped a given number of times before it was pulled tight. The concept of zero was apparently understood and shown by the absence of any knot in the expected position while place value is indicated by any particular knot's distance from the main cord. Census records of population and produce were of considerable importance to the Inca Empire, leading to the development of a *quipu-mayoc*—an elite group of accountants. *Quipu*s were also mnemonic aids for the recitation of ancient legends, genealogies, and ballads. They have survived better here on the coast than in the mountains and the Ica collection is one of the best in the country.

Other Museums, and Winery Tours

To see another, smaller archeological museum, the **Museo de Prospero Belli**, you'll need to make an appointment (☎ Campo 2293), and if you've still got enough energy and enthusiasm there's a rather bizarre and controversial third museum back on the Plaza de Armas. This, the **Museo de Piedra** (Bolivar 174, daily 9am–1pm and 4–9pm; $5, including a guided tour), consists of Javier Cabrera's private collection of engraved stones—which, so he claims, are several thousand years old. Despite his being a well-respected member of the community—and a descendant of Ica's heroic founder—few share his belief. Some of the stones depict patently modern surgical techniques and, perhaps more critically, you can watch artisans turning out remarkably similar designs over on the *pampa* at Nazca. Nevertheless, the stones are remarkable pieces of art and an enthusiastic local guidebook claims that "dinosaur hunts are portrayed, suggesting that Ica may have supported the first culture on earth"!

The best way imaginable of escaping Ica's hot desert afternoons, however, is to wander about the cool chambers and vaults, and sample the wines, at one or other of the town's **bodegas** or wineries. The most accessible—and very good too—is *Vista Allegre* (daily 9am–5pm; ☎23-1432). It's easily reached by walking down Avenida Grau from the main plaza, crossing over the Río Ica bridge, then turning left. Follow this road for about twenty minutes until you come to a huge yellow colonial gateway on your right (or take the orange microbus from town—#8); the arch leads via an avenue of tall eucalyptus trees to the *bodega* itself, an old *hacienda* still chugging happily along in a forgotten world of its own. There's usually a guide who'll show you around free of charge, then arrange for a wine and *pisco* tasting session at the shop. You don't have to buy anything, but you're quietly expected to tip.

If you follow the road up beyond Vista Allegre for another 6km you'll come to **Bodega Tacama**, a larger and slightly more important wine producer with the same basic procedure regarding guided tour and opening times. An interesting aspect of Tacama is that their vineyards are still irrigated by the **Achirana** canal, which was built by the Inca Pachacutec (or his brother Capac Yupanqui) as a gift to Princess Tate, daughter of a subjugated local chieftain. According to Inca legend it took 40,000 men only ten days to complete this astonishing canal which brings cold pure water down from some 4000m in the Andes to transform what was once an arid desert into a startlingly fertile oasis. Clearly a romantic at heart, Pachacutec is supposed to have personally named it *Achirana*—"that which flows cleanly toward that which is beautiful."

Huacachina

During the late 1940s, **HUACACHINA**, only 5 or 6km outside Ica, was one of Peru's most elegant and exclusive resorts—a lagoon with a delightfully old-world atmosphere surrounded by palm trees, sand dunes, and waters long famous for their curative powers. Since then the lagoon's subterranean source has grown erratic and its waters are perhaps less inviting—at best they are a murky green, and when really low can become a positively thick, viscous syrup—red in color and apparently radioactive. However, though visitors these days are few, it's a place that retains considerable mystique, and is a delightfully quiet, secluded spot if you want to rest up. On my last visit freak weather conditions had actually raised the level of the waters and people were bathing again to test its powers.

There are two long-established **hotels**. The most stylish, the *Mossone*, was once the haunt of politicians and diplomats, entertained by concerts on the colonial-style veranda overlooking the lagoon; rooms here go for around $7 single and $11 double. Alongside is the *Salvatierra*, cheaper at only $4 for a single room with shower, but becoming a little decrepit. In the last (or first) resort it's also possible to **camp** in the sand dunes around the lagoon—very rarely is it cold enough to need more than a blanket and you may even get cured in the bargain.

To get to Huacachina, jump on the **red bus** in Ica, either from its starting point outside the *Sanctuario de Luren* or as it passes through the Plaza de Armas; the bus runs about every fifteen minutes.

The Nazca Lines

One of the great mysteries of Peru, indeed of South America, the **Nazca Lines** are a series of animal figures and geometric shapes, none of them repeated and some up to 200m in length, drawn across some 500 square kilometers of the bleak, stony *Pampa de San José*. Each one, even such sophisticated motifs as a spider monkey or a hummingbird, is executed in a single continuous line, most often created by clearing away the brush and hard stones of the plain to reveal the fine dust beneath. They were likely a kind of agricultural calendar to help regulate the planting and harvesting of crops, while perhaps at the same time some of the straight lines served as ancient sacred paths connecting *huacas*, or power spots. One theory proposes that the Lines were used as running tracks in some sort of sporting competition; whichever theory you end up favoring, they are among the strangest and most unforgetable sights in the country.

Getting to the Lines

South from Ica, the Pan American Highway cuts across the *Pampa de San José*, quickly leaving the oasis fields behind through a long stretch of bleak wilderness. Amidst this the one settlement breaking out from the barren life is OCUJAJE, a former *hacienda* and another of Peru's finest wine and *pisco* producers. Shortly afterwards you pass the village of SANTA CRUZ, where a bad track leads up into the hills to reach **TIBILLO** (68km), a small place surrounded by minor sites from the Nazca culture. At 2000m, it was apparently the highest region these people lived in. If you make it up here there's good scope for **camping**, but it's fairly isolated and you'll need to take most of your own food and water.

The Lines begin on the tableland above PALPA, where there's a small *hostal* amid the orange groves. You probably won't want to stay here, however, since it's another 20km until you can actually see them. This, to be exact, happens at km 420, where a tall metal-framed **mirador** has been built above the plain. Unless you plan to go on a flight above the Lines from Nazca, or unless you've got the time to climb up onto one of the hills behind, it's the nearest and best view you'll get. Buses will let you off here, but they won't hang around, so if you're stopping en route you may have to hitch the remaining 20km to the town of Nazca. Alternatively, you can come back out by taxi.

If you've got the cash, three companies in Nazca will take you on **flights** over the Lines—they cost from $30 to $45 a person, and last from ten minutes to an hour so ask around before deciding. Also, it's worth knowing that the planes are small and bounce around in the changeable air currents, making many passengers airsick. The main private companies are *Aeroica* (Tacna 476, off the Plaza de Armas; ☎64) and *Aerocondor* (office at the airport; ☎134); or you can take the new plane run by the *Hotel Montecarlo*—whose English-speaking pilot has some interesting tales to tell and has probably photographed the Lines more than anyone else. Getting a seat is no problem, but it's best to book an early morning trip since the air gets hazier as the sun rises higher. The Nazca airport is about 3km down the main road south of town. *Aerocondor* also offer round-trip flights over the Lines from Pisco ($100) and Lima ($150).

Some Theories

The greatest expert on the Lines is undoubtedly **Maria Reiche**, who has worked at Nazca almost continuously since 1946, and who believes that the Lines and cleared areas were a sort of astronomical calendar, linked to the rising and setting points of celestial bodies on the east and west horizons. She considers these to be the most important features; next the animals and lastly the spirals. The whole complex, according to her theories, is designed to help organize planting and harvesting around the seasonal changes rather than the fickle shifts of weather. In most developed Central and South American cultures there was a strong emphasis on knowledge of the heavens, and in a desert area like Nazca, where the coastal fog never reaches up to obscure the night sky *pampa*, this must have been highly advanced.

In the late 1960s an American, **Gerald Hawkins**, computed that two mounds on the *pampa* were aligned with the Pleiades constellation in the era between A.D. 600 and 700—during the Nazca period. The Incas revered the Pleiades, calling them *Quolqua* (or granary) because they believed them to watch over and protect the seeds during germination. This kind of information, if it wasn't already common knowledge in ancient Peru, might have been adopted by the Incas from the Nazca culture when it was drawn into their empire in the fifteenth century. Hawkin's computers also suggested, however, that the occasional alignments of the Lines with the sun, moon, and stars are barely frequent enough to raise themselves above the level of chance.

In many cases the Lines connect with low hills on the plain or the foothills of the Andes along its edge. Fragments of Nazca pottery found around these hills suggest that they may have been sacred sites, perhaps as important in terms of ritual as the celestial movements. Recent theories regarding the Lines take this as evidence that at least some of them were *ceques*, or sacred pathways, between *huacas*. In Inca Cuzco, *ceques* radiated from the Sun Temple, Koricancha, to surrounding *huacas*, many of these being hills on the distant horizon. Each of the *ceques* was under the protection of a particular *allyu* or kinship group. This theory is all the more feasible since if the Lines were purely for astronomical observations they wouldn't need to be so long.

Tony Morrisson, one of the proponents of this idea, discovered many similar *ceques* in the mountains between Cuzco and La Paz. They were related to *huacas* and still "owned" by specific local kinship groups. Morrisson concludes that the various stone piles often found at the end of lines at Nazca were ancient *huacas*, and the lines are paths between these sacred places. They were in a straight line, he says, simply because this is the shortest distance between any two *huacas*. It follows that the cleared areas were ceremonial sites for larger *allyu* gatherings. The animal figures might be explained by them pre-dating the straight lines; this would fit into the early and late pottery phases (the former being most closely associated with animalistic motifs).

Maria Reiche's theory isn't necessarily contradictory. Many other alignments were confirmed by Hawkins's computer (particularly those for the solar solstices and the Pleiades) and even if the Lines and animal designs were made at different times, there's still a connection: designs like the spider and the monkey might be representations of the constellations of Orion and Ursa Major. It's difficult for a Western mind to visualize the constellations except through the stereotyped images we've grown accustomed to. The Nazca people, on the other hand, were free to impose their own ideas and there are remarkable similarities between the motifs they drew on the *pampa* and some of the major constellations.

On a slightly less esoteric level it's interesting to note how many of the extended lines are amazingly straight. One theory claims that they were made using three cane poles and a rope, in much the same manner as a surveyor uses ranging sticks and a theodolite; when Maria Reiche first came to Nazca some of the locals could indeed remember wooden poles at the end of certain lines—perhaps sighting posts for the stars. How long it took to construct them is a last, inevitable question—and since none of them can be properly seen from the ground it is tempting to believe they must have been the skilled product of numerous generations. In strictly physical terms this isn't necessarily so. A few years back a local school tried building its own line and from its efforts calculated that a thousand patient and inspired workers could have made them all in less than a month!

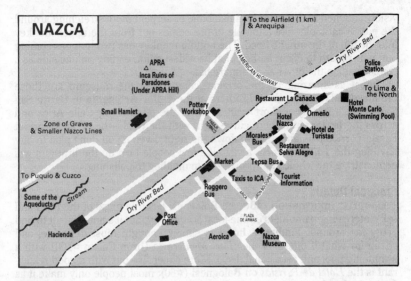

Nazca

Some 20km south of the mirador overlooking the Lines, the colonial town of **NAZCA** spreads along the margin of a small coastal valley. Although the river is invariably dry, Nazca's valley remains green and fertile through the continued application of an Incaic subterranean aqueduct. It's a small town— slightly at odds with its appearance on the maps—but an interesting and enjoyable place to stay. There are adobe ruins only a couple of kilometers outside, an excellent local museum, and two important Nazca culture archeological sites within an easy day's range.

Getting There

Roughly halfway between Lima and Arequipa, Nazca is easily reached by frequent **bus** (*Tepsa* or *Ormeño*), *colectivo* , or even small **plane** (from Lima *Aerocondor*, Hotel Sheraton Mall, Lima; ☎32-9050). It is possible not to notice the Nazca stop if the bus is going on to Arequipa and not pulling into town— ask the driver to tell you when to get off.

The Town

As you come into town, **Bolognesi**, the main street, leads straight into the **Plaza de Armas**. In the most impressive building here, its steps beautifully tiled with Nazca-style ceramic bird designs, you'll find the *Municipalidad* and the **Archeological Museum** (daily 10pm–noon and 2–6pm). The exhibits, crowded into one small room, include Nazca pottery, lengths of hair up to 2m long found in the graveyards, and large maps showing the layout of the Nazca Lines. One magnificent bulb-shaped pot, about half a meter tall, is stood upside down to display two beautifully stylized monkeys. Each one is visibly attached to the other by a fish-bone or serpent motif stretching around the pot. What looks like a tongue of fire comes out from the upper monkey into the top of the other's head. The bottom monkey has two tongues coming out of its mouth to encircle the pot at its widest point, ending on one side as a condor and on the other as a vampire bat.

Almost as amazing as the original ceramics in the museum are those produced today by a pair of brothers at the **Taller Artesania** in Barrio San Carlos. This is only a short walk south of the plaza along Calle Arica and across the bridge; from here curve right with the road—the ceramics are at Pasaje Torrico 240, about 200m down the right. Even if you don't plan to buy anything the *Taller* is worth a visit; if a few people turn up the brothers will demonstrate the whole craft process from molding to polishing.

Practical Details

The **tourist information office** on Bolognesi has free maps of the town and sells interesting pamphlets on the local archeology, but it's not difficult to find your way around. Finding a **hotel** is simple enough: most desirable, and cheap for what if offers, is the *Hotel Montecarlo* (Jirón Calao; ☎100) with a swimming pool and occasional disco. More expensive but with a good restaurant is the *Hotel de Turistas* on Bolognesi (☎60); most people only make it as far as the bar here to have a drink and to meet Maria Reiche who may still give nightly talks and slide shows about the Nazca Lines (she also sells her own book, *Mystery in the Desert*). Among the cheaper places is the *Hostal el Sol* on the Plaza de Armas and the popular *Hotel Nazca* (Jirón Lima 438; ☎85), run by a friendly woman who seems to have a finger in most pies (she exchanges dollars and has contacts with the taxi drivers for tours of the nearby archeological sites, especially the Nazca Lines, and also arranges $30 deals on flights). If you phone her or speak to her in person in the afternoon she can usually set things up for the following morning.

There are two really good **places to eat**: the ramshackle *Selva Allegre* (opposite the Hotel Nazca) and *La Cañada* (near the *Hotel Montecarlo*). At *Selva Allegre* you get good roast *cuy* (guinea pig), *La Cañada*, on the other hand, is a *criolla* place—laid back and tropical with loud salsa music and spicy seafood or the traditional *rocoto relleno*.

There are several **bus services** to Lima, Cuzco or Arequipa, once again operated by several companies: *Ormeño* (offices near the *Hotel Montecarlo*—the best), *Morales Moralitos* (near the Hotel Nazca), *Roggero*, and *Tepsa*. **Colectivos** for up or down the coast generally wait in Jirón Lima, not far from the *Hotel Nazca*.

Los Paradones, the Graveyard, and the Inca Canal

The most impressive **archeological sites** around Nazca are some distance out—dealt with in the following section and best reached with one of the taxi-guides. If you have an afternoon to spare, though, or just feel like a walk, there are a few interesting spots you could take in. The route covered below will take a leisurely three to four hours on foot—if you don't end up spending the day at the Cantay Cooperative's swimming pool half way along.

LOS PARADONES was an Inca trade center where wool from the mountains was exchanged for cotton grown along the coast; a modern road, following the same trail as the ancient route from Nazca to Cuzco, passes just below the ruins. Follow Calle Arica from the Plaza de Armas, cross the bridge, and keep going straight (off the main road which curves to the right). The ruins are about a kilometer directly ahead of you at the foot of the sandy valley mouth, underneath a political slogan—APRA—etched into the hillside.

The buildings, made from adobe with stone foundations, are in a bad state of repair and the site dotted with *huaquero*'s pits, but if you follow the path to the prominent central sector you can get a good idea of what the town must have been like. Overlooking the valley and roads, it's in a commanding position—a fact recognized and utilized by local cultures long before the Incas arrived.

Another 2km up the Puquio road from Los Paradones there's a **Nazca graveyard**, its pits open and burial remains spread around. Though much less extensive than the cemetery at Chauchilla (see the following sections), it is still of interest—with subterranean galleries to explore if you can find them.

Across the valley from here is the former *hacienda* of **Cantay**, now a model cooperative. A short walk through the cotton fields and along a track will bring you to its central plaza and **swimming pool**—one of the previous owner's more luxurious hand-me-downs. Just a little farther up above the co-operative settlement, you can make out a series of inverted conical dips, like swallow-holes in the fields. These are the air vents for a vast underground canal system which siphons desperately needed water from the Bisambra reservoir; designed and constructed by the Incas, it is possibly even more essential today. If you want, you can get right down into the openings and poke your head or feet into the canals—they usually give off a pleasant warm breeze, and you can see small fishes swimming in the flowing water. The canals are well built of cut stones, usually about 90cm by 60cm, just large enough for a person to climb in when they need cleaning or fixing; they run underground in a gentle zigzag fashion, slowing down the flow and avoiding rapid silting.

Archeological Sites Around Nazca

Chauchilla and **Cahuachi**, after the Lines the most important sites associated with the Nazca culture, are both difficult to reach by public transportation, and unless your energy and interest are pretty unlimited you'll want to arrange for a **local guide**-cum-taxi driver to show you around. This is easily enough done in Nazca, since they generally advertise themselves by loud, tuneful horn-honking. If you need to search one out ask Sra. Fernandez, who runs the Hotel *Nazca*, or look up María Raúl Pino Etchebarne (Jirón Los Espinales 101, Nazca)—he's a good driver and a reliable guide to the Lines, Chauchilla cemetery, Cahuachi, or the nearer (walkable) ruins detailed above.

Chauchilla Cemetery

Roughly 30km south of Nazca along the Pan American Highway, then out along a dirt road beside the Poroma riverbed, **CHAUCHILLA CEMETERY** is a place that takes a definite commitment to visit. It's well worth the effort, though, because once you reach the atmospheric site you realize how considerable a civilization the riverbanks must have maintained in the time of Nazca culture. Scattered about the dusty ground are literally thousands of graves (most of which have been opened, leaving the skulls and skeletons exposed to the sun), along with broken pieces of pottery, bits of shroud fabric, and lengths of braided hair, strangely unbleached by the desert sun. Farther up the track, near Trancus, there's a small ceremonial **temple**—*Huaca del Loreto*; and beyond this at Los Incas you can find Quemazon **petroglyphs**. The guide will want more than the standard $5 a person fare to take you to these last two, but if you bargain with him when you get to Chauchilla he may prove willing.

Cahuachi

The ancient center of Nazca culture, **CAHUACHI** lies to the west of the Nazca Lines, only 17km from modern Nazca, but a good four-hour round trip ($7 a person by taxi).

The site consists of a religious citadel split in half by the river with its main temple (one in a set of six) constructed around a small natural hillock. Adobe platforms step the sides of this 20m mound and although they're badly weathered today, you can still make out the general form. Attached to each of the six pyramids a separate courtyard can be distinguished—but exactly what their use was we'll probably never know.

Quite close to the main complex is a weird temple construction known as *El Estaqueria*, "the Place of the Stakes," and still retaining a dozen rows of *huarango* log pillars. *Huarango* trees (known in the north of Peru as *algarrobo*) are the most common form of desert vegetation. Their wood, baked by the sun, is as hard as any, though their numbers have been much reduced by locals who use them for fuel.

Cahuachi is typical of Nazca ceremonial centers in its exploitation of natural features to form an integral part of the structures. The places where they lived showed no such architectural aspirations—indeed there are no major towns associated with the Nazcas, who tended to live in small clusters of adobe huts, villages at best. One of the largest of these, the walled village of **Tambo de Perro**, is to be found in Acari, the next dry valley. Stretching for over a mile, and situated next to an extensive Nazca graveyard, it was apparently one of their most important dwelling sites.

Until 1901, when Max Uhle "discovered" the Nazca culture, a group of beautiful **ceramics** had been hanging around in Peru's museums unidentified and unclassifiable. With Uhle's work all that changed rapidly (though not quickly enough to prevent most of the sites being ransacked by *huaqueros* before proper excavations could be undertaken) and the importance of Nazca pottery came to be understood. Many of the best pieces were found here in Cahuachi.

Unlike contemporaneous *Mochica* ware, Nazca ceramics rarely attempt any realistic reproduction of images. The majority—painted in three or four earthy colors, then given a resinous surface glaze—are relatively stylized or even completely abstract. Nevertheless, two main categories of subject matter recur: naturalistic designs of bird, animal, and plant life, and motifs of mythological monsters and bizarre deities. In later works it became common to mold effigies onto the pots, and in Nazca's declining phases, under *Huari-Tihuanuco* cultural influence, workmanship, and design became less inspired.

The style and content of the early pottery phases, however, shows remarkable similarities to the symbols depicted in the Nazca Lines, and although not enough is known about this culture to be certain, it seems reasonable to assume that the early Nazca people were also responsible for those mysterious drawings on the Pampa de San José. With most of the evidence coming from their graveyards, though, and that so dependent upon conjecture, there is little to characterize the Nazca and little known of them beyond the fact that they collected heads as trophies, that they built a ceremonial complex here in the desert at Cahuachi, and that they scraped a living from the Nazca, Ica, and Pisco valleys from around A.D. 200 to 600.

The Hills Above Nazca: The Pampa Galeras Vicuña Reserve and Lake Parinacochas

Just inland from Nazca, the **PAMPA GALERAS** is one of the best and most easily accessible places in Peru to see the **vicuña**, the finest-woolled member of the cameloid family. Here, in a reserve where they have lived for centuries and which is now maintained as their natural habitat, there are over 5000 of the creatures.

Well signposted at km 89 of the Nazca-Cuzco road, the reserve is easily reached by hopping off one of the many buses that run past. If you want to stay indoors at the *Park Camp* it's advisable to have obtained written permission in advance, from the Ministry of Agriculture and Fauna in Lima, as they have few beds; if you're happy to **camp** you'll probably be allowed in without a permit.

The **vicuña** themselves are not easy to spot. When you do see a herd, if you catch its attention you'll see it move as if it were actually one organism. They flock together and move swiftly in a tight wave, bounding gracefully across the hills. The males are strictly territorial, protecting their patches of scrubby grass by day, then returning to the rockier heights as darkness falls.

Puquio and Lake Parinacochas

Going on another 55km from the reserve you reach **PUQUIO**. As soon as you cross over the metal bridge at the entrance to the town, you'll sense that it's very different from the hot desert town of Nazca. Puquio was an isolated community until 1926 when the townspeople built their own road link between the coast and the sierra. There are three *hostals* in the town, none of them particularly enticing; however, this is a potential journey breaker and a good place to stock up or have a hot meal.

The road divides at Puquio with the main route continuing over the Andes to CUZCO (see p.78) via ABANCAY; a side road goes south along the mountains about 140km to LAGO PARINACOCHAS—**Lake of Flamingoes**. Although frequently destroyed by mudslides in the rainy season, this road always seems full of passing trucks which will usually take passengers for a small price.

Fifty kilometers before you get to Parinacochas, the road passes the small provincial capital, **CORACORA**, a remote town with only one hotel. Around the plaza there are some reasonable restaurants but there's little here to interest most travelers. Far better to continue the 16km to **CHUMPI**, an ideal place to camp amid stunning sierra scenery. Nearby are the thermal waters of **Bella Vista**; and the amazingly beautiful lake of **Parinacochas**, named for the many flamingoes who call it home and probably one of the best unofficial nature reserves in Peru, is within a few hours' walk.

From Chumpi you can either backtrack to PUQUIO and then go on to CUZCO or NAZCA, or continue down the road, passing the lake before curving down another 130km back down to the coast at CHALA.

South to Arequipa—The Pan American Highway

There's very little in the 170km of desert between NAZCA and CHALA, and what there is can be avoided without regret—PUERTO SAN JUAN, the one place of any size, is a modern industrial port for the local iron-ore and copper mines.

The first break in this stark area, known for its winds and sandstorms, are the olive groves of the Yauca valley as you approach Chala. Just beyond this, at km 595, is a strange uplifted zone, a natural moisture-gathering oasis in the desert with its own microclimate stretching for about 20km. It's a weird but fascinating place to spend some time **camping** and exploring; there are Inca and pre-Inca ruins hidden in the *lomas*, but today the area is virtually uninhabited.

CHALA, the main port for CUZCO until the building of the Cuzco-Arequipa railroad, is now an agreeable little fishing town. If you want to stay over awhile there's a two-star **hotel**, a couple more rather basic ones, and as much fresh **seafood** as you could want.

Continuing toward AREQUIPA the road keeps close to the coast wherever physically possible, passing through a few small fishing villages and over monotonous arid plains before eventually turning inland for the final uphill stretch into the land of volcanoes and Peru's second largest city. At km 916 a road leads off into the Maches canyon towards the Toro Muerto **petroglyphs** and the Valley of the Volcanoes (see p.153)—a good place to hitch inland from, but a very remote spot.

AREQUIPA AND AROUND

It's not certain—but it seems probable—that the name **Arequipa** is derived from the Quechua phrase "*Are quepay*," meaning "OK, let's stop here." Sited well above the coastal fog bank, at the foot of an ice-capped volcano—*El Misti*—the place has long been renowned for having one of the most pleasant settings and climates in Peru.

The Incas were not alone in finding Arequipa to their liking. When Pizarro officially "founded" the city in 1540 he was moved enough to call it *Villa Hermosa*, "Beautiful Town," and despite a disastrous earthquake in 1687 it's still endowed with some of the country's finest colonial **churches** and **mansions**, many of which are constructed from white volcanic *sillar*, cut from the surrounding mountains and often flecked with black ash. These buildings—particularly the **Monastery of Santa Catalina**, a majestic complex that encloses a complete world within its thick walls—constitute the city's main appeal to travelers, but the startlingly varied countryside **around Arequipa**, from the incredible gorge of **Colca Canyon** to the eerie isolation of the **Valley of the Volcanoes**, is definitely worth a look if you can spare a day or two.

Arequipa

An active city, with a population well over three-quarters of a million, **AREQUIPA** maintains a rather aloof attitude toward the rest of Peru. Most Arequipans feel themselves distinct, if not culturally superior, and resent the idea of the nation revolving around Lima. With **El Misti**, a 5821m dormant volcano poised above like a melting ice-cream cone, the place *does* have a rather legendary sort of appearance.

But besides its widespread image as the country's most attractive big city, Arequipa has some very specific historical connotations for Peruvians. Developing late as a provincial capital, and until 1870 connected only by mule track with the rest of Peru, it has acquired a reputation as *the* center of **right-wing political power**: while populist movements have tended to emerge around Trujillo in the north, Arequipa has traditionally represented the solid interests of the oligarchy. Sanchez Cerro and Odria both began their coups here, in 1930 and 1948 respectively, and Belaunde himself sprung into *politicas* from one of the wealthy Arequipa families. In recent years, at least among the local students, things seem to be changing—in 1983 demonstrations against police harassment brought the city to a standstill.

Practical Details: Hotels, Restaurants, and Nightlife

Finding a **place to stay** in Arequipa is rarely a problem and there's a fairly clear range from which to choose. The *Pensión Guzman* (Calle Jerusalen 408; ☎23-7142) is very reasonably priced with shared rooms set around an attractive sunny colonial courtyard; there's often hot water, and the staff will do your washing quite cheaply, and will even buy your train tickets for you. A slightly cheaper place, friendly but nothing very special, is the *Hotel Mercaderes,* just off the plaza. The *Hostal Tradicional* (on Bolivar between San Augustin and Bolognesi, within a block of the Plaza de Armas) is very inexpensive for such a central location. One of the most popular places these days, and excellent value from around $6 double—including breakfast in bed if you want—is the hotel *La Casa de Mi Abuela* (Jerusalen 606; ☎22-3194). The *Hotel de Turistas* (Plaza Bolivar, Selva Alegre; ☎21-5110) has a swimming pool and a beautiful setting on the spur above the Barrio San Lazaro, surrounded by the eucalyptus trees of Selva Alegre park where young couples and families take a stroll in the afternoons and on Sundays; not surprisingly, it's a little on the expensive side.

There are all sorts of **restaurants** dotted about the town supplying a wide variety of foods, but Arequipa is particularly famous for a dish called *ocopa*, a cold appetizer made with potatoes, eggs, olives, and a spicy (not *too* spicy) yellow chili sauce. For this or other traditional dishes try *Bonanza* on block one of Jerusalen (open until late), or the *picantería Sol de Mayo* (Jerusalen 107, Yanahuara, off Avenida Ejercito, about 15 minutes stroll from the plaza). More central is the slightly crummy, very small *La Esquina* (corner of block two of San Juan Dios) and, on Calle San Franciso, *Manolo's* is *the* place for snacking and meeting friends. *La Vie Claire* (Pasaje la Catedral 113) is central and strictly **vegetarian**, as is *Govinda*, on block four of Jerusalen. For quiet snacks, and space to write letters, try the *Salon de Té* on Jerusalen block three, and for excellent Italian food in the evenings head for *La Pizza Nostra* (Portal de San Augustin) on the Plaza de Armas. *Restaurant La Monza* on Santa Domino is recommended for local dishes. For **drinking** try *La Nueva Taberna* (San Juan de Dios 204).

A strong tradition of folk singing and poetry is reflected in several *peñas* that are the focus of Arequipan **nightlife**. *El Rome* (opposite the Plazuela de San Francisco) starts around 8pm and warms up a few hours later with good food and music (liveliest on weekends); another with a good atmosphere and strong *pisco sours* is opposite Santa Catalina in Calle Santa Catalina. For less traditional stuff there's also the town disco,*Carnaby Club*, on block one of Jerusalen.

The City: Churches, Mansions, and Museums

Among the huge number of religious buildings spread about the old colonial center of Arequipa there is one, the **Monastery of Santa Catalina**, of outstanding beauty and interest. The finest and most prestigious establishment in Peru, it is covered individually in a separate section following this town account. Within a few blocks of the Plaza de Armas, though, there are half a dozen churches well deserving a brief visit, and a couple of superb old mansions.

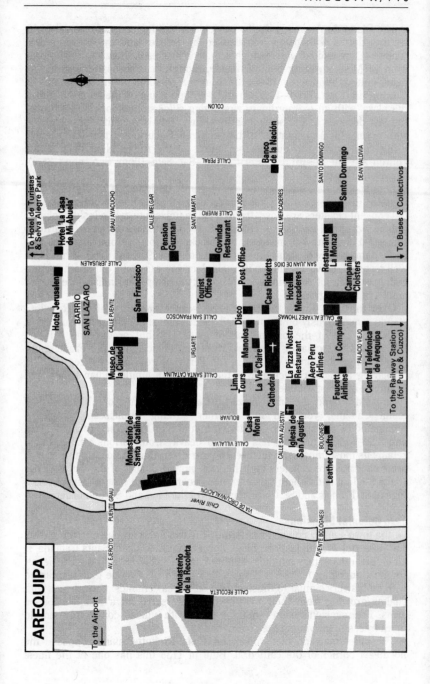

AREQUIPA

To the Airport

Monasterio de la Recoleta

CALLE RECOLETA

AV. EJERCITO

PUENTE GRAU

Chili River

VIA DE CIRCUNVALACION

PUENTE BOLOGNESI

Monasterio de Santa Catalina

Museo de la Ciudad

CALLE PUENTE

BARRIO SAN LAZARO

Hotel Jerusalen

San Francisco

CALLE JERUSALEN

GRAU AYACUCHO

CALLE MELGAR

SANTA MARTA

Hotel 'La Casa de Mi Abuela'

To Hotel de Turistas & Selva Alegre Park

Pension Guzman

Govinda Restaurant

CALLE RIVERO

CALLE SAN JOSE

CALLE MERCADERES

COLON

CALLE PERAL

Banco de la Nación

SANTO DOMINGO

DEAN VALDIVIA

Santo Domingo

To Buses & Collectivos

Restaurant La Monza

Compañia Cloisters

Hotel Mercaderes

SAN JUAN DE DIOS

Casa Ricketts

Post Office

Tourist Office

CALLE SAN FRANCISCO

Disco

URGARTE

CALLE SANTA CATALINA

Cathedral

Manolos

La Vie Claire

Lima Tours

La Pizza Nostra Restaurant

CALLE ALVAREZ THOMAS

Aero Peru Airlines

La Compañia

PALACIO VIEJO

Central Telefonica de Arequipa

To the Railway Station (for Puno & Cuzco)

Faucett Airlines

BOLIVAR

Casa Moral

CALLE SAN AGUSTIN

Iglesia de San Agustin

CALLE VILLALVA

Leather Crafts

BOLOGNESI

The **Plaza de Armas** is itself a particularly striking array of colonial architecture, dotted with palms and flanked by arcades and by the **cathedral** (daily 6–11am and 5–7pm)—which actually manages to draw your sight away from El Misti towering behind. Inside, though, it is disappointing, having been gutted by fire in 1844. Much more exciting is the elaborate **La Compañía** (Mon.–Fri. 9–11:30am and 3–5:30pm), just off the opposite side of the plaza, with an extraordinary zigzagging *sillar* stone doorway. Built over the last decades of the seventeenth century, this is magnificently sculpted with a very local inspiration of baroque relief—curiously two-dimensional, using shadow only to outline the figures of the frieze. Next door to the church are fine **Jesuit Cloisters** (Mon.–Sat. 8am–10pm; Sun. noon–8pm), again superbly carved.

Less spectacular, but nonetheless elegantly designed, is the **Iglesia San Agustin** (daily 4–9pm) on Calle San Agustin, one block west of the plaza; its old convent cloisters are now attached to the university, while inside only the unique octagonal sacristy survived the 1868 earthquake. **Santa Domingo** (daily 7–11am and 3–6pm; free), two blocks east of La Compañía, was also badly damaged by quakes—but more recently, in 1958 and 1960. It has been well restored, however, and on its main door you can make out another interesting example of Arequipa's *mestizo* craftsmanship—an Indian face carved amid a bunch of grapes.

Over the Chili River, the large Franciscan **Monastery of La Recoleta** stands conspicuously on its own (daily 9am–1pm; small charge). Founded in 1648, not one of the original buildings is left, but around the Mission Cloisters is a fascinating **Amazon Museum**, dedicated to the Franciscans' long-running missionary activity in the Peruvian tropical forest regions and displaying artifacts collected over the years from jungle Indian tribes, and examples of forest wildlife.

Situated around the small plaza off Calle Melgar, just one block east of Santa Catalina, you can find another striking Franciscan complex—dominated by the sixteenth-century church of **San Francisco** (daily 6–11am and 3:30–7pm). This, too, has suffered heavily from various quakes but it retains its most impressive feature—a pure silver **altar**. Adjoining the church are rather austere cloisters and the very simple Chapel of the Third Order (daily 8–11am and 3–5pm), its entrance decorated with modest *mestizo* carvings of St. Francis and St. Clare, founders of the First and Second orders.

Two Colonial Mansions

Of the town's many colonial **mansions**, the two finest are open to the public. **La Casa del Moral**, just one block down from the walls of Santa Catalina, is an eighteenth-century building, restored and refurbished with period pieces. Its most engaging feature is a superbly worked *sillar* stone gateway carved with motifs very similar to those shown on Nazca ceramics: puma heads with snakes growing from their mouths curiously surround a Spanish coat-of-arms. The mansion's name—nothing to do with ethics—comes from an old mora tree, still thriving in the central patio.

The other mansion that's open, **La Casa Ricketts**, stands opposite the northeast corner of the cathedral. Built in 1738 this has one of the finest facades in Peru—much more intricate and harmonized than the Moral, if in its content (a Jesuit monogram) less inspired. Owned by the *Banco Continental*—banks are major arts patrons throughout Peru—it houses a small **museum** and art gallery (Mon.–Fri. 9am–3pm and 5–8pm).

Arequipa's Museums

The city museum, the **Museo de La Ciudad** (Mon.–Fri. 8:30am–1pm and 4–6:30pm), devotes itself principally to Arequipa's local heroes—army chiefs, revolutionary leaders, presidents, and poets (including the renowned Mariano Melgar); it's just above Santa Catalina on the Plazuela de San Francisco. More interesting to most tastes are the universities' **archeological museums**, located in the suburbs on either side of the city.

San Agustin is the largest, with good collections of everything from mummies and replicas of Chavin artwork to colonial paintings and furniture. Stuck out in the campus along Avenida Independencia (by the corner with Victor Morales) it's not very far from the road to Paucarpata and the exit route across the mountains to Puno and Cuzco; **opening hours** are officially 8:30am–12:30pm and 3–5pm but it's best to phone for an appointment (☎ Arequipa 29-719).

The other museum belongs to the Catholic University of Santa Maria (Mon.–Fri. 8am–noon) and concentrates on items from pre-Conquest cultures such as the Huari, Tiahuanuco, Chancay, and Inca. It is a little difficult to find: out across the Puente Bolivar (south of the Bolognesi), and amid the university buildings a few hundred meters to the right.

Barrio San Lazaro and the Suburbs

The oldest quarter of Arequipa—the first place where Spaniards settled in this valley—is the **Barrio San Lazaro**, an uncharacteristic zone of tiny, curving streets stretching around the hillside at the top end of Calle Jerusalen. If you feel like a walk, and some good views of *El Misti*, you can follow the streambed from here to Puente Grau—a superb vantage point. From here, a longer stroll takes you across to the west bank of the Chili, along Avenida Ejercito and out to suburbs of **Cayma** and **Yanahuara**, quite distinct villages until the railroad boom of the late nineteenth century, which brought peasant-migrants to Arequipa from as far away as Cuzco. Both are built up now, though they still command stunning views across the valley, above all from their **churches**; at Cayma's you can climb up to the rooftop (daily 9am–4pm), while Yanahuara's possesses the famous mirador from which all the postcard views of Arequipa seem to be captured.

Santa Catalina Monastery

Just two blocks north of the Plaza de Armas, the vast protective walls of **Santa Catalina Monastery** (daily 9am–6pm, last entrance at 4pm; $2) sheltered as many as five hundred nuns in seclusion until they were opened to the public in 1970. It's architecturally the most important and impressive religious building anywhere in Peru; it takes a good hour or two to wander around the enormous complex of rooms, cloisters, and tiny plazas—an altogether extraordinary and haunting microworld. Nuns still live here today, but they're restricted to the quarter bordered by Calles Bolivar and Zela, worshiping in the main chapel only outside of opening hours.

The most striking general feature of the monastery's architecture is its predominantly "Mudéjar" style, adapted by the Spanish from the Arabic Moors, but rarely found in their colonial buildings. The quality of the design is emphasized and beautifully harmonized by an incredible interplay between the strong sunlight, white stone, and brilliant colors—in the ceilings and in the deep blue sky above the maze of narrow interior streets. You notice this at once as you enter, filing left along the first corridor to a high vaulted room with a ceiling of opaque *Huamanga* stone imported from the Ayacucho valley. Beside here are the **locutorios**—little cells where on holy days the nuns could talk, unseen, to visitors.

The **Novices Cloisters**, beyond, are built in solid *sillar*-block columns, their antique wall paintings depicting the various qualities to which the devotees were expected to aspire. Off to the right, surrounding the **Orange Tree Cloister**, a series of paintings show the soul evolving from a state of sin through to the achievement of God's grace—perhaps not certain to aid spiritual enlightenment, but at least a constant reminder of the Holy Spirit's permanent existence. In one of the side rooms dead nuns were mourned, before being interred within the monastic confines.

Along **Calle Malaga** (beyond the doorway marked "M. Colores Llamosa") there's an interesting old mud-brick oven; opposite, in the **Sala Zurbaran** you can find original robes, Cuzceño paintings, and some fine crockery displaying luxurious scenes from the grandeur of early colonial days.

Calle Toledo, a long street brought to life with permanently flowering geraniums, connects the main dwelling areas with the *lavandería*, or communal washing sector. There are several rooms off here worth exploring, including small chapels, prayer rooms, and a kitchen. The **lavandería** itself, perhaps more than any other area, offers a captivating insight into what life must have been like for the closeted nuns—open to the skies and city sounds yet bounded by high walls.

If you're feeling a bit thirsty by this stage, there's a little **restaurant** just off to the left along the broad Calle Granada. Straight on is the **Plaza Socodobe**, a fountain courtyard to the side of which is the **bañera** where the nuns used to bathe. Around the corner, down the next little street, are **Sor Ana's rooms**. Dying at the age of 90, in 1686, Sor Ana was something of a phenomenon, leaving behind her a trail of prophecies and cures. Her own destiny in Santa Catalina, like that of many of her sisters, was to castigate herself in order to offer up her torments for the salvation of other souls—wealthy Arequipan patrons who paid handsomely for this privilege. Sor Ana is currently being considered in Rome, and is said to be "well on her way to being named a saint."

The **refectory**, immediately before the main cloisters, is deceptively plain—its exceptional star-shaped stained glass shedding dapples of sunlight through the empty space. Nearby, confessional windows look into the **main chapel**, but the best view of its majestic cupola is from the top of the staircase beside the cloisters. An interesting little room underneath these stairs has an intricately painted wall niche with a centerpiece of a heart being

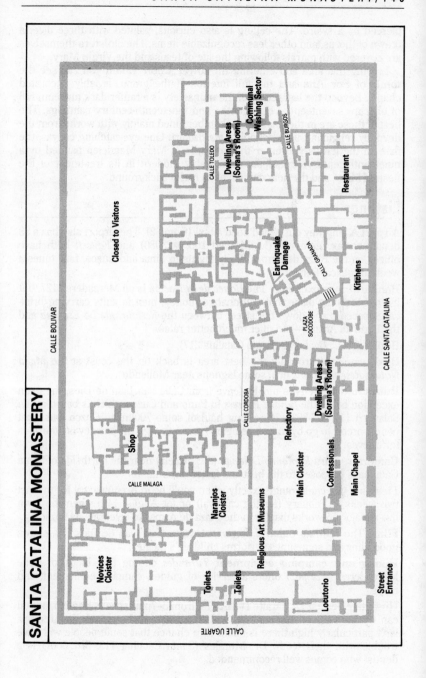

pierced by a sword. The ceiling is also curious, painted with three dice, a crown of thorns, and other less recognizable items. The **cloisters** themselves are covered with murals following the life of Jesus and the Virgin Mary.

Leaving this area and entering the **lower Choir Room** you can see the **tomb of Sor Ana** and the full interior of the grand, lavishly decorated chapel. Beyond the last sector of the monastery is a rather dark museum full of obscure seventeenth-, eighteenth-, and nineteenth-century paintings. The best of these are in the final outer chamber, lined mainly with works from the devoutly religious Cuzco school of *mestizo* art. One eye-catching canvas, the first on the left as you enter this room, is of Mary Magdelen painted by a nineteenth-century Arequipan, remarkably modern in its treatment of the flesh of Mary, and the near cubism of its rocky background.

Listiings

Airport A long way out, you'll need a taxi (from $2). The airport also has a $3 departure tax. *AeroPeru* (La Merced 106; ☎23080) and *Faucett* both have offices on the Plaza de Armas. Daily flights to Lima and Cuzco, four times a week to Juliaca/Puno.

Banks/Money exchange The *Banco de la Nación* is on Mercaderes 127, but it's not the only place that will change money; men in suits carrying brief-cases pace up and down the street between the *Restaurante La Esquina* and the Plaza de Armas—and offer much better rates.

Books *A.B.C. Bookstore* (Santa Catalina 217).

Bird watching Probably the best area is back on the coast at the *Mejia Nature Reserve* (1 to 2 hr.), some lagoons near Mollendo.

Buses and colectivos mostly leave from Calle San Juan de Dios, the main exception being the *Juliaca Express* to Puno and Cuzco which is based at Av. Salaverri 11 (☎27-893). It's a long haul of some 700km to Cuzco and most people prefer to go by train (see below), even though the journey is notorious for thieves.

Camera repairs *Fernando Delange* (303 at Zela) near the northside of Santa Catalina is supposed to the best and fastest around.

Fiestas If you can arrange exactly when you'll be in Arequipa, try for the last two weeks in Febuary (for the carnival) or for August 14th when the town has a major fireworks display in the Plaza de Armas to celebrate its founding.

Films The *Instituto Cultural Peruano-Aleman*, San Juan de Dios 202, shows good films and sometimes performs children's theater.

Hiking and camping equipment *Turandes* on the first block of Calle Mercaderes (☎22-962) offers a service of guides, camping equipment, and maps.

Hospital/Dentist Dr. Jaraffe (☎21-5115; from 3–7pm) speaks English, or you can try the General Hospital (☎23-1818). Although the altitude in Arequipa isn't particularly high there is still a slim chance that some people will have trouble with their teeth; Dr. Morales (Santa Catalina 115; 3rd floor) is a dentist who comes well recommended.

Information The Guardia Civil on block three of Jerusalen are pretty helpful. They have information, sometimes free maps, and will be able to help out if you get ripped off (see *Thieves* below). **Tourist information** comes officially from the office by the Plaza (La Merced 117; daily 8:30am–noon and 2:30–3:30pm).

Market For shopping or merely wandering around in an interesting, lively atmosphere there's nowhere better than the **Central Market**, a couple of blocks down from Iglesia Santa Domingo. One of the largest in Peru, with all sorts of foods, leather work, musical instruments, hats, herbal stalls, and cheap shoe repairs (up on the balcony at the bottom end)—I've even seen llama and alpaca meat on sale. Even with police surveillance in the market, however, this is the most likely spot in Arequipa for gringos to get ripped off, so keep everything valuable in money belts, out of sight, and covered with as many layers of clothing as possible! All the same, the atmosphere here is a good one. Some of the old *quechua* ladies serve excellent fruit juices and special mixtures including eggs and stout beer.

Post office The central post office is on Calle San Jose/Moral 118, 1½ blocks up from the plaza—open Mon.–Sat. 8am–7pm.

Shopping *Artesania* and alpaca goods from *Casa Secchi* (Mercaderes 111) and *Alpaca 111* (San Juan de Dios 111).

Telephones for long-distance calls are in the *Entel Peru* offices on Avarez Thomas, 1½ blocks straight downhill from the square.

Thieves If no one's told you on the way, be warned that Arequipa is one of the worst places for thieving in Peru—a distinction it shares with Cuzco and Lima. Working in pairs the pickpockets have become very skillful in recent years—one distracting your attention while the other does the job. Wherever you go, and above all in the market or train station, keep anything you don't want to give away well hidden. See *Information*, above, for the address of the *Guardia Civil* police.

Trains Dangerous though it is in terms of rip-offs, the Arequipa–Puno railroad is a journey most people are going to want to make. The **train station** is on Avenida Tancna y Arica, seven blocks south of the Plaza de Armas, and is always packed first thing on Mon., Wed., and Fri. when the train leaves (at around 8am) for the 10-hour trip to Puno. It's best to buy tickets in advance whenever possible and to be at the station an hour before departure so you can be at the front of the line when the rush to get on begins—a particularly vulnerable time. The night-train to Puno, which leaves around 9:30pm, is best avoided. Whenever you go, stock up on glucose tablets—at altitudes of up to 4476m you might need them.

Travel agencies Among the better ones are *Transcontinental* (Santa Catalina 213; ☎21-3843), *Receptur* (General Moran 118; ☎21-5752), and *Lima Tours* (Santa Catalina 120; ☎22-4210).

Water Arequipa's tap water is supposed to be safe for drinking, but locally bottled spring water and *Arequipeña* beer taste a lot better.

Around Arequipa

Arequipa is one of those towns where it's all too easy to pass the time; the only view many travelers get of the spectacular countryside around is from the train on the way in and out. But if you've got a couple of days or more to spare try to do otherwise, for there are some particularly exciting and adventurous possibilities around. Climbing **El Misti** is a demanding but rewarding trek, but the Inca ruins of **Paucarpata** at the volcano's foot give good views and are archeologically fascinating.

Farther out, the **Colca Canyon**—nearly twice the size of Arizona's Grand Canyon—is one of the country's most extraordinary natural sights; or you can explore the amazing petroglyphs of **Toro Muerto**, perhaps continuing on to hike amid the craters and cones of the **Valley of the Volcanoes.**

UNUSUAL EXCURSIONS

If time is limited, or you lack the energy to fit in with the sparse transportation and meager facilities around any of these places, you might want to consider the unlikely titled *Holley's Unusual Excursions*, and be driven in a Land Rover from Arequipa by an extremely knowledgeable Englishman, Anthony Holley. These are all more than reasonable in price, and range from morning trips to the Inca terraces of Paucarpata and *sillar* quarries around rural Arequipa, to all-day excursions out to Toro Muerto or the flamingo-packed Salinas Lake in the shadow of Mount Ubinas—Peru's most active volcano. All passengers are insured and oxygen is available. The only condition is that a minimum of six people (maximum 12) get together for any one trip. To get in touch with Anthony Holley, look for his Land Rover parked outside the Santa Catalina monastery or phone him at Arequipa ☎22-4452.

El Misti

If you feel absolutely compelled to climb **El Misti**, bear in mind that it's considerably farther and taller (5821m) than it looks. It is a perfectly feasible hike, but you will need two days for the ascent and another day to get back down. Buses to the trailhead leave from Avenida Sepulveda for Chiguata (1 hr.), from where there's a seven- or eight-hour hike to base camp. To spend the night here you'll need at least food, drink, warm clothing, boots, and a good sleeping bag. Your main enemies will be the altitude and the cold night air, and during the day strong sunlight requires you to wear some kind of hat, a good pair of sunglasses, and a strong sunscreen. From the base camp it's another breathless seven hours to the summit, with its excellent panoramic views. *Turandes* (Mercaderes 130) in Arequipa can arrange for walkers to be dropped off at a higher starting point than Chiguata, cutting off a few hours of the first day.

Paucarpata

For an afternoon's escape into the countryside, **Paucarpata** is perhaps the best target. About 9km out of central Arequipa (an hour's walk or a quick ride on a local bus), it's a large village surrounded by farmland based on perfectly regular pre-Inca terraces—*paucarpata*, the Quechua word from which it takes its name. Set against the backdrop of El Misti, this is a fine place to while away an afternoon with some wine and a picnic. Or, a little farther out there's the old colonial mill at **Sabandia** (round-trip taxi from $5), another excellent place for an *al fresco* lunch, and the nearby (expensive) restaurant has its own swimming pool. Beyond here there's a colonial museum at the **Casa del Fundador** (10km).

Chapi

CHAPI, 45km southeast of Arequipa, is just a short trip by bus—easily manageable as a day's excursion. Though less dramatic than the Colca Canyon, the landscape here is still magnificent. Chapi itself is famous for its white church, the **Sanctuary of the Virgin**, set high above the village at the foot of a valley which itself is the fountain of a miraculous natural spring. Thousands of pilgrims come here annually on May 1 to revere the image of the Virgin, a marvelous burst of processions and fiesta fever. There's no hotel, so if you intend to stay overnight you'll need a tent. Buses leave Arequipa from the *Empresa Zevallos* terminal at San Juan de Dios 621.

Chivay, Cabanaconde, and the Colca Canyon

Reputedly the deepest canyon in the world, the **Colca Canyon**, about 150km north from Arequipa, is a vast and incomparable place, its sharp terraces still home to more or less traditional Indian villages. Using local transportation you have a choice of taking a bus (Cruz del Sur, for instance) to CHIVAY or to CABANACONDE, 50km farther on; both leave Arequipa daily from the terminal on San Juan de Dios.

Taking the seven-hour bus from Arequipa to **CABANACONDE** you can see condors diving down into the gorge, but only around sunrise and at sunset, so you'll have to spend the night here to be sure of seeing one. Cabanaconde is the best option if you just want to take a look over the canyon—it's positioned close (some four hours' walk) to an amazing clifftop where it is possible to camp above the canyon. Another option is to stay in the small *pensión* back in the village for $2.50 a night.

CHIVAY, in the upper Colca valley, is, however, closer to Arequipa and set in the finer hiking country, surrounded by some of the most impressive and intensive ancient terracing in South America. There's an old bridge down in the canyon, and numerous small villages on either side

Toro Muerto and the Valley of the Volcanoes

Even if most archeological sites or geological phenomena leave you unmoved, it's difficult not to be overwhelmed by the sheer size and isolation of **Toro Muerto** and the **Valley of the Volcanoes**, and though it's a long and exhausting trip out from Arequipa it has to be one of the most exciting in southern Peru. To combine both sites you'll need at least six days: leaving

Arequipa on the afternoon **bus** (3:30pm every Sun., Wed., and Fri.), wandering around the petroglyphs on days two and three, and catching the next bus on to the Valley for another couple of days' camping and hiking before returning to Arequipa on a Monday, Thursday, or Saturday. You could theoretically cut down on this by hitchiking one or more of these stages, but don't depend on it. *Holley's Unusual Excursions* (see box above) takes groups out as far as Toro Muerto on day trips but rarely ventures as far as the Valley. The **Andagua-Oropampa bus** operated by the *Delgado* bus company covers the whole of this route in what makes quite a grueling overnight journey.

The Road from Arequipa

Leaving Arequipa the bus follows the Lima road to SIGUAS, a small oasis town where you can see the drainage channels cut into the hillside waiting for water to irrigate the desert *pampa* north of the town. At present the fertile strip of Siguas is very narrow—little more than 200m in width in 1983—but recently sprinklers have begun to water the sandy plain above and small patches of alfalfa have been planted with a view to producing a humus-rich soil. This is the first stage of the vast $650-million **Majes Project**, which plans to irrigate 150,000 acres in the dry *pampa*, build two hydroelectric power plants, and develop a number of new towns to house some 200,000 people. With costs escalating to over $10,000 an acre, it is considered by many people to be a complete waste of time, and it seems slightly strange that so much effort, worry, and controversy should surround plans very similar in theory to successful Inca irrigation projects, such as the Achirana aqueduct, which still maintains the Ica oasis after 500 years.

Just beyond the sprinklers, a few kilometers north of Siguas, the bus turns off the Pan American Highway to head east across stony desert. After around 20km you find yourself driving along the top of an incredible cliff, a sheer drop of almost 1000m separating the road from the Majes valley below. This amazing contortion was created by a fault line running down the earthquake belt which stretches all the way from Ayacucho. Descending along winding asphalt, you can soon see right across the well-irrigated valley floor, the cultivated fields creating a green patchwork against the stark dusty yellow moonscape. At the bottom, a steel-webbed bridge takes the road across the river to the small village of PUNTO COLORADO, dwarfed below a towering and colorful cliff—an ancient river bluff.

The Toro Muerto Petroglyphs

For the Toro Muerto petroglyphs you'll have to hop off the bus a few kilometers down the wide dirt track that continues from Punto Colorado towards CORIRE and APLAO (and on into the hills to the Valley of the Volcanoes). The driver should know the best spot to drop you but even so the petroglyphs are difficult to find, and since it's usually dark by the time the bus arrives you are probably better off spending the night at **PUNTO COLORADO**. You can camp here, stock up with water and supplies, and walk on in the morning. There's another lure in the fresh crayfish caught locally and served up at a restaurant called *Condesuyos*, on the left just after the bridge.

When I first visited **Toro Muerto**, I was expecting to see a few indecipherable etchings on an outcrop of rock. Much to my amazement the site is strewn over a kilometer or two of hot desert and more than a thousand boulders have been crudely yet strikingly engraved with a wide variety of distinct representations. No archeological remains have been directly associated with these pictures but they apparently date from between 1000 and 1500 years ago. The engravings include images of humans, snakes, llamas, deer, parrots, sun disks, and simple geometric motifs. Some of the figures appear to be dancing, their shapes almost moving as you watch; others look like spacemen with large round helmets—obvious potential for Eric Von Daniken's extraterrestrial musings, particularly in view of the high incidence of UFO sightings in this region.

Curiously, and perhaps the main clue to their origin, there are no symbols or pictures relating to coastal life—not one seabird or fish. One possibility is that they were a kind of communal drawing session during a tribe's long migration from the mountains towards the coast. Some of the more abstract geometric designs are very similar to those of the Huari culture who may well have sent an expeditionary force in this direction, across the Andes from their home in the Ayacucho basin, around A.D. 800. To be certain, however, archeological traces would have to be found along the route, and no such work has been undertaken. The petroglyphs are not among Peru's best known or visited sites.*

There's no very clear **route to the petroglyphs**, which are a good hour's walk from the road, and at least 500m above it. What you're looking for is a vast row of **white rocks**, which were presumably scattered across the sandy desert slopes by some mammoth prehistoric volcanic eruption. After crossing through corn, bean, and alfalfa fields on the valley floor, you'll see a sandy track running parallel to the road along the foot of the hills. Follow this to the right until you find another track heading up into a large gully towards the mountains. After about a kilometer—always bearing right on the numerous crisscrossing paths and trying to follow the most well-worn trail—you should be able to see the line of white boulders: over 3000 of them in all. The natural setting is almost as magnificent as the glyphs themselves, and even if you were to camp here for a couple of weeks it would be difficult to examine every engraved boulder.

Unless you have excellent luck hitchiking you'll have to flag down **the bus** on a Monday, Thursday, or Saturday evening if you want to go straight **back to Arequipa**, or on a Sunday, Wednesday, or Friday evening to go on to the Valley of the Volcanoes. Check the exact times with the driver on the way out since they tend to vary.

---

* During the late 1980s the petroglyphs have been severely damaged, and many of the boulders have been smashed to make portable souvenirs, presumably for the tourist market. Don't buy any if you're offered them! That way perhaps such shortsighted, and highly illegal, "entrepreneurial" behavior will stop and the remaining petroglyphs be saved.

The Valley of the Volcanoes

Going on to the **Valley of the Volcanoes**, the bus winds endlessly uphill through the darkness for at least another ten hours. After tracing around Mount Coropuna, the second highest Peruvian peak at 6450m, the little town of **ANDAGUA** (337km from Arequipa) appears at the foot of the valley. Most passengers get off here, though the bus also goes on a little farther to ORCOPAMPA, a good starting place if you have the energy to walk the whole way down the valley. The Mayor of Andagua offers a roof and meals to travelers when he's in town, but there are **no hotels** as such. However, all the local people are generally very hospitable, often inviting strangers they find camping in their fields to sleep in their houses. Because this is a rarely visited region where most of the locals are pretty well self-sufficient, there are only the most basic of shops—usually set up in people's houses.

To continue on beyond Orocampa, your only chance would be to catch a ride with one of the rare trucks that climbs up the rough track to CAILLOMA, from where there's a bus service to Chivay; otherwise you have to backtrack to Arequipa.

Exploring the Volcanoes

At first sight a pleasant enough Andean valley, the *Valle de Los Volcanos* is also one of the weirdest geological formations you're ever likely to see, its surface scored with extinct craters varying in size and height from 2m–300m yet perfectly merged with the environment. The main section is about 65km long; to explore it in any detail you'll need to get **maps** (two adjacent ones are required) from the *South American Explorers Club* or the *Instituto Geográfico* in Lima, or from the *Instituto de Cultura* in Arequipa. The best overall view can be had from Anaro Mountain (4800m), looking southeast towards the Chipchane and Puca Maura cones.

Camping here, or at the petroglyphs, you won't need a tent—a sheet of plastic and a good sleeping bag will do—but you will need good supplies and a sun hat; the sun beating down on the black ash can get unbelievably hot at midday.

South from Arequipa: Tacna and the Chilean Frontier

The one possible attraction south of Arequipa, and even this only really in the summer months (Dec.–Apr.), is **MOLLENDO**—a coastal resort, reachable by train, with hotels, restaurants, and nearby nature reserve lagoons at Mejia. Most people go straight past on the bus with only one intent—to cross into Chile.

The Pan American Highway runs south from Arequipa about 200km to MOQUEGA—once a quiet colonial town, with winding street and houses roofed in thatch and clay, it's now dominated by the nearby copper mines. **Tacna**, some three to four hours and 150km farther on across desert landscape, is the last stop in Peru, a notoriously expensive place that's renowned among travelers for its pickpockets. Tacna offers little incentive to hang around before getting a shuttle bus to the frontier, and happily the border crossing itself is a relatively simple affair, involving no more than a bus or *colectivo* ride from Tacna to a customs control where virtually all nationalites (except those in the Communist Bloc) are given a routine 90-day tourist card.

Tacna

The main focus of activity in the sprawling city of **TACNA** is around the Plaza de Armas and along the tree-lined Avenida Bolognesi. Fronting the square is the **cathedral**, designed by Eiffel in 1870 (though not completed until 1955), and around the corner a *Casa de Cultura* where, if you have an hour to spare, they have pre-Conquest artifacts and exhibitions related to the wars with Chile.

If you need a **hotel**, the cheap and reasonable *Hotel International* and *Las Vegas* are just off the plaza, while the *Hostal Junin* (near the plaza on the corner of San Martin and Menendez; $4 triple room) is even better value if there are a few of you. The *Comedor* in the market is the best place to get a decent **meal** at the right price. **Tourist information** (8am–3pm; ☎71-3501) is available from the office out of the town center at Av. Bolognesi 2088. Scores of money changers hang around in Bolognesi and Mendoza, while the *Banco de la Nacion* is on the Plaza de Armas. It's a good idea to get rid of your extra *intis* before going into Chile (exchanging them preferably for U.S. dollars or, if not, Chilean *pesos*), and if you're coming into Peru from Chile the money-changers usually offer a better rate of exchange than in Santiago or Arica.

Crossing into Chile

The **frontier** (daily 7am–11pm) is about 40km south from Tacna. There are regular buses and *colectivos* to ARICA (20km beyond the border) and two trains a day (8:30am and at 2:30pm). At around $2 the train is the cheapest option but it's slow and you have to take care of your passport business before leaving Tacna with the Passport and Immigration Police (on the plaza) and the Chilean Consulate (five long blocks from the plaza, just off Coronel Albarracin). *Colectivos* (normally $8—leaving from the Avenida Bolognesi) are slightly more expensive than the bus but the extra expense is well worth it given the hassle saved, since they'll wait at the border controls while you get a Peruvian exit stamp and Chilean tourist card. They are also a lot quicker.

ARICA, just across the border in Chile, is often described as a fun town, and being a free port (and gambling resort) with no taxes on booze it's admittedly a good place to get acquainted with the excellent Chilean wines.

Coming back into Peru from Arica is as simple as getting there. *Colectivos* run throughout the day and the train leaves at the same times as the one from Tacna. Night travelers, however, might be required to have a *salvoconducto militar* (safe-conduct card), particularly in times of tension between the two countries. If you intend to travel at night, check first with the tourist office in Arica (Calle Prat 375, on the second floor). The border closes at midnight.

East to Puno and Lake Titicaca

Heading east from Arequipa, you cross the 4500m high *Meseta del Collao* through some stunning scenery, though it's a long and not particularly pleasant journey, either by train or by bus. The train is the more popular alternative, allowing you to stop off at the hot springs near **Yura** or to have a look at the rock paintings in the mountains around **Sumbay**. You're nominally less likely to get ripped off—the train journey is as bad as any in Peru for thievery—if you take the bus, which is slower and less comfortable than the train.

Arequipa to Puno by Train

It's a ten-hour trip from **Arequipa to Puno**, which means that if you take the morning train (officially 8am) you'll arrive sometime in the evening. It's a rare event if the train actually leaves Arequipa much before 9 or 10am. Tickets are all cheap and you have a choice of three classes: buffet (around $18), first ($12), and second ($6). Second class is all right if you don't mind chickens scrambling over your feet all day but it's quite a battle getting on, since seats are unreserved.

YURA, only 30km up the tracks, is perched right on the side of Mount Chachani, and although marred by a modern cement plant it offers a really stupendous view. There are fairly well-maintained **thermal baths** here, as well as a *Hotel de Turistas* and a more basic *hostal*, but it's not a very inviting place to stay and there are regular buses back into Arequipa if you're not going on.

Beyond Yura you're into an almost continual ascent for the next five hours, a strange process that never really gives you the feeling of entering the mountains. Instead you edge slowly through a series of deceptively small-looking hills and across apparently flat *pampa*. The tufted grass looks like electrified sea urchins, with powerful sprays extended towards the sun, and you can get occasional glimpses of vicuña herds, darting away *en masse* when they spot the train's approach. There are llamas, too, along with alpacas, sheep, and cows, tended by the occasional herder, sitting here on top of the world.

SUMBAY, which the train reaches after about three hours, is very basic and little visited, and to stay here you'll be **camping**, which is really the best way to see the place—waking up to the morning sun on this high *pampa* is always exhilarating. Close to Sumbay are a series of 8000-year-old rock paintings, mostly found in small caves, representing people, pumas, and vicuñas. The surrounding countryside is amazing in itself: herds of alpacas roam gracefully around the plain looking for *itchu* grass to munch and vast sculpted rock strata of varying colors mix smoothly together with crudely hewn gullies as reminders of their primeval formation through immense heat and constant shattering blasts.

In another couple of hours the train stops briefly at CRUCERO ALTO, the highest point on the track at 4476m. At this altitude many people are feeling pretty terrible—see Paul Theroux's account for the full horrors—and the only thing for it is a cup of *maté de coca*, served on the train, and a packet of glucose tablets. If you can stomach it, food is also served around this point.

After crossing an even sparser stretch of *pampa*, covered in vast volcanic boulders, the train stops at IMATA—a largish settlement dependent upon the railroad, and surviving on sheep and alpaca wool spinning. From here on it's all downhill into the lakeland region of the Titicaca Basin: another shift of scene to a landscape which, if it weren't for the flamingos, would resemble nothing so much as the Scottish Highlands.

SANTA LUCIA (7½ hours from Arequipa) is a lively, tin-roofed town with a small hotel, closely followed by the old colonial buildings of CABANILLOS. It's under 100km from here to Puno, but at 3885m the air is still quite thin.

Juliaca

It's another hour to JULIACA, the junction for Cuzco, where there's often a long wait as scores of Indian women pile onto the train to peddle their ponchos, scarves, sweaters, and socks. Initial prices are reasonable, but they get even better as the train begins to pull out for the last section of the journey. Unless you're making a connection (trains to Cuzco leave at 9am) there's no particular reason to stop here, though the Monday market is one of the cheapest around for woollen goods, and the daily market around the station sells everything—even stuffed iguanas.

If you get stranded (trains can leave without warning) try the *Hostal Peru* on the plaza—cheap, comfortable, and one of the safest. Also on the same plaza you'll find the *Hotel Benique* and the *Hostal Sakury*, both reasonable. *Colectivos* for Puno and Lake Titicaca leave the plaza frequently, and money can be changed two blocks away on M. Nuñez, just around the corner from the *Hotel El Sur*. *AeroPeru*'s office in Juliaca (daily twenty minute flights to Arequipa) is within a block of the train station, just beyond the *Aquarius Disco*.

By Bus

The road between Arequipa and Puno runs parallel but mostly to the south of the railroad—crossing the *pampa* at TOROYA (4693m). **Buses** are much less comfortable than the train, and usually take a bit longer, but they do go past the spectacular Lake of Salinas, in the shadow of the active Ubinas Volcano and normally covered with thousands of deep-pink flamingos.

Buses from Arequipa are operated by *Morales Moralitos* at Nicolas de Pierola and *Cruz del Sur* (San Juán de Dios). Or, alternatively, you could hitch this route quite easily, starting at the police control point on the outskirts of Arequipa.

PUNO AND LAKE TITICACA

The first Spanish settlement at **Puno** sprang up around a silver mine discovered by the infamous Salcedo brothers in 1657, a camp that forged such a wild and violent reputation that the Lima viceroy moved in with a force of soldiers to crush and finally execute the Salcedos before things got too out of hand. At the same time—in 1668—he created Puno as the capital of the region and from then on it developed as the main port of Lake Titicaca and an important town on the siver trail from Potosi. The arrival of the railroad, late in the nineteenth century, brought another boost, but today it's a relatively poor, rather grubby sort of town, even by Peruvian standards, and a place that has suffered badly from recent drought and an inability to manage its water resources.

On the edge of the town spreads the vast **Lake Titicaca**—enclosed by white peaks and dotted with the somewhat weird **floating islands**, basically huge rafts built out of reeds and home to a dwindling and much-abused Indian population. Densely populated since well before the Incas, the Titicaca region is also dotted with **Chullpa Tombs**, often battlement-like rings of burial towers.

Puno

With a dry, cold climate—frequently falling below freezing in the winter nights of July and August—Puno represents no more than a crossroads to most travelers, en route between Cuzco and Bolivia or Arequipa and maybe Chile. In some ways this is fair, for it's a breathless place, full of pickpockets (beware the bus and train terminals), and not well known for its ancient past. Yet the town has its own attractive traditions: it's famed as the folklore capital of Peru, with its own **folk music cooperative** (just off the main plaza), and most nights you can find a group of musicians playing somewhere.

The Town

There are three points of reference in Puno: the central plaza with its **cathedral**, the **railroad station**, and the **port**. It all looks an impressive sight from a distance but in fact the real attractions, beyond the basic provision of places to sleep, eat, and drink, are few and quickly seen.

The seventeenth-century **cathedral**, built with an exquisite baroque facade, is, unusually for Peru, very simple and humble inside, in line with the local Aymara Indians' austere attitude to religion. Opposite its north face, at Conde de Lemos 284, is the **Museo Municipal** (Mon.–Sat. 8am–12:30pm and 2–5:30pm) with an interesting collection including grave goods from the *chullpas*. An **artesania shop** between here and the large Prefectura building sells good craft items, but the **market** (between the railroad tracks and the port) has a wider and cheaper range.

Practicalities: Hotels and Restaurants

A common sight around Puno—and if you're loaded with baggage and struggling to find a hotel room, a welcome one—are **bicycle carts**. For a small fee the cart boys will carry your gear anywhere in town.

Most of the cheaper **hotels** are strung out between the train station and main plaza on Calles Deustua and Moquegua. The very cheapest hotels, not exactly recommended, are along Avenida Tacna, but for a few dollars more

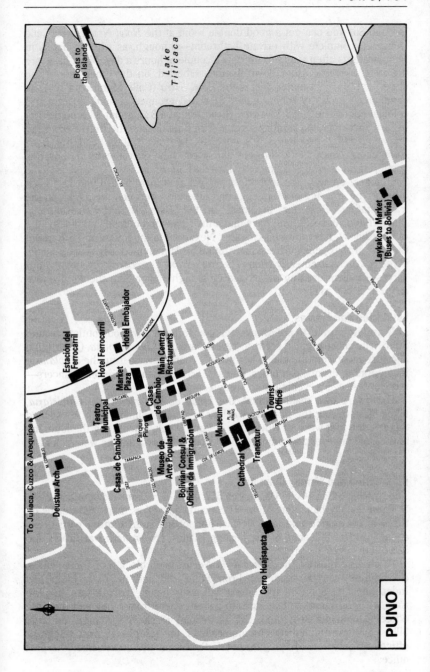

PUNO

Lake Titicaca

Boats to the Islands

To Juliaca, Cuzco & Arequipa

Deustua Arch

Teatro Municipal

Casas de Cambio

Estación del Ferrocarril

Hotel Ferrocarril

Hotel Embajador

Market Plaza

Casas de Cambio

Parque Pino

Museo de Arte Popular

Bolivian Consul & Oficina de Inmigración

Main Central Restaurants

Museum

Cathedral

Tranextur

Tourist Office

Cerro Huajsapata

Laykakota Market (Buses to Bolivia)

(around $5) you can get a good double room at the *Hotel Nesther* (on Calle Deustua), complete with private bathroom—although, as with all hotels in Puno, water is often available for only a couple of hours a day. More basic are the *Hotel Torino* (farther down Avenida Libertad, on the other side of the street) and an even better deal is the *Hotel Extra* (Calle Moquegua 124), its communal dormitory rooms under $1 a bed grouped around an attractive colonial patio. The *Hotel Samaray* (Jirón Deustua 323, about $3 a night) has its own snack bar and laundry service. Other options are the *Hotel Ferrocarril* for value and convenience (it's opposite the train station) and the *Hotel Europa* (on Ugarte; hot showers and great view over the lake). For real comfort from around $12 single try the *Hotel Sillustani*.

Strangely enough, the four most popular **restaurants** in Puno face each other at the crossing of Moquegua and Libertad—between the plaza and the train station. Best for breakfast is the *Bar-Cafe Delta;* restaurants *International* and *Sillustani* have much the same kind of food and quality; the other, *Club 31*, has rather less to offer. Next door to the *Restaurant Sillustani*, the *Cafe Misky* opens for breakfast around 5:30am on most days—very handy if you're catching an early train. The *Restaurant Ferrocarril* (by the station) serves excellent evening meals and most nights after 8pm there's live *folklorica* or *criolla* music.

Folklórica and Fiestas

Folk-music concerts are always being advertised at various outlets around Puno. The most regular seem to revolve around *Club Samana* (Jiron Puno 334; just down from the main plaza) where there's music from the *altiplano*—incorporating drums, pan pipes, flutes, *churrangos*, and occasional dancers—more or less every evening from around 9pm.

The town's own main **festival**, the *Fiesta de la Virgen de la Candelaria*, takes place during the first two weeks of Febuary, climaxing on the second Sunday; the first week of November is Puno Week, celebrating the founding of the city and legendary emergence of Manco Capac from the waters of Lake Titicaca.

Information and Money Changing

The **tourist office** (Calle Cajamarca 527; Mon.–Fri. 8am–12:30pm and 2:15–5:30pm) usually has information on concerts as well as maps and details on travel in the region and local fiestas. For further **information**, particularly about **tours** to Sillustani of the floating islands, try *Tranextur* at Jiron Puno 525 (off the Plaza de Armas).

To **change money**, the *Banco de la Nación* is on block 5 of Tacna; **casas de cambio** can be found at Jiron Puno 280 and on both Junin and Independencia. Some of the hotels will also change cash dollars (try the *Europa*). Mail seems to take ages to get anywhere from Puno, and the **post office** (Moquegua 264; Mon.–Sat. 8am–5pm) rarely has change for large bills. For more immediate communications, the **telephone and telegram offices** are also on Moquegua, but farther from the center than the post office.

Lake Titicaca

Though its name has long been the source of prepubescent giggles and school kids' jokes, **Lake Titicaca** is an impressive sight: the world's largest high-altitude body of water, some fifteen times the size of Lake Geneva in the Swiss Alps, higher and slightly bigger than Lake Tahoe. The villages that line its shores depend mainly on grazing, since the altitude limits the growth potential of most crops. What's fascinating to most travelers are the Inca-built **Chullpa burial tombs** that circle the lake and the many man-made **floating islands**, inhabited for centuries since their construction by retreating Uros Indians. They are, quite literally, floating platforms—built from layer upon layer of *tortora* reeds, the same organic material used for the local fishing rafts.

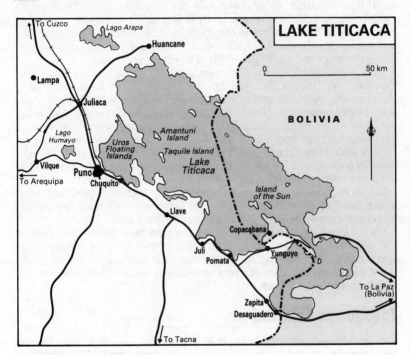

The Floating Islands

There are over forty *tortora* islands, but most trips limit themselves to the largest one, **Huacavacani**, where several Indian families live, rather bizarrely, alongside a floating Seventh Day Adventist missionary school. Short three to four hour trips can be arranged either through a tour agency, or directly with the skipper of one of the many launches that leave about every half hour from the jetty in Puno—look for the only woman pilot; she's one of the best ones! To get to the scruffy-looking port, walk down Avenida Titicaca, a continuation of Calle Deustua from the Plaza de Armas.

There are only a few hundred Uros Indians living on the islands these days, and many of the ones you might meet on the island actually live on the mainland, only traveling out to sell their wares to the tourists; most are a mixture of the original Uros and the larger Aymara tribe. When the Incas controlled Collao, they considered the Uros so poor—almost subhuman—that the only tribute required of them was a section of hollow cane filled with lice.

Life on the islands has certainly never been easy. The inhabitants have to go at least 2km to find fresh water, and the bottoms of the reed islands rot rapidly, requiring fresh matting to be constantly added above. Struggling amid this vegetable decay, over half the islanders have converted to Catholicism, and the largest community is very much dominated by its evangelical school. The islanders generally sit in lines selling tons of craft-work and woollen goods—most of it cheaper in Juliaca or Puno, although the children's drawings and the brilliant stylized tapestries are unique.

Only twenty years ago the Uros were a proud fishing tribe, in many ways guardians of Titicaca. But visiting the islands these days, particularly Huacavacani, leaves an ambivalent aftertaste. The 1980s, particularly, have seen a rapid devastation of their traditional values. Many foreign visitors are put off by what they experience on landing at the island—a veritable mobbing by young children speaking a few words of English ("sweets," "money," "what's your name?" and "give it to me") and fighting each other for your material possessions. It's not the fact that the children are in such great need that turns visitors off—for many of them it's a morning's fun and games, with relatively high economic returns. The underlying distaste comes from recognizing that they are actually reflecting the values of a civilization that used to be beyond them—the world where the tourists come from.

On the one hand, the Indian communities have been turned into a human zoo and have learned to squeeze as much from visitors as possible (they appreciate money, sweets, and, better for their teeth, fresh fruit); on the other, you do get a glimpse of a very unusual way of life—and the opportunity to ride on a *tortora* reed raft.

Taquile and Amantini

Two genuine—nonfloating—islands in Titicaca can also be visited. **Taquile** and **Amantini**, peaceful places that see fewer gringos, are both around 25km across the water from Puno on the outer edge of the Gulf of Chucuito. Amantini is the least visited of the two and, consequently, has fewer facilities and costs slightly more to reach by boat.

Boats for these islands leave early every morning, around 6 to 9am; a four- to five-hour trip costs from $4. The sun's rays reflected off the lake can burn even well-tanned skins so it's a good idea to protect your head and shoulders during this voyage. Most boats return after lunch the same day, but since this doesn't give you enough time to look around, most people prefer to stay a night or two in bed and breakfast accommodation (from around $1). Sleeping bags are recommended for the cold night air, and toilet paper is never a bad idea to take along, both for personal use and for bartering. Fresh fruit and vegetables are warmly appreciated by the host-islanders. There is no electricity, so take a flashlight and candles. There are no medical facilities, hotels, or shops either—though there is a small store and a few **places to eat** (honey pancakes a specialty) in the small plaza.

TAQUILE has a population of some 1200 people on less than 100 acres of land. Most of them are weavers and knitters of fine alpaca wool—renowned for their excellent cloth and unusual designs. On arrival at the island it's a long haul up a flight of stone steps from the port to the settlement where you're met by a committee of Campesinos who delegate various native families to look after particular travelers. The view from the top is spectacular.

Conquered by the Incas in the thirteenth century, Taquile was Quechua-speaking when the Conquistadores first arrived. The island was "bought" by Pedro Gonzalez de Taquile in 1580. The 1930s saw Taquile used as a safe exile/imprisonment center for troublesome characters like the ex-president Sanchez Cerro, but these days it's mostly European and North American tourists who while away some time soaking up the beauty of the island. It wasn't until 1937 that the residents—the local descendants of the original Indians—regained the legal ownership by buying it back. As far as agriculture is concerned, the main crops include potatoes, corn, broad beans, and the hardy *quinoa*.

The local people are proud and gracious, and generally very friendly and hospitable. But staying with a family who might not even speak Spanish (Quechua being the first language in Taquile) and under conditions you're not used to can be a very trying experience. Keep cool and treat it as exactly that—an experience. Remember you're their guest, and that it's probably a trying episode for them too. Watch them drop-spin, a common form of hand spinning that produces incredibly fine thread for their special cloth. They may be into the wristwatch and radio culture a little these days but they are still among the most skilled weavers in the Andes.

Both Taquile and **AMANTINI**, the nearby basket-weavers' island, have managed to maintain some degree of cultural isolation and autonomous control over the tourist trade. Only by arrangement may boatsmen bring in groups of travelers. The women dress in fine colorful cloths, very distinctly woven. The ancient agricultural terraces are maintained in excellent condition and traditional crafts of stone masonry are still practiced. Taquile, which is where most of the boats go, also has a few scattered pre-Inca and Incaic ruins, including some burial towers.

The **Island of the Sun,** largest and most sacred, in Inca times, of all the islands, lies to the southeast in Bolivian waters and can best be visited from Copacabana, just over the border from Yunguyo. Boats from there take about six hours and cost roughly $3 to $6 per person. Tours can be arranged through *Tranextur* (Plaza de Armas, Puno).

The Chullpa Tombs of Sillustani

Chullpas, built by the *Collao* tribe who dominated this region before the Incas arrived, are scattered all around Lake Titicaca. Some of these ancient funeral towers stand 10m in height—the largest built in white stone for local chieftains.

Those at **Sillustani**, set on a little peninsula in Lake Umayo overlooking Titicaca some 30km from Puno, are the most spectacular. A battlement-like ring, they have guarded this land of the dead for over five hundred years—some occasionally tumbled by earthquakes or, more recently, by *huaqueros* intent on repossessing the rich grave goods (ceramics, jewelry, and a few weapons) buried with important mummies. Two main styles predominate at this site: the honeycomb *chullpas* and the Inca stonework types. The former are set aside from the rest and characterized by large stone slabs around a central core; some of them are carved, but most are simply plastered with white mud and small stones. The Inca-type stonework is more complicated and in some cases you can see the elaborate corner jointing more typical of Cuzco masonry.

You can get to the site by local bus from Puno, but a more efficient service is offered as an afternoon trip by **minibus** ($4), which can be booked from one of the agencies or most hotels. *Tranextur*, just off the Plaza de Armas, normally runs a bus at 2:30pm for around $2 per person for a three- to four-hour tour. If you want to **camp** overnight at Sillustani (remembering how cold it can be) the site guard will show you where to pitch your tent. It's a magnificent place to wake up, with the morning sun rising over the snow-capped Cordillera Real on the Bolivian side of Titicaca.

On from Puno: Some Travel Details

Puno is one of the few towns in Peru where you have any real choice about where or how to move on. To **Arequipa** or **Cuzco**, the early morning **train** is the obvious choice—both roads are rough and you can always see much more from the train. The train **to Arequipa** leaves on Tuesdays, Thursdays, and Saturdays at 7am, or there's a night train (rife with thieves) daily at 7:45pm. **To Cuzco**, departures are Monday through Saturday at 7am (arriving around 5:30pm). Tickets can and should be bought the evening before departure (**ticket office** Mon.–Sat. 6:30–8am, 9:30–11:30am, 2–5pm, and 7–8:30pm; Sun. 6–8am, 2–4pm, and 7–8:30pm).

Heading **south to Bolivia** there are two options: you can go any day of the week by road via either DESAGUADERO or YUNGUYO. These are both fascinating routes and are detailed below. The steamer ship service **across Lake Titicaca** connecting Puno with Guaqui in Bolivia no longer operates but if you don't want to miss out on the lake you could always take a trip out to one of the islands, or cross the Straits from Yunguyo. **Tickets** for the steamer and train to La Paz used to be obtainable from the jetty in Puno ($10–$25 depending on class), and it's worth checking with the tourist office or at the jetty for up-to-date information on this service.

The Train North to Cuzco

The railroad journey from Puno to Cuzco can be as enjoyable as any in the world. From the desolate *pampa* of the Lake Titicaca valley, the train climbs over the 4300m La Raya pass before dropping down into the magnificient Vilcanota valley and on to Cuzco.

Trains run every day of the week except Sunday, leaving Puno for the eleven-hour journey: first class costs a mere $4.50, and traveling to one of the intermediate stations—Juliaca, Ayaviri, or Sicuani—costs virtually nothing. However, it's best to buy your seats in advance—Mon.–Sat. 9:30–11am or 3–5pm, Sun. 8–10am. If you want to sit in the Buffet Wagon, with the relatively meaningless advantage of being near to the kitchen doors (it means that you finish your food first only to get battered by the waiters as they serve everyone else), it's an extra $1.50. As with all train journeys in Peru, this is renowned for its thieving activities: keep anything valuable well hidden and a good eye on your gear as you board the carriage and find your seat.

The Journey

The first town out of Puno, JULIACA, is only an hour away across a grassy *pampa* where it's easy to imagine a straggling column of Spanish cavalry and footmen followed by a thousand Inca warriors—Almagro's fated expedition to Chile in the 1530s. Today, much as it always was, the plain is scattered with tiny isolated communities, many of them with conical kilns, self-subsistent even down to kitchenware.

Passing beyond here through a magnificent glacial landscape, the train pulls up outside AYAVIRI station (3903m). Once a great Inca center with a palace, sun temple, and well-stocked storehouses, it's now a market town, notable for the women's weird and wonderful hats. You can see an interesting old church from the train—low but with two stone towers and a cupola. This is a good place to buy meat, even through the carriage window, and a perfect place for **trekking** if the urge has grabbed you.

Next stop is **LA RAYA**, a scenic pass between the Vilcanota valley in the Amazon watershed and the Titicaca Basin which flows down into the Pacific. Enclosed by towering mountains, some of them snowcapped, it's the sort of spot that makes you feel like leaving the train and everything else behind just to head for the horizon. The villages north of La Raya pass have already been dealt with in the Cuzco chapter.

Into Bolivia: Desaguaderos and Yunguyo

You can sometimes travel directly to Bolivia by boat—across Titicaca to GUAQUI. Much the most interesting routes, however, involve at least some overland travel, crossing the frontier at either **Yunguyo** or at the river border of **Desaguaderos**. En route to either you'll pass by some of Titicaca's more interesting colonial settlements, each attractively individual in its architecture.

Several of the Puno **bus companies** cover these routes, two of them, *4 de Noviembre* and *Cruz del Sur*, taking in the detour to YUNGUYO from where a minibus service connects with COPACABANA, just a short distance away. Several companies can help arrange this, though it can be done by public transportation quite easily without their help: try *Tranextur* (on the plaza), *Puno Travel* (Tacna 254), *Transturin* (on Ugarte), or the *Co-op Dos de Febrero* (Libertad 113). If you're in a hurry you'll want to go via Desaguaderos, and several companies including *Cruz del Sur*, *Morales Moralitos*, and the *Juliaca Express* **colectivos** run right through to La Paz. All buses for Bolivia and either border crossing leave from **Laykakota market** down Avenida Tacna.

Chucuito and Juli

CHUCUITO, 20km out of Puno, is dwarfed by its intensive hillside terracing and by huge igneous boulders poised behind the brick and adobe houses. Early in the morning, small blotchy-cheeked Aymara children clamber onto the stone walls around their homesteads to bask in the sun's first warming rays. Chucuito was once a colonial town and its main plaza retains the *picota* (pillory) where the severed heads of executed criminals were displayed.

From here the road cuts 60km across the plain to JULI, a larger town nestling between gigantic round-topped and terraced hills. There are a few *hostals* here (a basic one on the main plaza), a *Hotel de Turistas* , and a very expensive (up to $80), somewhat out of place, **hovercraft service** to Copacabana which often isn't running. The Jesuits chose Juli as the site for their training center, which prepared missionaries bound for the remoter regions of Bolivia and Paraguay. The concept they developed, a form of community evangelization, was at least partly inspired by the Inca organizational system and extremely influential through the seventeenth and eighteenth centuries.

Fronting the large open plaza are the parish church of San Pedro and the amazing-looking **Casa Zavala** ("House of the Inquisition") with thatched roof and fantastically carved double doors. Juli's other churches are worth a look too, if you're breaking the journey here, each having served its own quarter of the town for some three centuries. So too is **POMATA**'s pink granite *iglesia*, 20km on, from where you may want to make the connection on to YUNGUYO.

Crossing the Border

The **YUNGUYO–COPACABANA** crossing is by far the most enjoyable route into Bolivia, though unless you intend staying overnight in Copacabana (or taking the 3-hr.Puno–Copacabana minibus) you'll need to set out quite early from Puno; the actual **border** (open 8am–6pm) is a 2km walk from Yunguyo. The Bolivian passport control, where there's usually a bus for the 10km or so to Copacabana, is a few hundred meters on; only change enough money to carry you to LA PAZ at the stalls in Yunguyo's plaza.

The cheap afternoon service across Titicaca from Copacabana takes you through some of the most exciting scenery of the basin. At TIQUINA you leave the bus briefly to take a passenger ferry across the narrowest point of the lake, the bus rejoining you on the other side from its own individual ferry. Officially all travelers have to report to the Bolivian Naval Office—this is one of the few landlocked countries in the world which has a navy—beside the passenger ferry terminal before crossing the lake; but in practice there are often too many people and there's a very real danger of missing the bus (and your luggage) on the other side by hanging around in a hopeless line; once across the lake it's a four- to five-hour haul on to La Paz.

Quicker but less interesting, allowing you to get from Puno to LA PAZ inside twelve hours with a minimum of delays and changing (as opposed to the more complicated Copacabana route), the **DESAGUADEROS CROSSING** sees most of the traffic across the Peru-Bolivia border. If you're on one of the *Morales Moralitos* buses (Sun.–Tues. and Thurs.; $20 to La Paz) or *Juliaca Express colectivos* (daily but slightly more expensive) all you'll need to do is get a stamp in your passport; the Peruvian control is by the market, the Bolivian one just across the bridge. If you arrive here by local bus—or by one of the new minibuses from Peru—it's a short walk between the two and you can pick up an *Ingravi* bus on to La Paz (more or less hourly). Money can be changed on the bridge approach but the rates are poor, so buy only as much as you'll need to get you to La Paz.

For anyone **coming into Peru from Bolivia** by either route, the procedure is just as straightforward, only reversed. One real difference worth noting is that when leaving COPACABANA there is a customs and passport check for all those going into Peru. This takes place in two little huts on the left just before the exit barrier. Now and again Bolivian customs officials take a heavy line (probably when their rent's due) and thoroughly search all items of luggage. In some cases bribery has to be resorted to, simply to avoid undue hassle or delay. If you get stranded crossing the border there are some basic **hostals:** the *Hotel Amazonas* in YUNGUYO; the sordid *Alojamiento Internacional* at DESAGUADEROS; or several places in COPACABANA.

travel details

Buses and Colectivos

From Pisco Several daily to Lima (3 hr.) and on to Ica and Nazca (1–3 hr.); Ayacucho (1 daily; 14 hr.) and Huancavelica (1; 14 hr.).

From Nazca To Arequipa (nightly; 12 hr.) and Cuzco (every other day; 35 hr.). Several daily to Lima (5 hr.).

From Arequipa To Tacna (several daily; 5 hr.), Puno (daily; 12 hr.), Cuzco (daily; 20 hr.) and Lima (several daily; 14 hr.).

From Puno To Cuzco (1–2 daily; 12–15 hr.) and La Paz (several daily either direct or via connections at Desaguaderos, Yunguyo and Copacabana; 12 hr. upwards)

Trains

From Arequipa Day train leaves Mon., Wed., and Fri. at 8am (officially), arriving at Yuma (1 hr.), Sumbay (3½ hr.), Santa Lucia (7 hr.), Juliaca (9 hr. connection to Cuzco) and Puno (10 hr.). Not recommended is the *night train* leaving Arequipa every evening at 9pm (arriving Juliaca at 6am, and Puno at 7am).

From Puno to Arequipa trains leave at 7:25am Tues., Thur., and Sat. The night train departs 7:45 pm daily.

From Puno to Cuzco trains leave Mon.–Sat. 7am, arriving 6pm—via Juliaca (1½ hr.) and Sicuani (6½ hr.).

Flights

From Arequipa Daily with both *Faucett* and *AeroPeru* to Lima and Cuzco; four times a week with *AeroPeru* to Puno.

From Puno (Juliaca airport) Daily to Lima and Cuzco with *AeroPeru*. Four times a week to Arequipa.

CHAPTER FOUR

ANCASH AND HUANUCO

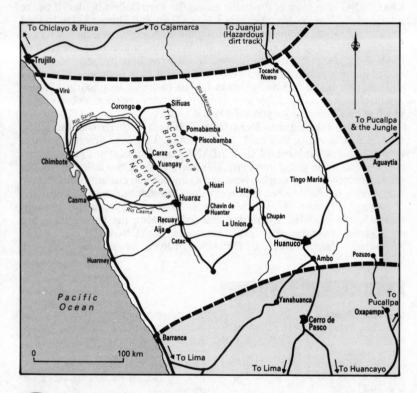

S liced north to south by parallel ranges of very high Andean peaks, this notably stunning part of central Peru offers more in terms of flora and fauna, glaciated valleys, history, and living traditions than most entire countries could. But despite their central location—dividing Lima from the coastal attractions around Trujillo to the north, and bounded on the east by the central jungle zone of Pucallpa—the *departmentos* of Ancash and Huanuco are remarkably little visited.

Ancash stretches itself along an immense desert coastline, where pyramids and ancient fortresses are scattered within easy reach of several small resorts which are, in turn, close to vast and perfectly empty Pacific beaches. Behind range the barren heights of the Cordillera Negra, and beyond that the spectacular backdrop of the snowcapped Cordillera Blanca; between the two cuts the **Callejón de Huaylas**—a 200km-long natural corridor some 3000m above sea level which also happens to have some of the very best hiking and mountaineering in South America. **Huaraz**, the vital center of this inland region, makes an excellent base, within easy reach of the mountain trails and also of **Chavin de Huantar**, an impressive stone temple complex which was the heart of a puma-worshiping religious movement some 2500 years ago.

Separated from the coast by the western Andes, and with a distinct cultural tradition, **Huanuco** is even less well known than Ancash. Nevertheless it's an obvious staging point en route to the central jungle and a range of fascinating nearer sites. From the eponymous regional capital—the thriving market city of **Huanuco**—it's possible to visit a series of unique archeological ruins, above all the huge and puzzling complex at **Tantamayo**, and the deserted expanse of **Huanuco Viejo**, a remarkably well preserved Inca city. It's just a short trip from Huanuco down to **Tingo Maria** and the luxuriant rainforest regions, where the eastern slopes of the Andes merge into the jungle of the Amazon Basin.

The connecting road between Huanuco and Huaraz via La Unión is little more than a delicate thread connecting two large but separate economic and political entities. Some terrorist activity has been reported in this quite remote mountain area, but the route was still being traveled safely by the occasional backpacking gringo back in 1988—get a political update from the South American Explorers Club and/or your embassy in Lima, or ask at the nearest tourist office (Huaraz or Huancayo).

THE ANCASH COAST

Most people traveling along the Ancash coast between Lima and Trujillo do the whole trip in a single nine-hour bus ride along the Pan American Highway. If you're short of time you'll probably want to do the same, but it's worth at least considering a stop at the small beach resort of **Barranca**, or at the farming- and fishing-based villages of **Casma** or **Chimbote**, all three of which have some intriguing archeological sites nearby, as well as offering alternative routes up into the **Callejón de Huaylas**. The provision of facilities is hardly overwhelming, but this zone is nevertheless relatively well serviced considering how few tourists make it here.

Barranca and Paramonga

North of Lima, **The Fortress of Paramonga** is the first site of real interest, the best preserved of all Peru's coastal outposts, built originally to guard the southern limit of the powerful Chimu Empire. To explore the ruins, the easiest plan is to get off the bus at **BARRANCA**, where there's a surprising choice of hotels and restaurants, or even the chance to rent a beach-villa (sometimes advertised in local hotels and papers). *Hotel Chavin* is cheap and good, and there's an excellent *chifa* restaurant on the main street. Buses and *colectivos* on their way between Lima and Trujillo or Huaraz will nearly all stop at Barranca.

For Paramonga, or the smaller town of Patavilca (5km north), there is an efficient local bus service. **PATAVILCA**, the village where Bolivar planned his campaign to liberate Peru, is also a possible alternative base with a cafe, small museum, and the rudimentary *Hostal del Sol*.

The Fortress of Paramonga

Less than a kilometer from the ocean, the **Fortress of Paramonga** looks in many ways like a feudal castle. Constructed entirely from adobe, its walls within walls run around the contours of a natural hillock—similar in style and situation to the Sun Temple of Pachacamac, near Lima. There are differences of opinion as to whether the fort had a military function or was purely a ritual center, but bearing in mind the tendency most pre-Conquest cultures had of worshiping while utilizing the natural personality of the landscape and environment (rocks, water, geomorphic oddities, etc.), it seems likely that the Chimu built it on a more ancient *huaca*, both as a well-protected and fortified ritual shrine and to delimit the southern boundary of their empire. It was conquered by the Incas in the late fifteenth century, the new overlords maintaining a road down from the Callejón de Huaylas and another that ran along the sands below the fortress.

Hernando Pizarro was the first Spaniard to see Paramonga, arriving in 1533 during his exploratory journey from Cajamarca to Pachacamac. He described it as "a strong fort with seven encircling walls painted with many forms both inside and outside, with portals well built like those of Spain and two tigers painted at the principal doorways". There are still red- and yellow-based geometric murals visible on some of the walls in the upper sector, as well as chess-board patterns.

As you climb up from the road, by the small site **museum** (daily 8am–5pm) and ticket office, the main entrance is to the right. Heading into the maze-like **ruins**, the rooms and sections get smaller and narrower the closer you get to the top—the original palace-temple. From here there were once commanding views across the desert coast in either direction; today, looking south, you see vast sugar-cane fields, now farmed by a co-operative, which used to belong to the U.S.-owned Grace Corporation, who then controlled nearly a third of Peru's sugar production. In contrast to the verdant green of these fields, irrigated by the Río Fortaleza, the fortress stands out in the landscape like a huge, dusty, yellow pyramid. If you're traveling straight through, you can't miss it from the passing bus; it's best seen from the right-hand windows.

Casma, Sechin, and Chanquillo

North of Paramonga, sand dunes encroach on the main coastal road as it continues past Paramonga to **HUARMEY** (km 293). As well as exhilarating and usually deserted beaches (La Honda, El Balneario, and Tuquillo), you'll find the *Hotel Venus* here and a 24-hour restaurant, *El Piloto*, geared towards serving truckers.

Leaving Huarmey the road closely follows the shoreline, passing by the magnificent **PLAYA GRANDE**, a seemingly endless **beach** with powerful rolling surf—often a luminous green at night due to phosphorescent plankton being tossed around in the white water crests—and a perfect spot for getting off the bus to camp. The road, straight as far as the eye can see, seems to have a life and tempo of its own; for the bus, truck, and *colectivo* drivers this is where they have spent and will spend most of their lives, winking and waving as they hurtle towards each other at combined speeds of 200km per hour. Some of the desert you pass through has no plant life at all beyond the burned-out tumbleweed that rams around the humps and ridge-backed undulations fringed with curvy lines of rock strata—intrusions of volcanic power from the ancestral age. In places huge hills crouch like sand-covered jellyfish squatting on some vast beach.

Casma

CASMA, the next town from Huarmey, marks the mouth of the well-irrigated Río Sechin valley. Surrounded by corn and cotton fields, this small place is peculiar in that most of its buildings are just one story tall and all of them are modern. For a long time the port for the Callejón de Huaylas, it was razed by the 1970 earthquake, and there's not a lot of interest here except the temple complex of SECHIN, 5km southeast of the town, and the **Pañamarca Pyramid** over 20km north. With a few roadside cafes and a couple of **hotels** (*El Farol*—with a decent restaurant of its own—or the more basic *Hotel Central* on the plaza) this is another potential journey-breaker. **Buses** run to Lima, Huaraz (a scenic but dusty trail over the Cordillera Negra via the Callan Pass), Chimbote, and Trujillo.

The Sechin Ruins

SECHIN (daily 8am–5pm) is a long hour's walk from Casma, south along the Pan American for a couple of kilometers then up the side road to Huaraz for about the same distance. The main section of **the site**, unusually stuck at the bottom of a hill, consists of an outer wall clad with around ninety tall monolithic slabs engraved with eerie, sometimes monstrous, representations of bellicose warriors with trophy heads, and mutilated sacrificial victims or prisoners of war. Some of these stones, dated to about 750 B.C., stand 4m high.

The carvings have a very characteristic style, curvier than the complicated Chavin designs found in the sierra, and more than a little sinister. Although they have no feline features and are not really similar to the contemporaneous Chavinoid engravings, some small objects discovered on the coast do contain designs which link the two cultures. Little, however, is known about the symbolizm involved or the militaristic (perhaps sadistic) cult which surely must have built Sechin.

Behind the standing stones an interesting-looking inner sanctuary lies hidden—a rectangular building consisting of a series of superimposed platforms with a central stairway on either side. The sanctuary has been closed to the public for some time and you get the impression that the restoration of this site bears little relation to how it originally looked.

Chanquillo and the Sechin Valley

Out in the Sechin Valley there is a maze of ancient sandy roadways, and it seems that this area was an important pre-Inca junction where a coastal road merged with one from the sierra. Several other lesser-known sites dot the region. A huge complex of dwellings can be found on the **Pampa de Llamas** and there's a terraced, stone-faced pyramid with stone stairs and feline and snake designs at **Mojeque**. Some 12km from Casma lies the ruined, possibly pre-Mochica, fort of **CHANQUILLO**—to which there are trucks every morning at around 9am from the *Petro Peru* garage in Casma—;ask the driver to drop you off *El Castillo* (a half hour walk uphill). It's an amazing ruin set in a commanding position on a barren hill with four concentric ring walls and watch towers in the middle keeping an eye over the desert below.

The Pyramid of Pañamarca

Heading north from Casma, the first major landmark is the Nepeña valley. At km 395 on the Pan American Highway there is a turnoff that leads 11km to the ruined adobe pyramid structures of **PAÑAMARCA**. Three large painted panels were found here and on another wall a long procession of warriors was depicted—but both have been badly damaged by rain. Although an impressive monument to the Mochica culture (A.D. 500) it's not an easy site to visit; you'll have to make it a day trip from either CASMA or CHIMBOTE and rely on your hitching skills or try to wave down one of the passing long-distance buses.

Chimbote and the "Great Wall of Peru"

Until recently one of the biggest industrial fishing ports in the world, **Chimbote** is a sprawling city characterized more by the stench of fish than anything of interest to the majority of tourists. Hardly ever visited, but surprisingly close to Chimbote, the surrounding desert area is littered with archeological remains including an enormous defensive wall probably built over 1000 years ago.

Chimbote

From the turnoff to Pañamarca, **CHIMBOTE** is another 25km to the north. Now a modern city and the site of the country's most spectacular urban growth outside of Lima, it was a quiet fishing port and favorite honeymoon spot until the early part of this century. Its ugly, sprawling development—which reeks of fish-processing and canning factories—was stimulated by the Chimbote–Huallanca railroad (1922), the hydroelectric plant in the Cañon del Pato, and by government planning for an anticipated boom in the anchovy and tuna fishing industry. The population rose rapidly from 5000 in 1940 to 60,000 in 1961 (swollen by squatter settlers from the mountains), nearly tripling in the next decade to an incredible 159,000—making it Peru's fifth largest city, despite the destruction in 1970 of nearly every building by an earthquake whose epicenter was not far off shore.

Chimbote's fish-packing factories, over thirty of them, utilize some of the world's most modern canning equipment, one of the nation's pride and joys. Unfortunately the fishing industry has been undergoing a crisis since the early 1970s: overfishing and *El Niño* (the changing off-shore sea current) have necessitated the imposition of bans and strict catch-limits for the fishermen. Yet over 75 percent of Peru's fishing-related activities continue here.

Finding a Room
It smells too awful to stay very long in Chimbote (although the locals say you get used to it after a while) and travelers remain overnight at most, continuing as soon as possible to Lima, Huaraz (perhaps via the stupendous Cañon del Pato), or north to Trujillo. The *Hotel Venus* on Avenida Prado (the main street) is bearable and not too expensive, or there's the noisy *Hostal Los Angeles* near the market half a block from Prado (on Galvez). The *Hotel de Turistas* (Plaza 28 de Julio) is reasonably priced at around $8, and its restaurant, though not exactly cheap, serves some of the best food in town.

Onward travel
Cars to Trujillo (only two or three hours) leave regularly from opposite the *Hostal Los Angeles* (slightly up towards the market): the drivers make themselves known by shouting out their destinations. **Buses** for Trujillo leave from just outside the Hostal, while for Caraz and Huaraz they leave from the corner of Galvez over the other side of Prado and on block 7 of Bolognesi. The *Tepsa* buses (north and south) stop briefly just off the Plaza 28 de Julio on Bolognesi. *Trans Moreno* run buses to Huaraz from Jiron Pardo (between Galvez and Ruiz). **Colectivos** to Lima hang around on Manual Ruiz, one block towards the sea off Avenida Prado. The **tourist office** (Bolognesi 421) can advise on transportation to sites nearby and sometimes stock town and departmental maps. The **post office** is on Prado just a block from the Plaza 28 de Julio.

The Great Wall of Peru

North of Chimbote, the coast road crosses a rocky outcrop into the Santa Valley, where the **GREAT WALL OF PERU**—a stone and adobe structure more than 50km long—rises from the sands of the desert. The enormous wall was first noticed in 1931 by the Shippee-Johnson Aerial Photographic Expedition, and there are many theories about its construction and purpose. Julio Tello thought it was pre-Chimu since it seems unlikely that the Chimu would have built such a lengthy defensive wall so far inside the limits of their Empire. It may, however, have been constructed prior to a second phase of military expansion or, as the chronicler Garcilaso de la Vega believed, the Spaniards might have placed it here against the ever-increasing threat of Inca invasion either from the coast or down from the Callejón de Huaylas.

In its entirety **the wall** stretches from Tambo Real near the Santa's estuary up to Chuqucara where there are scattered remains of pyramids, fortresses, temples, and stone houses. The best surviving section lies just to the west of the Hacienda Tanguche, where the piled stone is cemented with mud to more than 4m high in places.

Finding the Ruins

There's a bridge over the river Santa about 20km from Chimbote: simply head upstream to find the ruins. It's an interesting desert region, which offers the opportunity to spot wildlife—the desert fox, a condor or two if you're lucky—while exploring the valley for pre-Columbian sites. The climate is hot but ideal for sleeping out, and the only things you'll need to carry are your own food, bottled drinking water, and a sleeping roll (blanket and mat). **Maps** of the region are available in Lima from the *Instituto Geográfico Militar* (see BASICS).

Higher up the valley lies a double-walled construction with outer turrets, discovered by Gene Savoy's aerial expedition in the late 1950s. Savoy noted 42 stone-built strongholds in the higher Santa Valley in only two days' flying, evidence that supports the chronicles' claim that this was the most populated valley on the coast prior to the Spanish Conquest of Peru. Hard to believe today, it seems more probable if you bear in mind that the zone is still fed by the largest and most reliable of the coastal rivers. In 1962 Savoy led an expedition into the area on foot, finding that most of these parapeted defensive structures were well hidden from the valley floor. Once you climb up to them, however, you can see (on a clear day) the towering peaks of the Cordillera Blanca to the east and the Pacific Ocean in the west.

North to Trujillo: The Viru Valley

Continuing north, the road cuts up the normally dry river-bed of Chau, a straggling, scrubby green trail through the absolutely barren desert of the **Viru Valley**. In the Gallinazo period the Viru Valley saw great developments: dwelling sites became real villages (basically large groups of adjacent rooms and stone pyramids); improved irrigation produced a great population increase; and a society with a stronger tendency towards control of labor and distribution began to arise. The Gallinazo started to build defensive walls just prior to being invaded by the Mochicas (around A.D. 500) on their military conquests south as far as the Santa and Nepeña valleys. Later on, during the Chimu era, the population was dramatically reduced again, perhaps through migration north to Chan Chan, capital of this highly centralized pre-Inca state.

Viru

The main town here is **VIRU**, a small place along the roadside at the north end of the valley (km 515), with a bridge over the river bed that, in the dry season, looks as though it has never seen rain. An impressive cultural center around A.D. 300 when it was occupied by the Gallinazo or Viru people, the town today offers very little. Nearby, however, there are abundant **archeological remains**, two of which are within easy reach of Viru.

Closest to town is **CERRO PRIETO**, near the fishing village of Guanape— a short walk from the northern side of the bridge towards the mouth of the Río Viru. This ancient rubbish dump was the site of an agricultural settlement around 1200 B.C. and some of the earliest ceramics on the coast were found here.

A more interesting and visual ruin is the **GRUPO GALLINAZO** near Tomabal, 24km to the east of Viru up a side road just north of the bridge. Here you can see the dwellings, murals, and pyramids of a significant relig- ious and administrative center, its internal architectural layout derived from kinship networks. It's built entirely of adobe, with separate cultivation plots irrigated by an intricate canal system.

From Viru the Pan American cuts across a desert plain, close to the sea. Before reaching Trujillo there is a huge multi-crescent dune to the left, which shelters a chicken farm on the sands below. The road then runs down into the expansive plains of the Moche valley with the great Mochica temples of the Sun and Moon (see p.215) a couple of kilometers to the right under Cerro Blanco, and the very likable city of TRUJILLO (km 561) spread out in front.

THE CALLEJÓN DE HUAYLAS: HUARAZ AND THE CORDILLERA BLANCA

Situated in the steeply walled valley of the Callejón de Huaylas, **Huaraz** is the focal point of inland Ancash. Although it is hardly one of Peru's most interest- ing towns, the surrounding mountains and the lively atmosphere make Huaraz the ideal springboard for exploring the region, dominated as it is by the **Cordillera Blanca**, the highest tropical mountain range in the world, and **Huascaran**, Peru's highest peak at 6768m. Only a day's bus ride from Lima or Trujillo, it's one of *the* places to base yourself if you have any interest at all in South American hiking. The best weather in the Callejón de Huaylas, and in Huaraz, comes between May and September when the skies are nearly always blue and it rains very little.

Besides the beckoning mountain scenery, there are spectacular ruins such as **Chavin de Huantar**, natural thermal baths, and immense glacial lakes. Throughout the whole region, too, you come upon traditional mountain villages, unusual and exotic flora like the weird and unique *Puya Raymondi* bromeliad, and unwritten legends encapsulated only in the ancient carved stones.

Huaraz

Less than a century ago **HUARAZ** was still a fairly isolated community, barri- caded to the east by the dazzling snowcapped peaks of the *Cordillera Blanca* and separated from the coast by the dry, dark *Cordillera Negra*. Between these two mountain chains is a single corridor, the **Callejón de Huaylas**— fountainhead of the largest river in Peru, and a region with strong traditions of local independence. In 1885 the people of the Callejón waged a guerrilla war against the Lima authorities, which saw the whole valley in rebel hands for several months, when a revolt was sparked off by a native leader, the charismatic Pedro Pablo Atusparia, and thirteen other village mayors, who protested over excessive taxation and labor abuses. Sent straight to prison and humiliated by having their braided hair (a traditional sign of status) cut off, the local peasants reacted by overrunning Huaraz, freeing their chieftains, and expelling all officials before looting the mansions of wealthy landlords and merchants (many of them expatriate Englishmen who had been here since the Wars of Independence). The rebellion was eventually quashed by an army battalion from the coast which recaptured Huaraz while the Indians were celebrating their annual fiesta. But even today, Atusparia's memory survives close to local hearts, and village peasants remain distinctly unimpressed by the claims of central government.

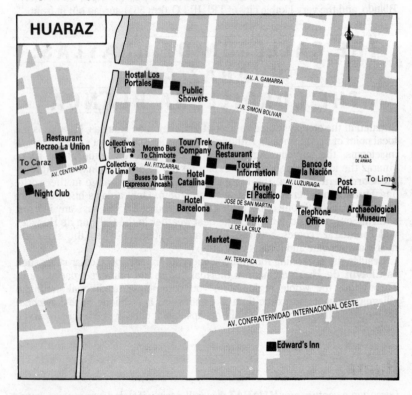

The Town

High above sea level at some 3060m, **the town** of Huaraz has become almost cosmopolitan—developing commercially and in terms of the tourist trade since completion of the highway through the river basin from Paramonga. Virtually the entire city was leveled by the 1970 earthquake, and the old houses have been replaced with single-storied modern structures topped with gleaming tin roofs.

Surrounded by eucalyptus groves and fields, it must have been really beautiful once—and still is a fine place in which to rest up after the rigors of hard travel. There are any number of easy trails just outside of town, and if you'd like nothing more than an afternoon's stroll you can simply walk out to the eastern edge and follow one of the paths or streams uphill.

The only place really worth checking out is the **Regional Museum** (daily 10am–6pm) beside the modern Plaza de Armas. Apart from a superb collection of ceramics (including many from the little-known Recuay culture) it has gardens and an abundance of the finely chiseled stone monoliths typical of this mountain region, most of them products of the incredible Chavin culture.

Modern Huaraz is a noted **crafts** center, too, producing such things as tooled leather goods (custom made if you've got a few days to wait around) very cheaply. Other quality bargains include woolen articles, embroidered blankets, delicious local honey, *manjar blanco*, and, if you've got the room, interesting replicas of the Chavin stone carvings.

Fiestas occur year round in the town and surrounding villages and hamlets. They are always particularly bright, energetic occasions in this region, with *chicha* and aguardiente flowing freely, roast pigs, bullfights, and vigorous communal dancing with the town folk dressed in outrageous masks and costumes. The main festival for Huaraz is usually in the first week of February, but September seems to be a lively month for rural get-togethers, which you'll often come across en route to the various sites and ruins in the Callejón de Huaylas.

Finding a Room

Even in the high season around August, it's rarely difficult to find a room at a reasonable price. Within the center of town, from the Plaza de Armas along Luzuriaga, there are countless **hostels** and many smaller places seeking to earn some spare cash; outside of high season it is often possible to bargain for a room, especially if there are a few of you to share it. *Pepe's Palace*, one of the traditional gringo dives, has moved to the *Hotel Catalina* (Raymondi 622, two doors away from its old home in the *Hotel Barcelona*). They still speak English, serve great food, and can help arrange for hiring, buying, and selling of equipment, guides, and mules for trekking. Another excellent place, though much quieter, is *Edwards Inn* (off Avenida Confraternidad, one block from Raimondi); this pleasant hostel is excellent value at around $3 per person, has its own restaurant, and is run by climbers and guides. It's also very clean and a safe place to leave baggage while you go off trekking or on day trips. Alternatively try the *Hotel el Pacífico* (on Avenida Centenario), which has hot water and is quite reasonable.

For a little more luxury, though not as dauntingly plush as it looks at first glance, try the *Hotel Monterrey*, about 7km farther north into the valley with regular bus connections (#1) to Huaraz center; this has a swimming pool and some superb thermal baths—very clean and civilized with individual and communal tubs. If you can afford it, the *Monterrey* makes a perfect base for trekking (☎ Lima 40-4630 for advance reservations). The *Turistas Hotel* (Avenida Centenario, block 10; ☎72-1640) on the northern edge of Huaraz is a bit expensive, but serves some delicious Peruvian criolla dishes.

Upscale rooms in Huaraz include the three-star *Hostal Los Portales* (Raymondi 903; ☎72-1402) and *Hostal Colomba* (Francisco de Zela 210; ☎72-1501). The *Hostal Andino* (Pedro Cochachin 357; ☎72-1662) also comes recommended. If you just want to clean up after a week in the backcountry, *Baños Raymondi*, near to Pepe's Palace, offers good **public showers**.

Eating and Nightlife

There's no shortage of **restaurants** in Huaraz, though they do vary considerably in value and quality. The *Chifa Familiar* (on the corner of Raymondi and Luzuriaga) is better than most, *Pizzeria Mama Mia* (Luzuriaga 808) is good, and for local fare an excellent spot is *El Recreo Union* on Manco Capac or *La Familia* (Luzuriaga 431). There are several **discos** scattered about the center including *Tabariz* (Avenida Centenario, from 11pm) with dancing, music, and an occasional live band. The *Peña El Rizzo* (Luzuriaga 455) holds folklore and *criolla* performances on weekends (don't arrive before 9:45pm).

Hiking and Camping: Supplies, Information and Maps

If you intend **to hike** at all it's essential to spend at least a couple of days acclimatizing to the altitude beforehand. Huaraz itself is (just) 3000m above sea level but most of the Cordillera's more impressive peaks are over 6000m. A number of places give free **information**, including the shops at Luzuriaga 459 (☎ 72-2394), Fitzcarral 458 and Pomabamba 415, the Municipal Building on the plaza, and *Ancash Tours* on Jr. Francisco de Zela 210 (☎72-2310). There are at least three or four places selling and hiring **camping equipment**—notably *Andean Sports Tours* (Luzuriaga 571) but also try *Pepe's Palace* (Hotel Catalina) and the shop at Fitzcarral 458. The going price for tent, mat, sleeping bag, and a stove is about $4 to $5 per person each day; mules can be had from $3 a day and guides charge about $8.

If you intend to trek in the Huascaran National Park (which encompasses virtually the whole Cordillera Blanca; see below) you should register beforehand with the **Park Office** (Av. Centenario 912 at the top end of Raymondi) where you can also get information and friendly advice. Ideally you should have detailed maps and one or other of the excellent guidebooks, *Backpacking and Trekking in Peru and Bolivia* or *Trails of the Cordillera Blanca and Huayhuash* (see p.317). These aren't currently available in Huaraz, though you should be able to get them in Lima at the *South American Explorers' Club* on Av. Portugal 146. **Maps**, too, are available from them, or in Huaraz from *Hostal Andino* (Pedro Cochachin 357).

Other Things

You can exchange money at the **Banco de la Nación** is on Luzuriaga (half a block north of the plaza); also, the **post office** is next to the Municipal Building (on the plaza), and the **telephone office** is just off Luzuriaga (slightly downhill and opposite the side of the post office).

Buses going north down the Santa valley to YUNGAY and CARAZ leave more or less hourly from the market area and Avenida Fitzcarral, and buses or trucks bound for RECUAY and CATAC can be picked up at the southern exit to town where Luzuriaga merges with the Avenida Confraternidad

Internacional Oeste. Two other bus companies that might come in useful are: *Empressa Soledad* (to Casma), Raymondi 336; and *Moreno* (to Chimbote), Av. Fitzcarral. Two bus companies run daily **to and from Lima**, eight hours away: *Expresso Ancash* (Carlos Zavala 177) and *Transportes Huaraz* (Leticia 655).

Around Huaraz

There are a number of fascinating sites within a day's easy reach of Huaraz. Less than 3km from the Plaza de Armas the *Rataquena Mirador* (an ancient lookout tower) is a perfect spot for taking in the broad panorama of the Callejón de Huaylas. Only 7km away is the dramatic **Wilkawain temple**, its inner labyrinths open for exploration, while on the other side of the valley, just half an hour by bus, **Punta Callan** is another ideal locale for magnificent views and long range photography across the Cordillera Blanca. To the north are the alluring thermal baths of **Chancos** and to the south the weirdly intriguing cactus-like *Puya Raymondi* of the **Huascaran National Reserve**.

The Temple at Wilkawain

WILKAWAIN can be reached from the center of Huaraz by following Avenida Centenario downhill from Fitzcarral, then turning right up a track (just about suitable for cars) a few hundred meters beyond the *Hotel de Turistas*. From here it's about an hour's stroll, winding slowly up past several small hamlets, to the sign-posted ruins. If there are four or five of you, a taxi there and back shouldn't come to more than about $3 each.

The temple is an unusual two-story construction, with a few small ancient houses around it, set against the edge of a great bluff. With a flashlight you can wander around some of its inner chambers, checking them out along with ramps, ventilation shafts, and the famous stone nails that hold it all together. Most of the rooms, however, are still inaccessible—filled with the rubble and debris of at least a thousand years.

The temple base is only about 11m by 16m, sloping up to large slanted roof slabs that create a gable-type protection, long since covered with earth and rocks to form an irregular domed top. In short, the construction is unmistakably a small replica of the Castillo at Chavin de Huantar—with four superimposed platforms, stairways, a projecting course of stones near the apex, and a recessed one below it. There was once a row of cats' heads tenoned in beneath this, typical of classic Huari-Tiahuanucu culture masonry; a cultural influence that spread up here from the coast some time between A.D. 600 and 1000. Continuing on from the ruin another 20km you come to the remote and high *Laguna Llaca*.

Punta Callan

PUNTA CALLAN is reached by a short bus ride from Raymondi 336—ask the driver to drop you off at CALLAN, shortly before the village of Pira along the road to Casma. There's no other spot that can quite match the scintillating views of the Cordillera Blanca from here, so save it for a really clear afternoon when the opportunities for capturing Huascaran's towering ice-cap on celluloid are at their best. From Punta Callan you can sense how the snowy range across the valley is dependent on the Cordillera Negra for protection against the drier coastal climate. Around Callan and Pira is grazing land as pleasant as you could find for a picnic and it's a relatively easy walk of a few hours back down the road to Huaraz. Passing trucks or buses will usually pick up anyone who waves them down along the way.

Chancos and the "Fountain of Youth"

For **CHANCOS** take any of the frequent valley buses heading towards Yungay or Caraz from the market area or along Fitzcarral. Get off at MACARA and follow the track uphill, passing small peasant settlements beside the stream for about 4km, until you reach the **Baños de Chancos** situated in a beautiful *quebrada* below the village of Vicos. Above, the Nevado Copa glacier looms another 3000m over these thermal waters. The baths at Chancos, known traditionally as the **"Fountain of Youth,"** claim to be excellent for respiratory problems, but with natural saunas and great pools gushing hot water you don't have to be ill to enjoy them. The valley bus service is good enough to get you back to Huaraz within an hour or so, but if you want to **camp**, that's all right, and there are a couple of basic **restaurants** on hand.

From Chancos a small track leads off to the hamlet of ULLMEY following the contours of the Legiamayo stream to the upper limit of cultivation and beyond into the barren puna zone directly below the glaciers. Keeping about 500m to the right of the stream, it takes 1½ to 2 hours to reach **Laguna Legia Cocha**, a lake hung between two vast glaciers, receiving their icy meltwater at 4706m above sea level. It's an exhilarating spot, with the added bonus of amazing views across the Santa Valley—to Carhuaz in the north, Huaraz in the south, and Chancos directly below. If you leave Huaraz early one morning, this is the ideal place to stop for lunch, leaving time to get down to Chancos for a stimulating bath before going on to Macara to catch the bus back into town.

The Huscaran National Reserve

A lengthier excursion is a visit to the pride and glory of the **Huascaran National Reserve**—the *Puya Raymondi*, a plant which most people take to be a cactus, but which is technically a bromeliad, or member of the pineapple family. With an early start from Huaraz you could get there and back in a day; or you can camp on the site, either returning the next day or continuing to La Unión (and Huanuco). The cheapest access from Huaraz is hitching or the local bus (along the Lima road) as far as CATAC (45km), where you can get the *San Cristobal* bus down the La Unión road; or keep going another 5km from Catac to PACHACOTO (where there are a couple of cafes often used as pit-stops by truck drivers) and hitch from here along the dirt track which turns off the main road across the barren grasslands of the low puna. This road is fairly well traveled by trucks on their way to the mining settlements of Huansalla, before it turns south to Huallanca and La Unión.

About 15 to 20km down the track—roughly an hour's drive—you're surrounded by the gigantic bromeliads, some of them reaching 12m into the rarefied air. This incredible plant, the world's largest bromeliad, is called *cuncush* or *cunco* by the locals (and *Pourretia gigantea* by botanists). It only grows between altitudes of 3700m and 4200m and is unique to this region.

May is the best month to see the Puya Raymondi, which is usually in full bloom by then—averaging an unbelievable 8000 flowers and 6,000,000 seeds per plant. There's not a lot more one can say about it except perhaps that you have to see it to believe it. In many ways the plants look like upside-down trees, the bushy part for a base and a phallic flowering stem pointing to the sky. Dotted about the Quebrada Pachacoto slopes like candles on an altar, each one has a life span of around 40 years, and there's nothing else in sight except grasses, rocks, lakes, snowy mountain crests, llamas, and the occasional hummingbird. Isolated as the area is, it's a good idea to take along something warm, something waterproof, and something to eat. For a leisurely look at this marvelous countryside, very different from the Santa valley, you'll need to take a tent and stay a day or two.

Returning, you should be able to hitch back to the main road at Huaraz— or alternatively you could go on farther to the **Quebrada Pasto Ruri** where it's possible to walk up to the spectacular glacier used in the region's annual skiing competition every June; or you might feel up to making it all the way on to La Unión (see p.192)—without undue problems. Rather than having to rely on buses and trucks, though, it might be worth going along to *Ancash Tours* (Jr. Francisco de Zela 210, Huaraz) where $10 could save a lot of hassle. Outside of late April, May, and early June, the Puya Raymondi can prove disappointing, often becoming burned-out stumps after dropping their flowers and seeds, but the surrounding scenery remains sensational.

Yungay, Caraz, and the Cordillera Blanca

No one comes to the Callejón de Huaylas without visiting the northern valley towns and many travelers will want to use them as bases from which to explore one or more of the ten snow-free passes that join the Pacific and Amazonian watersheds across the Andes. Simply combining almost any two of these ten passes makes for a superb week's trekking.

Yungay and **Caraz**, although not very far down the Santa valley from Huaraz, are quite distinct little settlements—visible contrasts to the larger market town and each a popular base from which to begin treks into the Cordillera Blanca. Physically they have little in common—Yungay the sad site of several catastrophic natural disasters, Caraz surviving the centuries as one of Peru's prettiest little towns—but to understand either properly they have to be considered in relation to the overwhelming mountain range that divides them from the Amazon Basin.

The **Cordillera Blanca**—the highest range in the tropical world—consists of some 35 peaks poking their snowy heads over the 6000m mark. Until 1918 it was possible to see this white crest from the Pacific, but since then the glaciers have receded, leaving *cochas* that feed the Río Santa with meltwater all year round. Of the many mountain lakes, Lago Paron, poised dangerously above Caraz, is renowned as the most beautiful. Recently, fears have begun to spread about Paron's dam of ice and glacial moraine collapsing, leaving the waters free to gush down the hills and engulf Caraz, but the chances of this happening in the course of your stay are very remote. Above Yungay, and against the sensational backdrop of Peru's highest peak (**Huascaran**, 6768m), are what many people consider to be the equally magnificent **Llanganuco Lakes**: more often than not an emerald green, their waters change color according to the time of year and the sun's daily movements.

Fortunately, most of the Cordillera Blanca falls under the auspices of the **Huascaran National Park**, and as such the habitat has been left relatively unspoiled. Among the more exotic **wildlife** that hikers can hope to come across are such creatures as the viscacha, vicuña, gray deer, pumas, foxes, the rarer spectacled bear, and several species of hummingbirds. All of these animals are shy, so you'll need a good pair of binoculars and a fountain of patience to get close to any of them.

The number of **possible hikes** into the Cordillera is virtually infinite, depending more than anything else on your own initiative and resourcefulness. Maps of the area, published by the *Instituto Geográfico Militar*, are good enough to allow you to plot your own routes confidently if you wish, or you can follow one of the more standard paths outlined by the expert trekkers—Hilary and George Bradt or Jim Bartle (see p.317). The following sections outline a couple of possible treks, including what is probably the most popular one—the **Llanganuco to Santa Cruz Loop**—which begins at Yungay and terminates at Caraz.

Yungay

YUNGAY was a mere 58km down the Santa valley from Huaraz until 1970, when it was obliterated in seconds during Peru's last major earthquake. Long before its final destruction the "Pearl of the Huaylas Corridor" had shown itself to be most unwisely situated: in 1872 it was almost completely wiped out by avalanche, and on a fiesta day in 1962 another avalanche buried the tiny neighboring village of Ranrahirca. The merciliess 1970 quake also arrived in the midst of a festival, and although casualties proved impossible to calculate with any real accuracy, it's thought that at least 70,000 people died—locals, their friends, relatives, and visitors.

The new town, an ugly conglomeration of modern buildings—including some ninety prefabricated cabins sent as relief aid from the USSR—around a concrete Plaza de Armas, lies a little farther north, still cowering beneath the threat of Huascaran but hopefully sheltered from further dangers. Just before you reach it there's a parking lot and memorial monument to the dead, while in a rather morbid way the buried **old town** has developed into one of the region's major tourist attractions. Its site is covered with a gray flow of mud and moraine, now dry and solid, with a few stunted palm trees to mark where the Plaza de Armas once stood. Local guidebooks show before and after photos of the scene, but it doesn't take a lot of imagination to reconstruct the horror.

Modern Yungay has a helpful **tourist office** (Mon.–Sat. 9am–5pm) on the Plaza de Armas, where you can get free **maps** and information on the area. Nearby, and also on the plaza, is a reasonable cafe—*El Padmero*—which usually has a few rooms available. The only reason to stay here, though, is to make the trip up to lakes Llanganuco and Huascaran; trucks leave most mornings from outside *El Palmero*.

Llanganuco Lakes

The lakes, only 26km from Yungay, take a good hour and a half to reach by bus or truck, on a road that crawls up beside the canyon with a long history of avalanches—created by thousands of years of Huascaran's meltwater. On the way you get a dramatic view across the valley and can clearly make out the path of the 1970 devastation. The last part of the drive slices through rocky crevices and snakes around breathtaking precipices, not much fun for anyone suffering from even the faintest trace of vertigo. Eventually reaching **Chinan Cocha**, the first of the two Llanganuco lakes, the track continues around its left bank and on to the second—**Orcon Cocha**—where the road ends and the **loop trail** begins (see below).

Immediately to the south of the lakes is the unmistakable sight of the massive **Huascaran ice cap**, teasingly tempting yet a very difficult 3000m climb to the top. This imposing peak is much higher than Mount McKinley in Alaska—the highest peak in North America—and an explicit display of the fact that the Andean crests are second only to Himalayan peaks. Surrounding Huascaran are scores of lesser glaciated mountains stretching almost 200km and dividing the Amazon Basin from the Pacific watershed. Although there are some three hundred glacial lakes in the Cordillera Blanca, those of Llanganuco are the most accessible and the most majestic of them all.

Hiking: The Llanganuco to Santa Cruz Loop

To have a crack at the **Llanganuco to Santa Cruz loop** you simply follow the clear trail that leads off from the end of the road along the left bank of Orcon Cocha. The entire trek shouldn't take more than about five days for a healthy (and acclimatized) backpacker, but it's a perfect hike to take at your own pace: some will probably manage it in three days if they push it, others will prefer to take a whole week, savoring every moment. It is, however, essential to carry all your food, camping equipment, and, ideally, a medical kit and emergency survival bag. Throughout the trail there are hundreds of potential **camp sites**, each one as enchanting as the next. The best time to attempt this trek is between April and October, in the dry season, unless you enjoy getting struck in mud and spending several days soaked to the skin.

From Orcon Cocha the main path climbs the **Portachuelo de Llanganuco pass** (4767m) before dropping to the enchanting beauty of the **Quebrada Morococha**, through the tiny settlement of VAQUERIA. From here you can go on to Colcabamba and Pomabamba (in the Callejón de Conchucos—not advisable in the rainy season when you may well find yourself stranded) rather than continuing back to the Callejón de Huaylas via Santa Cruz. The Loop Trail heads north from Vaqueria up the **Quebrada Huaripampa** and around the ice cap of **Chacraraju** (6000m)—a stupendous rocky canyon with a marshy bottom, snowy mountain peaks to the west, and Cerro Mellairca to the east. Following the stream uphill, keeping the lakes of Morococha and Huiscash to your left, you pass down (via Punta Union, 4750m) into the Pacific watershed along the **Quebrada Santa Cruz**. Emerging eventually beside the calm waters of **Laguna Grande**, you go around the left bank and continue down this perfect glacial valley about another eight hours' walk to the village of **SANTA CRUZ**. From here it's just a short step (about 2km) to the by now extremely inviting thermal baths of **Shangol**, and there's a road or a more direct three-hour trail across the low hills south to Caraz.

Caraz and Lago Paron

The town of **CARAZ**, a little less than 20km down the Santa valley from Yungay, sits quietly below the enormous Huandoy glacier. Palm trees and flowers adorn a classic colonial Plaza de Armas, and the small market is normally vibrant with gentle activity. Close to the main square stands the attractive old *Hotel la Suiza Peruana*, cheap and basic but with an excellent restaurant, while on the other side of the plaza the cafe *El Paris* serves good sandwiches and other snacks. Most of the bus companies have offices on the main square too, but for the *Banco de la Nación* you have to head ten blocks north, then two blocks right and it's opposite the track to the lake.

Unless you've traveled miles for the delicious honey produced in this little town, you're probably here to visit **Lago Paron**, the deep-blue lake sunk resplendently into a gigantic glacial cirque and hemmed in on three sides by some of the Cordillera Blanca's highest ice caps. The lake is only accessible on foot by climbing straight up the Río Paron gorge from town. Taxis and *colectivos* (coming to about $6 per person when full) leave daily or you can walk it: the best part of a day's hike. You'll need to take food and a tent since the **tourist lodge**, a cabin with views across the lake, is often closed.

Just across the Río Santa from Carza, set on the lower slopes of the Cordillera Negra, is the small settlement of HUATA, a typical rural village with regular truck connections to Caraz and the rest of the Callejón de Huaylas. From here there are a number of easy walks, such as the 8km stroll up to the unassuming lakes of **Yanacocha** and **Huaytacocha** or, perhaps more interesting, north about 5km along a path up Cerro Muchanacoc to the small Inca **ruins of Cantu**.

Another short trip from Caraz is to the village of SANTA CRUZ (buses around midday from Huaraz market) where you can sample the **hot springs** at nearby Shangol and try out your legs on pleasant country paths. If you're up for camping in glorious glacial scenery without doing a major hike—like the Llanganuco loop trip described above—it's an easy day's stroll up the Quebrada Santa Cruz to **Laguna Grande**, a perfect spot to pitch a tent and soak in the clear mountain air. Back down in Santa Cruz there is basic accommodation available, although, unless you've got a tent, Caraz is a much more comfortable place to stay.

North of Caraz

North of Caraz the first major settlement is **HUALLANCA**, where the road to CHIMBOTE (another 140m) begins. The main attraction of the entire Caraz-Chimbote route is this first 40km stretch, squeezing through the spectacular **Cañon del Pato** (*Duck's Canyon*). An enormous rocky gorge, cut out of solid rock by the Río Santa's struggle to get to the Pacific, it curves around the Cordillera Negra for most of the way between Caraz and Huallanca. Sheer cliff faces rise thousands of meters on either side while the road passes through some 39 tunnels—an average of nearly one every kilometer. Situated within the canyon is one of Peru's most important hydroelectric power plants; the heart of these works, invisible from the road, is buried 600m deep in the cliff wall. The road is undoubtedly one of Peru's most exciting journeys, and although severely damaged by the 1970 earthquake, the tunnels and road surface are in fairly good condition. Even if you don't intend going all the way to Chimbote it makes a good day trip from Caraz and can also be taken en route to CORONGO and the Callejón de Conchucos.

The Temple Complex at Chavin de Huantar

Possibly the most fascinating archeological site north of Lima, the magnificent temple complex of **CHAVIN DE HUANTAR** (daily 8am–4pm) evolved and elaborated its own brand of religious cultism during the first millenium B.C. Around 300 B.C. it was at its height of power and importance and must have been one of the largest religious centers in the world at that time, with about 3000 live-in priests and temple attendants.

Only five hours by bus southeast of Huaraz, the village and ruins are the most important site associated with the Chavin cult, and although partially destroyed by earthquakes, floods, and erosion from the Mosna river, enough of the ruins survive to make them a fascinating must for anyone even vaguely interested in Peruvian archeology. The religious cult that inspired Chavin's construction also influenced subsequent cultural development throughout Peru right up until the Spanish Conquest some 2500 years later, and the temple complex of Chavin de Huantar is equal in importance, if not grandeur, to most of the sites around Cuzco.

The Temple Ruins

The **main temple** at Chavin shows several stages of construction between about 1000 and 200 B.C., although the complex has always maintained its roughly east–west orientation. Julio Tello first looked at the site in 1919 when the temple was still buried under cultivated fields; during 1945 a vast flood reburied most of it and the place was damaged again by the 1970 earthquake and the rains of 1983. Undaunted, it remains a palatial ruin.

Excavation work at Chavin carried out by the University of California, Berkeley, in 1984 has established some very important insights into the historical development and social structure of this ancient pilgrim sanctuary. Located in a relatively fertile valley, Chavin was only two hours' walk from pasture on the upper Andean slopes while just seven hours downriver tropical fruits and other produce were abundant. Although its population was relatively large, it alone could never have been responsible for the megalithic temples.

Evolving between 850 B.C. and 200 B.C. the site began with a small temple area separated from a village dwelling complex. Over the centuries the village was abandoned in favor of occupation sites focusing around the temple itself. Among the fascinating recent finds at Chavin are bone snuff tubes, beads, pendants, needles, ceremonial spondylus shells (imported from Ecuador), and some quartz crystals associated with ritual sites. One quartz crystal covered in red pigment was found in a grave, placed after death in the mouth of the deceased. Contemporary anthropological evidence suggests that quartz crystals played an important role in the shamanic ceremonies in Peru, as in the Americas in general, Australia, and parts of Asia. The Desana forest Indians of Colombia still see crystals as "a means of communication between the visible and invisible worlds, a crystallization of solar energy or the Sun Father's semen that can be used in esoteric undertakings."

The main construction consists of a central rectangular block with two wings projecting out to the east. The large, southern wing, known as the **Castillo**, is the most conspicuous feature of the site: enlarged three times it now stands some 10m high. Massive, almost pyramid-shaped, the platform is built of dressed stone with gargoyles (nearly all removed now) tenoned in. Throughout the buildings are inner chambers on various levels connected by ramps and steps: in the seven major subterranean rooms you'll need a flashlight to get a decent look at the carvings (even when the electric lighting is switched on) while all around you can hear the sound of water dripping, a chilling experience that modern travelers can share with the ancient pilgrims. Still in its original underground site, too, is the awesome *Lanzon*, a prism-shaped block of carved white granite which tapers nearly 4m down from a broad feline head to a point stuck in the ground.

Some way in front of the Castillo, down three main flights of steps, is the **Plaza Hundida**, or sunken plaza, covering about 250 square meters with a rectangular, stepped platform to either side. Here, almost certainly, the thousands of pilgrims thought to have worshiped together at Chavin would gather during the appropriate calendrical *fiestas*. And it was here that the famous Tello Obelisk (now in the Archeology Museum in Lima) was found, next to an altar shaped to represent a jaguar and bedecked with seven cavities forming a pattern very close to that of the Orion constellation.

Another large stone slab discovered at Chavin in 1873—the *Estela Raymondi*, also now in the Lima Museum—was the first of all the impressive carved stones to be found. This too seems to represent a monstrous feline deity, the same one that recurs with awesome frequency both in human form with snake appendages and as a bird figure, sometimes both at the same time. The most vivid of the carvings remaining at the site are the gargoyles (known as *Cabeza Clavos*), guardians of the temple that again display feline and birdlike characteristics.

Most theories about the **iconography** of these stone slabs, all of which are very intricate, distinctive in style, and highly abstract, agree that the Chavin people, whoever they were, worshiped **three major gods**: the Moon (represented by a fish), the Sun (depicted as an eagle or a hawk), and an overlord, or creator divinity, normally shown as a fanged cat, possibly a jaguar. It seems very likely that each god was linked with a distinct level of the Chavin cosmos: the fish with the underworld, the eagle with the celestial forces, and the feline with earthly power. This is only a calculated guess, and ethnographic evidence from the contemporary Amazon Basin suggests that each of these main gods may have also been associated with a different moiety (or subgroup) within the Chavin tribe or priesthood as a whole.

The **Chavin cult** had a strong impact on the Paracas culture, and later on the Nazca and Mochica civilizations. Theories as to the origin of its religious inspiration range from extraterrestrial intervention to the more likely infiltration of ideas and maybe individuals or entire tribes from Central America. There is an extraordinary affinity between the ceramics found at Chavin and those of a similar date from Tlatilco in Mexico, yet there are no comparable Mexican stone constructions as ancient as these Peruvian wonders. More probable, and the theory expounded by Julio Tello, is that the cult initially came up into the Andes (then down to the coast) from the

The Fanged Deity (Chavin Raymondi Stone)

Amazon Basin via the Marañón valley. The inspiration for the beliefs themselves may well have come from visionary experiences sparked by the ingestion of **hallucinogens**: one of the stone reliefs at Chavin portrays a feline deity or fanged warrior holding a section of the psychotropic mescalin cactus—*San Pedro*—still used by *curanderos* today for the invocation of the spirit world. This would make sense in terms of an Amazonian link since many of the tribes living in the forest also traditionally use hallucinogens (*Ayahuasca* and *Datura*) to contact the spirits—their ancestors.

Chavin itself may not have been the center of the movement, but it was obviously an outstanding ceremonial focus: the name Chavin comes from the Quechua *Chaupin*, meaning navel or focal point. As such it might have been a sacred shrine where natives flocked in pilgrimage during festivals, much as they do today, visiting important *huacas* in the sierra at specific times in the annual agricultural cycle. The appearance of the Orion constellation on Chavin carvings fits with this since it never fails to appear on the nighttime skyline just prior to the traditional harvest period in the Peruvian mountains. During these pilgrimages the people would also have brought food and artifacts for sale or barter, and this may have been the moment, too, for marriage rituals and even intergroup truces. In order to have organized the building of the complex there must have been a high priesthood wielding enormous political power and, presumably, able to control the labor of thousands of pilgrims—the local population was far too small to have done it alone.

Getting to Chavin

From Huaraz, the road to Chavin leaves the main highway at CATCA before heading through the Cordillera Blanca via the impressive Cahuish tunnel, 4178m above sea level. **Buses** leave Huaraz every morning around 10am (*Empresa Condor de Chavin*, Tarapaca 312; ☎2039; or *Empresa Huascaran*, Tarapaca 133; ☎2208), and *Ancash Tours* has a faster, though more expensive, run.

A more adventurous way to reach Chavin is by following the two- or three-day **trail over the hills** from OLLEROS. Trucks leave Huaraz market every day for this small village (two hours) and the hike from there is fairly simple, and clearly marked all the way. It follows the Río Nearo up to Punta Yanashallash (at 4680m), cuts down into the Marañón watershed, and from there traces the stream to the ruins another 1500m below. Hilary and George Bradt give a good account of this walk in *Backpacking and Trekking in Peru and Bolivia* and the South American Explorers' Club in Lima will be happy to give advice and information about it.

Rooms and Camping

CHAVIN DE HUANTAR itself is a pretty little village only a couple of hundred meters from the ancient remains. Hidden behind its white-washed walls and traditional tiled roofs is a deceptively good supply of amenities for the traveler: the *Hotel Monte Carlo* is clean and quite cheap; there's a neat and pleasant little *albergue* just an hour or so's walk along the road to Huare; or you can **camp** by the thermal springs some 20 minutes' stroll from the village. For food the best bet is to try the *Co-operativo* behind the main church, but there are several other places to choose from if this is full or closed.

The Callejón de Conchucos and Pombabamba

To the east of the Cordillera Blanca, roughly parallel to the Santa valley, runs another long natural corridor, the **Callejón de Conchucos**. Virtually inaccessible in the wet season and off the beaten track even for the most hardened of backpackers, it's nevertheless a challenging target, with the town of **Pombabamba** in the north and Chavin de Huanatar just beyond its southern limit. This is also one of the few regions of Peru where the bus drivers sometimes allow passengers to lounge around on the roof as they career along precipitous mountain roads, bowing their heads and crossing themselves before plummeting into each steep drop of the dusty track: an electrifying experience with the added bonus of a 360-degree, ever-changing view.

Until the Conquest, this zone was also the center of one of the most notoriously fierce of the ancient tribes—the Conchucos—who surged down the Santa valley and besieged the Spanish city of Trujillo as late as 1536. By the end of the sixteenth century, however, even the fearless Conchuco warriors had been reduced by the colonial *encomendero* system to virtual slavery: besides a vast array of agricultural and craft produced, the area's annual levy demanded the provision of eighty people to serve as laborers, herders, and servants in the distant town of Huanuco. In his excellent book *The Conquest of the Incas*, John Hemmings gives a succinct account of exactly what the natives could expect in return for their tribute: the *encomendero* was charged "to instruct the said natives in the tenets of our Holy Catholic Church." Wary of strangers and reluctant to be pushed around, the people of the Callejón de Conchucos nevertheless remain manifestly proud of their heritage.

Pomabamba

POMABAMBA itself is a small town, 3000m up in dauntingly hilly countryside, surrounded by little-known archeological remains which show common roots with Chavin de Huantar. Its very name—originally *Puma Bamba*—means the Valley or Plain of the Pumas, and may reveal direct links with the ancient Chavin cult of the feline deity. Today the town is a valuable trekking base, though one that's seldom used by travelers. From here you can connect with the **Llanganuco to Santa Cruz Loop** (see p.185) by following trails southwest to either COLCABAMBA or PUNTA UNION. Or, a hard day's hike above Pomabamba, are the unstudied stone remains of **YAINO**, an immense fortress of megalithic rock, its buildings are locked into labyrinthine formations. On a clear day you can just about make out this site from the Plaza de Armas, appearing as a tiny rocky outcrop high on the distant horizon. The climb takes longer than you might imagine, but locals will point out shortcuts along the way.

Practical Details

Most days a bus leaves the main plaza in CARAZ at around 5:30am for CORONGO via the Cañon del Pato; from here there are fairly regular trucks (at least between April and October) on to POMABAMBA. Alternatively, Pomabamba can be reached from HUARAZ via CHAVIN, where a bus coming all the way from Lima goes north up the Callejón de Conchucos more or less every other day—thrillseekers will ask to ride on the roof!

There are a couple of small **hostels** in Pomabamba, one of them just off the main square, the other on the edge of town; and there are good thermal baths as well. As with the rest of Ancash and Huanuco, though, you'll undoubtedly have a better time, and enjoy greater flexibility, if you take a tent and ask the locals for good camping spots.

Between Pomabamba and the exceptional attractions of Chavin de Huantar, there's little in the way of specifics to detain you. The village of **PISCOBAMBA** (Valley or Plain of the Birds) doesn't have a great deal to offer and nor does **HUARI**, though you might want to stop and **eat** here because it's a long haul (141km) over barren mountains between the two. From Huari, Chavin is only another 30km.

HUANUCO

On the main road from Lima to the central jungle region of Pucallpa and the vast Río Ucayali, **Huanuco** is usually reached via the Central Highway, or train, to La Oroya, then north through the Cerro de Pasco; it's also a well-serviced stopping point on the way to the jungle town of **Tingo Maria** and the coca-growing slopes of the upper Huallaga river. However, for anyone already in and around Huaraz, or those willing to risk possible hardship and delays in return for magnificent scenery, there is a direct route over the Cordillera Blanca which takes you to **La Unión** and the preserved Inca ruins of **Huanuco Viejo** before continuing to the modern city. The area offers the possibility of several more fascinating excursions—the 4000-year-old **Temple of Kotosh** and the impressive ruins at **Tantamayo**, to name two—as well as the option of penetrating the jungle regions of the Amazon basin.

Huaraz to La Unión

The dusty minor road from Huaraz to La Unión sets off along the same path as that to the Huascaran National Reserve (see p.182)—into the Pachacoto *quebrada* via the turnoff beyond Catac. From here it's a matter of hitching a ride in a truck on to the rather cold, bleak, and miserable mining settlement of HUANSALLA (another hour or two)—try not to get stuck here overnight, as there are virtually no facilities for travelers except occasional floor space—then walking, or busing it, 10km farther to Huallanca where there are frequent trucks all the way to La Unión. It's fairly complicated, but this whole journey can be completed in about six to nine hours and is only some 120km in all.

In **LA UNION** there are a couple of **hotels** (try the *Dos de Mayo* or the clean, simple and surprisingly cheap *Hotel de Turistas*—from around $1.50 a night) and several reasonable **restaurants** (*El Danubo*, near the market, is central and quite good) but it's not the nicest of towns. You should keep a watchful eye on your gear and make the two- or three-hour hike to the ruined city of Huanuco Viejo as soon as possible. There's a nightly bus on to HUANUCO (the modern town) that takes about eight hours, or you can ride on top of a truck which leaves La Unión market most mornings.

Huanuco Viejo

Situated well above La Unión, the superb Inca stonework of **HUANUCO VIEJO**, virtually untouched by the Spanish conquistadores and without any later occupation, lies on the edge of a desolate pampa. The gray stone houses and platform temples are set out in a roughly circular pattern radiating from a gigantic *unsu* (Inca throne) in the middle of the plaza. To the north are the military barracks and beyond that the remains of suburban dwellings. Directly east of the plaza is the palace and temple known as *Incahuasi*, and next to this the *Acllahuasi*, a separate enclosure devoted to the "Chosen

Women" or "Virgins of the Sun." Behind this and running straight through the Incahuasi is a man-made water channel diverted from the small Río Huachac. On the opposite side of the plaza you can make out the extensive administrative quarters.

Without a doubt one of the most complete existing examples of an Inca provincial capital and administrative center, Huanuco Viejo gives a powerful impression of a once-thriving city—you can almost sense the activity even though it's been a ghost town for four hundred years. Poised on the southern hillside above the main complex are over five hundred storehouses which, in daily use, must have provided for a rapid turn-over in all sorts of produce and treasure—tribute for the Emperor and sacrifices to the sun. Well away from the damp of the valley floor, and separated from each other by a few meters to minimize the risk of fire, they also command impressive views across the plain.

Arriving here in 1539, the Spanish very soon abandoned the site of Huanuco Viejo to build their own colonial administrative center—León de Huanuco—at a much lower altitude, more suitable for their unacclimatized lungs and with slightly easier access to Cuzco and Lima. **Spanish Huanuco**, built along the standard city plans specified by Royal Decree, grew into a thoroughly rich *encomienda*: nevertheless, the colonists always regarded it as one of those remote outposts (like Chile) where Spanish or mestizo criminals, or anyone unpopular with officialdom, would be sent into lengthy exile.

The region remained a center of native dissent too—in the early years Illa Tupac, a relative of the rebel Inca Manco and one of the unsung heroes of the Indian resistance, maintained clandestine Inca rule around Huanuco Viejo until at least 1545. And as late as 1777 the royal officials were thrown out of the area in a major—albeit shortlived—insurrection.

The City of Huanuco

The charming modern city of **HUANUCO**, more than 100km east of the deserted Inca town, is relatively peaceful nowadays—depending for its livelihood on forestry, tea, and coca, along with a little low-key tourism. Its old narrow streets ramble across a handful of small plazas, a pleasant environment where travelers often spend days just roaming the bars and cafes on an endless round of trail tales.

There are no singular attractions in the town, but a couple of old churches, convents with airy cloisters, a small **natural history museum,** and a **cathedral**, whose altarpieces have the saints counterposed by Inca deities of the Sun and Moon, do offer some focus for activity. The church of **San Cristobal** is actually built on the foundations of the site where the *Curaca de los Chupacos* once lived and where the Portuguese Pablo Coimbra celebrated the first mass in the region. **San Francisco**, meanwhile, shows a strong indigenous influence, its altars richly carved with native fruits—avocados, papayas, and pomegranates. The church also boasts a small collection of sixteenth-century paintings.

Practical Details

As far as **hotels** go, always a good bet are the clean but basic *Hostal Europa* (Calle Huanuco, two blocks from the plaza toward the market) or the less expensive, sometimes noisy, *Hostal Internacional* (opposite the market on Huallayco). The *Hostal Confort* (Jr. Huanuco 608; ☎2404) isn't bad, or you could try the more basic *Bella Durmiente* (opposite the market on Jr. Arequipa) and *Hotel Astoria* just two blocks from the plaza (General Prado 988; ☎2310). If you prefer to **camp**, this is permitted down by the Rio Huallaga near the stadium, but you'll have to cope with the insects that sometimes overrun the site.

El Café is a good **restaurant** on the main square, though *Bar Venecia* (on Dos de Mayo) offers a more entertaining atmosphere in the evenings. *Huanuco Tours*, near the *Hostal Confort*, offer **tourist information** and **money exchange**. The **post office** and **telephones** are alongside each other, two blocks up Jr. Castillo from the plaza.

Huanuco carnival week begins around August 15 when the town's normal tranquillity explodes into a wild fiesta binge. Peruvian Independence Day (July 28) is also a good time to be here, with opportunities to see traditional dances like the *Chunco*; and at Christmas the children put on their own performances.

If you've come directly up from Lima via La Oroya and want to visit Huanuco Viejo, **buses** leave for La Unión every morning at 8am from the lively market area—a nine-hour ride, if there are no delays.

The Temple of Kotosh and Tomay Qichua

Only 8km from Huanuco along the road to La Unión, the fascinating, though poorly maintained, **Temple of Kotosh** lies in ruins on the banks of the Río Tingo. At over 4000 years old, this site predates the Chavin era by more than a thousand years. Between 1960 and 1962 a team of Japanese archeologists excavated the large mound which had been created by the fallen debris of the original temple: its occupation proved to span six phases, the first town of which falls into the Early Agricultural Period when the ceramic arts were beginning to develop rapidly. Potsherds found here bear clear similarities to works from the lower jungle areas.

The first evidence of massive stone constructions (from about 2000 B.C.) suggests that complicated building work began here many centuries before it started anywhere else on the American continent, and more or less permanent settlement continued through the Chavin era (though without the monumental masonry and sculpture of that period) and, with Inca occupation, right up to the Conquest. One unique feature of the Kotosh complex is the **crossed-hands symbol** carved prominently in stone—the gracefully executed insignia of a very early culture about which archeologists know next to nothing.

An equally easy trip from Huanuco—less than 30km south, just off the road to La Oroya—is the village of **TOMAY QUICHUA**, birthplace of Santa Rosa's grandmother and of the infamous *La Perricholi* mestizo actress and seductress. Legend has it that in a valley not far from Tomay Qichua the Indians cultivate a secret medicine which magically cures all ills—its Quechua name means "this plant is more powerful than God"!

Tantamayo

About 150km north of Huanuco, poised in the mountainous region above the higher reaches of the Marañón river, the small village and extensive ruins of **TANTAMAYO** make a rather longer excursion. Nevertheless, a regular bus service from Huanuco makes it easy enough to do—some fourteen hours' travel over poor roads. In the **village** local guides are available for the two- to three-hour hike to the scattered site, and excellent accommodation is offered at the Swiss-style **tourist lodge** for anyone without a tent.

The Ruins

The precise age of this remote pre-Columbian complex is unknown. Its buildings appear to fit into the later Tiahuanuco-Huari phase, which would make them some 1200 years old, but physically they form no part of this widespread cultural movement and the site is considered to have developed separately, probably originating among tribes migrating to the Andes from the jungle and adapting to a new environment over a long period.

At Tantamayo the architectural development of some four centuries can be clearly seen—growing from the simplest of structures to really complex edifices. Tall buildings dot the entire area—some clearly **watchtowers** overlooking the Marañón, others with less obvious functions, built for religious reasons as temple-palaces, perhaps, or as storehouses and fortresses. One of the major constructions, just across the Tantamayo stream on a hill facing the village, was named *Pirira* by the Incas who conquered the area in the fifteenth century. At its heart there are concentric circles of carved stone, while the walls and houses around are all grouped in a circular formation—clearly this was once an important center for religious ritual. The **main building** rises some 10m on three levels, its bluff facade broken only by large window niches, changes in the course of the stone slabs, and by centuries of weathering.

A detailed archeological survey of the ruins may well reveal links with Chavin and Kotosh. In the meantime, the more than thirty separate, massive constructions make up an impressive scene, offset by the cloud-forest and jungle that begin to flourish along the banks of the Marañón just a little farther to the north.

Into the Jungle

The spiralling descent north **from Huanuco** is stunning, with views across the jungle, as thrilling as those from a small plane, highlighted in the **Pass of Padre Abad** with its glorious waterfalls. By the time the bus reaches Tingo Maria (4–5 hours) the Huallaga has become a broad tropical river, navigable downstream in shadow canoes or by balsa raft. And the tropical atmosphere, in the shadow of the forested ridges and limestone crags of the *Bella Durmiente* (Sleeping Beauty) mountain, is delightful. Nevertheless, as anything more than an overnight stop to break the journey from Lima (or Huanuco) to PUCALLPA, the town has nothing much to recommend it.

Tingo Maria

Once an attractive town, the ramshackle settlement of **TINGO MARIA** lies at the foot of the mountain where, according to legend, the lovesick Princess Nunash awaits the waking kiss of Kunyaq, the sorcerer. These days it welcomes few travelers due to the proliferation of the **cocaine trade** that surrounding regions have succumbed to during the 1980s, and the inherent dangers that go hand in hand with big money and Mafia-type control of such large-scale illicit operations. Nevertheless, it's a strikingly well favored setting—670m above sea level on the forested eastern slopes of the Andes, amid the fecund tropical climate of the *ceja de selva*—and Tingo Maria *was* once known as the Garden City. Today, though, the ravages of Western civilization have left their mark. Dominated by sawmills and plywood factories financed by multinational corporations, and with a booming trade in stolen goods and cocaine, Tingo Maria displays all the symbols of relative affluence, but the tin roofs below the forest of TV aerials spattered across the township betray the poverty of the majority.

For sightseeing there's little beyond the rather sorry zoo and botanical gardens attached to the university or—about 14km out of town—the **Cueva de las Lechuzas** (Owls' Cave); vast, picturesque, and dark (you'll need a flashlight). **Bed and breakfast** is available at Av. Benavides 263, or the *Hotel Viena* (Tulumayo 245; ☎194) which is reasonably priced, as are *La Cabaña* (Av. Raymondi 342; ☎146) and the *Hotel Royal* (Av. Benavides 206; ☎66). For Western **eating** it's hard to beat the *Café Rex* (Raymondi 500), while *La Cabaña* also serves up tasty food. The last week in July is Tingo Maria's major **fiesta** period, but on no account leave your gear unattended at this time.

Pucallpa and the Amazon Jungle

PUCALLPA, second largest town in the Peruvian Amazon region, is another eight to ten hours on the bus—260km directly northeast through virgin forest (much of which is in the process of being cleared). Since 1980, and months of local protests and strikes against paying taxes to Iquitos, it has been capital of the newly created Departmento of Ucayali. Quite apart from any intrinsic interest, this is the ideal point to find embarkation up the Ucayali to IQUITOS and from there on to Brazil, or to set off on expeditions deeper into the seemingly limitless wilderness of tropical forest (for full details see *The Jungle* chapter).

It's often difficult to get seats on the **buses** from Tingo Maria to Pucallpa since nearly all of them arrive full on their way from Lima via Huanuco. However, if you book in advance at one of the offices in town and you're pushy enough as you struggle on board, you should be able to secure a seat or two. If you do get stuck you can always fly there (see travel details below) or go back to Huanuco (or Lima!) and start again.

travel details

Buses and/or *Colectivos*
From Barranca to Lima (several daily; 3 hr.); Casma/Chimbote (several daily; 2 hr./3 hr.); Huaraz (several daily; 4 hr.).

From Chimbote to Trujillo (several daily; 3 hr.); Lima (several daily; 6 hr.); Huaraz (1 or 2 daily; 7 hr.).

From Huaraz to Lima (several daily; 7 hr.); Casma (daily; 7 hr.); La Unión for Huanuco (trucks and buses—see text above).

From Huanuco to Lima (daily; 12 hr.); Tingo Maria/Pucallpa (several daily; 4 hr./12 hr.); Tantamayo (more or less daily; 14 hr.).

From La Unión to Huanuco (daily; 7 to 8 hr.) ; Huaraz (trucks via Huansalla—see text above).

Flights
From Chimbote, **Huanuco** and **Tingo Maria** Daily to Lima.

CHAPTER FIVE

TRUJILLO AND THE NORTH

Though far less known—and much less visited—than the regions around Cuzco or Lima, the northern reaches of Peru are well worth some time. It's an immensely varied, often compelling, and always intriguing corner of the country, ranging from the handful of cities that stand out as welcoming oases along the desert coast, up to secluded villages in the Andes where you may well be the first *gringo* to pass through for years. On top of this, the entire area is chock full of Inca and pre-Inca sites, making it perhaps the most historically and archeologically important part of Peru.

Trujillo, which rivals Arequipa for the title of Peru's second city, is one of Peru's undiscovered jewels, located on the seaward edge of the vast desert plain at the mouth of the Moche valley. It's an attractive colonial city, with all the usual modern amenities, and one of the friendliest and most interesting places in the country—something of a northern capital. Few people have heard of it before they arrive, but almost everyone seems to spend more time here than planned. The attractions of Trujillo are partly in nearby **ruins**, notably **Chan Chan** and the huge pyramids of the **Temples of the Sun and Moon**, partly in the city itself, and partly in its **beaches**—some of the best around. **Huanchaco**, 12km from Trujillo and an alternative base, is a good case in point, still essentially a fishing village, and an enormously likable travelers' resort within walking distance of sandy beaches and massive ancient ruins.

The so-called "Northern Circuit" is a variety of long-established touring routes through the Andean region above Trujillo, all of which take the beautifully situated mountain town of **Cajamarca** as their main focus. It was here that Pizarro first met up with and captured the Inca Emperor Atahualpa to begin the Spanish conquest of Peru, and around the modern city are a number of fascinating Inca ruins—many linked with water and ritualized baths. Cajamarca is also the springboard for the smaller town of **Chachapoyas** and the ruined city complex of **Kuelap**; it is perhaps the single most overwhelming prehistoric site in Peru. Beyond, there are two possible routes down Amazon headwaters to the jungle town of **Iquitos**— both long and arduous, but well worthwhile if you have the time, enthusiasm, and necessary equipment. Alternatively, you can head back to Trujillo overland through the colonial outpost of **Huamachuco** and—for the really adventurous—perhaps pay a visit to the remote and newly discovered ruins of **Gran Pajaten**.

The coastal strip north of Trujillo, up to the Ecuadorean border, is for the most part a seemingly endless desert plain, interrupted by many small isolated villages but only two real towns, **Chiclayo** and **Piura**. You may well decide to pass straight through on the 1000km Pan American Highway, but you'd miss out on a number of interesting **archeological sites**, a couple of adventurous **routes into the Andes**, and, the best reason to stop, a number of personable, village-like **beach resorts**—the only ones in Peru where the sea is ever really warm.

TRUJILLO AND AROUND

Peru's northern capital, **Trujillo** may be small but it has the real feel of an active regional city—very lively and cosmopolitan, but friendly too, with locals offering you drinks in bars and inviting you back to their homes for a meal. Perhaps it's because of the **climate** here, probably the most pleasant on the whole Peruvian coast, warm and dry without the fogs you get around Lima, but not as hot as the deserts farther north.

Trujillo's most interesting attractions are without a doubt the numerous **archeological sites** dotted around the nearby Moche and Chicama valleys. There are three main zones of interest within easy reach, first and foremost being the massive adobe city of **Chan Chan** on the northern edge of the modern town. To the south, standing alone under Cerro Blanco you can find the largest mud-brick pyramids in the Americas, the **Temples of the Sun and Moon**, while farther away to the north of Trujillo, in the **Chicama valley**, the incredible remnants of vast pre-Inca irrigation canals, temples, and early settlement sites stand in stark contrast to the massive green sugar-cane plantations of the *haciendas*. In many ways these sites are more impressive than the ruins around Cuzco—and most are more ancient too—yet apart from Chan Chan they have been strangely underplayed within the scheme of Peruvian tourism.

Buses and **colectivos** connect the center of town with the Chan Chan complex and the Temples of the Sun and Moon, but reaching the Chicama valley is a little more complicated.

Some History
Pizarro, on his second voyage to Peru in 1528, sailed by the site of ancient Chan Chan, then still a major city throbbing with life as an important regional center of Inca rule. He returned to establish a Spanish colony in the same valley, naming it Trujillo after his birthplace in Estremadura, but a year later, in 1536, the town was besieged by the Inca Manco's forces during the second rebellion against the Conquistadors. Many thousands of Conchuco Indian warriors, allied with the Incas, swarmed down to Trujillo, killing Spaniards and collaborators on the way and offering their victims to Catequil, the tribal deity. Surviving this attack, Trujillo grew to become the main port-of-call for the Spanish treasure fleets, the sailors wining and dining here on their way between Lima and Panama.

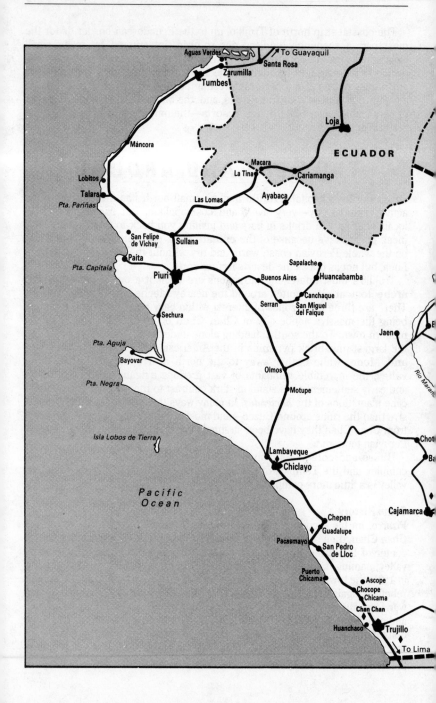

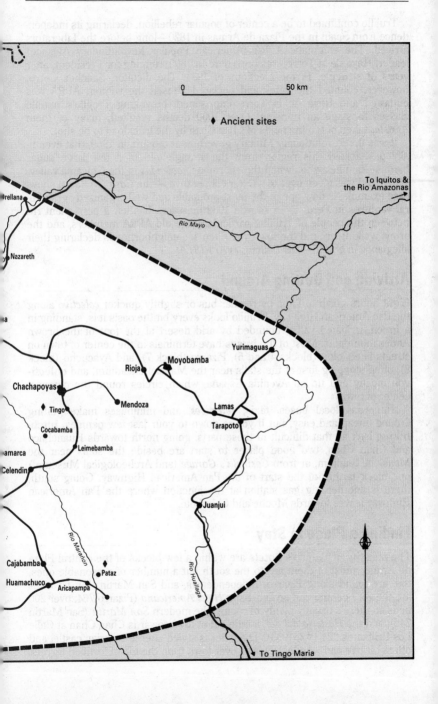

Trujillo continued to be a center of popular rebellion, declaring its independence from Spain in the Plaza de Armas in 1820—long before the Liberators arrived. The enigmatic APRA (American Popular Revolutionary Alliance) leader, Haya de la Torre, was born here in 1895, running for President, after years of struggle, in the elections of 1931. The dictator, Sanchez Cerro, however, counted the votes and declared himself the winner. APRA was outlawed and Haya de la Torre imprisoned, provoking Trujillo's middle classes to stage an uprising. Over 1000 deaths resulted, many of them *Apristas* taken out to the fields of Chan Chan by the truckload to be shot.

It was the Revolutionary Military government though, in 1969, that eventually unshackled this region from the stranglehold of a few large sugar barons—families who owned the enormous *haciendas* in the Chicama valley. Their land was given over to worker cooperatives—the *Casa Grande*, a showcase example, is now one of the most profitable and well-organized agricultural ventures in Peru. Even so, the 1932 massacre has left a permanent rift between the people of Trujillo, particularly the old APRA members, and the army; walking around the town you often see neighborhoods declaring their allegiance in graffiti—*Las Delicias es APRISTA!*

Arriving and Getting Around

Eight hours north of Lima by regular bus or slightly quicker *colectivo* along the Pan American Highway, Trujillo looks every bit the oasis it is, standing in a green, irrigated valley bounded by arid desert at the foot of the brown Andes mountains. Most of the **buses** have terminals in the center of town on streets like Colón (blocks 4 and 5), Pizarro (block 7), and Ayacucho (block 8), often stopping first at the stalls near the Mansiche stadium, and **colectivos** mostly end up on Avenida España, which circles round the compact center of town.

Numerous local buses, taxis, *colectivos*, and minibuses make getting around cheap and easy, but if you're down to your last few pennies, **hitchhiking** isn't all that difficult in these parts: going north towards Huanchaco and Chan Chan, two good places to start are beside the stalls near the Mansiche Stadium, or from *Casinelli's Garage* (and Archeological Museum!) one block farther at the start of the Pan American Highway. Going south, there is another big gas station at the junction where the Pan American Highway leaves towards Moche and Chimbote.

Finding a Place to Stay

The majority of Trujillo's **hotels** are within a few blocks of the central Plaza de Armas: most of them are to the south but a number of reasonable ones, too, are found along Pizarro, Independencia, and San Martin. My favorites are the very central and stylish 1-star *Hotel Americano* (Pizarro 764; over 200 beds so there's usually plenty of room); the modern *San Martin* (San Martin 745); and the *Hostería del Sol*, a little out of town towards Chan Chan at Calle Los Brillantes 224 (☎231933). The latter is styled after a Bavarian castle, and offers bizarre and wonderful views over town from the top of fortified turrets, as well as some of the cleanest rooms in Peru. It also runs a bus to an annex some 140km away into the mountains (in the village of COINA—at 1500m) where in a dry, subtropical microclimate you can visit thermal waters, a trout farm, and several ancient ruins.

More expensive hotels, but still offering good value, include the ubiquitous *Hotel de Turistas* on the Plaza de Armas (from $7.50 single), the *Hotel Continental* (on Gamarra) and the *Hotel Opt Gar* (Gamarra 595).

Eating, Drinking, and Nightlife

There's no shortage either of **bars** or **restaurants** in Trujillo—some of the liveliest are on streets like Independencia, Pizarro, Bolivar, and Ayacucho, to the east of the Plaza de Armas. Seafood is good and quite reasonably priced at the *Costa Azul* restaurant (on the little plaza between Orbegozo's house and the central market), although it is probably even better eaten on the beach, at Huanchaco, Moche, or Buenos Aires (see *Beaches* below). Some tasty **vegetarian** dishes are offered all day long by a small restaurant on the seventh block of Bolivar; there's also a **pool hall** just around the corner from here on Colon.

In addition to the bars there are several **discos** in town. *Billy Bobs*, small, friendly, and long-lived, stays open late (Av. Nicolas de Pierola 716). *Nancy's* is more central at Av. España 303. Out at Huanchaco there are also *Charly's* and a folklore *peña* (held in the French restaurant on Friday and Saturday nights).

More than any other town in Peru, Trujillo is good for **movies**. There are several theaters, clustered within a radius of a few blocks from the Plaza de Armas, that show all sorts of films from great classics to Hollywood comedies, Italian soft porn, and Bruce Lee specials. Audience participation is the most enjoyable thing about going to the movies here. Way back in the 1950s, the writer George Woodcock noted, after a few nights at local theaters, that the uninhibited and infectious response of Trujillo's movie-going audiences "made one realize how much the use of sound in films had turned audiences into silent spectators instead of vociferous participants." Trujillo's audiences are still undaunted by the technology of the screen: however boring the film, you always leave with a feeling you've shared a performance, and perhaps rattled a few barriers with laughter.

Banks and Information

The **banks** are all within a couple of blocks off the Plaza de Armas but just on the square you'll find a **casa de cambio** (cash only changed). The **post office** is on the corner of Independencia with Bolognesi, 1½ blocks from the plaza, and *Entel*, for international telephone calls, is at Puerta Aranda 680.

Tourist information is officially available from *Foptur* (Independencia 628; ☎24-1936), but, although you can sometimes get free maps of the town, it's actually more of a tour agency. Maps and information are also available from the *Touring and Automobile Club* (Almagro 707), and there are two helpful and well-informed local **tour guides**, *Trujillo Tours* (Gamarra 440, ☎23-

3069) and *San Valentín Tours* (Orbegoso 585, ☎23-2812), both of whom double as travel agents.

If you need **medical attention** the best place is the *Clinica Peruana-Americana* (block 8 of Mansiche, on the right just beyond Casinelli's garage); if the nurse at reception isn't very receptive, go to the emergency door where they'll usually see you right away if they have nothing more serious to deal with.

The Town

From the graceful colonial mansions and baroque churches at its heart, **TRUJILLO's** grid system gives way to commercial buildings, light industry, and shantytown suburbs, before thinning out into rich sugar-cane fields that stretch far into the neighboring Chicama valley. It hardly seems a city of nearly a million inhabitants—walk twenty minutes in any direction and you're out in the *campo*, open fields hedged by flowering shrubs. At its center—a dominating force—is the university *La Libertad*, founded by Bolivar in 1824, and around it spread rather elegant, Spanish-style streets, lined with ancient green ficus trees and overhung by long wooden-railed balconies. Most of the older *calles* are named after famous men, liberators, and heroes in the Trujillo fashion. **Gammarra** is the main commercial drag, with ugly, modern, brick-and-glass buildings, shops, hotels, a pinball arcade, and restaurants (one claims to be open 24 hours a day). And life still revolves within the limits of the old town—falling roughly between San Martin, Ayacucho, Almagro, and Colón.

The Plaza de Armas

Commissioned and built by Miguel de Estete, Trujillo's **Plaza de Armas** is a modern square, packed with sharp-witted shoeshine boys playing around the central statue—the *Heros of the Wars of Independence*, created by a German sculptor. Although fairly recent, this statue—indeed the entire plaza—is sinking noticeably year by year. Subsidence, however, doesn't seem to have affected the colonial mansions which front the square, two of which, tastefully restored by banks, now host small **museums** (Mon.–Fri. mornings). Also on the Plaza de Armas is the city's **cathedral**, built in the mid–seventeenth century and substantially rebuilt the following century after earthquake damage. It seems almost plain by Peruvian standards, but houses some colorful baroque sculptures and a handful of paintings by the Quiteña School. Perhaps more impressive are the big, white outside walls splashed with political graffiti in huge red-painted letters.

You can't visit it—though it too has been extensively rebuilt (this time after flood damage)—but the most architecturally interesting of the city's churches is the **monastery of Santa Clara**. A five-minute stroll north from the Plaza de Armas, this really stands out as something special within the confines of the old city. The chapel has an interesting altar covered with gold-leaf and a pulpit with high relief carvings. Perhaps the most stunning of the city's edifices, however, is the **Monastery and Church of El Carmen**; the

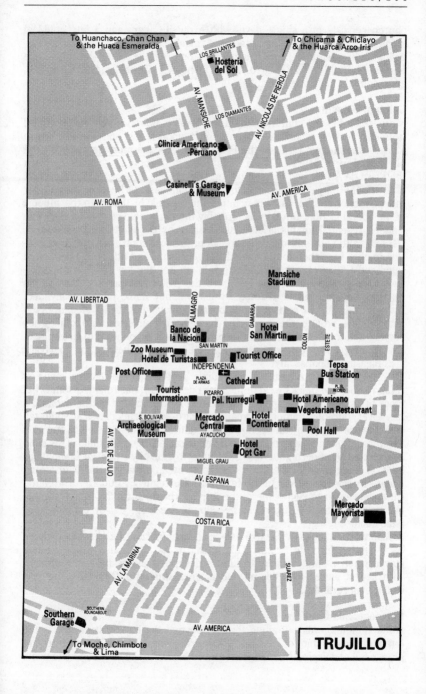

To Huanchaco, Chan Chan, & the Huaca Esmeralda

To Chicama & Chiclayo & the Huarca Arco Iris

LOS BRILLANTES

Hosteria del Sol

AV. NICOLAS DE PIEROLA

AV. MANSICHE

LOS DIAMANTES

Clinica Americano-Peruano

Casinelli's Garage & Museum

AV. AMERICA

AV. ROMA

Mansiche Stadium

AV. LIBERTAD

ALMAGRO

GAMARRA

Hotel San Martin

COLON

ESTETE

Banco de la Nacion

SAN MARTIN

Zoo Museum

Hotel de Turistas

INDEPENDENIA

Tourist Office

Tepsa Bus Station

Post Office

PLAZA DE ARMAS

Cathedral

P. EL RECREO

Tourist Information

PIZARRO

Pal. Iturregui

Hotel Americano

Vegetarian Restaurant

S. BOLIVAR

Archaeological Museum

Mercado Central

AYACUCHO

Hotel Continental

Pool Hall

AV. 18. DE JULIO

Hotel Opt Gar

MIGUEL GRAU

AV. ESPANA

Mercado Mayorista

COSTA RICA

AV. LA MARINA

SUAREZ

SOUTHERN ROUNDABOUT

Southern Garage

AV. AMERICA

To Moche, Chimbote & Lima

TRUJILLO

church consists of a single nave, with exquisite altars and a fine gold-leaf pulpit. The monastery is home to some valuable antique paintings and interesting figures carved from Huamanga stone. Of the other churches, the Iglesia de La Merced (Pizarro, block 5) houses a priceless rococo organ, apparently the only one in Trujillo.

Colonial Mansions

More than for its churches, though, Trujillo is renowned for **colonial houses**, most of which have been kept in good repair and are still in use today. After the two right on the Plaza de Armas, the most impressive—the old **mansion of Marshal Don Luis José de Orbegozo**—stands between the Plaza de Armas and the central market, at Calle Orbegozo 553. Born into one of the city's wealthiest founding families, Orbegozo fought for Independence and became president of the republic in 1833 with the support of the liberal faction. But he was probably the most ineffective of all Peruvian leaders, resented for his aristocratic bearing by the *mestizo* generals; from 1833–39, although still officially president, he lost control of the country—first in **civil war**, then to the invited Bolivian army, and finally to a combined rebel and Chilean force. Orbegozo's rule marked the low point in his country's history, and he disappeared from the political scene to return to his mansion here in disgrace. Today even his family home has been invaded. Although it's still in perfect condition and outstanding in its elegance, the main rooms around the courtyard have been converted into offices for lawyers and the *Colonial Rent-a-Car* company. Still, if you want to sit and read a while, or get your bearings away from the turmoil of the city, the courtyard is as pleasant a spot as any.

The **Palacio Iturregui**, an incredible mid-nineteenth-century mansion (Pizarro 688; two blocks west of the Plaza de Armas), has retained somewhat more of its splendor. Despite being painted a horrific blue on the outside, it has a very striking, almost surreal courtyard—in pseudoclassical style, tall columns are topped by an open roof, and under the blue desert sky one gets the impression of being on Mount Olympus rather than in Trujillo. This patio is encircled by superb galleries. Used today by the city's *Central Club*, it was built, as were most of the city's mansions, by an army general with a long name—in this case Don Juan Manuel de Iturregui y Aguilarte. Today the Club allows you to visit some of the interior rooms in the mornings (Mon.–Fri. only), but the courtyard can be seen all day long, just by popping your head inside.

Also worth a look—at Pizarro 446—is a last mansion, **La Casa Urquiaga**, back by the Plaza de Armas. This is said to be the house where Bolivar stayed when visiting Trujillo. Inside it's decorated and restored throughout, with period pieces to set it off and a small **museum** (Mon.–Fri.) of pre-Columbian ceramics.

Museums and Markets

A few minutes' walk out along Pizarro, beyond the Palacio Iturregui, is the diminutive old square of **Plazuela El Recreo**, where huge old ficus trees are always full of chirping birds. Another three blocks to the south and you come to the limit of the old town and a piece of the original **city wall** to prove it. The wall used to surround the city in a more or less circular route but today the crumbling ruins are a sorry sight, a last-minute attempt at conservation and patchy restoration stuck in the middle of the busy Avenida España beltway.

Probably the best, and without a doubt the most curious, museum in Trujillo is underneath José Casinelli's *Petro Peru* gas station and garage. Set right in the middle of the road, just north of the large Mansiche stadium, it's impossible to miss. Stuffed with ceramics collected over many years from local *huaqueros*, **Casinelli's museum** (in the basement of the gas station at Nicolas de Pierola 601; Mon.–Sat. 8:30–11:30am and 3–5pm; small fee) houses pottery and artifacts spanning literally thousands of years. The Salinar, Viru, Mochica, Chimu, Nazca, Huari, Recuay, and Inca cultures are all represented.

Particular favorites are the **Mochica pots** with their graphic images of daily life, people, animals, and anthropomorphic deities. There are two very Chinese-looking ceramic men, one with a fine beard, the other with a moustache and sitting in a lotus position, while on another shelf Sr. Casinelli (who often shows his visitors around personally) has displayed a range of **Chimu silver objects** including a tiny set of pan pipes. Also of note are the owl figures, symbols for magic and witchcraft, and the perfectly represented **Salinar houses**, which give you an idea of the ancient culture much more successfully than any site restoration.

The **university** also runs two free museums for the public, both somewhat more central than Casinelli's. The **Archeological Museum** (weekdays 9am–noon and 4–5:30pm, Jan.–Mar. 8am–1pm only) is on block 3 of Pizarro and specializes in ceramics, early metallurgy, textiles, and coral. The other building, just behind the Plaza de Armas on block 3 of San Martin, is a fascinating **zoological collection** (same hours), full of dozens of very bizarre stuffed animals, the likes of which you'll have never seen before.

There are two large **markets** in Trujillo, the **Mercado Central**, on the corner of Ayacucho and Gammarra, and the busier **Mercado Mayorista**, on Avenida Costa Rica in the southeast corner of town. The central market, more convenient, sells most essentials (juices, food, clothing, etc.) and has an interesting line in the herbal stalls around it, not to mention unionized shoe-cleaners!

Haciendas and Festivals

Until recent years Trujillo still had a British-owned-and-operated railroad connecting it with the sugar-growing **haciendas**, whose lumbering old wagons used to rumble down from the plantations full of molasses and return loaded with crude oil; they were, incidentally, never washed between loads. Things have changed in the last twenty years, with Trujillo now specializing in wheat, rice, and mechanical engineering as well as producing nearly half of Peru's sugar. And the old haciendas, *Casa Grande, Cartavio* and *Laredo*, are all viable agricultural collectives—converted in 1969 into CAPs (*Co-operativas Agrarias de Producción*). If you feel like taking a look at one, there are regular *colectivos* from the Avenida de España.

The region around **Paijan**, in the Chicama valley, is the heart of this vast sugar-cane zone—and also a special place for the breeding of *Caballos de Paso*—horses reared in the colonial tradition for competing in "who-can-trot-the-nicest" contests. This long-established sport is still popular with high society here and around Lima. Most of the Caballos de Paso meetings are held during Trujillo's **spring festivals**—when teams of horses are trotted around paddocks looking as if their feet never actually touch the ground.

The **September fiestas** are also celebrated with a number of regional dances; particularly noteworthy is the **Marinera**, a famed Peruvian dance that originated in Trujillo and turns up at some point during any musical evening here. A combination of Andalucian, African, and aboriginal music combining the *cajón* (rhythm box) and guitar, its dancers hold handkerchiefs above their heads and skillfully prance around each other. Energetic and very sexual, the *Marinera* is performed in *peñas* all over the country but rarely with the same spirit and conviction as here.

Trujillo's main **fiestas** turn the town into even more of a relaxed playground than it normally seems. September is the main month for festivities with the *International Spring Fair* being held from September 29 until October 3. The main religious fiestas are in October and December. October 17 is generally set aside for the procession of *El Señor de Los Milagros*; while in Huanchaco, the first two weeks of December are devoted to their patron saint—another good excuse for wild parties. February, as everywhere, is carnival time and among the highlights of this are the national *Marinera* dancing competitions.

The Beaches: Huanchaco

Although not exactly a tropical paradise these days, **HUANCHACO** is still a beautiful and relatively peaceful little resort, and, only twenty minutes by bus from Trujillo, offers a viable alternative to staying in the city. It makes an equally good base for visiting many of the sites around the region—in fact it lies just beyond the ruins of Chan Chan—and though it's possible to **camp** here, there are at least three small, fairly cheap **places to stay** which, despite growing popularity, usually have room. Probably the most popular is the *Hotel Bracamonte*, which has a pool and a decent snackbar—clean and friendly, from $1.50. If this is full try the *Hostal Caballito de Tortora* (Av. La Rivera 219; ☎ Lima 28-6314 for reservations).

Only fifteen years ago Huanchaco was a tiny fishing village, quiet and hardly ever seeing tourists. Today it is one of the fastest growing settlements in Peru, with land being sold off for the construction of weekend beach houses, and hotels and restaurants. This, however, hasn't yet diminished the intrinsic fishing village appeal. There is a long jetty where fishermen are usually jostling for the best positions, and stacked along the back of the main beach are rows of *caballitos del mar*—the ancient seagoing rafts used by the Mochicas and still used by locals today. They are basically constructed out of four cigar-shaped bundles of *tortora* reeds, tied together into an arc tapering at each end. The fishermen kneel or sit at the stern and paddle, using the surf for occasional bursts of motion. The local boat builders here are the last people left who know the craft of making *caballitos* along the design of the Mochica prototype.

There are seafood **restaurants** all along the front, a few of them with verandas actually extending to the beach. Most strongly recommended are the *Restaurante Colonial Club*—which serves amazing lobsters, scallops, etc.—and *Walter's Beach Hut*, run by a Californian who prepares a mean fish, it's very reasonable and he's good company when not too busy. Crab is the local specialty and you can often see groups of women and children up to their waists in the ocean picking them and other shellfish with one hand, while holding baskets, alive with claws, in the other.

The very best time to visit Huanchaco is during its **June fiesta** week, or the first two weeks of December, but the town is always alive in a quiet way with people on the beach, others fishing, and usually a few travelers hanging around the restaurants. As far as nightlife goes, there's *Charly's* nightly disco and a new weekend folkore *peña* at the French restuarant. I met one traveler who had been "stuck" in Huanchaco for two years, he liked the place so much.

Huanchaco is connected to Trujillo by an unusually frequent and very regular orange-and-yellow **microbus** from the corner of Avenidas España and Mansiche. On the way out to Huanchaco the bus travels the whole length of Calle Estete (returning via Colón); to get back into town there's normally a line of micros picking up passengers from along the waterfront.

Other Beaches: Buenos Aires and Las Delicias

Closer to the center of town than Huanchuco is the beachfront *barrio* of **Buenos Aires**, 5km of sand just north of Trujillo—very popular with locals and constantly pounded by a not very pacific surf. Like other coastal resorts, its seafood restaurants are a big attraction.

To the south, after crossing the Río Moche's estuary, you come to the settlements of MOCHE and **Las Delicias**, another fine beach—though little more than that—and a handful of restaurants. The famous healing wizard **El Tuno** lives in Las Delicias; his house, which also serves as a restaurant and "alternative" doctor's office, is right on the beach, its walls painted with Mochica designs. At *El Tuno*'s a year or so ago I witnessed a diagnostic session while eating a *ceviche*. An apprentice healer—*curandero*—first rubbed a live guinea pig over the patient's body, then split the animal open—removing its innards for inspection while the heart was still pumping. It didn't do much for my appetite, but did seem to reveal the patient's problems and he was given a prescription and sent away with a mix of healing herbs.

The Chan Chan Complex

The ruined city of **CHAN CHAN** (daily 8:30am–4pm) stretches across a large sector of the Moche valley, beginning almost as soon as you leave Trujillo on the road to Huanchaco. A huge complex, it needs only a little imagination to raise the weathered mud walls to their original grandeur; in fact, I've always thought of the city much like one from an Edgar Rice-

Burroughs story—highly civilized and rule-bound, slaves carrying produce back and forth while artisans and courtiers walk the streets slowly, stopping only to give orders or chat with people of similar status. On certain preordained days there were known to have been great processions through the streets, the priests setting the pace, loaded down with gold, silver jewelry, and flowing, brightly-colored feather cloaks as they all made their way to one of the principal temples along roads between 10m-high adobe walls.

Chan Chan was the capital city of the **Chimu Empire**, an urban-minded civilization which appeared suddenly on the Peruvian coast around A.D. 1100. The Chimu built cities and smaller towns throughout the region, stretching from Tumbes in the north to as far south as Paramonga. Their cities were always extremely elaborate with large, flat-topped buildings for the elite nobility and intricately decorated adobe pyramids serving as temples. They tended to develop methods of social control rather than new technologies, and thus their artwork, particularly ceramics, was essentially mass produced, with quantity being much more important than quality. Food was rationally distributed among the population that grew it, while nobles involved themselves in politics, religion, and the high art of commerce—bringing treasures such as skins, gold, silver, gems, and plumes into the heart of the empire.

Recognized as fine goldsmiths by the Incas, the Chimu used to panel their temples with gold and "cultivate" palace gardens where the plants and animals were made from precious metals. Even the city walls were brightly painted, and the style of architecture and relief decoration is sometimes ascribed to either the Mochica or Chimu having migrated from Central America into this area, bringing with them knowledge and ideas from a more advanced civilization, like the Maya. But although this is a possibility, it's not really necessary to look beyond Peru for inspiration and ingenuity, as the Chimu must have inherited ideas and techniques from a host of previous cultures along the coast and, most importantly, stood on the shoulders of many generations of trial and experiment in irrigating the Moche valley. In the desert, organization, and access to a regular water supply were critical in the development of an urban civilization like that of Chan Chan, whose very existence depended on extracting water not only from the Moche river but also, via a complicated system of canals and aqueducts, from the neighboring Chicama valley.

Without written records, the **origin of Chan Chan** and the orders for its construction are mere conjecture, but there are two traditional local legends. According to one, the city was founded by a certain **Naymlap**, who arrived by boat with his royal fleet; after establishing an empire, he left his son, Si-Um, in command and then disappeared into the western horizon. The other has it that Chan Chan was inspired by an original creator deity of the same name, a dragon who made the sun and the moon and whose earthly manifestation is a rainbow—sign of life and energy, evidence of the serpent's body. Whatever the impulse behind Chan Chan, it remains one of the world's marvels and, in its heyday, was one of the largest pre-Columbian cities in the Americas.

The events leading to the city's demise are better known: in the 1470s Tupac Yupanqui led the Inca armies down from the mountains in the east and cut off the aqueducts supplying Chan Chan with its vital water supply. After lengthy discussions, the Chimu council managed to persuade its leader against going out to fight the Incas. You could say that the Chimu succumbed to the Inca deterrent—they knew full well how the Incas met resistance with brutality and surrender with peaceful takeover. The Chimu were quickly deprived of their chieftains, many of them taken to Cuzco (along with the highly skilled metallurgists) to be indoctrinated into Inca ways. These turbaned aliens from the coast must have formed a strange sight there—strutting around its cold stone streets with huge golden nose ornaments dangling over their chins. Sixty years later when the first Spaniards rode through Chan Chan they found only a ghost town full of dust and legend.

Fish in a wave (Adobe relief at Chan Chan)

The Ruins

Of the three main sectors specifically opened up for exploration, the **Tschudi temple-citadel** is the largest and most frequently visited. Not far from Tschudi, the **Huaca Esmeralda** displays completely different features, being a ceremonial or ritual pyramid rather than a citadel. The third sector, the **Huaca Arco Iris** across on the other side of this enormous city, was similar in function to Esmeralda but has an entirely unique design which has been restored with relish if not historical perfection. One **ticket**, bought for $1.75 at any of these three sites, covers the entrance to all of them. **Guided tours** are easily arranged (guides often hang around at Tschudi but are willing to tour the others) for a few dollars—well worth the money if you can afford it.

The Tschudi Temple-Citadel

TSCHUDI is the best place to get an idea of what Chan Chan must have been like—even though it's now stuck out in the desert among high ruined walls, dusty streets, gateways, decrepit dwellings, and open graves. Only a few hundred meters from the Pacific Ocean at Buenos Aires beach, and bordered by corn fields, this was once the imperial capital and power base from which the Chimu elite ruled their massive domain. To reach Tschudi take the orange-and-yellow Huanchaco-bound **microbus** from Avenida Mansiche in town, getting off at the concrete Tschudi/Chan Chan signpost about 2km beyond the outer suburbs. From here you just follow the track to the left of the road in a straight line until you see the ticket office (on the left) next to the 9m-high defensive walls around the inner temple-citadel.

All the inner courtyards and passages of the **citadel** are laid out according to some well-ordered and preordained plan—and all have been carefully restored and enclosed. This area of the ruins is located only ten or fifteen minutes' walk off the main road between Trujillo and Huanchaco. Beyond it extend acres of ruins, untended and, according to the locals, **dangerous** for gringos—some certainly have been robbed after wandering off alone. This is frustrating, since Tschudi is thought to have been the central citadel among a major group of at least ten complexes, each divided by wide streets and clearly forming separate wards or sacred urbanizations.

Like Tschudi, each of these distinct sectors was designed along typical Chimu lines—with a rectangular layout and divided by enormous trapezoidal walls. As you walk from the road towards Tschudi, although it's difficult to make them out at all clearly, you are actually passing at least four of the other citadels: **Bandelier** and **Uhle** to the left, **Velarde** and **Laberinto** on the right. Each of these individual complexes was most likely based around a royal clan with its own retinues.

Very little is known about the history or even the daily life of those who lived in Tschudi; unfortunately, the Chimu didn't leave us such a graphic record as the earlier Mochica culture whose temples were built on the other side of the Moche valley. But following the marked route around the citadel through a maze of corridors, chambers, and amazingly large plazas, you will undoubtedly begin to form your own picture of this ancient civilization. In a courtyard just past the entrance gateway, some 24 seats are set into niches at regular intervals along the walls, and you can experience an unusual acoustic effect: by sitting in one niche and whispering to someone in another you'll find that this simply designed **council room** cleverly amplifies all sounds, i.e., the niches appear to be connected by adobe intercoms.

La Huaca Esmeralda

One of the most beautiful, and possibly the most venerated, of Chimu temples, **LA HUACA ESMERALDA** lies in ruins a couple of kilometers before Tschudi, just off the main Huanchaco road from Trujillo. Unlike Tschudi, the *huaca* is actually on the very edge of town, stuck between the outer suburbs and the first corn fields. Getting off the orange-and-yellow **microbus** (again, catch this from Avenida Mansiche) where the road begins to narrow, only a block or so beyond the *Hostería del Sol*, the first thing you

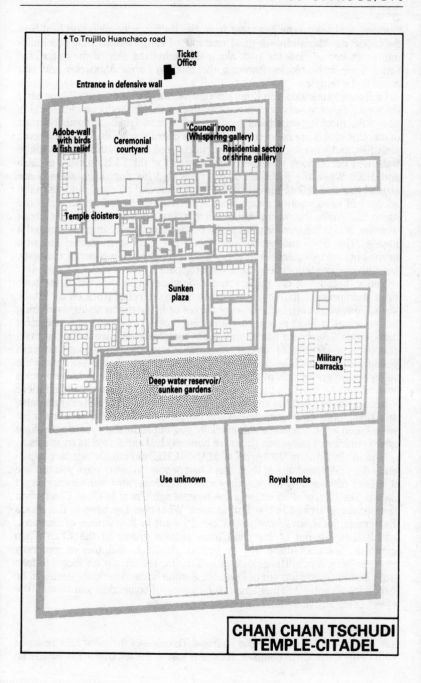

↑ To Trujillo Huanchaco road

Ticket Office

Entrance in defensive wall

Adobe-wall with birds & fish relief

Ceremonial courtyard

'Council' room (Whispering gallery)

Residential sector/ or shrine gallery

Temple cloisters

Sunken plaza

Military barracks

Deep water reservoir/ sunken gardens

Use unknown

Royal tombs

CHAN CHAN TSCHUDI TEMPLE-CITADEL

can see, set back to the left away from the traffic, is the old church of **San Salvador de Mansiche**—a good example of early colonial religious building. From here, follow the path along the right-hand side of the chapel for some three small blocks (through the modern *barrio Mansiche*) and you come to the temple.

La Huaca Esmeralda, the Emerald Temple, was built in the twelfth or early thirteenth century—at about the same time as the Tschudi complex—and is one of the most important *huacas* scattered around Trujillo. Unusually, most of its relief motifs are concerned solely with ocean-marine life, related human activities, and wave formations. It was uncovered only in 1923, but its adobe walls and decorations were severely damaged in the El Niño rains of 1925 and 1983. While the guardian of the ruins and his dog, Lilly, showed me around this site, telling me about the freak rains and pointing out where the adobe had been washed away, I suddenly realized the full meaning of the name. *El Niño*, the warm water current that causes the periodic freak weather, is also the term applied to the bad weather itself. Simply translated it means "The Boy" and people see it just like that—a frustrated kid who pushes his warm waters south every now and again, merely out of curiosity, but with dire consequences whenever it happens.

Today, because of the rains, you can only just make out what must have been an impressive multicolored **facade**. All of the **relief work** on the adobe walls, however, is original, showing friezes of fishnets containing swimming fishes, waves, a flying pelican, and frequent repetitive patterns of geometrical arabesques. The *huaca* has an unusually complex **structure**, with two main platforms, a number of surrounding walls, and several sloping pathways giving access to each section. From the top platform you can see across the valley to the graveyards of Chan Chan, out to sea, over the cultivated fields around the site, and into the primitive brick factory next door. Standing there it seems obvious that the site was a place for adoration, possibly serving also as a royal tomb. Only some shells and *chaquiras* (stone and coral necklaces) were found when the *huaca* was officially dug out some sixty years ago—long after centuries of *huaqueros* (treasure hunters) had exhausted its treasures.

The locals living in the barrio of **MANSICHE**, next to the site, are apparently direct descendants of the Chan Chan people. In many ways you can see it in their faces and by the way they walk. Mansiche, now with strange street names like Liverpool Street, was the nearest settlement to Chan Chan when the Spaniards arrived in the Trujillo area. Whenever I've been to the Huaca Esmeralda, local boys have asked me if I want to buy strings of *chaquira*, which they sift out of the sand from remote graves in the Chan Chan complex. Some of these are in perfect condition and they're generally cheaper here than at Huanchaco or in Trujillo. Technically it's illegal to take pre-Columbian artifacts out of Peru, but a stone or coral necklace seems to be generally acceptable. Then again, the chance of something you buy on the street being anywhere near that old is very remote.

La Huaca Arco Iris

LA HUACA ARCO IRIS—the Rainbow Temple—is the most fully restored ruin of the Chan Chan complex. Its site is just to the left of the Pan American

Highway about 4km north of Trujillo in the middle of the urban district of LA ESPERANZA. There's a regular bus service (red-and-blue **microbus**, Comite 19) which you can catch from the center of Trujillo or across the road from Casinelli's gas station–cum–museum. The ruins are indicated by a blue concrete sign at the side of the main road. Get off the bus here and you'll see the *huaca* set back behind a sandy vacant lot and surrounded by a tall wall.

The *huaca*, or temple, flourished under the Chimu between the twelfth and fourteenth centuries. No one knows exactly what to call it since several interpretations have been made of the central motif, which is repeated throughout the pyramid. It has been called a dragon, a centipede, and, more recently, a rainbow. In fact, the dragon and the rainbow need not exclude one another, both possibly representing the creator divinity. However, local legend has it that the rainbow is the protector of creation and, in particular, fertility and fecundity. The centipede, however, is a fairly widespread motif (notably on the Nazca ceramics) whose original meaning seems to have been lost. Large poisonous centipedes, up to 20cm long, do live in the Andes, and they're still looked upon with some awe because of the way they move and control their myriad legs—people are very careful not to tread on them.

Most of the main **temple walls** have been restored, and they are covered with the recreated "rainbow" design. Originally, the outer walls were decorated in the same way with identical elaborate friezes cut into the adobe, in a design that looks like a multi-legged serpent arching over two lizard-type beings. Each of the serpents' heads, one at either end of the arc, seems to be biting the cap (or tip of the head) off a humanoid figure.

There are two tiers to the temple, the **first platform** consisting of fourteen rectangular chambers, possibly used for storing corn and precious metals for ritual purposes. A path slopes up to the **second tier**, a flat-topped platform—the ceremonial area where sacrifices were held and the gods spoke. From here there is a wide view over the valley, towards the ocean, the city, other *huacas* and the city of Chan Chan.

Down below you can visit the small **site museum**, built while the *huaca* was being restored in 1964 and housing a minor selection of ceramics from the site itself and some interesting wooden idols found in a tomb here. Fifteen minutes' walk down the main road, back towards Trujillo, brings you to the **Pedro Puerta gallery** where you can usually find English-speaking **guides** to any of the Trujillo ruins; the gallery, however, was closed on my last visit—and may still be so (ask at the museum).

The Temples of the Sun and Moon

Located south of Trujillo beside the Moche river in a barren desert landscape, these two temples bring ancient Peru to life. The stunning **Temple of the Sun** (*La Huaca del Sol*) is the largest adobe structure in the Americas, and easily the most impressive of the many pyramids on the Peruvian coast. Its twin, the **Temple of the Moon** (*La Huaca de la Luna*), is smaller, but more complex and brilliantly frescoed.

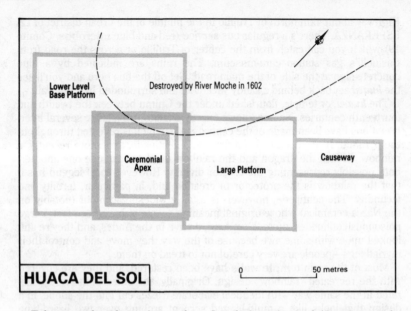

Lower Level Base Platform

Destroyed by River Moche in 1602

Ceremonial Apex

Large Platform

Causeway

HUACA DEL SOL

0   50 metres

Taken together these sites make a fine day's outing and, if you've got the time, really shouldn't be missed. To reach these sites—**entrance** to which is currently free and unrestricted—take one of the direct *colectivos* from the first block of Avenida Suarez in Trujillo. They leave throughout the day and cost about 25¢. Or save a dime by taking the yellow-and-green **microbus** (marked *Salaverry* or *Moche*), which leaves town by the southern traffic circle at Avenida America and Avenida La Marina. About 1km beyond the bridge over the Moche a sandy track turns off the main Pan American High-way to the left—you can already see the *Huaca del Sol* to the left of a conical white hill (Cerro Blanco). Just follow the track through corn fields and small gardens for about half an hour until you reach the foot of the pyramid.

With the *huacas* being so close to the coastal villages of MOCHE and LAS DELICIAS, it's a good idea to combine a visit to the ruins with a stop at one of the local *picanterías* for a bite to eat. Walking back from the Temple of the Sun to the Pan American Highway, you can pick up the yellow-and-green **microbus** without much problem and get into **MOCHE**, a small settlement with lots of big restaurants, all serving freshly prepared seafood. There are a couple of restaurants on the beach on the next settlement, **LAS DELICIAS**, one of which (see p.209) is run by the famous Trujillan *curandero* El Tuno.

The Temple of the Sun

The Temple of the Sun was built by the Mochica around A.D. 500 and, although very weathered, its pyramid edges still slope at a sharp 77° to the horizon. The larger part of the structure, which you come to first, is made up of a lower level base-platform. On top of this is the demolished stump of a four-sided, stepped pyramid, which is surmounted about 50m above the surrounding desert by a ceremonial platform. On the other side of the base platform is another larger one leading off down to a causeway at the end; from the top you can see how the river Moche was diverted by the Spanish way back in 1602, in order to erode the *huaca* and find treasure. They were quite successful at washing away a large section but found precious little, except adobe bricks. The first scientific archeological work here was done by Max Uhle in the early 1900s; he discovered over 3400 objects and ceramics, most of which were removed to the University of California at Berkeley museum.

Estimates of the pyramid's **brickwork** vary, but it must contain somewhere between 50 and 140 million adobe blocks, each of which was marked in any one of a hundred different ways—probably the maker's distinguishing signs, used in the counting of tribute. It must have required a massively well-organized labor supply to put together—Calancha, one of the Spanish chroniclers, wrote that it was built in three days by 200,000 Indians! Three days might actually mean three stages, but even so, someone must have been working on those bricks for a long time. It would be interesting to know exactly how the Mochica priests and architects decided on the shape. If you look at the form of the *huaca* against the silhouette of Cerro Blanco from the main road there is a remarkable similarity between the two, and if you look at the *huaca* sideways from the vantage point of the Huaca de La Luna, it has the same general outline as the hills behind.

The Temple of the Moon

Clinging to the bottom of Cerro Blanco, just 500m from the Sun Temple, is another Mochica edifice—**The Temple of the Moon**. Again, this was probably a sacred building, quite separate from the *Huaca del Sol* though constructed in the same era. It may even have been an administrative center when the Priest-Lord was in residence. The Temple of the Moon is only the visible part of an older complex of interior rooms; ceramics dug up from the vast graveyard that extends between the two *huacas* and around the base of Cerro Blanco suggest that this might have been the site for a cult of the dead.

You can still scramble about on the *Huaca de la Luna* (unless the Tourist Police have closed it off for restoration work) but you'll need a flashlight to find your way around the rooms and cave niches inside. The interior rooms

Litter Bearers (design from Mochica ceramic)

are in a bad state: in one you can just see the top of a mural poking above a pile of rubble.

Behind the Temple of the Moon some frescoed rooms were discovered by a *huaquero* in 1910 and more were found in 1925, displaying murals with up to seven colors (mostly reds and blues). The most famous of these paintings has been called *The Rebellion of the Artifacts* because, as you find on some Mochica ceramics, all sorts of objects are depicted attacking human beings, getting their revenge, or rebelling: there are war clubs with faces and helmets with human legs chasing after people.

The Chicama Valley

Chicama is the next valley north of the Moche river, 35km from Trujillo and the heart of its fertile plain. In the Mochica and Chimueras eras the Chicama river was connected to the fields of Chan Chan by a vast system of canals and aqueducts over 90km long, and **remains** of this irrigation system, fortresses, and evidence from over 6000 years of residence can still be seen around the valley. Today, however, the region is most striking in its appearance as a single enormous sugar-cane field, although in fact it's divided among a number of large sugar-producing cooperatives, again originally family-owned *haciendas* that were redistributed during the military government's agrarian reforms in 1969. The sugar cane was first brought to Peru from India by the Spaniards and quickly took root as the region's main crop. Like the Moche, the Chicama valley is full of *huacas* and the locals have a long tradition as *huaqueros*. Rumors abound about vile deaths from asphyxiation, a slow process sometimes lasting days, for anyone who ventures into a tomb. "*Le llamó la huaca*," they say—the *huaca* called him!

Three important ancient sites—**La Huaca Prieta**, **Chiquitoy**, and **Ascope**—and the isolated seaside village of **Puerto Chicama** make a trip out here worthwhile. For the villages of CHICAMA, PAIJAN, or ASCOPE you can pick up **buses** in Trujillo across the road from Casinelli's garage, or from around the main market (where most of them start). **Colectivos** to CARTAVIO leave from the Avenida Espana, and are best if you want to start off at Chiquitoy or the Huaca Prieta. The whole valley is also served by local *colectivos* so it's quite easy to get from one center to another, although there is always a little walking to do: from Cartavio to the Huaca Prieta, for instance, is half an hour or so of easy walking.

La Huaca Prieta

La Huaca Prieta, quite literally, is a heap of rubbish—right next to the *Playa El Brujo* at the edge of the ocean. But it's a garbage dump redeemed by the fact that it has been accumulating for some 6500 years, and is crowded with evidence and clues about the evolution of culture and human activity on the coast.

The usual way to get here is by *colectivo* to CARTAVIO, then a short walk via the *hacienda*/co-op of MAGDALENA DE CAO. **La Prieta** is a small, dark hill about 12m high, its coloration due to thousands of years of decomposing

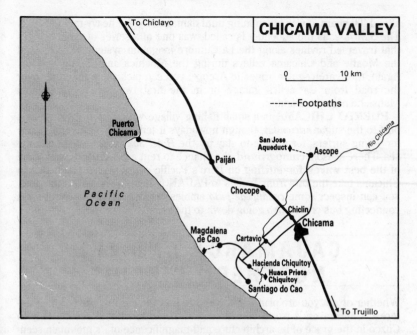

CHICAMA VALLEY

0   10 km

------ Footpaths

To Chiclayo

Puerto
Chicama

San Jose
Aqueduct

Ascope

Rio Chicama

Paiján

Chocope

*Pacific
Ocean*

Chiclin

Chicama

Magdalena
de Cao

Cartavio

Hacienda Chiquitoy
Huaca Prieta
Chiquitoy

Santiago do Cao

To Trujillo

organic remains. On the top part there are signs of subterranean dwellings, long since excavated by Larco Hoyle and Junius Bird.

Chiquitoy

The well-preserved ruins of **CHIQUITOY** are rarely visited—stuck out as they are on an empty desert plain unconnected by any road. To reach the site you'll need to take a *colectivo* to CARTAVIO and then walk to the HACIENDA CHIQUITOY. You should be able to find someone there who'll put you on the right track, which leads off into the desert; follow this across the flat *pampa* for about 5 or 6km (45 minutes' walk) and you can't miss the ruins.

Chiquitoy's ruins are comprised of a temple complex with a three-tiered pyramid—very Mayan-like—in front of a walled, rectangular sector. There is evidence of some dwellings and a large courtyard, too, though little is known about its history.

If only because of its location and the good condition of the pyramid, Chiquitoy is well worth the walk; alternatively, you can usually find **taxis** in Chocope or Chicama who'll take you to this site for a few dollars per person, the more people the cheaper.

Ascope and Puerto Chicama

The two other places of interest around the Chicama valley are Ascope and Puerto Chicama. Near to **ASCOPE**, just a couple of kilometers out of the settlement, is a great earthen **aqueduct**, standing 15m high, which used to carry water across the mouth of this dry valley. Still an impressive site even after 1400 years, it was functioning until damaged by the heavy rains of 1925. The *San Jose*, as the aqueduct is called, was one of a series of canal bridges that traversed ravines along the La Cumbre irrigation system, which joined the Moche and Chicama valleys during the Mochica and Chimu periods. Again, there are regular **buses** to Ascope; you can pick them up either over the road from Casinelli's garage or in the first two blocks of Avenida Mansiche near the stadium.

PUERTO CHICAMA is a small fishing village which used to serve as a port to the sugar *haciendas*, though nowadays it tends to be a meeting place for young surfers; for a place to stay try the *Hotel Sony* which overlooks the sea. There's also a **campground**, the chance to rent a **beach hut** , and some of the best **waves for surfing** on Peru's Pacific coastline. To reach Puerto Chicama take the **bus** from Trujillo to PAIJAN (where, if you've got the time, you can inspect some *caballo de paso* stables or stud farms) and wait for a connecting bus or *colectivo* going down to the coast.

CAJAMARCA AND THE NORTHERN CIRCUIT

Whether or not you are planning to venture into the eastern sites or the rainforest, **Cajamarca** is worth considering—a *sierra* town, it is second only to Cuzco in the grace of its architecture and magnificence of its mountain scenery. From Trujillo there are two main routes, each exciting and spectacular, and many travelers choose to make a loop, the **Northern Circuit**, going up by one and returning by the other. The speediest is up from the coast at Pacasmayo along a relatively new paved road which follows the Jequetepeque River, passing small settlements and families at work in terraced fields along precipitous valley walls. There are *colectivos* this way from Trujillo and from Chiclayo, in the Northern Desert, each route taking about eight hours. The more interesting but slower route (two days at least) is by bus along the old road from Trujillo through **Huamachuco** and **Cajabamba**.

One of Peru's proudest and most historic cities, Cajamarca has barely been affected by the tourist trade, despite its increasing popularity as a base for visiting the exciting ruins of **Chachapoyas**, and as the last taste of civilization before the jungle regions around **Tarapoto** and **Yurimaguas**. From there boats head downstream as far as IQUITOS—the capital of the vast *Departamento de Loreto*—on the Amazon, in the heart of the Peruvian rainforest.

Cajamarca

An attractive little city, almost European in appearance, **CAJAMARCA** squats placidly below a high mountain in a neatly organized valley. The stone-based architecture of the town seems to reflect the cold nights up here, over 2700m above the Pacific Ocean. Charming as it all is—elaborate stone filigree mansions and churches and old baroque facades wherever you look—most buildings are actually quite austere in appearance. Easily reached by *colectivo* or bus from Lima and/or Trujillo, or by plane with *Aeroperu* (Tues., Thurs., and Sat. mornings), Cajamarca is rarely overcrowded with tourists. The narrow streets are, however, usually thronged with locals going to market.

Hotels, Eating, and Practical Details

Since most of the places of interest are in the center of Cajamarca, the best **hotels** are those on the main square. The *Hostal Casablanca*, a colonial mansion right on the Plaza de Armas, is excellent value, one of the best cheaper hostels at $2 a night, single. Cajamarca has one of the few state-run *Hotel de Turistas* which is relatively reasonable ($4–$5; with good hot baths). The *Gran Hotel Plaza*, too, is stylish and cheap with hot showers; cheaper, yet still on the main square, the *Hostal Peru* is also recommended. Just slightly farther out, the *Hotel Continental* (Calle Amazonas, block 7) costs less than $5; the *Hostal Atahualpa* (Pasaje Atahualpa) has rooms from around $2; and the *Hostal Cajamarca* (Calle Dos de Mayo) has clean but simple accommodations for about the same price. Two of the cheapest places in town, though still acceptable to most budget travelers, are the *Hotel Jusoui* (Amazonas 637, just a block down from the plaza) at around 50¢ single and the *Turismo* (four blocks down Dos de Mayo from the plaza), also under $1.

Within a stone's throw of the cathedral are several good **restaurants**; one of the most popular, and generally good value, is *La Taverna*. Other recommendations include *Restaurante El Cajamarquez* (Calle Amazonas, block 7); *Restaurante Salas* , a classical eating house on the main plaza with decent set menu; and *La Namorina* (on the exit towards the Inca Baths), a delicious *picantería* serving typical Peruvian food. *El Buen Amigo* (Dos de Mayo, just above the plaza) is a modest but friendly spot for lunch.

You can get free **maps** and **information** from FOPTUR (Jr. Silva San Tisteban 138/144) or in the *Conjunto de Belén*, just around the corner from the plaza on Calle Belén. *Cajamarca Tours* (2 de Mayo 323) is also very helpful and can advise on arranging trips to most of the nearby sites.

The **Banco de la Nación** is at Jirón Tarapaca 647 and the **post office** is nearby, on block 4 of Calle Lima. Domestic and international **phone calls** can be made from *Entel-Peru's* offices at Jirón San Martin 363. The **central market**, a flurry of activity in the mornings, is on the corner of Apurimac and Amazonas, within three minutes' walk of the Plaza de Armas.

Fiestas and Annual Events

If you can arrange it, the best time to visit Cajamarca is during the months of May or June for the **Festival of Corpus Christi**. Until eighty years ago this was the country's premier festival, coinciding with the traditional Inca sun festival and led by the elders of the Canachin family who were directly descended from local pre-Inca chieftains. The procession still attracts Indians from all around, but one gets the impression that increasing commercialism has eaten away at its traditional roots. Nevertheless it's fun, with plenty of parties, bullfights, *Caballo de Paso* meetings, and an interesting trade fair. **Cajamarca Day**, usually around February 11, is celebrated with music, dancing, procession, and fireworks.

The Town

The town is laid out in a grid system centered around the **Plaza de Armas**—built on the site of the original triangular courtyard where Pizarro captured the Inca leader Atahualpa in 1532 (see the section immediately following for more on this). Four centuries on, the battle scene looks rather different—and distinctly sad. On one side of the plaza is a late–seventeenth-century **cathedral**, its walls incorporating various pieces of Inca masonry, its internal atmosphere lifted only by a splendid Churriguerresque altar created by Spanish craftsmen. On the other is the strange-looking **San Francisco**, in whose sanctuary are thought to be the bones of Atahualpa—who was originally buried in the church's cemetery.

One of Cajamarca's unique features was that, until relatively recently, none of the churches had towers—a concerted effort to avoid the colonial tax rigidly imposed on "completed" religious buildings. The eighteenth-century chapel of **La Dolorosa**, next to San Francisco, followed this pattern; it does, however, display some of Cajamarca's finest examples of stone filigree, both outside and in. The church of **Belén**, just around the corner on Calle Belén, also boasts a lavish interior.

Even more stylish than the churches, and a superb example of colonial stonecraft, is the **Palacio de los Condes de Ucedo** on Calle Apurimac, one block from the plaza. A splendid colonial mansion, this has been taken over and conserved by the *Banco de Credito*. Not far away is the **University Museum** (Jirón Arequipa, 1½ blocks from the plaza, by the central market; Mon.–Sat. 8am–noon and 2–5pm), particularly interesting for the breadth of its collections of ceramics, textiles, and other objects, spanning some 3000 years of culture in the Cajamarca basin. If the director, Rodolfo Ravines, is around he is always very eager to chat about archeology and local sites, something he probably knows more about than anyone else alive. **San Francisco convent**, by the plaza, has a separate museum devoted to religious art, not as good as the one in Cuzco but an insight, nevertheless, into the colonial mind.

By far the most famous site in town is the so-called **Ransom Room**, *El Cuarto del Rescate* (Jr. Amalia, Puga 722; closed Tues.), the only Inca construction still standing in Cajamarca. For a long while this was claimed to be the room which Atahualpa, as Pizarro's prisoner, promised to fill with gold in return for his freedom. Although fitting the dimensions described in detail by the chroniclers (not surprisingly, considering the symmetry and repetitiveness of Inca design), historians now agree that this was in fact Atahualpa's prison cell. Its bare Inca masonry is notably poorer than that which you find around Cuzco, and the trapezoidal doorway a post-Conquest construction (probably Spanish rather than native).

Some History—Atahualpa and Pizarro

The fertile Cajamarca basin was domesticated long before cows arrived to graze its pastures, or the white fences parceled up the flat valley floor. As early as 1000 B.C. it was occupied by well-organized tribal cultures—the earliest sign of the Chavin culture's influence on the northern mountains. The existing sites, scattered all about this region, are evidence of advanced civilizations capable of producing elaborate stone constructions without hard metal tools, and reveal permanent settlement from the **Chavin era** right through until the conquering **Inca** army arrived in the 1460s. Then, and over the next seventy years, it developed into an important provincial garrison town, evidently much favored by the Inca emperors as a stopover on their way along the Royal Highway between Cuzco and Quito. With its hot springs, it proved a convenient spot for resting up and licking wounds after the frequent Inca battles with "barbarians" in the eastern forests. The city was endowed with sun temples and sumptuous palaces, and their presence must have been felt even when the supreme Lord was over 1000km away to the south, paying homage to the ancestors in the capital of his empire.

Atahualpa, the last Inca Lord, was in Cajamarca in late 1532, taking it easy at the hot springs, when news came of **Pizarro** breathlessly dragging his 62 horsemen and 106 foot soldiers up into mountains higher than most Europeans even realized existed. Atahualpa's spies and runners kept him well informed of the Spaniards' movement, and he could quite easily have destroyed the small band of weary aliens in one of the rocky passes to the west of Cajamarca. Instead he waited patiently until Friday, November 15, when a disheveled group entered the silent streets of the deserted Inca city. For the first time, Pizarro saw Atahualpa's camp, its cotton tents "extending for a league, with Atahualpa's own in the middle. All his men were standing outside the tents and their arms, which were spears as long as pikes, were stuck in the earth." Estimates varied, but there were between 30,000 and 80,000 effective Inca warriors—outnumbering the Spaniards by some two hundred to one.

Pizarro meanwhile was planning his coup along the same lines that had been so successful for Cortés in Mexico: he would capture Atahualpa and use him to control the realm. The square in Cajamarca was perfect for the following day's operation: "Long low buildings occupied three sides of it, each some 200 yards long. Pizarro stationed the cavalry in two of these, in three contingents of 15 to 20."

The next morning nothing happened. Pizarro became anxious; his plans could easily be foiled. In the afternoon, however, Atahualpa's army began to move in a ceremonial procession, slowly making their way across the plain towards the city of Cajamarca. Tension mounted in the Spanish camp. As the Indians came closer they could be heard singing a graceful lament and their dazzling regalia could be made out. "All the Indians wore large gold and silver disks like crowns on their heads . . . In front was a squadron of Indians wearing a livery of checkered colors, like a chessboard."

Leaving most of his troops outside on the plain, Atahualpa entered with some 5000 men, unarmed except for small battleaxes, slings, and pebble pouches. He was being carried by eighty noblemen in a ornate litter—its wooden poles covered in silver, the floor and walls with gold and brilliantly colored parrot feathers. The emperor himself was poised on a small stool, dressed richly with a crown placed upon his head and a thick string of magnificent emeralds around his aristocratic neck. Understandably bewildered to see no bearded men and not one horse in sight, he shouted— "Where are they?"

A moment later, the Dominican friar, Vicente de Valverde, came out into the plaza; with the minimum of reverence to one he considered a heathen in league with the devil, he invited Atahualpa to dine at Pizarro's table. The Lord Inca declined the offer, saying that he wouldn't move until the Spanish returned all the objects they had already stolen from his people. The friar handed Atahualpa his Bible and began a Christian discourse which no one within earshot could understand. After examining this "strange" object Atahualpa threw it on the floor, visibly angered, probably more at the friar's spoutings than at the holy book. Vicente de Valverde, horrified at such a sacrilege, hurried back to shelter screaming—"Come out! Come out, Christians! Come at these enemy dogs who reject the things of God."

Two cannons signalled the start of what quickly became a massacre. The Spanish horsemen flew at the 5000 Indians, hacking their way through flesh to overturn the litter and capture the emperor. Knocking down a 2m-thick wall, many of the Inca troops fled onto the surrounding plain with the cavalry at their heels. The foot soldiers set about those left in the square with such speed and ferocity that in a short time "most of them were put to the sword." Not one Indian raised a weapon against the Spaniards.

To the vain Spanish, it was patently obvious why Atahualpa, an experienced battle leader, had led his men into such an obvious trap. He had underestimated his opponents, their crazy ambitions, and their technological superiority—steel swords, muskets, cannons, and horse power. On the other hand, perhaps the Inca Lord knew that the inevitable was about to happen— the oracles had warned him. He could kill Pizarro but there were doubtless others, maybe even more ruthless, where these strange foreigners on four-legged monsters had come from. Whatever the explanation for what must surely be one of the world's biggest ever massacres of indigenous people, it was a bloody beginning to Cajamarca's colonial history. (Excerpts here are from John Hemming's translations of the original Chronicles in *The Conquest of the Incas*.)

Inca Ruins, Hot Springs, and Some Local Hikes

A short stroll from Cajamarca's central plaza, two blocks along Avenida Dos de Mayo, brings you to the path up the **Cerro Santa Apolonia**, the grassy hill that overlooks the town and offers by far the best view across the valley. On top, originally a sacred spot, you'll find what is thought to have been a sacrificial stone used by the ancients around 1000 B.C. It is popularly called the "Inca's Throne," and if you sit in it for a while you'll see why.

Just 2km to the southwest of this hill, along the road to Cumbemayo, is a group of other ruins—prominent among them an old pyramid. Little is known about this, which the Spanish used to call a temple of the sun, but the locals today use the name *Agua Tapada*, "covered water." Quite possibly, there is a subterranean well below the site—they're not uncommon around here and it might initially have been a temple related to some form of water cult.

Many of the ruins around Cajamarca are in fact related to water, in a way that seems both to honor it in a religious sense and to use it in a practical manner. Only 5km away from the city are the **Inca Baths** where Atahualpa was camped when Pizarro arrived, and from where the Inca army marched, or paraded, to their doom. You can take a taxi or *colectivo* out here very cheaply; or you can walk, which is probably a better way to appreciate the thermal waters when you arrive. To reach the baths, follow Amazonas east from the market five blocks until you reach the corner with Cinco Esquinas; turn up here, then immediately make a right onto Calle El Inca—this is laid on the foundations of the old Inca road and will take you all the way up in about an hour-and-a-half. For a small fee you can still use the baths—which are of pure thermal waters (hot, cold, or a mixture) as they bubble straight out of the mountain. The adjoining *Hotel Chavez* seems to have something of a monopoly over the springs but this doesn't spoil either the beneficial effect or the pleasure of using them.

An enjoyable two-hour walk from the Inca baths, following the Río Chonta gently uphill to its source brings you to another important site—the **Ventanillas de Otuzco**. The *Ventanillas* ("Windows") are a huge pre-Inca necropolis where the dead chieftains of the Cajamarca culture were buried in niches, sometimes meters deep, cut by hand into the volcanic rock. If you want to go directly back into town from here, a road goes all the way (about 12km), becoming the Avenida Aviación and coming out on Avenida Arequipa four blocks north of the Plaza de Armas.

Cumbemayo and Kuntur Huasi

About 20km by road northwest of Cajamarca is **CUMBEMAYO**, an ancient canal stretching for over a kilometer in an isolated highland dale. There are no buses from Cajamarca and only infrequent trucks, but you can walk or hitchhike in around three to four hours, depending on how many short cuts you find across the bends in the road—starting from the back of Cerro Santa Apolonia on the southwest side of town. Alternatively, if you don't want to walk and there are four or five of you, it's not difficult to find a taxi willing to do the trip for around $3 per person (or *Cajamarca Tours* run trips which cost $5 each).

Just before you reach Cumbemayo there is a weird natural rock formation, the **Bosque de Piedras** ("Forest of Stones"), where clumps of eroded limestone taper into thin, figure-like shapes—known locally as *los fraillones* ("the friars"). A little farther on is the well-preserved and incredibly well made water channel, **El Cumbemayo**, built perhaps 1200 years before the Incas arrived here. The amount of meticulous effort which must have gone into constructing this, cut as it is from solid rock with perfect right angles and precise geometric lines, suggests that it was more for a ritual or religious function than simply for irrigation purposes. Water was certainly a very important, probably sacred substance for the ancient cultures of Peru; there are many examples of whole citadels designed around natural springs. Sites like Cumbemayo and Tipón (near Cuzco) illustrate how fruitless it sometimes is to try to differentiate between the practical use and religious adoration of natural phenomena in attempting to understand nonindustrial cultures. In some places along the canal there are rocks cut into what look like tables: in fact these forms were left by the quarrying of stones during the building of the canal. Cumbemayo originally transferred water from the Atlantic to the Pacific watershed (from the eastern to the western slopes of the Andes) via a complex system of canals and tunnels, many of which are still visible and in some cases operational. An extravagant project, the waterway displays an unsurpassed knowledge of surveying and engineering.

To the right-hand side of the aqueduct (with your back to Cajamarca) there is a large face-like rock on the hillside, with a manmade **cave** cut into it. This contains some interesting 3000-year-old petroglyphs etched in typical Chavin style (you'll need a flashlight) and dominated by the everpresent feline features.

Kuntur Huasi

From Cumbemayo it's possible to walk to a second ancient site—**KUNTUR HUASI**—in the upper part of the Jequtepeque river valley, to the east of the Cajamarca Basin. This, however, takes three or four days so you'll need a tent and food. Hilary and George Bradt's *Backpacking and Trekking in Peru and Bolivia* has a good detailed description and sketch map of the trail: you'll need this, or at least a survey map of the area since neither site is marked.

An easier way of getting there, though much less spectacular, is to take a bus from Cajamarca to CHILETE, a small mining town about 50km along the paved road to Pacasmayo. At Chilete you can connect with a bus to the village of SAN PABLO (two **hotels**) from where it's just a short downhill walk to the ruins.

Although Kuntur Huasi has lost what must once have been a magnificent temple, you can still make out a variation on Chavin designs carved onto its four stone monoliths. Apart from Chavin itself this is the most important site in the northern Andes related to the feline cult; golden ornaments and turquoise were found in graves here, but so far not enough work has been done to be able to give a precise date to the site. The anthropomorphic carvings indicate differences in time—perhaps Kuntur Huasi belonged to the late Chavin era, placing it around 400 B.C. Whatever its age, the pyramid is an imposing ruin amid quite exhilarating countryside.

Farther Afield: The Ruins of Gran Pajaten

It's a major expedition from Cajamarca, or anywhere else for that matter, to the relatively recently discovered ruins of **Gran Pajaten**. If you're seriously interested in visiting these incredible but extremely remote ruins of a sacred city, information and advice can be found from the universities and the *Instituto de Cultura* in Lima, Trujillo, or Cajamarca. Permission to visit must also be obtained from them—it's best to ask the South American Explorers' Club in Lima for details before setting off.

Reaching **the ruins** is no easy task: from Cajamarca it's an eight-hour bus ride to CAJABAMBA (*Hotel Flores* on the main plaza), from where it's another three hours to **HUAMACHUCO**; here there is a reasonable hotel, *La Libertad*, and quite a good restaurant, *La Caribe*. From here, you can take a two-hour walk to the amazing circular pre-Inca fort of *Marca Huamachuco*. Trucks connect Huamachuco with the village of **Chagual** (around twelve very bumpy hours) where it is possible to hire mules and guides (from $5 a day per mule) for the four- or five-day (each way!) trek via the settlments of **Pataz** (20km or 6-hr. walk from Chagual) and **Los Alisos** (another 8km or 3-hr. walk). Los Alisos is the true trail head—another three or four days' walk to the ruins.

Alternatively, it's possible to take a twelve hour bus ride (with *Empressa Antisuyo*) from Trujillo to Huamachuco.

Chachapoyas and Its Mountaintop Ruins

Chachapoyas, the unlikely capital of *El Departmento de Amazonas*, is poised on an exposed plateau between two river gorges, over 2300m above sea level. In the mountain language of the Aymaru Indians, Chachapoyas evidently means "the cloud people," a description, perhaps, of the fair-skinned tribes who used to dominate this region, living in at least seven major city complexes, each one located high up above the Utcubamba valley on prominent, very dramatic peaks and ridges.

The town today, although very friendly and attractively surrounded by wooded hills, is of no particular interest to the traveler except as a base from which to explore the area's wealth of archeological remains, above all the ruins of **Kuelap**. Other no doubt equally spectacular monuments also exist in this area but they're yet to be surveyed. If the pioneering spirit takes you, the local inhabitants—many of them with light-colored hair and remarkably pale faces to this day—are the best source of information about the ruins.

Getting There

There are two **land routes** up to Chachapoyas from the coast, both of them arduous, bumpy, and meandering. By far the easiest is the **northern route** from Chiclayo via Olmos and Jaen. Though less spectacular than the approach from Cajamarca, it involves fewer climbs and crosses the Andes by the Porculla Pass, the lowest possible track across the Peruvian Andes, obviously a better alternative for those travelers worried by *soroche* (mountain sickness). There are daily **buses** this way (15 hr. in the dry season, 20–25 from Nov.–Mar. due to frequent *huaycos*, landslides, along the road), and it's worth knowing that every seat on the bus is reserved about four days in advance. **Flights** (from Lima and Chiclayo every Wed.) are full about two weeks ahead.

The **road from Cajamarca** is certainly memorable—crossing into the Marañon valley beyond LEIMABAMBA along winding mountain roads and nearly achieving 4000m before descending to the town of Chachapoyas. The whole trip lasts a minimum of 20 hours (plus another 8 hours from Trujillo and the coast) and there are only two buses a week. Trucks along this road are cheaper and more frequent than the buses but slower and somewhat less reliable; both buses and trucks usually break the journey overnight at **CELEDIN** (*Hotel Celedin* on the plaza and the *Hotel Amazinos* nearby) which has a daily bus service connecting it to Cajamarca. If you get stuck here there's a fascinating and wild market every Sunday.

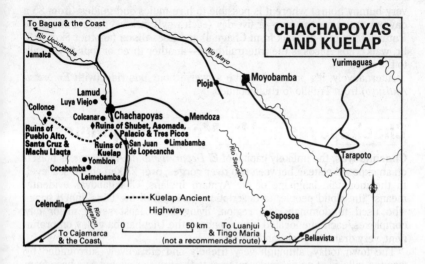

CHACHAPOYAS AND KUELAP

To Bagua & the Coast
Rio Ucubamba
Jamalca
Rio Mayo
Yurimaguas
Pioja
Moyobamba
Lamud
Luya Viejo
Collonce
Colcanar
Chachapoyas
Mendoza
Ruins of Shubet, Asomada, Palacio & Tres Picos
Ruins of Pueblo Alto, Santa Cruz & Machu Llaqta
Ruins of Kuelap
San Juan de Lopecancha
Limabamba
Tarapoto
Yomblon
Rio Saposoa
Cocabamba
Leimebamba
Celendin
Rio Marañon
Kuelap Ancient Highway
Saposoa
0   50 km
To Cajamarca & the Coast
To Luanjui & Tingo Maria (not a recommended route)
Bellavista

If you're more bothered about retreading old ground than *soroche*, there is no need to choose between these routes—you can reach Chachapoyas from the coast via one and return by the other. Going from Chachapoyas to Cajamarca *Transportes Rojas* leaves most Wednesday mornings around 2am (via TINGO, for the Kuelap ruins), and *Olano* leaves daily at 10am for Chiclayo.

Chachapoyas

Once a colonial possession rich with gold and silver mines as well as extremely fertile alluvial soil, **CHACHAPOYAS** fell into decline during the Republican era. Recently, however, with the building of the Cajamarca road and the opening up of air travel, it has developed into a thriving, if small, market town with a mostly Indian population of some 7000—said by many to be among the most friendly and hospitable in Peru. As the center of a military zone, the town has a **PIP** (*Policia de Investigaciones*) office—where all travelers should go upon arrival to present their passports.

Fronting the main square, the *Hotel Amazonas* is cheap, pleasant, and one of the few places in town with a decent bed; the *Hotel Continental* is another, less good, possibility (both from $1 a night). Both are on the **main plaza**, where you'll also find some pretty good, if limited, **restaurants** including the *Restaurante Kuelap*. For **information** on sites stop by the *Instituto Nacional de Cultura* office in the second block of *Avenida Libertad*.

As a gringo you're likely to attract lively curiosity from the local folk; travelers are still a rare sight. In general, though, this entire area is best visited with your own tent, sleeping bag, and cooking gear. There's a lot to see, distances are great, and there are almost no facilities for travelers outside the town.

The Ruins at Kuelap and Gran Vilaya

The main reason for most travelers to be in the Chachapoyas region is the unrestored archeological ruin of **Kuelap,** among the most overwhelming prehistoric sites in Peru. Anyone intending to go beyond Kuelap itself to the more remote site of **Gran Vilaya** should first obtain **permission to visit** from Dr. Torres at the *Instituto Nacional de Cultura* in Chachapoyas. An excellent **book** on the region's archeological sites has been published by Canadian explorer Morgan Davis—usually available from Martin Antonio Oliva (Av. Libertad 361; $10).

Only 40km south of Chachapoyas (along the Cajamarca road), Kuelap sits above the tiny village of TINGO in the verdant Utcubamba valley, remote and only "discovered" in 1843. To reach the village take one of the trucks that cruise around the main square in Chachapoyas around 9am every morning, picking up passengers for the long journey along the road to Celedin; ask someone to give you a nudge when you get to Tingo. The village now has a small *pensión* and a few hostels, notably the *Hostal El Viajero,* run by a former policeman. It's reasonable value and also a good place to make inquiries about hiring mules and guides.

A road giving access to the scattered ancient sites collectively known as Kuelap was under construction until 1981 when the project was (for good or bad) abandoned. Consequently, the actual site is reached only by a hard, 1500m climb (around four hours up and almost two back down) from the west bank of the Utcubamba river.

Kuelap

The ruined fortress of **KUELAP** is situated high on a ridge, commanding terrific views of the surrounding landscape, but it is the structure itself which immediately arrests your attention. It really is enormous, with walls towering to 20m in height, constructed with gigantic limestone slabs arranged into geometric patterns. Some sections of the walls are faced with rectangular granite blocks over forty layers high, and going inside the ruins you come across hundreds of round stone houses decorated with a distinctive zigzag pattern (like the local modern ceramics), small carved animal heads, condor designs, and intricate serpent figures. There are also various enclosures and large crumbling watchtowers partly covered in wild subtropical vegetation, shrubs, and even trees. One of these towers is an inverted, truncated cone containing a large, bottle-shaped cavity, probably an ancient reservoir.

It has been calculated that some 40 million cubic feet of building material was used at Kuelap, three times the volume needed to construct the Great Pyramid of Egypt. It is the strongest, most easily defended of all Peruvian fortress cities and, occupied from about A.D. 1000 by the Chachapoyas tribe, is thought to be the site which the rebel Inca, Manco, considered using for his last-ditch stand against the Conquistadores in the late 1530s. He never made it here, ending up instead in the equally breathtaking Vilcabamba area, northeast of Cuzco.

It comes as a surprise to most visitors to find soft drinks and even beer on sale near the top of the ruins. The only residents in the actual ruins today are the guardians, who can provide a little food (though don't depend on it; they might be off duty) and they have recently finished building a small **hostel** (a hut really) to accommodate anyone who would prefer to sleep in the ruins (and hasn't got a tent) rather than back down in Tingo. You can also camp, but either way you'll be best off with your own sleeping bag. The guardians (including the friendly José) are familiar with other, smaller ruins in the immediate vicinity such as **Revash**, near the village of SANTO TOMAS.

Gran Vilaya

The site guardians at Kuelap will also direct those who are prepared for longer expeditions to the village of CHOCTAMAL (a five-hour walk). Guides and mules (check with Carlos Cruz, an interesting and very reliable guide) are available from here at around $3 to $5 each per day, to take you to remote, largely unexplored, and very hard-to-find sites within another five hours' walk.

These sites—known collectively as **GRAN VILAYA** since Gene Savoy claimed to have "discovered" them in 1985, though many gringos have been hiking into this area for years and there were several sketch maps of the ruins in existence years before Savoy arrived—form an incredible complex of almost entirely unexcavated ruins. Despite *El Comercio*'s claim that Savoy discovered over 100,000 buildings, a more conservative estimate puts the archeological record at some 150 sites divided into three main political sections. About thirty of these sites are of particular note and about fifteen of them are of definite archeological importance.

Other Sites

Going on from Choctamal with a guide, some of the most impressive ruins— **Santa Cruz**, **Machu Llacta**, and **Las Pilas**—are two relatively easy one day walks from the *Abra Yumal* (a 3500m pass). Beyond the pass the trail begins to make its way into the stunning cloud forest towards the small settlements of TRIBULON and PUEBLO NEGRO located below the ruins. It's often hard to use money in remote regions such as this, so it can prove extremely handy to have some trade goods with you—pencils, fresh fruit, chocolate, fresh bread, canned fish, or cookies. Apart from these, the usual camping gear is essential unless you want to be completely dependent on the local hospitality: this is usually abundant, but the more trekkers that arrive here the less true this will probably be (in any case it isn't reasonable for travelers automatically to expect a roof over their heads, much less to expect to be fed).

Purunllacta and El Pueblo de los Muertos

Among other charted ruins in the Utcubamba valley are those of the archaic metropolis of **PURUNLLACTA**. This can be reached fairly easily from Chachapoyas by taking the daily bus to PIPOS on the MENDOZA road; getting off here you can walk to the village of CHETO, from where it's a short climb to the ruined city itself. The return trip is possible the same day, though it's more enjoyable to camp at the site. Purunllacta—probably the capital—was one of the seven major cities of the Chachapoyas culture, before all of them were conquered by the Inca Tupac Yupanqui in the 1470s.

The **site** consists of numerous groups of buildings scattered around the hilltops, all interconnected by ancient roads and each one surrounded by elegant agricultural terraces. At the center of the ruined city you can clearly make out rectangular stone buildings, plazas, stairways, and platforms. The most striking are still two-stories-high, constructed in carved limestone blocks. The explorer Gene Savoy estimated that the entire complex covered about 150 square km—and even if the truth amounts to only a third of this calculation, it is an astonishing accomplishment.

Another characteristic of the Chachapoyas region is the **necropoli**, full of elaborately molded, anthropomorphic coffins, often stuck inaccessibly into horizontal crevices high up along cliff faces and painted in vivid colors. A fine example—and yet another rewarding excursion from Chachapoyas—is the **PUEBLO DE LOS MUERTOS** ("City of the Dead") some 30km to the north. This is positioned a short way above the **Lake of Tingobamba**, easily enough reached by taking the CHICLAYO bus to PUENTE TINGOBAMBA or by hitching on one of the many trucks along this road. The **sarcophagi** are about three hours from Puente (ask directions there): up to 2m high, carved with human faces, they stare blankly across the valley from a natural fault in the rock face. Each one has been carefully molded into an elongated egg-like shape from a mixture of mud and vegetable fibers, then painted purple and white with geometric zigzags and other superimposed designs. Savoy described them aptly as "standing like ten pins in a bowling alley," and most of them are still intact. If you get close you can see that the casings are hollow, some containing mummies wrapped in funerary shrouds, others just filled with sun-bleached bones. Protected as they are from the weather by an overhang, these ancestors of the Chachapoyas race may well be watching over their land for another thousand years yet.

Into the Jungle: Two River Trips to Iquitos

Two rough, very adventurous **journeys by land and river** will take you on from CHACHAPOYAS to the Peruvian jungle capital of IQUITOS, not far from the Brazilian border on the Amazon river. It's difficult to estimate the duration of each trip—there are always inevitable waits for connections and embarkations—but you'd be unlikely to do either in less than a week's hard traveling. Unless, of course, you take the easy way out: at Moyabamba and Yurimaguas there are a number of air strips with scheduled internal **flights**.

A WORD OF WARNING

There were reports of increasing violence and terrorist/drug-trafficking problems in this region—particularly around **Tarapoto**—during the late 1980s. Check with the tourist and/or police authorities in Lima, Cajamarca, Chiclayo, or Chachapoyas before departing for this area or immediately on arrival.

The Moyabamba–Yurimaguas Route

The main overland route to Iquitos, this involves one of the best of Peru's Amazon River trips—not as long as most, and reasonably straightforward. You begin, however, by taking a series of trucks and *colectivos*: first (by truck) from CHACHAPOYAS along the Mayo river valley to RIOJA/MOYABAMBA, then (by *colectivo*) to TARAPOTO, and finally north (by truck) to the end of the road at YURIMAGUAS.

Rioja/Moyabamba

It takes about twelve hours in the dry season (though it's often impassable when rainy) to reach **RIOJA/MOYABAMBA**, twin towns set just above the Río Mayo in a hot, humid, tropical forest environment. Moyabamba is the older of the two, founded in 1539 by Don Alonso de Alvarado on one of his earliest explorations into the Amazon jungle. Although a small town, it is the capital of a large, though for the most part sparsely populated, *departmento*, San Martin. During the colonial period it was a camp for pioneers, missionaries, and explorers—like Pedro de Urzúa, who used it as a base in his search for the "Land of Cinnamon," one of the tempting carrots cleverly used by Pizarro to keep his men happy and busy. Having noticed Indians using dry buds that tasted of cinnamon in cooking, Urzúa conceived a goal almost as alluring and potentially as lucrative as El Dorado's gold. If he had been successful in finding cinnamon plantations in the jungles, where the Indians traded for it, then the Portuguese monopoly with the Spice Islands could have been challenged, Columbus's original aspirations fulfilled, and Moyabamba might have become a rich city. As you can see today, however, Urzúa failed in his attempt, and Moyabamba is much the same as any other jungle town—hot, muddy, and laid back, with a cathedral and a cheap **hotel**, the *Monterrey*, on the Plaza de Armas.

Tarapoto

From Moyabamba there are regular **colectivos** to **TARAPOTO** (4–5 hr.), a larger town with a *Hotel de Turistas* (complete with swimming pool) and an **airport** with regular flights to Iquitos and the coast. The town is located only 420m above sea level, yet the Huallaga River flows on from here, via the Amazon, until it finally empties into the Atlantic Ocean. A strange sort of place, Tarapoto has a large **prison** and a big drug-smuggling problem, with people flying coca paste from here to Colombia, where it is processed into cocaine for the U.S. market. There are a few **hotels**—the *Hotel Grau* on the main plaza is reasonable—but, transit connections aside, the town doesn't have a lot of interest for travelers.

You could, however, make a trip to the nearby village of **LAMAS**, about 30km up into the forested hills. This is a small, exotic, native settlement whose inhabitants are reputed to be direct descendants of the Chanca tribe who escaped from the Andes to this region in the fifteenth century, fleeing from the clutches of the conquering Inca army. The people still keep very much to themselves, carrying on a highly distinctive lifestyle which displays an unusual combination of jungle and mountain Indian cultures—the women wearing long blue skirts and colorfully embroidered blouses (more typical of the Ecuadorean Sierra), the men adorning themselves on ceremonial occasions with strings of brightly plumed, stuffed macaws. Everyone goes barefoot and speaks a curious dialect, a mixture of *Quechua* and *Cahuapana* (a forest Indian tongue), and the town is traditionally renowned for its *brujos* (wizards) who use a potent hallucinogen, *Ayahuasca*, for their nighttime divinatory and healing sessions. The best month to visit is August when the village's **festival** is in full swing. The days are spent dancing, and drinking, and most of the tribe's weddings occur at this time. There's no hotel here, but if you ask nicely someone may let you camp in the garden; alternatively, you can easily make it here and back from Tarapoto in a day. The **porters** in Lamas are renowned all over Peru as the best—able to carry large loads quickly over vast distances, never using river transportation if it can be avoided.

Yurimaguas

From Tarapoto it's another 140km by rugged road to **YURIMAGUAS**. In the dry season you can make this by truck in about six hours, but from November until March it's more likely to take between ten and fifteen. There are **hotels** in Yurimaguas (the *Estrella* is best) but I would recommend going straight to the port to look for **boats downstream to Iquitos**. These leave regularly though not at any set times; it's simply a matter of finding a reliable captain (preferably the one with the biggest, newest, or fastest-looking boat) and arranging details with him; the normal price is about $15—which isn't bad for a four-day trip, including food. All you absolutely need to take is a hammock and sun hat, but some extra things to eat, bottles of drink, and canned fish—and if you want to try fishing yourself, a line and hooks (sold in the town's *fereterías*)—will make this magnificent, but tiring, river journey all the more enjoyable. The scenery en route is electric: the river gets steadily wider and slower, and the vegetation on the river banks more and more dense. Remember, though, that during the day the sun beats down intensely and wearing a sunhat is essential to avoid **river fever**—cold sweats (and diarrhea) caused by exposure to the constant strong light reflected off the water.

An Alternative—Via Oracuzar

An even more sensational route to Iquitos, but really only for the seasoned outward-bound traveler, is **from Chachapoyas via Oracuzar**. The first stage here is relatively simple—you take the daily **Chiclayo bus** to BAGUA GRANDE or JAEN and then pick up a truck bound for ORACUZAR. Shortly before arriving at Oracuzar you pass through **PUERTO DELPHUS** (250km from Chachapoyas). At this small port (ask in the restaurants if you need a room) you can find **boats going down the Marañon river**. Only a few will be going all the way to Iquitos, so you'll have to decide on the spot whether to risk doing the journey in stages (which can involve many days of waiting in river settlements) or to stick it out in Puerto Delphus until someone offers to take you the whole way.

The **river trip** never fails to be an experience. In the first couple of days you'll shoot numerous rapids, before the Marañon smooths out into a pacific snake of water, gliding slowly on towards Iquitos, Brazil, and the Atlantic. The whole expedition should take around six days on the river, more if you choose to do it in stages with smaller craft. You'll need all the things that were required for the Yurimaguas-Iquitos journey, but here especially it is advisable to take enough **food** for at least ten days (and lots of **mosquito repellent**) just in case you get stuck for a week on the riverbank literally in the middle of nowhere (which is far from unlikely). Only one thing is certain about this route—when you arrive in Iquitos (see p.278) after a week or so of eating only fish, yucca, and bananas, it'll appear to be the biggest, best-stocked city you've ever come across.

THE NORTHERN DESERT

For all the travelers who pass through it, the **Northern Desert** remains one of the least visited areas of Peru. This is as much a result of its distance from Lima and Cuzco as it is of a lack of obvious attractions, and despite the fact that it offers a considerable amount in terms of landscape, wildlife, and history—with a complex cultural identity that's quite distinct and strongly individualistic—its popular image is of a desolate zone of scattered rural communities, a myth that belies both past and present. Before Pizarro arrived here in the sixteenth century to begin the Conquest, the Northern Desert had formed part of both Inca and Chimu Empires and hosted a number of local pre-Columbian cultures. Today, its main cities of **Chiclayo** and **Piura** are both important and lively commercial centers—serving not only the desert coast but large areas of the Andes as well.

The **coastal resorts** are probably the best reason for stopping—though very small, there's usually at least basic provision for travelers and, most importantly, the ocean is warmer here than anywhere else in the country. With the Andes rising over 6000m to the east, this northern coastal strip of Peru has always been slightly isolated and access even today is restricted to just three **roads**, the main north–south Pan American Highway and two minor routes straggling over the Andes and down to sites reached along the navigable jungle rivers.

If, like so many travelers, you decide to bus straight through from Trujillo to the Ecuadorean border town of **Tumbes** (or vice versa) in a single journey, you'll be missing out on all of this—and also the region's strong sense of **history**. It was at Tumbes that Pizarro's Andalucian sea pilot Bartholomew Ruiz discovered the first evidence of civilization south of the equator—a large balsa sail raft—in 1527. And here too, five years on, the *conquistadores* set anchor before the northern city outposts of the Inca kingdom.

The one serious drawback to travel in the region is the likelihood of extremely heavy **rain**. Rainfall is always high here: in 1983 even the normally arid coast around Piura and Tumbes was flooded, crops destroyed, and roads and bridges washed away.

The Pan American Highway from Trujillo to Chiclayo

The **Pan American Highway**, mainstay of the north's transportation system, offers the fastest route north from Trujillo, passing through an impressively stark and barren landscape of few villages and no towns—though the valleys here have yielded notable archeological finds dating from Peru's "Early Formative" period.

SAN PEDRO DE LLOC, the first settlement of any real size, stands out from miles around with its tall, whitewashed buildings, its old town wall, and its railroad station (now inactive but a National Monument). A quiet little village, San Pedro has one small hotel and a reputation for its local delicacy of stuffed lizards—something I've yet to find on any menu. If you're around here in late June it may be worth some planning to coincide with the town **Fiesta**, held on the 29th amid colorful religious processions.

Pacasmayo and the Ruins at Pacatnamú

Ten kilometers to the north a huge cement plant heralds the approach of **PACASMAYO**, a growing port and town with a rather grim roadside appearance. Despite this it's not unattractive, particularly if you've time to wander down to the old jetty, and it's a useful point to get trucks up to CAJARMACA (though buses are easier from Trujillo or Chiclayo). If you need to stay overnight there a few small **hotels**, though it's unlikely that you'll get stranded.

The one site along this stretch of road is only a few kilometers beyond, just before you reach the village of GUADALUPE. At the beginning of a large curve in the road a track leads off left, towards the coast. This runs down to the well-preserved ruins of **PACATNAMÚ** ("The City of Sanctuaries"), overlooking the mouth of the Jecetepeque river. Ubbelohde-Doering excavated these remains in 1938 and 1953, showing them to be a great complex of pyramids, palaces, storehouses, and dwellings. Digging up the forecourts in front of the pyramids and some nearby graves, he discovered that the place was first occupied during the Gallinazo period (around A.D. 350). It was subsequently conquered by the Mochica and Chimu cultures.

Being off the main road and not too close to any towns, Pacatnamú has survived relatively untouched by archeologists, treasure hunters, or curious browsers—a very abandoned city. If you can get here by *colectivo* or bus fairly early one morning it is possible to check out the ruins and hitch on, or back to Trujillo or Chiclayo, without much problem. The road is busy with plenty of trucks, some half-empty *colectivo*s, buses, and private cars—but it gets very hot without shade around midday and if you're going to linger you should take your own food and drink.

There are more ruins, probably of similar age, at ZAÑA—right beside the small town of MOCUPE (several kilometers before Chiclayo)—but effectively destroyed by floods in the eighteenth century, these present only an eerie half-outline.

Chiclayo and Lambayeque

Some 770km north of Lima, and rapidly becoming one of Peru's larger cities, **Chiclayo** is an active commercial center thanks more to its strategic position than to any industrial development. Originally it was just a small annex to the old colonial town of **Lambayeque**, 12km north, but things have swung the other way over this century, and all the vibrancy and energy are now concentrated in Chiclayo.

Chiclayo

As ever the heart of **CHICLAYO** is the **Plaza de Armas**, where you'll find the cathedral and municipal buildings, most of the banks, and at least one decent restaurant—*El Cordano*. The main focus of activity is along the main **Avenida Jose Balta**, between the plaza and the town's fascinating *mercado central*. Packed daily with food vendors at the center, and other stalls around the outside, this is one of the best **markets** in the north—and a revelation if you've just arrived in the country. A kind of rayfish known as *la guitarra* is hung up to dry in the sun before being sold to make one of the favorite local specialties—*pescado seco*. There's a whole section of live animals, including wild fox cubs, canaries, and even the occasional condor chick. One famous baby condor was bought here several years ago and has been reared to work in an amazing circus act, terrifying the spectators as it swoops down from a trapeze with its 3m wing span fully spread. But probably the most compelling displays are the herbalists' shops, selling everything from herbs and charms to whale bones and hallucinogenic cacti. The Chiclayo area, and more specifically Lambayeque (see below), is a center for *curanderos* and traditional folk-medicine in general.

On weekends, families crowd out to the **beaches** of SANTA ROSA and LA PIMENTEL—each well served by buses from the market area. Santa Rosa is the main fishing village on the Chiclayo coast and scores of big, colorful boats go out early every morning—along with the occasional *caballito de tortora*, reed canoes that have been used here for almost two thousand years. If you ask local permission it's usually all right to camp out at either beach, or there's a cheapish **hotel** at Santa Rosa. On weekends, too, *Chiclayanos* congregate for the Sunday afternoon **horseraces** at the town's *Santa Victorial Hipodromo*, 2km south of the Plaza de Armas just off the Avenida Roosevelt.

Sleeping, Eating, and Nightlife

Finding a place to stay is a relatively simple matter in Chiclayo. Most of the good, reasonably priced **hotels** are around the Plaza de Armas (particularly the *Hotel Royal*) or along Avenida José Balta, the street leading towards the market, where the *Mediterranea* is recommended. The *Hotel Venezuela*, two blocks and a bit from the plaza (on Lora y Cordero), is also friendly and quite reasonable. More comfort for more money can be found at the *Hotel de Turistas* (Avenida Salaverry; ☎23-4911) or the *Costa de Oro* (Balta 399; ☎23-2869).

Among Chiclayo's **restaurants**, *Mario's*, just a few blocks down Avenida Balta from the Plaza, is open 24 hours a day and provides interesting eating. Also on Avenida Balta, but one block nearer the center, the *Restaurante Roma* is very good value. Right on the Plaza de Armas try *El Cordano*, which prepares excellent fresh fish, or *Restaurante Las Americas* .

A few **peñas** in Chiclayo are worth a look, especially *Los Hermanos Balcazar* at Lora y Cordero 1150 and *Brisas del Mar* on Elias Aguirre. This region is renowned for its religious **festivals**, not least that of the *Cruz de Chaplon*, which is celebrated twice a year in Motupe—for details ask at the tourist office.

Information and Practical Details

Tourist information is available from two offices: one on Las Acacias 305 (☎23-4409), and the other in the street behind the cathedral, Sáenz Peña 838. For further information, and if you want to arrange tours in and around Chiclayo, contact *Indiana Tours* (Elias Aguirre 830; ☎23-4921). The **post office** is seven blocks west of the plaza, just before the *Hotel de Turistas* on the Avenida Felipe Santiago Salaverry (a continuation of Elias Aguirre). Money can be exchanged in most of the **banks** near the plaza or (all day long) at the travel agent next to the *Hotel Royal*.

Many of the **buses** (particularly those going north) and some **colectivos** leave from the market area, but a number of companies (mainly dealing with southern traffic) are also based at the southern entrance to Chiclayo—for example *Empresa Olano* and *Peru Express* (both on Bolognesi). The main exceptions are *colectivos* to Trujillo, which run from the Plaza de Armas.

Lambayeque

Only a short *colectivo* ride from Chiclayo market, **LAMBAYEQUE** is a rather forlorn old colonial town, quite a grand place in the seventeenth century but fallen well into decay for most of the years since. Its main draw, beyond a handful of fine old mansions, is the unexpectedly modern and extremely well stocked **Brunning Museum** (Mon.–Sat. 9am–noon and 3–5pm; Sun. 9am–noon). Named after its founder, a successful businessman and expert in the ancient Mochica language and culture, the museum boasts superb collections of early ceramics and metal work. The Lambayeque valley has long been renowned for turning up pre-Columbian metallurgy—particularly gold pieces from the neighboring hill graveyard of **Zacame**—and local *huaqueros* (treasure hunters) have sometimes gone so far as to use bulldozers to dig them out.

On an incidental and rather more prosaic note, Lambayeque is also known for its sweet pastry cakes—filled with *manjar blanca* and touted under the unlikely name of *king-kongs*! Between here and Lima, traveling on the buses or walking the streets of any town, you're bound to be bombarded by *ambulantes* (street vendors) pushing out piles of the cake, shouting "King-Kong! King-Kong!"

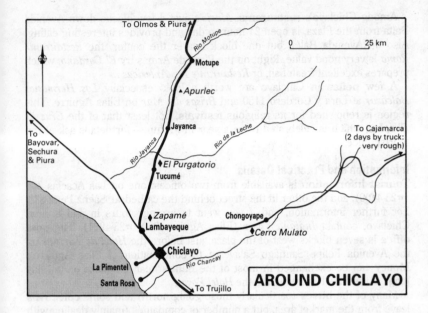

To Olmos & Piura

Río Motupe

Motupe

▲Apurlec

0   25 km

To Bayovar, Sechura & Piura

Río Jayanca

Jayanca

Río de la Leche

To Cajamarca
(2 days by truck:
very rough)

◆El Purgatorio
Tucumé

◆Zapamé
Lambayeque

Chongoyape

◆Cerro Mulato

Chiclayo

Río Chancay

La Pimentel

Santa Rosa

To Trujillo

AROUND CHICLAYO

Around Chiclayo: Archeological Sites

The northern base of successive ancient cultures, it was in the Chiclayo area that Pizarro and his mob turned inland in search of the city of Cajamarca, the Inca overlord Atahualpa, and the legendary treasures. There is some dispute among historians as to which route they in fact took into the mountains but it's generally accepted to have been along the course of either the Chancay or Saña rivers—both just south of modern Chiclayo.

A similar route today to CAJAMARCA (see p.220) takes the best part of two days by local trucks, a rough and exhausting journey. You can get an

Chavinoid design (from a vase discovered at Chongoyape)

initial sense of it, however, just by traveling up to **CHONGOYAPE**—an attractive journey that follows the climb of the Chancay valley. The road at this stage, 80km out of Chiclayo, is paved and there's regular service by bus or *colectivo*. Chongoyape itself is a bright little hill town close to the site of **Cerro Mulato**, where you can see some impressive Chavin petroglyphs (engraved stones). Around the region, too, archeologists have uncovered a number of graves, their finds indicating that the Chavin feline cult survived well into the fifth century B.C., the latest yet recorded.

If you're waiting for a truck on to Cajamarca, you could camp at Chongoyape or at nearby **TINAJONES**, site of a massive new irrigation project, where a new **tourist center** offers swimming, sailing, and waterskiing facilities. For most travelers, though, the **Chimu culture ruins** en route to Piura are likely to prove more immediate and accessible destinations.

El Purgatorio and Apurlec

Both **El Purgatorio** and **Apurlec** can be visited in a day trip from Chiclayo (*colectivos* from Pedro Ruiz between the plaza and market, or local bus to Olmos), or if you start early in the day you could just about take them in and continue on to Piura. Whichever way you do it, take some drink and a sunhat: neither site has any shade and for the onward journey you'll probably have to hang around waiting to wave down a bus or truck.

EL PURGATORIO, just outside TUCUME (20km north of Lambayeque), was a major Chimu city—second in size and splendor only to the great capital of Chan Chan (see p.209). Spread on and around the base of a hill, it remains an extensive site, the ruins of adobe pyramids, raised platforms, walls, and courtyards all quite visible. It has apparently yielded few archeological remains and virtually no treasure—nothing like the riches found at the hill-grave of Zapame by Lambayeque—but it's a place with a reputation of great local power. *Curanderos*, healing wizards, still perform their magical rites here. Near the site is the **Huaca Pintada**, an adobe temple, also of Chimu construction, which was covered with beautiful colored murals when it was unearthed in 1916.

El Purgatorio was part of an enormous Chimu irrigation complex that took water from the rivers Chancay and Lecche to sustain the cultivated areas essential for a developing urban population. **APURLEC**, another vast adobe city a little farther north, was another link in the chain. First occupied in the eighth century B.C., it seems still to have been flourishing 500 years later under the great Chimu planners and architects. There are remains here, scattered over a huge area, of pyramids, forts and palaces, temples, and store houses, and long city streets. Built throughout from adobe, mud-bricks raised from the dust, its walls have been eroded over the years by heavy rains but they remain quite recognizable.

North to Piura: Through the Sechura Desert

Buses and *colectivos* between Chiclayo and Piura can take any of three different routes: that via OLMOS outlined above; the new *Expreso* section of the Pan American Highway, right through the middle of the Sechura desert; or around its edge, down to the sea near the old refineries of BAYOVAR and on along the coast past a series of small fishing hamlets to the town of SECHURA. If you particularly want to take one or other of these routes you'll have to check the bus schedules beforehand. Times of travel vary between around four to six hours and though the desert scenery is impressive, in all cases you'll want to keep some reading matter on hand.

Along the Coast to Sechura

The route via Sechura is a slightly strange one. The buses run quickly towards the turnoff to **BAYOVAR** (which is itself a forbidden zone) and then switch up to the coast at a vast obelisk and traffic circle right in the middle of nowhere. To the south, accessible only on foot, are the **Sechura hills**—an isolated and unoffical wildlife reserve of wild goats and foxes, and the occasional condor come to feast on washed up, rotting carcasses of whales and sea lions. There is **no water** in the region, and it's a good three-day walk from the road to the beach; maps are available in Lima, however, if you're interested in a serious exploration.

North of the traffic circle there is little more—just a handful of hermit goat-herders and two or three scattered groups of roadside restaurants—until you approach the edge of the town of SECHURA. As you do, there are a few tiny hamlets—basically clusters of huts on the beach—often inhabited by the same fishing families since no one knows how long before the Conquest. The last of these, **PARACHIQUE**, has recently developed into a substantial port with its own fishmeal factory; the others are all very simple, their inhabitants mostly using sailing boats to fish, and often going out to sea for days at a time.

Sechura

SECHURA itself is not a large place, though the tall twin towers of its seventeenth-century church lend it a definite air of civilization. Local legend has it that the church was built over an ancient temple, from which an underground tunnel leads out to the ocean and where, no doubt, treasure was once reputed to be hidden. To the south of the town—between the sea and road—a long line of white crescent **dunes**, or *lomas*, reaches into the distance: they are another link with the past according to local people who claim that they were used by Incas as landmarks across the desert. If you want to take a closer look at the dunes it's possible to rent four-wheel-drive cars in town. Just a few kilometers to the east there's a huge, supposedly enchanted, star-crescent dune—reached along soft sandy tracks which are too much for most vehicles. If you want to stay overnight here it's possible to **camp** anywhere (including the beach), or to stay in a small **hostel**. The town's **food market** is a good one and there are also several **restaurants**, the best probably *Don Gilberto's* on the main plaza. Unless the desert excites you, however, there's a lot more life and interest in PIURA, a fast 52km bus ride to the north.

Piura and Around

The city of **Piura** feels very distinct from the rest of the country, cut off to the south by the formidable Sechura Desert, to the east by the Huancabamba mountain. The people here, too, see themselves primarily as Piurans rather than Peruvians, and the town itself has a strong oasis atmosphere, entirely dependent on the vagaries of the Río Piura—known since Pizarro's time as the *Río Loco*, "Crazy River." Despite this precarious existence, Piura is the oldest colonial town in Peru. And this century—despite weathering at least two serious droughts and seven major floods (the last in 1983)—it has grown into a *departmento* of over a million people, around a quarter of whom actually live in the city. With temperatures of up to 100° from January to March the region produces more limes than any other, and it also has spawned a particularly wide-brimmed straw sombrero, worn by everyone from the mayor to local goat herders.

Francisco Pizarro spent ten days here in 1532 on his way to the fateful meeting with the Inca overlord, Atahualpa, at Cajamarca. Beginning life as San Miguel de Piura, the town had well over two hundred Spaniards by 1534, including the first Spanish women to arrive in Peru. All were hungry for a slice of the action—and treasure—but although Pizarro kept over 57,000 pesos for himself, he only gave 15,000 to the Piurans; the cause of some considerable resentment, and possibly the origin of the town's isolationist attitude. Pizarro did, however, encourage the development here of an urban class, drawn from the sick or invalided, and destined for trade rather than war. As early as the 1560s there was a flourishing trade in the excellent indigenous Tanguis cotton, and Piura today still has a third of the nation's cotton production.

The Town

Modern **PIURA** is divided in half by the river, with most of the action and all the main hotels, bars, restaurants, etc. on the west bank. Within a few blocks of the middle bridge is the main square, a very attractive **Plaza de Armas** shaded by tall tamarind trees planted well over a hundred years ago. On the plaza you can see the "Statue of Liberty," nicknamed *La Pola* ("The Pole") by Piurans, and, as usual in Peru, the **cathedral**. Though not especially beautiful, the impressive bronze nails decorating its main doors are striking, and inside, the gilt altars and intricate wooden pulpit are spectacularly tasteless.

Perhaps more interesting from a traveler's point of view are the museums. The **Museo Grau** (Mon.–Sat. 9am–6pm) on Avenida Tacna occupies the nineteenth-century home of Miguel Grau, one of the heroes of the War of the Pacific (1879–80) in which Chile successfully took control of Peru's valuable nitrate fields in the south and permanently cut Bolivia's access to the Pacific. A British-built ship—the *Huascar*—was Peru's only successful blockade runner, and a model is displayed here, along with various military artifacts and a small archeological section. Stronger on the region's archeological finds—and in particular the ceramics from Vicus (see below)—is the museum in the **Municipalidad** (3rd floor; Mon.–Fri. am only). A third museum, with extensive Inca sections, is on Avenida Loreto 818.

Other points worth checking out while you're in town are two neatly laid out **parks** dedicated to the *Conquistadores*, Pizarro and Cortés, and the old bridge connecting the main part of Piura with the less aesthetic east-bank **Tacala** quarter. Tacala is renowned for the quality and strength of its fermented *chicha* beer and on Friday afternoons you'll find the bars here packed with thirsty people beginning the weekend with a tangy jar.

Other **local specialties** include *natilla*, a rather tasty sweet toffee. Apart from this you can buy very well made straw hats (invaluable in the desert), ceramics made in the village of Simbila, and a variety of leather crafts. The best place to buy stuff like this is the town's **market**, one block before the Pan American heads north.

Practicalities: Rooms and Food

Hotels are well spread over Piura but most of them, including some of the more reasonably priced, are within a few blocks of the Plaza de Armas, an area roughly delineated by Avenidas Sanchez Cerro, Grau, Loreto, and the river. The *Hotel San Jorge* on Plaza Grau and the *San Martin* on Avenida Cuzco are among the best cheap possibilities. Slightly more expensive but quite a bit better is the *Hotel Cristina* (Jr.Loreto, between Ica and Callao). Nearer the top of the range there's the *Hotel Tangara* (by the corner of Arequipa and Ica, just a few blocks from the Plaza de Armas) and the *Hotel de Turistas* on the plaza itself.

Restaurants are mostly in the same area. For a cold draft **beer** (*chop*) on a hot afternoon or sultry evening, and there are plenty of these in Piura, try the *Choppería Munich* close to the *Hotel Tangara*. Even cooler, the *Heladería Chalan* on the plaza and the *Venecia* just a couple of blocks away on Libertad both dish up delicious ice cream.

As far as **nightlife** goes, there are a couple of theaters that often have good visiting shows (details from the tourist office), but the "in" places to hang out are a handful of nightclub-discos—try *El Tiburon*, 2km south along the Pan American Highway, or *Hector's Bar*, nearer the center at Av. Sanchez Cerro 408. Most Piurans, however, tend to spend their evenings strolling around the main streets, chatting in the plazas, and drinking in the relatively cheap **bars** along roads like Jiron Junin.

More down-to-earth matters are easily dealt with. The **post office** is right on the Plaza de Armas, and there's a **money exchange** section in the bank on the first floor of the *Municipalidad*. **Tourist information** and maps can be obtained from the official office (Calle Libertad 945; ☎32-6761) or from a desk at the airport. The main **festival** time is *Piura Week*, which takes place during the first two weeks of October: you'll find the town in high spirits, but beds scarce and travelers' checks difficult to change. Most of the **buses**—including those to Paita, Tumbes, and Chiclayo—leave from a station by the Plaza Grau.

Catacaos

Just 12km south, down the Pan American Highway, **CATACAOS** is well worth some of your time. It's a friendly, dusty little place with a public TV in the main plaza—a gift from the mayor—and an excellent market just off it, which sells everything from food to crafts, even filigree gold and silverwork. A good buy are the hammocks hanging colorfully about the square, and the town itself is the best place around to have lunch, famous for its *picanterías* (spicy seafood **restaurants**), which serve up all sorts of local delicacies.

Among these are *tamalitos verdes* (little green-corn pancakes), fish-balls, *chifles* (fresh-made banana or sweet potato chips), and superb goat (*seco de cabrito*). While you're here you can also try the sweet medicinal drink *algarrobina*, made from the berries of a desert tree. A last peculiarity of the village—not meant to be eaten!—are the amazing metallic-looking lizards: young boys try to sell them to everyone who arrives.

There are regular *colectivos* to Catacaos from the Avenida Tacna in Piura.

Vicus

At **CERRO VICUS**, 27km east of Piura on the old route to Chiclayo, there is an interesting pre-Inca site 500m to the left of the main road. According to the kilometer marker (which is calculated from Trujillo) this is at km 449.

There are no buildings associated with the site, probably due to the occasional heavy rains—which can destroy adobe ruins—but there are a number of L-shaped tombs, some up to 15m deep. These graves contained ceramics and metal artifacts revealing several styles, early Mochica the most predominant, superbly modeled in a variety of human, animal, and architectural forms; there are good examples in the Piura museum and in Lima, Trujillo, and Lambayeque.

To reach Cerro Vicus you can take any of the Olmos buses or *colectivos*. Ask to be dropped off at km 449 (making sure they don't drive past), then walk across the sand to the tombs on the hill. Most buses, and some trucks, will stop if you wave them down beside the road for the return trip to Piura.

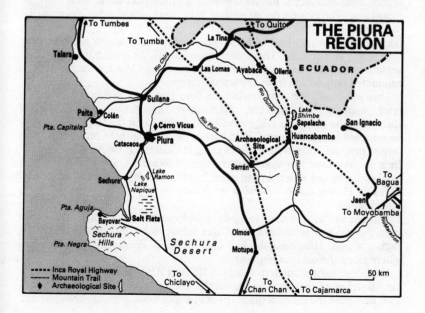

Serran and Huancabamba

One of the more adventurous routes around Piura takes you into the hills to the east and—after some 215m and up to fifteen hours by bus or truck—to the remote village of **HUANCABAMBA**. According to the chronicler Cieza de Leon, the Inca Topa Yupanqui (1471–93) expanded his empire into this region, taking "five moons" to subdue the local tribe. The subsequent Inca lord, Huayna Capac, was also forced to return here to restore order.

Up until the Spanish Conquest, the town of Huancabamba was an important crossroads on the Royal Highway. This traversed the Andes, connecting the Inca Empire from Santiago (Chile) to Quito in Ecuador: at Huancabamba one side road went down to the coast, linking with the ancient desert highway at Zaran (modern Serran), the other east to Jaen along the forested Marañon watershed, a trading link with the fierce jungle headhunters of the Aguaruna tribe. Even before the Incas arrived the Huancabamba had an extremely active trade, ferrying goods such as feathers, animal skins, medicines, and gold from the jungle Indians to the coastal cultures of the Mochica, and, later, Chimu.

It was at **SERRAN**, then a small Inca administrative center, that in 1532 Pizarro waited for Hernando de Soto and a small troop whom he had sent up the Inca road on a discovery mission. Some of this highway was wide enough for six horsemen to ride abreast and it took de Soto just two days and a night to reach the town of Cajas, not far from Huancabamba. Here they gained a first insight into the grandeur and power of the Inca empire, although, under orders from Atahualpa, the 2000-warrior garrison had slunk away into the mountains. The Spaniards, given free rein, were not slow to discover the most impressive Inca buildings—a sacred convent of over 500 *mamaconas* (virgins of the sun) who had been chosen at an early age to dedicate their lives to the Inca religion. The soldiers raped at will, provoking the Inca representative with de Soto to threaten that they would die for such sacrilege committed only 300km from Atahualpa's camp.

This was exactly the information de Soto had been seeking. And after a brief visit to the adjacent, even more impressive, Inca town of Huancabamba—where a tollgate collected duties along the Royal Highway—he returned to rejoin Pizarro. With him de Soto brought the Inca envoy, who invited the Spaniards to Atahualpa's camp at Cajamarca. On behalf of the lord Inca he presented two stone fortress-shaped fountains, some "fine stuffs of wool embroidered with gold and silver," and "a quantity of goose-flesh scent." In return Pizarro made somewhat symbolic gifts of a crimson cap and cheap glass jewelry.

You can still see the ruins of the Inca settlement of **Zaran**, just a short walk from the modern settlement, but **Cajas** seems to be temporarily lost in the region around Huancabamba and Lake Shimbe. Presumably it lies somewhere along the old Inca highway.

In places near the modern village of **HUANCABAMBA** you can still make out stretches of that thoroughfare in the ancient stone slabs, quite easy to spot alongside the modern road. The actual Inca town here has been lost but, being well made of stone, it too must still be around somewhere. Today, the village, which is apparently slipping down its hill on very watery foundations, is famous throughout Peru for its **curanderos**—healing wizards or curers, who utilize herbal and hallucinogenic remedies in conjunction with ritual bathing in sacred lagoons such as Lake Ahimbe, 2000m and seven hours' mule ride above the town. These *curanderos* are visited by Peruvians from all walks of life who want to be cured of ailments that don't respond to modern medicine.

The name *huancabamba* means "valley of the stone spirit guardians": quite fitting, since you can still see the tall, pointed stones guarding fields in the sheltered valley. The lake area above the town is much less hospitable, around 4000m above sea level, and with sparse marshy vegetation. It is usually possible to rent mules and a guide to take you up to the lakes—or even on the five-day trek, keeping close to the old Royal Highway, to AYABACA and the nearby Inca fortress of AYAPATE. These routes, though, are only for the really explorer-minded, and you should come equipped with maps from Lima (see p.58). It's not a good idea to take the trip alone or without a local guide.

AYABACA can also be reached by road by **bus or truck**, a fifteen-hour journey if you're lucky: for HUANCABAMBA transportation leaves from around Piura's market area. Both towns have small **hostals**, but don't expect comfort. **Information** on both places, and a booklet on the Ayapate fortress (*Las Ruinas de Ayapate* by Mario Polia, 1972), can be obtained from the University in Piura.

North of Piura: Paita, Talara, and Cabo Blanco

Leaving Piura, the Pan American Highway heads directly north, steering well clear of **PAITA**, which for centuries has been Piura's port and the closest major settlement. Set on a small peninsula at the mouth of the Río Chira, it has good roads to both PIURA (50km) and SULLANA, and is still a major center— the country's fifth port. But Paita is best known to many Peruvians as the former home of **Manuela Saenz**, the tragic mistress of Simon Bolivar during the Wars of Liberation. After the 1828 skirmishes with Colombia (of which Bolivar was dictator), Manuela was ostracized by Peruvian society, dying here in poverty in 1856. You can visit her house in the old quarter of town.

Overlooking Paita to the north is a small Spanish fortress built to protect the bay from pirates, and just beyond it is the once elite bay of **Colan**. This is still a good place to swim, though the old wooden beach huts which used to echo with the chatter of wealthy land-owning families are now pretty well destroyed. They were washed away in 1983 by the swollen river Chira amid the dramatic floods of that rainy season. Other good beaches nearby include YACILA, HERMOSA , and ESMERALDA.

Back on the highway **SULLANA**, only 40km from Piura, is a major transit junction, quite a large town overlooking the usually dry, but occasionally flooded, riverbed. Here the Plaza de Arnas and the old church of La Santisima Trinidad are worth a quick stroll while you're changing transportation—but otherwise, or if your ride takes you straight through, the town has little of interest to travelers. It's at Sullana, however, that you'll emerge if you have just entered Peru at the LA TINA border.

TALARA, some 70km farther, is distinctly attractive—taking its name and function from Peru's most important coastal oilfield. It was no more than a small fishing hamlet until 1940, though its deep-water harbor and tar pits had been used since Pizarro's time for caulking wooden ships. Pizarro in fact chose the site to build the first Spanish settlement in Peru but it proved too unhealthy and he was forced to look elsewhere, eventually hitting on what is today the city of Piura.

Talara's oil reserves, now a national refinery, were directly responsible for the last military coup in 1968. President Belaunde, then in his first term of office, had given subsoil concessions to the multinational company IPC, declaring that "if this is foreign imperialism what we need is more, not less of it." A curious logic, based on his impressions of superior conditions at the plant, it led to the accusation that he had signed an agreement "unacceptable to true Peruvians." Within two months of the affair, and as a direct consequence (if not perhaps the underlying cause), he was deposed and exiled. One of the initial acts of the new revolutionary government was to nationalize IPC and declare the Act of Talara null and void. Today the town is highly industrialized, with fertilizer plants as well as the oil business. If you need to spend the night, there are a few reasonable **hotels** in the commercial center. The nearest unpolluted beach is 2km away at LA PENA.

Thirty kilometers or so beyond, with the road still running away from the beach, there is a short turnoff to EL ALTO and the old fishing mecca of **CABO BLANCO**. It is just off the cape here that the cold Humboldt Current meets the warm equatorial El Niño—a stroke of providence that creates an extraordinary abundance of marine life. Thomas Stokes, a British resident and fanatical fisherman, discovered the spot in 1935, and it was a very popular resort in the postwar years. Hemingway stayed some months in 1951, while two years later the largest fish ever caught with a rod was landed here—a 710kg black marlin. Changes in the off-shore currents have brought decline in recent years but there are still international competitions and the area is much reputed for swordfish. The fishing club has one of the few official **campgrounds** in Peru, and there is a handful of **hotels** too.

From here to Tumbes the Pan American cuts across a farther stretch of desert, for the most part keeping tight to the Pacific coastline. It's a straight road, but not a dull one, with immense views along the rolling surf and, if you're lucky, the occasional school of dolphins playing close to the shore. To the right of the road looms a long hill, the *Cerro de Amotape*, the largest bump along the entire Peruvian coast that isn't actually a proper Andean foothill. Amotape was a local chief whom Pizarro had killed in 1532—an example to potential rebels; just to the north of this wooded hill, the ancient Inca highway can still be seen (though not from the road) on its way down the coast.

Tumbes and the Border Crossings

About 30km from the Ecuadorean border, and usually considered a mere pit-stop for overland travelers, the city of **TUMBES** nevertheless has a significant and interesting history. It was the first town to be "conquered" by the Spanish and has maintained its importance ever since—originally as the gateway to the Inca Empire, more recently through its strategic position on the controversial frontier with Ecuador. Despite two regional wars—in 1859 and 1941–42—the exact line of the border remains a source of controversy. Maps of the frontier vary depending on which country you buy them in, and the dispute occasionally breaks out on the surface—the last time in 1981 when military skirmishes closed the border for a month.

The traditional enmity between Peru and Ecuador, and the continuing dispute over the placing of the border (the two sides put it hundreds of miles apart in places) means that Tumbes has a strong army presence. There is a strict policy of no photography anywhere near military or frontier installations. Tumbes, then, is very much a border town, most of its 85,000 population seemingly engaged in either transportation or petty trading across the frontier. In many ways the people here are quite cut off from mainstream Peru, connected only by the Pan American Highway, and considerably nearer to Quito than to Lima. It is a surprisingly elegant place, however, at least in the center with its broad plaza and long **Malecon** promenade built along the high riverbanks—the kind of town where, although there is nothing much to do, there is always something going on. In the rural areas around, nearly half of Peru's tobacco leaf is produced. Down the coast are some of the best **beaches** in the country, among them CALETA DE LA CRUZ, reputed to be the bay where Pizarro first landed. You can get out here by *colectivo* from the central plaza; there are restaurants and **rooms** to let if you want to stay.

Central Tumbes is itself well endowed with restaurants and **hotels**. The *Hotel Estoril*, two blocks off the Plaza de Armas, is as good as any, cheap and clean. In the same range there's also the *Hotel Italia* (Grau 733) some four blocks from the plaza, or the *Hotel Pilsen* on the plaza itself. A little more expensive again are the *Hostal Toloa* (Teniente Vasquez), four blocks north of the plaza, or *Residencial Internacional*, beside the Plaza Bolognesi near the more expensive *Hotel de Turistas*. Cheaper than the *Turistas*, but excellent value, the *Hostal Roma* on the Plaza de Armas is relatively luxurious by Tumbes's standards.

The best place to try some of the traditional local **food** is probably *Peko's* which regularly serves both *ceviche de conchas negras* (black scallop ceviche) and *caldo de bolas de platano* (banana ball soup). Either of these can be washed down—at your peril—with *Chinguirito*, a cocktail of coconut juice with fiery *aguardiente*. The traveling crowd tends to hang out around the central plaza, drinking ice-cold beers at *Monkey's Restaurant*: when there's a war on, all Ecuadoreans are called monkeys—*monos*—by Peruvians. Facing onto the Plaza de Armas the restaurants *Zurich* and *Europa* are probably the best bet, though for excellent fish dishes try *Titos* (Alfonso Ugarte 212).

The official money exchange, the **Banco de la Nación**, is just off the main square, although the border and sometimes the town are usually milling with **black market** dealers. Be wary: these are renowned for trying to rip you off if they can. The best rates can usually be found on the street at **Aguas Verdes** on the actual frontier. The **post office** is on San Martin, less than two blocks from the Plaza de Armas.

Pizarro and the Inca City of Tumbes

Pizarro didn't actually set foot in Tumbes when it was first discovered in 1527. He preferred to cast his eyes along the Inca city's adobe walls, its carefully irrigated fields, and its shining temple, from the comfort and safety of his ship. However, with the help of translators he set about learning as much as he could about Peru and the Incas during this initial contact. An Inca noble visited him aboard ship and even dined at his table. The noble was said to be especially pleased with his first taste of Spanish wine and the present of an iron hatchet.

The Spaniards who did go ashore—a Captain Alonso de Molina and his black servant—made reports of such grandeur that Pizarro at first refused to believe them, sending instead the more reliable Greek cavalier, Pedro de Candia. Molina's descriptions of the temple, lined with gold and silver sheets, were confirmed by Candia. He also gave the people of Tumbes their first taste of European technological might—firing his musket to smash a wooden board to pieces. With this Pizarro had all the evidence he needed; after sailing another 500km down the coast, as far as the Santa valley, he returned to Panama and then back to Spain to obtain royal consent and support for his projected conquest.

The Tumbes people hadn't always been controlled by the Incas. The area was originally inhabited by the Tallanes, related to coastal tribes from Ecuador who are still known for their unusual lip and nose ornaments. In 1450 they were conquered for the first time—by the Chimu. Thirteen years later came the Incas, organized by Topac Inca, who bulldozed the locals into religious, economic, and even architectural conformity in order to create their most northerly coastal terminus. A fortress, temple, and sun convent were built, and the town was colonized with loyal subjects from other regions—a typical Inca ploy, which they called the *Mitimaes* system. The valley had an efficient irrigation program, allowing them to grow, among other things, bananas, corn, and squash.

It didn't take Pizarro long to add his name to the list of conquerors. But after landing on the coast of Ecuador in 1532 with a royal warrant to conquer and Christianize the land of Peru, his arrival at Tumbes was a strange affair. Despite the previous friendly contact, some of the Spanish were killed by Indians as they tried to beach, and when they reached the city it was completely deserted with many buildings destroyed, and, more painfully for Pizarro, no sign of gold.

It seems likely that Tumbes's destruction prior to Pizarro's arrival was the result of intertribal warfare directly related to the Inca Civil War. This, a war of succession between Atahualpa and his half-brother, the legitimate heir, Huascar, was to make Pizarro's role as conqueror a great deal easier.

Tumbes itself he took without a struggle. Leaving a contingent behind to turn it into a "real town," he set off down the coast, sending a squad under Hernando de Soto to survey the mountainous inland area.

The ruined **Inca city** of Tumbes lies 5km southwest of the modern town and although there's not a lot that you can make out these days it's a pleasant walk and both the temple and fortress are recognizable. The ruins are bisected by the modern Pan American Highway, and cows and goats from the nearby hamlet of San Pedro wander freely among the ancient adobe walls, devastated by centuries of intermittent flooding.

If you've never seen a mangrove swamp, **PUERTO PIZARRO** too is worth a visit, 7km farther. Buses and *colectivos* go regularly from Tumbes (Comite 6, Avenida Piura or from the *Roggero* bus depot) to this ancient fishing port, a commercial harbor until swamps grew out to sea, making it inaccessible for large boats and permanently disconnecting Tumbes from the Pacific. You can take short boat trips out to see the *rhizopora* mangle tree's dense root system and wildlife, take part in organized shark fishing and waterskiing, or just dangle your own hook and line into the warm water.

If it's just a **beach** you're interested in—and the sea is pleasantly warm around Tumbes—there are buses for the coastal settlements of **Caleta La Cruz** (23km; 45 min) and **Zorritos** (34km; 1 hr.) regularly every day from the market.

The Tumbes Border

Crossing the border (open at the Peruvian end from 9am–noon and 2–5:30pm) is relatively simple in either direction. On the Peruvian side, some 2km before **Aguas Verdes** proper, you'll find the Peruvian *migraciones* where you get an exit (or entry) stamp and tourist card for your passport and go through the usual customs procedures. Once past these buildings it's a fifteen-minute walk or a short drive to the busy frontier settlement at Aguas Verdes. From here you just walk over the bridge into Ecuador and **Huaquillas**, the Ecuadorean border town and the immigration office (open in Ecuador from 9am–noon and 2–5pm) where you'll get your entry (or exit) stamps and tourist card.

In both directions the authorities sometimes require that you show an onward ticket (bus or plane) out of their respective countries. Unless you intend to recross the border inside a week or two it's not worth taking out any local currency: changing Peruvian *soles* in Ecuador or Ecuadorean *sucres* in Peru usually involves a substantial loss, and inflation is such that even two weeks can make quite a difference.

There are **buses** and **colectivos** several times an hour between Tumbes and Aguas Verdes (some 25km) from the corner of Bolivar and Piura for less than $1, or you can take a **taxi** for around $5.

La Tina: The Alternative Border

The crossing at **LA TINA**, to the east of Tumbes, is a longer route out of Peru but a fairly spectacular one—particularly in the scenery on the Ecuadorean side. The main disadvantage is the road up from SULLANA, an unbelievably bumpy eight-hour ride. **Buses** and **trucks**, however, travel daily in both directions—and though the service tends to be erratic (frequent breakdowns), everyone gets there in the end. The route became quite popular in 1983 as travelers tried to avoid some of the rain-devastated zones between Piura and Tumbes, but in normal times it's a somewhat eccentric option and there have been reports that it is now quite a dangerous zone, due mainly to drug smuggling.

Crossing over from LA TINA to the Ecuadorean town of LA MACARÁ there is a 2km walk (or overpriced taxis) at the International Bridge over the Macará River. If you're coming in the other direction, (a somewhat adventurous possibility) **onward from La Tina**, the Inca fortress of **AYAPATE** is near the town of AYABACA, to the east along the frontier. It is possible to get transportation from Las Lomas.

t‑avel details

Buses and/or *Colectivos*
From Trujillo Lima (several daily; 9 hr.); Chiclay/Puira (several daily; 3 hr./7 hr.); Cajamarca (several daily; 8 hr.)

From Cajamarca Lima (several daily; 17 hr.); Celedin (daily; 5 hr.); Chachapoyas (Every Tue. and Sun; 20 hr.); Chiclayo (daily; 7 hr.)

From Chachapoyas Chiclayo (daily via Jaen; 17 hr.); Rioja/Moyabamba (irregular trucks; 12 hr.; thence on to Tarapoto and Iquitos—see p.232).

From Chiclayo Piura/Tumbes (several daily; 4 hr./10 hr.); Trujillo/Lima (several daily; 3 hr./14 hr.); Cajamarca (several daily; 8 hr.); Chachapoyas (daily; 17 hr.; Huancabamba 9 every Tues. and Fri.; 15–20 hr.).

From Piura Tumbes (several daily; 4–6 hr.); La Tina; (every morning from Sullana; 6–8 hr.); Chiclayo (several daily (4 hr.).

From Tumbes Aguas Verde (at least hourly; 20 min.); Lima (several day and night; 23 hr.).

Flights
From Trujillo Daily to Lima; Mon., Wed. and Fri. to Trujillo. **From Cajamarca** Mon., Wed. and Fri. to Trujillo and Lima.

From Rioja/Moyabamba Daily to Lima (except Thurs. and Sat.); Tues. and Sat. to Chiclayo.

From Tarapoto Daily to Lima; Wed. and Fri. to Trujillo; Tues., Thurs., Fri., and Sat. to Iquitos.

From Yurimaguas Daily to Lima (except Thurs. and Sat.); Tues. and Sun. to Iquitos.

From Chiclayo Daily to Lima, Trujillo, Piura and Talara; Tues. and Sat. to Rioja/Moyabamba; Mon. and Fri. to Tarapoto.

From Piura Daily to Lima, via **Chiclayo**.

From Tumbes Daily to Lima.

CHAPTER SIX

THE JUNGLE

F ew people think of Peru in terms of jungle, yet despite the inroads of colonists and the ever-advancing lumber industry, almost two-thirds of the country is still covered by dense **tropical rainforest**—the beginnings of a vast Amazon flood plain that emerges from myriad Andean streams and extends right across the South American continent until it reaches the Atlantic over 4000km away. Known to Peruvian outsiders as *El Infierno Verde*—"the Green Hell"—the jungle zone has, until recent decades, been left alone, its exotic plants, insects, birds, wild animals, and scattered native tribes living much as they have for thousands of years. The usually placid rivers—still the basis of jungle transportation—fall in places through tumultuous rapids, called *pongos*, like the Manseriche and Mainique, and beyond the main waterways much is still unexplored. Jaguars, anteaters, and tapirs roam the forests, huge anaconda snakes live in the swamps, toothy cayman (the South American crocodile) crawl along riverbanks, and trees like the giant Shihuahuaco, strong enough to break an axe head, grow as high as 50m.

Whether you look at it up close, from the ground or a boat, or fly over it in a plane, the rainforest looks endless. In fact, the jungle is disappearing at an alarming rate. Partly because of the imminent danger of its total destruction, and the awareness of the jungle's importance—not just as a unique eco-system but as a vital component of the global environment—the rainforest is increasingly *the* place for travelers to go. In terms of accessibility, range of ecological niches, wildlife, and beauty it's hard to beat the Peruvian edge of the Amazon. Flying to one of the main jungle towns is surprisingly cheap and can save an arduous two- or three-day journey, but although there are a number of quick and satisfying excursions into the nearby jungle, by far the best way to really experience the wilderness is to spend a week or so travel-ing by canoe or motor boat through the untouched inner sanctum of the rainforest.

Cuzco is the best base for trips into the southern jungle, with the only road across the continent leading to the frontier town of **Puerto Maldonado** and on into Bolivia and Brazil. A more adventurous trip—taking a week at least—will bring you into the amazing **Manu National Park**, quite possibly the most exciting nature reserve in South America. For a quick taste of the jungle, you can stay on the train beyond Machu Picchu to the end of the line at **Quillabamba**, on the Río Urubamba. The Urubamba flows north along the foot of the Andes, through the dangerous but unforgettable white water of the *Pongo de Mainique*, before merging with the Río Ucayali to flow past

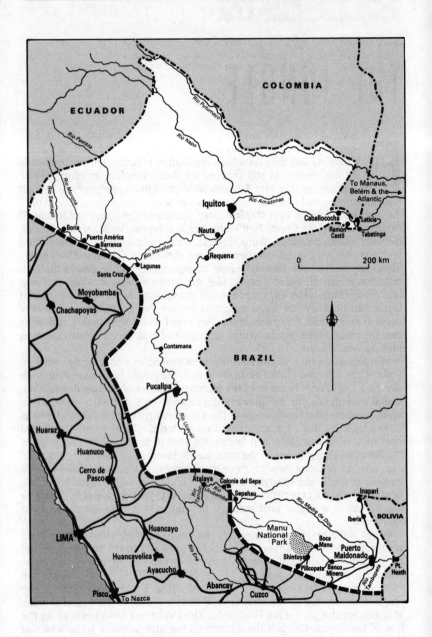

Pucallpa, the fastest-growing town in the country, and nearby **Lake Yarinacocha**, an attractively developed tourist resort. Farther north, the Ucayali merges with the equally broad Río Marañon to form the mighty Río Amazon itself, just outside the jungle's only real city, the regional capital **Iquitos**. One of Peru's most welcoming cities, despite the presence of oil wells and cocaine traffickers, Iquitos—accessible by a daily, one-hour flight from Lima—is the most organized of the Amazon's tourist destinations, with several different companies offering a wide range of jungle visits from luxury lodges to rugged jungle survival expeditions.

Some Background

Outside the few main towns there are still hardly any sizable settlements, and the jungle population remains dominated by around 35 **indigenous tribes**, each with its own distinct language, customs, and style of dress. After centuries of external influence (missionaries, gold seekers, rubber barons, soldiers, oil companies, anthropologists, tourists . . .) many jungle Indians speak Spanish and live conventional, Westernized lives, preferring to wear jeans and drink instant coffee. But others, increasingly under threat, have been forced to struggle for their cultural identities and territorial rights, or to retreat well beyond the new frontiers of "civilization."

For most of these traditional or semi-traditional tribes, the jungle offers a semi-nomadic existence. Communities are scattered, with groups of between ten and two hundred people, and their sites shifted every few years. For subsistence they depend on small cultivated plots, fish from the rivers, and game from the forest, including wild pigs, deer, monkeys, and a great range of edible birds. The main species of jungle fish are *sabalo* (a kind of salmon), *carachama* (an armored fish), the feisty piranha (ravenous meat eaters, so take care when swimming), and the giant *zungaro* and *paiche*—the latter, at up to 200kg, the world's largest freshwater fish. Food is so abundant that jungle dwellers generally spend no more than three to four days a week engaged in subsistence activities.

It's difficult to say for sure but many archeologists think that the initial spark for the evolution of Peru's **high cultures** came from the jungle. Evidence from Chavin, Chachapoyas, and Tantamayo seems to back up such a theory, and the **Incas** were certainly unable to dominate the jungle tribes—their main contact was one of peaceful trade in treasured items such as plumes, gold, medicinal plants, and the sacred coca leaf. At the time of the **Spanish Conquest** fairly permanent settlements seem to have existed along all the major jungle rivers, the people living in large groups to farm the rich alluvial soils. Only with the arrival of the Europeans—and the incursions of the nineteenth-century rubber boom—do they appear to have broken up into smaller and scattered groups.

Prior to the onslaught of the rubber collectors, the Peruvian jungle had resisted major colonization. Alonso de Alvarado, in 1537, had led the first Spanish expedition, cutting a trail through from Chachapoyas to Moyabamba, but most **expeditions** ended in utter disaster, defeated by the ferocity of the

/text continues on page 257

JUNGLE ESSENTIALS AND PRACTICALITIES

Ignored by most travelers, the Peruvian jungle is nonetheless the most exciting of all the country's regions—and the most exotic in every respect. If you go even a little off the beaten track, this is *real* traveling, through an environment extraordinarily intense in its mesh of plant, insect, and animal life. It is also, of course, an environment not to be taken lightly—the image of poisonous snakes, jaguars, and mosquitoes is based on fact. However, once you're there, the myth usually seems to be dispelled as you realize that these dangers don't actually come hunting for you. And if you just want to take a look at the place, exploring the immediate environs of Puerto Maldonado, Pucallpa, or Iquitos, you can do so with relative ease.

HAZARDS The most likely is **river sickness**, a general term for the effect of the sun's strong rays reflected off the water. After several hours on the river, particularly at midday without the shade of a hat, you may get the first irksome symptom—the trots—sometimes followed by nausea or shaking fever; in extreme cases these can last for a day or two. If you're traveling Lomotil, etc. will help; otherwise just treat by drinking fluids. Water-born **parasites** are quite common, so it's best to boil all drinking water and use sterilizing tablets or crystals. Also, get a medical checkup when you return home. **Jiggers**, small insects that live in cut grass, can also be a very irritating problem. They stick to and bury their heads in your ankles before slowly making their way up your legs to the groin, causing you to itch furiously. You can either pick them out one by one as the natives do, or apply sulphur cream (ask for the best ointment from a *farmacia* in the jungle town). It's unlikely that you will encounter any **snakes**. If you do, nearly all of them will disappear as quickly as they can—only the *shushupe* (a bushmaster) is fearless. If anyone does get bitten, the first thing to remember is to keep calm—most deaths result from shock, not venom. Try to kill the snake for identification, but more important, apply a temporary tourniquet above the bite and find medical help. Some natives have remedies even for a potentially deadly *shushupe* bite.

TRANSPORTATION The two most common forms of river boats are **canoes** and **launches**, either with a Briggs and Stratton *peque-peque* nine-horsepower engine or more powerful outboard motor. The latter is obviously faster and more maneuverable but a *peque-peque* is a lot cheaper; in the end your decision will probably be based on the price, your confidence in the captain, and his readiness for embarkation. If you're going to be traveling together for more than a day, it's a good idea to make sure you can get along well with the captain and that he really does know the rivers. Anyone who intends **hitching** along a river system should remember that the farther you are away from the town the harder it is to lay your hands on **gas** (even if you come across Shell drilling in the middle of the forest!). However much money you may offer, no one will take you up river if they're really short on gas—and most of the people are most of the time. Taking along your own supply, say a 55-gallon container, is a little difficult but it wouldn't be a bad idea if you're going somewhere really remote. As a last resort it's always possible to build or get hold of a **balsa raft** and paddle downstream from village to village, but this has obvious dangers in addition to rapids, etc.; you may well get stuck for the night on the river bank in some godforsaken place. This type of transportation isn't really advisable without the help of someone who knows the river extremely well.

There are a few other points worth knowing if you intend to do a lot of **river travel** in Peru. Firstly, you can save a lot of money on hotels by literally hanging around on the larger river boats (say between Pucallpa and Iquitos, or Iquitos and Tabatinga)—most captains allow passengers to sleep on board in hammocks for a few days before departure. Most of the bunks on the river boats are far too small for anyone six foot tall or more—best take a hammock in case. River boats traveling upstream tend to stay close to the bank, away from the fast central flow—this means upstream journeys may take longer but they're much more visually interesting, particularly on the larger rivers where it's often hard to make out even huts on the banks while you're moving down the middle of the river.

GETTING LOST in the forest is no fun and it can happen very easily. Just by straying a hundred meters from camp, the river, or your guide, you can find yourself completely surrounded by a seemingly impenetrable canopy of plant life. It's almost impossible to walk in a straight line through the undergrowth and one trail looks very much like the next to the unaccustomed eye. Your best bet, apart from shouting as loud as you can, is to find moving water and follow it downstream to the main river where someone will eventually find you waiting on the river bank. If you get caught out overnight the two best places to sleep are beside a fire on the river bank or high up in the boughs of a tree that isn't crawling with biting ants.

GUIDES A basic rule of thumb in the forest or on the rivers is to make sure that reliable guidance is always available—wherever you venture try to be with a local guide. They don't need to have official status—in fact natives are often the best guides—but they should be experienced in the region and willing to help out. There are several ways of enlisting this kind of help: by paying through the nose for an official **jungle tour**; by going to the port of a jungle town and searching for someone who will rent his **boat and services** as a guide; or by traveling within the boundaries of friendly human settlements, **hopping** along the rivers from one village to the next with someone who is going that way anyway and who will be able to introduce you to the villagers at each stage. The last option is obviously the most adventurous but will normally involve long waits in remote settlements for someone else to take you farther upriver. Whichever, bear in mind that the jungle is an essentially laid-back place: if there's one thing certain to get a *selvatico* (jungle dweller) mad, it's a gringo with a loud voice and pushy manner.

PERMITS To enter certain zones such as the *Manu National Park* or *Lago Valencia*, you'll need to obtain permission first, for details of which see the relevant sections. It's not usually difficult to get a permit unless there's a good reason, like suspected hostility from restless natives. In 1980 a German-led wildlife expedition entered the Manu Park without permission and was attacked by Indians—the first thing they knew about it was a sheet of arrows flying towards their canoe.

BOOKS For additional information, and an interesting account of a trip into the Manu Park, you might want to pick up Tanis and Martin Jordan's *South American River Trips II* (Bradt Publications: see p.317). The Jordans made their trip into Manu on a motorized rubber raft, which perhaps, in view of the above, isn't a very good idea!

INTO THE JUNGLE: THINGS TO TAKE

If you don't intend to go much beyond the frontier towns there's little that you'll have to take except the usual baggage. Outlined below, however, are three lists. If you're only going for a "conventional" visit to a town and staying maybe one night in a jungle lodge, the items on the first list should be adequate. If you're going to spend a little more time in the forest, the items on list two should be added to those on the first list. Anyone considering a serious jungle adventure of more than a few nights should take everything on all three lists. Probably the most important preparation, though, is a **mental** one: you should be prepared to respect (not fear) the rivers, the forest, and its inhabitants. The jungle is actually home for a large number of people, and by arriving ready to accept what comes you'll find most avenues open to you.

Items needed on any visit to the jungle
(even to a town and/or tourist lodge):

toilet paper

insect repellent

insect bite ointment (toothpaste will help in the last resort, but an antihistamine, tiger balm, or *mentol china* works better)

running shoes and sandals (ideally plastic or rubber)

waterproof overclothes

malaria pills (start course in advance as directed by prescribing doctor)

suitable clothing (although it might be warm, it's a good idea to wear socks and long sleeves in the evenings—that's when the mosquitoes come out).

Items useful for a semi-adventure jungle trip
(three to five days to a lodge or some similar basic facility):

something that works against diarrhea such as Lomotil or Imodium

a sun hat (especially for river travel)

good water sterilizers (tablets or crystals)

quick-dry clothing

candles

some luxury food and drink (assuming the basics are being provided; if not, then adequate basic food should obviously also be taken)

plastic bags to pack everything in (particularly important when traveling on the rivers)

a flashlight (plus spare batteries)

a multipurpose knife (with can and bottle opener)

waterproof matches and a back-up gas lighter

mosquito net (for sleeping inside)

waterproof box for camera equipment

a blanket for sleeping (unless you can be sure this is being provided)

Items needed on an adventure expedition
(five days or more away from any facilities):

adequate food supplies (mainly rice, beans, cans of fish, crackers, noodles, fresh fruits, etc.)

cooking pots (and either a stove or the ability to cook over a fire and a supply of dry wood)

a filled water container (a gallon a day)

adequate bedding (a blanket or two will usually do if you've got a hammock; something soft or a mat for underneath you plus the blankets otherwise)

good strong boots

some rope

fishing line and hooks (perhaps some unsalted meat for bait)

a first-aid box or medical kit (including tweezers, needles, scissors, Band-Aids, bandages, adhesive tape, sterile dressings, antiseptic cream, antibiotics, and painkillers)

gifts for people you might encounter (batteries, knives, fish hooks and line, Polaroid pictures, etc.)

a supply of fuel (gas for motor boats); it can be very scarce and consequently extremely handy on a jungle river—especially when bargaining for a ride with a boat owner

a good knife (sometimes also a machete)

a compass and a whistle (in case you get lost)

tribes, the danger of the rivers, climate, and wild animals—and perhaps as much by the inherent surrealism of the forest. Throughout the centuries, too, there have been significant uprisings. In 1742 a group of tribes drove out all nonnatives from their territories and chased the army back into the Andes as far as Tarma. And as recently as 1919 the Campa Indians were blockading the rivers and ejecting missionaries and foreigners from their ancestral lands.

The **rubber boom**, however, from the 1880s to just before World War I, had a more prolonged effect. Treating the natives as little more than slaves, the rubber barons—men like the notorious Fitzcarraldo—made overnight fortunes, and large sections of the forests were explored and subdued. It was a process that fell into decline when the British explorer **Markham** took Peruvian rubber plants—via Kew Gardens—to Malaysia, where the plants grew equally well but were far easier to harvest.

The Threat to the Forest

Over the last few decades the exploitation of the rainforest has been more dangerously and irreversibly repeated by the intrusion of oil corporations and lumber companies; even worse, vast tracts of forest are disappearing to make way for coca fields to supply North American and European cocaine habits. Successive waves of colonists—mostly landless mountain dwellers—have swept down from the Andes into much of the Peruvian Amazon over the last ten years, most of them clearing trees to grow cash crops. Coca seems to be the most viable these days, its black market price making it well worth the risk, particularly with the national economy in such a dire state. The way things are going, it's hard to see how much longer the indigenous peoples of the Peruvian rainforest can maintain their culture or their traditional territories. The present dwellers' children will be without a means of earning a living if the trees disappear. There is time to save the forest and there is a duty to respect its original inhabitants—arguably among the best guardians of a natural environment this world will ever see. We should be learning from them, not contributing to their destruction.

Campa face painting stamp

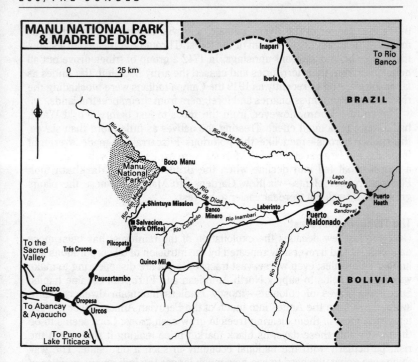

MANU NATIONAL PARK & MADRE DE DIOS

0   25 km

Inapari

To Río Banco

Iberia

BRAZIL

Río Manu

Río de las Piedras

Manu National Park

Boco Manu

Rio Alto Madre de Dios

Río Madre de Dios

Lago Valencia

Shintuya Mission

Banco Minero

Laberinto

Lago Sandoval

Puerto Heath

Salvacion (Park Office)

Río Colorado

Río Inambari

Puerto Maldonado

To the Sacred Valley

Trés Cruces

Pilcopata

Quince Mil

Río Tambopata

BOLIVIA

Paucartambo

Cuzco

Oropesa

To Abancay & Ayacucho

Urcos

To Puno & Lake Titicaca

THE SOUTHERN JUNGLE: MADRE DE DIOS

The comparatively small *departmento* of **Madre de Dios**, named for the broad river that flows through the heart of the southern jungle, is, like so many remote areas of Peru, changing extremely fast. It was one of the last zones affected by the rubber boom at the turn of the century, and natives here—many of whom struggle to maintain their traditional ways of life, despite the continuing efforts of colonists and Christian missionaries—were left pretty much alone until the push for oil here in the 1960s and 1970s brought roads and airplanes into what is now the most accessible part of the Peruvian rainforest. As the oil companies moved out, prospectors took their place, panning for flakes of gold along the river banks, while agribusiness moved in to clear groves of mahogany trees and harvest the bountiful Brazil nuts.

It's still very much a frontier zone, centered on the rapidly growing river city of **Puerto Maldonado**, founded by the legendary explorer and rubber baron Fitzcarraldo near the Bolivian border. As in all jungle regions, human activity here is closely linked to the river system, and though the scattered town and villages are interesting, even endearing, for their Wild West energy and spirit, most people who make the effort to get here come to see the **wildlife**, especially the three strictly protected national parks in which all development is banned. **Manu National Park**, quite possibly the most abundant jungle area in the world, is literally teeming with exotic plant and animal life. It's also the most easily accessible part of true jungle in Peru—a day by truck and two more by canoe from Cuzco, the nearest city. Other, less adventurous, but still rewarding trips head out from Puerto Maldonado to **Lago Valencia**, where you're likely to see at least a few cayman, capybaras, and jaguars ambling along the shore.

The Rivers

The **Río Madre de Dios** is fed by two main tributaries—the *Manu* and the *Alta Madre de Dios*—which roll off the Paucartambo Ridge just north of Cuzco. The ridge divides the tributaries from the Río Urubamba watershed, and delineates Manu National Park, one of the region's greatest attractions and still very much an expedition zone. Described in a following section, Manu National Park is usually approached by road from Cuzco and, permission having been obtained, entered by canoe with a guide from the village of Shintuya.

At Puerto Maldonado, four or five days downstream, the Madre de Dios meets with the **Río Tambopata** and the **Río de las Piedras**—and flows on to **Puerto Heath**, a day's boat ride away, on the Bolivian frontier. From here it continues through the Bolivian forest into Brazil to join the great **Río Madeira** which eventually meets the Amazon river near **Manaus**.

The Río Tambopata's rich forest flora and wildlife have, in a similar way to Manu, been turned into a national park, though it is increasingly under threat from colonists, and an expensive place to visit. More accessible, and the target for many travelers staying over in Maldonado, is the huge expanse of **Lago Valencia**, another extraordinary wildlife locale where, if you feel like it, you can even fish for piranha.

Indigenous People

Off the main waterways, within the system of smaller tributaries and streams, live a variety of different **native groups**. All are depleted in numbers due to contact with this century's Western influences and diseases, but while some groups have been completely wiped out over the last twenty years, several have maintained their isolation. A traditionally dangerous region, with a manic climate (usually searingly hot, but with sudden icy winds), the southern jungle has only been systematically explored since the 1950s and was largely unknown until Fitzcarraldo founded Puerto Maldonado in 1902.

Occasional "uncontacted" groups still turn up, although they are usually segments of a larger tribe split or dispersed with the arrival of the rubber barons, and they are fast being secured in controllable mission villages. Most of the native tribes that remain in, or have returned to, their traditional territories now find themselves forced to take on seasonal work for the colonists who have staked claims around the major rivers. In the dry season, from May through to November, this usually means panning for gold—the region's most lucrative commodity. In the rainy season the Brazil nut (or, rather, Peru nut) collections take over. The lumber industry, too, is well established—indeed most of the accessible large cedars have already gone.

If you go anywhere in the jungle, especially on an organized tour, you're likely to stop off at a **tribal village** for at least a half-hour or so, and you'll get more out of the visit the more you know about the people who live there. Downstream from the jungle town of Puerto Maldonado, the most populous indigenous group are the **Huarayos**. Originally seminomadic hunters and gatherers, the Huarayos were well-known warriors. They fought the Incas and, later on, the Spanish expedition of Alvarez Maldonado—eventually establishing fairly friendly and respectful relationships with both. Under Fitzcarraldo's reign in the region, they apparently suffered greatly. Today they live in fairly large communities and have more or less abandoned their original bark-cloth robes in favor of shorts and T-shirts.

Upstream from Puerto Maldonado live several native tribes known collectively as the **Mashcos** but actually comprising at least six separate linguistic groups—the *Huachipairi, Shireneris, Amaraceiris, Sapitoyeris, Arasayris*, and *Toyeris*. All of them typically use long bows—over a meter and a half—and equally lengthy arrows. Most settlements will also have a shotgun or two these days since less time can be dedicated to hunting when they are panning for gold or working lumber for colonists. Traditionally the Mashcos also wore long bark-cloth robes and had long hair; the men often stuck eight feathers into the skin around their lips—making them look distinctively fierce and cat-like. Having developed a terrifying hatred of white people during Fitzcarraldo's era, they were eventually conquered and "tamed" by missionaries and the army about thirty years ago.

Puerto Maldonado ... and Fitzcarraldo

With the local *concejo* still trying its utmost to play down the town's image as a Wild West frontier settlement, **PUERTO MALDONADO** is a slightly strange sort of place. Most of the people, riding coolly around on Honda 50s, are second-generation colonists, but there's a constant stream of new and hopeful arrivals—rich and poor boys from all parts of South America and even the occasional gang from the U.S. The lure, inevitably, is gold. Every rainy season the swollen *ríos* deposit a heavy layer of gold dust along their banks and those who have been quick enough to stake claims on the best stretches have made substantial fortunes.

It was rubber, however, that led to the town's establishment by Fitzcarraldo—though the old baron too, when he blundered upon the site, was actually after gold. Somewhere in the jungle hereabouts is reputed to be the site of the legendary "El Dorado" city of **Paititi**, the great quest of Spanish explorers through the centuries.

The Saga of Fitzcarraldo

Fitzcarraldo, while working rubber on the Urubamba river, caught the gold bug, hearing rumors from local Campa Indians of an Inca fort protecting vast treasures, possibly around the Río Purus. He set out along the Camisea, a tributary of the Upper Urubamba, managed to reach its source, and from there walked over the ridge to a new watershed which he took to be the Purus.

Leaving men to clear a trail, he returned to Iquitos and, in 1884, came back down the Camisea on a boat called *La Contamana*. He took the boat apart and, with the aid of over a thousand Campa and other Indians, carried it across to the "Purus," but as he cruised down, attacked by tribes at several points, Fitzcarraldo slowly began to realize that this river was not the Purus—a fact confirmed when he eventually bumped into a Bolivian rubber collector.

Though he'd ended up on the wrong river, Fitzcarraldo had discovered a trail link connecting the two great Amazonian watersheds. In Europe the discovery was heralded as a great step forward in the exploration of South America, but for Peru it meant more rubber and a quicker route for its export via the Amazon to the Atlantic—and the beginning of the end for the Madre de Dios's indigenous tribes. Werner Herzog, of course, thought it might make quite a good movie.

The Town

The main street of Puerto Maldonado, **Leon de Velarde**, immediately establishes the town's stage-set feel, lined with bars, hardware stores, and a poolroom. At one end is the **Plaza de Armas**, with a bizarre Chinese pagoda-type clocktower at its center, and along another side a modern *Municipalidad* where a TV is sometimes set up for the people to watch an all important event, like a soccer game. The streets, invariably muddy, show few signs of wealth despite the gold dust. For the Indians who now and then come upstream to sell a few grams at the *Banco Minero*, though, they hold some fascination. You sometimes see a small group, having traded for a few essentials like cloth, fish hooks, or machetes, leaning on the outside of restaurant windows, and watching with interest as the townspeople eat.

If you're considering a river trip, or just feel like crossing to the other side for a walk, follow Jiron Billingshurst down from the plaza to the **port**—one of the town's most active corners. There's a very cheap standard **ferry service** across the Madre de Dios to where the newish road to Brazil begins.

Arrival and Getting Around

Most of the **trucks** from Cuzco arrive at Puerto Maldonado market. It's a laborious two- or three-day journey down from the glacial highlands; after passing into cloud-covered high forest—the *ceja de selva*—the muddy track winds its slippery way through dense tropical vegetation, via the small settlement at QUINCEMIL. If you arrive **by plane** on the daily flight from Lima via Cuzco (less than one hour's flight from Cuzco), the blast of hot, humid air you get the moment you step out onto the runway is an instant reminder that this is the Amazon Basin. After picking up your luggage from the shack which serves as an airport building, the high cost of a taxi or *colectivo* into town ($2–$6) is another indication that you've reached the jungle.

The quickest way to get around the town and its immediate environs is by **renting a moped** (from $1 an hour—cheaper by the day). You'll find a reasonable (and central) place in an alleyway opposite the *Hotel Wilson* on Avenida Gonzalez Prada. Most of the machines are two-seaters so you can split the costs; if you're heading out of town, make sure there's ample gas in the tank. There are two main routes to follow: along Avenida Fitzcarraldo you come out at the cattle ranches on the far side of the airstrip, while if you turn off on 28 de Julio you can take the road as far as you like in the direction of Quincemil. A regular **bus** service now connects Puerto Maldonado with the upstream gold-mining frontier settlement of **Laberinto** (leaving from the *Hotel Wilson* on Avenida Gonzalez Prada).

Sleeping, Eating, and Nightlife

There are several **hotels** to choose from. A relatively good deal is the *Hotel Wilson* (cold shower and an electric fan in each room) on Avenida Gonzalez Prada, next to the *AeroPeru* office. Cheaper and with more jungle character, the *Hotel Moderno*, by the waterfront near the plaza, is modest but friendly. The *Hostel Oriental* on the plaza is more basic still. There are any number of other places—most of them, like much of the town's activity, within half a block of Leon de Velarde. At the far end of town, along Leon de Velarde to the banks of the Río Tambopata, you'll find the *Hotel de Turistas*, nothing special but all right (food sometimes quite good).

You should have no problem finding a good **restaurant** and the food in Puerto Maldonado is tastier than in any other jungle town. Delicious river fish are always available, even in *ceviche* form, and there's venison or wild pig, too, fresh from the forest (try *estofado de venado*). One of the best places is *El Danube Azul* (on the corner of the plaza and Leon de Velarde), run by Elba, a friendly woman who is often willing to arrange daily set meals at a very reasonable price if you're sticking around for a week or so. The *Savoy Restaurant* on Leon de Velarde, near the corner of Avenida Gonzalez Prada, serves traditional soup breakfasts but will also fix you a fried egg sandwich or something similar. More than for its food, though, this restaurant is worth visiting for the insight it gives into local images of the rainforest. Its walls are covered in paintings of a typical *selvatico* style, developed to represent and romanticize the dreamlike features of the jungle—looming jaguars, brightly plumed macaws talking to each other in the treetops, and deer drinking water beside a still lake. Farther up the main street, the morning **market** has excellent juices, fresh fruits, and vegetables.

There is very little **nightlife** in this laid-back town. Most people just stroll around, stopping occasionally to sit and chat in the plaza or in bars along the main drag. At weekends and fiesta times, however, it's possible to sample what for most people is one of the jungle's greatest delights—**chicha music**. Loud and easy to move to, you can usually pinpoint a concert just by following the sound of an electric bass guitar. The best place is probably the large pavilion off Jiron Daniel, less than three blocks from the plaza; shows normally continue into the very early hours of the morning and any *gringas* who go along can expect to be hounded for a dance without respite.

Other Things

Puerto Maldonado's **post office** is on the corner of Leon de Velarde and Jiron Jaime Troncoso. **Money** in dollars cash can often be changed privately (ask your hotel); for travelers' checks there are two **banks** on the plaza, *Banco Credito* and *Banco de la Nación*, both open weekday mornings.

River Trips

Puerto Maldonado has not really been developed for tourism, and the cost of living here is high, so you'll probably want to set about arranging a **river expedition** pretty quickly. You can do this in two ways: by arranging for your own boat and boatman or—considerably more expensive—taking an excursion up to one of the nearby tourist lodges. For most of the major river trips (including the most popular, Lago Valencia) you'll need to ask permission from the **Captain's Office** on Leon de Velarde, between Avenidas Gonzalez Prada and 2 de Mayo. This is normally quite straightforward, if it's often a battle to be heard over the *chicha* music on the captain's radio!

Something not commonly done by gringos, though a possibility, is to travel **by river into Bolivia** on one of the sugar boats that leave more or less every other week. Before embarking on this, however, you'll have to clear your passport and visa with the police and *inmigracion* offices near the Plaza de Armas. The Bolivian formalities can usually be dealt with at the frontier post of **Puerto Heath**, from where you continue by river to **Riberalta**. Here there are land and air connections with the rest of Bolivia as well as river or road access into Brazil via the Río Madeira or **Guajara-Mirim**.

Organized Tours

The two main **tourist lodges** in the jungle—*The Explorer's Inn* at the Tambopata Nature Reserve and *Cuzco Amazonica*, an hour down the Madre de Dios—are both very much the preserve of scientists, filmmakers, and well-heeled travelers and tourists. *Tambo Lodge* is a third and generally much cheaper option run by a couple of brothers from Cuzco.

The Explorer's Inn (contact and bookings through offices at G. de la Vega 1334, Lima; ☎31-6330; or Plaza San Francisco 168, Cuzco; ☎23-5242) runs tours through the jungle from around $36 a night for the privilege of Western luxury amid over 5000 hectares of virgin forest, and the chance to watch more than 500 species of birds—one-sixth of all those known in South America. *Cuzco Amazonica* (information and bookings through offices at Andalucia 174, Miraflores, Lima; ☎47-7193; or Procuradures 48, Cuzco; ☎23-2161), set up by a French-Peruvian venture in 1975 as "a journey within your journey," is a similar kind of set up but even more pricey and luxurious (upwards of $50 a night), with cocktail bars and all imaginable comforts.

Tambo Lodge (contact through agents in Cuzco at Portal de Panes 109; ☎22-2332; or at the airport—and via *El Danube Azul Restaurante* in Puerto Maldonado) is substantially more basic than the others as far as accommodation goes—wooden huts with bunks and mosquito nets—and not in quite such a beautiful location. It is nevertheless a jungle trip (if only 8km or so from town) that you can make for less than $30 a night without having to invest heavily in food or equipment. They provide a reliable service, have a boat, and run fairly complete schedules including transportation (bus and boat) between the airport at Puerto Maldonado and the lodge, jungle walks, and visits to *Lago Sandobval* and a gold-panning river beach upstream. Alternatively, if you have plenty of cash but are more interested in wildlife than cocktails, an American woman named Barbara, who knows the region extremely well, takes people out on **trips**. Contact is easiest made through Elba at the restaurant *El Danube Azul* in Puerto Maldonado.

Independent Travel

Fortunately it is still possible to get **your own expedition** together without spending a fortune. For limited excursions into the wilderness all you need is a boat, boatman, the Captain of the Port's permission, and basic essentials like a mosquito net, blanket, and some food. If you've got at least three days to spare (two nights minimum), the most rewarding trip by far is down to **Lago Valencia**, an ancient ox-bow lake near the frontier with Bolivia (detailed below). A shorter trip—five hours up and about two hours down—is to **Tres Timbales**, a small community on the Río Tambopata, where you can spend two or three spellbinding days watching for wildlife, walking in the forest, and fishing; from here, too, you can visit the native village of EL INFIERNO—which has become a little touristy in recent years. Much nearer still (less than an hour down, one and a half hours back up) is **Lago Sandobal**, a large lake in the forest where the Ministry of Agriculture have started farming paiche fish; by taking a ferry over the Tambopata it's also possible to walk here in around an hour. Alternatively there are dozens of other possible trips which the boatmen will discuss with you and negotiate.

Obviously one of the most important aspects of any boat trip is finding the right **boatman**. All you can really do is ask around in the town and go down to the port to speak to a few of the guys who have canoes and motors. Someone I've found very good is Alberto Amachi, a friendly man with many years of experience on all of these rivers. His services as boatman and guide come at $40 a day, more or less regardless of the size of the party; the boat takes ten people with relative ease. Another well recommended river guide is Victor Yohamona (Calle Cajamarca, Lado Hospital, Puerto Maldonado; you can also leave messages for him at the *Hotel de Turistas* on the edge of town on Avenida Leon de Velarde, ☎29). If there are a few of you, these do-it-yourself trips (always do it with a guide) can cost under $20 a day each all inclusive.

Lago Valencia

Leaving Puerto Maldonado by canoe (with a *peque-peque* motor) it takes the best part of a day to reach the huge lake of **Lago Valencia**. On the way you can stop off to watch some workers panning for gold on the Madre de Dios and visit a small settlement of Huarayo Indians; about a half-hour beyond, you turn off the main river into a narrow channel that connects with the lake. Easing into the lake itself, the sounds of the canoe engine are totally silenced by the weight and expanse of water.

Towards sunset it's quite common to see cayman (crocodiles) basking on the muddy banks, an occasional puma, or the largest rodent in the world, a capybara, scuttling away into the forest. Up in the trees around the channel lie hundreds of amazing Hoatzin birds, or *gallos* as they call them locally— large ungainly creatures with orange-and-brown plumage, long wings, and distinctive spiky crests. The strangest feature of the Hoatzin are the claws at the end of their wings; they use these to help them climb up into overhanging branches beside the rivers and lakes, and have almost lost the power of flight.

There's a **police control post** on the right as you come out onto the lake, where you must register passports and show your Port Captain's permit. Beyond, reached via a slippery path above a group of dugout canoes, is the lake's one real settlement: a cluster of thatched huts around a slightly larger schoolhouse. Fewer than fifty people live here—a schoolteacher, a lay priest, the shop owner, and a few fishing families. Alberto Amachi usually takes groups to stay in a small camp farther down, a seasonal nut-collectors' *campamento* comprising just one cooking hut with an adjacent sleeping platform.

By day most people take a stroll **into the forest**—something that's both safer and more interesting with a guide, though whichever way you do it you'll immediately sense the energy and abundance of life. Quinine trees tower above all the trails, surpassed only by the Tahuari hardwoods, trees so tall and solid that jungle *shamans* describe themselves in terms of their power. Around their trunks you'll often see *Pega-Pega*, a parasitic ivy-like plant that the shamans mix with the hallucinogenic Ayahuasca into an intense aphrodisiac. Perhaps more useful to know are the liana vines. One thin species dangling above the paths can be used to take away the pain from a *shushu pe* bite. Another, the *Maravilla* or *Palo de Agua*, issues a cool stream of fresh water: you chop a section, say half a meter long, and put it to your lips. You may come upon another vine, too—the sinister *Matapalo* (or *Renaco*), which sometimes extends over dozens of trees, sucking the sap from perhaps a square kilometer of jungle. Hideously formed, these *Renacals* are a place where demons dwell, zones where native children can mysteriously vanish.

There are plenty of other things to do at Lago Valencia. You can **canoe up the lake** for a bit of fishing, passing beaches studded with groups of lazy-looking turtles sunning themselves in line along the top of fallen tree trunks—when they notice the canoe each one topples off, slowly splashing into the water, one after another. It takes a bit more to frighten the white cayman away; many can be seen soaking in the sun's strong rays along the margin of the lake. Sometimes over 2m in length, they are a daunting sight although they are apparently harmless unless you happen to step on one! At night it's possible to glide along the water, keeping close to the bank looking for the amber glint reflected from a pair of cayman eyes as the beam from your flashlight catches them. This is how the locals hunt them, fixing the crocs with a beam of light, then moving closer before blasting them with a shotgun. Unless you're really hungry (the meat is something of a delicacy—it tastes like chicken), it's best just to look into their gleaming eyes in the pitch darkness. The only sound on the lake will be the grunting of corvina fish vibrating up through the bottom of the canoe.

Lago Valencia is also superbly endowed with **birdlife**. In addition to the Hoatzin there are kingfishers, cormorants, herons, egrets, pink flamingos, skimmers, macaws, toucans, parrots, and gavilans. And behind the wall of trees along the banks hide deer, wild pigs, and **tapir**. If you're lucky enough to catch a glimpse of a tapir you'll be seeing one of South America's weirdest creatures—almost the size of a cow with an elongated rubbery nose and spiky mane. In fact, the tapir is known in the jungle as a *sachavaca* (forest cow—*sacha* is Quechua for forest and *vaca* is Spanish for cow). The easiest **fish** to catch are the piranha—all you need is some line, a hook, and a chunk of unsalted meat (brought from Puerto Maldonado). Throw this into the lake and pull out a piranha!

Onward Travel: to Brazil

There are no buses from Puerto Maldonado **going on to the Brazilian frontier by road** and it's pretty unlikely that anyone would want to ride a moped even part of the way to **Iberia** (180km, dirt road), let alone to **Inapari** (another 70km), on the less frequented section. This route first opened for use by trucks in the late 1980s and is still not used by many vehicles, so hitchhiking can involve long delays or a lot of hiking. Generally speaking, though, most people manage to reach Inapari within two or three days. From here you can cross the Río Acre to **Assis** in Brazil and continue by bus or truck to **Brasileia** (by no means to be confused with the capital!), then **Xapuri** and **Río Branco** (totaling another day or two at most).

Manu National Park

Quite possibly the only accessible piece of virgin rainforest left in the world, **MANU NATIONAL PARK**, at the foot of the Andes, is a beautiful and entirely unspoiled corner of southeastern Peru. Created as a national park in the 1970s, it is still throbbing with wildlife—rich in macaw salt licks, otter lagoons, prowling jaguars, and all the usual Amazon flora and fauna—but accessible only by boat and only to the right kind of person or party: no settlers, no hunters, and no missionaries are allowed in. If you're a naturalist, photographer, or can demonstrate a serious interest, then it is sometimes possible to gain permission to enter the most restricted zones of the Manu National Park. Even with permission, however, any expedition is very much in the hands of the gods, thanks to the changeable jungle environment.

Within the park boundaries, cool cloud forest phases down into dense tropical jungle—a unique, varied, and untouched environment. The only permanent residents are the teeming forest wildlife, a few virtually uncontacted native groups who have split off from their major tribal units (*Yaminahuas, Amahuacas*, and *Matsiguengas*), the park rangers, and the scientists at a biological research station situated just inside the park on the beautiful lake Cocha Cashu, where flocks of macaws pass the time cracking open Brazil nuts with their powerful, highly adapted beaks.

Tours of the Park

There are three main agents running expeditions into Manu National Park from Cuzco: *Mayuc* (Procuradores 354), *Manu Nature Tours* (Portal de Panes 137 or at Av. Sol 627; ☎23-1549), and *Expediciones Manu* (Procuradores 50 or 372; ☎22-6671). The costs for a seven- to ten-day trip range from around $400 to $1000. If you are going to pay that much it's probably worth your while asking for Barry, the English guide and ornithologist of *Cross Keys* fame. If you decide to do the trip by yourself, or, more economically and much more fun, in a group of your own formation, it shouldn't cost much more than $300 including rental of equipment, gas, food, boat, and guide for two weeks. If you have your own equipment it should come out much cheaper.

Independent Travel into Manu

Going into the park on your own is a serious undertaking requiring all the proper expedition preparations. The first step to assure yourself of entry is **written permission** from the *Dirección General Forestal y del Fauna* (Jirón Natalie Sanchez 220, Jesus María, Lima; ☎32-3154). CENFOR also has an office in Cuzco (Calle Quera 235, 2nd floor; ☎23-3632 or 23-3653) where it's worth checking again before entering the park. Both offices have a radio link with the Manu office and should be up-to-date with the number of visitors or any unusual circumstances (such as landslides blocking the road to Shintuya). Check also with the **National Parks Office** on Calle Laderos, Cuzco, and the *South American Explorers' Club* in Lima.

Advance Preparations

The next stage of preparation is in Cuzco—the springboard city for Manu. Here you can buy or rent all of the necessary stores and equipment (there's nothing available at Shintuya or in the park itself). Basic provisions obviously include all food, the means to sterilize river water, waterproof clothing, camping and cooking equipment, mosquito nets (for the vampire bats!), eating utensils, cash to rent a canoe and guide, and, importantly, as much gasoline as you can muster (one of the 55-gallon drums is probably enough to barter with and will certainly make getting a boatman much easier and inevitably a little cheaper). Carry your gear and stores in baskets or something vaguely waterproof: whatever you do, don't use cardboard boxes since they dissolve on contact with an Amazon river or jungle shower. A good insect repellent is more or less essential, and a sleeping mat is a good idea even if only to sit on during the long journey by truck from Cuzco to Shintuya. If the truck is carrying fuel wear old clothes and cover your baggage properly. Not essential but a good idea in the circumstances are: fishing hooks and line, a back-up stove, waterproof box for camera equipment and other delicate valuables, and a waterproof lining (plastic trashcan liners will do) for your bags or backpacks. If you can afford one luxury, make it a sturdy pair of **binoculars**, preferably brought with you from home.

Getting There

Trucks, generally loaded to the brim with beer, fuel, and passengers, leave Cuzco from Avenida Huascar every Monday, Wednesday, and Friday for Shintura (around twenty to thirty hours in good conditions; $6). Most trucks these days break for the night in PILCOPATA, where there's a basic hotel, a few small shops, and a simple market. The following day takes you on to SALVACIÓN, 25km before Shintuya, only 15km but a good two-hour drive under normal conditions; ask the driver to stop here at the **ranger station**, where you'll be charged $1 a day for the anticipated duration of your stay. Trucks, mostly carrying lumber, return to Cuzco on Tuesday, Thursday, and Saturday.

Arriving in **SHINTUYA**, a mission settlement on the edge of the park, all that remains to do is to seek out a canoe and a reliable boatman/guide. There's **no hotel**, but no problem about pitching a tent if you ask permission—best spot is beside the small stream that enters the main river (the water is cleaner here). Keep a watchful eye on your baggage, as Shintuya also has a sizable transient population, passing to and from the gold mining areas downriver.

Renting a Boat

If you've brought some of your own gasoline to bargain with, it should be relatively easy to find a reasonably priced canoe and guide at the mission in Shintuya. The Moscosa family (especially Cesar, Pepe, and Darwin) are evidently reliable guides. **Boats** from Shintuya cost around $250 for a week—if the boat is big enough this can be shared between as many as seven or eight people and the price of an extra week isn't that much more. Remember that things happen on a different time scale in the Peruvian jungle, so get the boat organized as soon as you arrive in Shintuya, and try to make an early start the next day. If it can be arranged it's a good idea to take a small light-weight dugout canoe for entering into the smaller channels and lagoons.

From Shintuya it's one day down the Alto Madre de Dios to **BOCA MANU**. Little more than a small settlement of a few families living near the airstrip (built in the 1970s by an oil company and now used to fly in tourists on the more expensive Manu trips run by Cuzco agents), there is a small *tienda* (prices double those in Cuzco, with no guarantee of supply), but the population mainly serves the gold mining settlements downstream towards Puerto Maldonado. From Boca Manu you head up the Río Manu, to the ranger station outpost near the park boundary at ROMERO. This is a checkpoint for permits and has no other facilities. **Camping** is possible on the beach fifteen minutes up the river from Romero.

Entering the Park

This is where the real adventure begins. **Manu** covers an area larger than Lake Michigan and is one part of the jungle where you won't bump into missionaries, colonists, or gold panners. It's as much a reserve for the Indians as it is for the wild animals and so anyone or anything you do come across should be treated with the utmost respect. A few expeditions have been attacked in Manu over the past ten years, but in each case there were reports suggesting that the "victims" concerned were unnecessarily tampering with the native way of life—stealing food, molesting Indian women, or vandalizing Indian property.

The layout of Manu is quite complicated and it is absolutely essential to get a good **map** in Cuzco, or from the *South American Explorers' Club* in Lima, before you arrive in Manu. In the end, though, if you can't find your way around without a guide, the rangers at Romero will assist in giving specific directions. The main features of the park are a series of **cochas** or lakes, which afford excellent chances of spotting wildlife, including everything from a jaguar to several types of monkey (spider, howler, capuchin, titi, emperor tamarins, and squirrel), wild pigs, piranhas, otters, macaws, parakeets, parrots, herons, cayman, turtles, and even otters. Cocha Wasi, Cocha Otorongo, Cocha Juarez (where there's a basic tourist lodge operated by *Manu Nature Tours*), and Cocha Salvador are all good bets, and beyond the other park station at **Pakitsa** (no facilities) lies the inner scientific sanctuary of Cocha Cashu which is abundant in wildlife. You need a special permit to enter this part of the park.

Along the River to Puerto Maldonado

From Manu it is possible to go directly on to Puerto Maldonado via the Río Madre de Dios. Although you're more likely to find a boat going downriver from Shintuya, many will also pick up passengers from Boca Manu. The journey takes between two and five days—one day to the sleazy gold-mining town of **Banco Minero** at the mouth of the Colorado river—a $5 trip from Boca Manu, $12 from Shintuya. Banco has a very basic hotel and a couple of simple restaurants. It is possible to camp but, again, look after your gear well! From here it is at least one more day on to LABERINTO where it's a relatively short bus ride to Puerto Maldonado itself.

THE URUBAMBA RIVER

Traditionally the home of the *Matsiguenga* and *Piro* Indians, the **Urubamba River** is one of the most glorious and exciting in Peru. Going north from Cuzco the Urubamba rolls down from the Inca's Sacred Valley to the humid lower Andean slopes around the town of **Quillabamba**—the end of the railroad line. For the next eighty or so unnavigable kilometers, the Urubamba is trailed by a dirt road to the small settlement of **Kiteni**, where it meets with the tributary Río Koshireni. From Kiteni the river becomes the main means of transportation, a smooth 3500km through the Amazon basin to the Atlantic Ocean, interrupted only by the impressive **Pongo de Mainique**—dreaded white-water rapids, less than a day downstream, which are generally too dangerous to pass in the months of November and December.

Unlike the Manu National Park, most of the Urubamba has been colonized as far as the Pongo, and much of it beyond has suffered more or less permanent exploitation of one sort or another for over a hundred years (rubber, cattle, oil, and now gas). Consequently this isn't really the river for experiencing pristine virgin forest, but it is an exciting and remote challenge and a genuine example of what's going on in the Amazon today.

Quillabamba

Traveling by train from Cuzco, you'll see jungle vegetation beginning to cover the valley sides from Machu Picchu onwards; the weather gets steadily warmer and the plant life thickens as the train gradually descends the

Urubamba valley. The first sights of **QUILLABAMBA** are the old tin roofs and adobe outskirts, coca leaves drying in their gardens. The main town is on the top of a high cliff, a stiff climb up from the railroad station over a bridge then up a series of steps; the **Plaza de Armas** is just a few blocks ahead at the top.

A cock-fighting, market town growing fat on the proceeds of illicit cocaine production, Quillabamba's main attraction to tourists is a quick look at the *selva*. The only Peruvian jungle town accessible by railroad, it's a good place to get all the gear you need for going deeper into the jungle. The market sells all the necessities like machetes, fish hooks, food, and hats, and it's an enjoyable town in which to relax, spending afternoons down by the river, eating ice cream, or hanging out in one of the bars. Only about 4km from Quillabamba there's an attractive river beach at SAMBARAY (restaurant and drinks available) if this is as far as you want to go down the Urubamba. The going certainly gets tougher quickly from here on.

Practicalities

The *Hotel Cuzco* is good (near Plaza Grau, the market square), *Hotel Comercio* slightly cheaper, the *Hotel Alto Urubamba* (behind the church) a very good deal at around $1 a night; there are also three very basic **hotels** uphill between the Plaza de Armas and the market. By far the best **restaurant** is the *Astral* on the plaza, which offers excellent typical dishes, cheap set menus, and good drinks. The *Hotel Don Carlos* (a modern hotel just up from the Plaza de Armas) is a good place to make connections for organized and relatively costly overland trips to Kiteni, and jungle river trips on from there.

To get to KITENI, five to eight hours deeper into the jungle, **buses** (the *Alto Urubamba* service) and **colectivos** (trucks or faster station wagons) leave Plaza Grau every day between 8am and 10am. The road keeps more or less to the course of the Urubamba. Heading back to Cuzco, the *Hidalgo* bus leaves Quillabamba from the market area a few times a week; trucks are more frequent, but slower (from block 5 of San Martin), and there are three trains a day (departing 5:30am; 1:05pm; and 10:50pm), arriving in about seven hours.

Kiteni and the Pongo de Mainique

By the time you reach **KITENI**, the Urubamba River is quite wide and, with the forest all around, the valley is hotter, more exotic, and much greener. Still a small *poblado*, Kiteni was until recently a tiny *Matsiguenga* Indian village. And with its ramshackle cluster of buildings, all wooden except for the schoolhouse and the clinic (where you can get yellow fever shots if you haven't already done so), it is still a one-street town with more mules than cars.

Arriving, the truck or bus stops at a chain across the dirt track. Here you have to register with the *guardia* in their office on the right before walking into the town. Straight down the road, at the other end of town (about 100m away) is the basic dormitory-type **hostel**, the *Hotel Kiteni*—a cheap, friendly place, attractively situated beside the bubbling Río Koshireni, and serving good set meals; there are no doors for security, but my gear has always been safe here. Next to the Hotel Kiteni there's an *oroya* (stand-up cable car) for people to pull themselves across the river; a ten-minute stroll on the far bank takes you to an *albergue* which has been closed for several years but still occasionally offers seclusion, greater security, spoken English, and excellent food for only a few dollars a night (but only for trips organized in advance by agencies or groups from Cuzco).

The Pongo de Mainique

Kiteni's main draw—beyond the feel of a small jungle settlement—is as a jumping-off point for the awe-inspiring **PONGO DE MAINIQUE**, possibly the most dangerous 2km of potentially navigable river in the entire Amazonian system. Tours down the Urubamba to the *pongo* can be arranged with *Fitzcarraldo Adventure Travel* in either Cuzco (Calle San Augustin 737; ☎4229) or Quillabamba (Av. San Martin 411) from around $30 a day per person. Other private entrepreneurs may approach you either in Quillabamba (notably in the *heladería* on the main square) or Kiteni for a trip to the *pongo* and perhaps a little camping and fishing. The merits of these trips are entirely dependent upon the price you have to pay and the confidence you have in the guide. It is cheaper to get a canoe or launch which is going through the rapids anyway: boats are often more than willing to take extra passengers for a relatively small fee. If there are enough of you, it might be economical to rent a canoe (preferably with a powerful outboard motor) for a couple of days from around $35 a day, including boatman. To arrange any of these options you'll do best hanging around the port at Kiteni—the beach behind the *guardia*'s huts.

To go downriver without renting a boat or taking an organized trip, it's a matter of being at the dock early every morning and asking every boat that leaves if it's going to the *pongo*—have all your baggage with you in case one says yes (this way a round trip shouldn't cost more than about $30). If you want to go all the way to SEPAHUA—$40 one way as a passenger—you might have to wait a few days until there's one going all the way: this is much easier than going hungry on a desolate beach somewhere in between! Boats tend to arrive from downstream in the afternoon and it's often worth checking with them when they intend to go back. A boat with a powerful motor takes about five to six hours to reach the *pongo*; a *peque-peque* canoe will usually need around ten.

Just before the *pongo* there's a community of settlers at **San Idriato**. These people, known as the Israelites, founded the village around a biblical sect. The men leave their hair long and, like Rastas, they twist it up under expandable peaked caps. Not far from San Idriato there's a basic tourist lodge, again now out of general use, right at the mouth of the rapids—an amazing spot. On the opposite bank of the Urubamba from San Idriato the small community of **Shinguriato**, also upstream from the Río Yuyato mouth, is the official entrance to the *pongo* itself.

The Rapids

You'll have heard a lot about the *Pongo de Mainique* before you get there—from the boatmen, the local Matsiguenga Indians, colonists, or the Israelites. Impossible to pass during the rainy season (between the months of November and January), it is dangerous at any time of the year. As you get close you can see a forested mountain range directly in front of you. The river speeds up and as you approach closer still it's possible to make out a great cut made through the range over millenia by the powerful Urubamba. Then, before you realize, the craft is whisked into a long canyon with soaring rocky cliffs on either side. Gigantic volcanic boulders look like wet monsters of molten steel; stone faces can be seen shimmering under cascades; and the danger of the *pongo* slips by almost unnoticed, the walls of the canyon absorbing all your attention. The main hazard is actually a drop of about 2m which is seen and then crossed in a split second. Now and then boats are overturned at this drop—usually those that try the run in the rainy season—but even then natives somehow manage to come upstream in small, non motorized dugouts!

Beyond the *pongo* the river is much gentler, but on all major curves as far down as the Camisea tributary (about two days on a raft) there is white water. Settlements along the river are few and far between—mostly native villages, colonists, or missionaries. If your boat is going straight back through the *pongo* to Kiteni you'll have to make a quick choice about whether to try your luck going downstream or return to the relative safety and luxury of town. If it's going farther down anyway, the next large settlement is **SEPAHUA** where there's a **hotel**, a few shops and bars, and a runway with fairly regular flights to Satipo (for road connection with Lima). Sepahua, however, is a couple of days downstream by motorized canoe or about four days on a raft: to be dropped off in between could mean waiting a week on the riverbank for another boat or raft to hitch with, and so, to be on the safe side, you'll need food for at least ten days. From Sepahua it's possible to continue downstream for another couple of days to ATALAYA, another small and isolated jungle town with a growing reputation for lawlessness and drug trafficking (and for cheaper flights to Satipo). At Atalaya the Urubamba meets the Ene-Tambo River to form the Ucayali. It's another few days from here to PUCALLPA and five or six more to IQUITOS on the Amazon proper.

PUCALLPA AND
LAKE YARINACOCHA

In the heart of the Peruvian Amazon, and well endowed with attractions of its own, the jungle town of Pucallpa is also a main point of departure for river trips downstream to the more obvious destination of Iquitos, a 1000km, week-long journey. Both Pucallpa and Iquitos—the northern jungle towns—have good connections with Lima and elsewhere, and are considerably more developed than any of the towns covered earlier in this chapter. But their indigenous Indian life is becoming more and more Westernized, and with it their tourism gets increasingly packaged or, as they say in Peru, conventional.

Pucallpa, in fact, is one of Peru's fastest growing cities (its population of 85,000 is ten times what it was thirty years ago) and an interesting—if, to outsiders, somewhat sad—place in its own right. With its newly acquired status as the capital of the independent *departmento* of Ucayali, and its oil refineries and massive lumber industry, it is a city which more than any other seems to represent the modern phase of the jungle's exploitation. For travelers the big attraction in this region is the nearby lake of **Yarinacocha**—a huge and beautiful oxbow, where you can swim and rest up, watch schools of dolphin, and (if you've got the money) go on wildlife expeditions or visit some of the nearby native communities.

Pucallpa

Long an impenetrable refuge for *Cashibo* Indians, **PUCALLPA** was "tamed" and developed as a camp for rubber gatherers at the beginning of this century. In 1930 it was connected to Lima by road; since then its expansion has been intense and unstoppable. **Saw mills**—most of the parquet floors in Lima originate from the lumber industry here—surround the city and spread up the main highway towards Tingo María and the mountains, and an impressive floating harbor has been constructed at the new port of La Hoyada. It was, until 1980, a province in the vast Loreto *departmento* controlled from Iquitos, but months of industrial action eventually led to the creation of a separate province—Ucayali. With the end of financial restrictions from Iquitos, and the turn towards the Pacific (Iquitos exports down the Amazon to the Atlantic), this change is a significant one.

Although in many ways a lively and vibrant city, there is little here of great interest to travelers—most of whom get straight on a local bus for Yarinacocha (15km out; buses leave from the market square). If you stay over a while, though, it's difficult not to appreciate Pucallpa's relaxed jungle feel—nor the optimism in a city whose thick-red-mud-splattered streets are fast giving way to asphalt. The **post office** is at San Martin 418; **phone calls** can be made with *Entelperu* at Ucayali 357; and there's a **tourist information** office at Dos de Mayo 11 (☎6585). **Money exchange** can be found at the *Tienda Cisne* (Jr. Raymondi).

Outside the town, the port at LA HOYADA is quite a lively spot, while at BARBON COCHA (6km up the main highway) there's a small lakeside settlement and zoological park. If you have an hour or so to while away in the town itself both the modern and old **markets** have interesting and varied stalls.

Getting There
Connected by 850km of road to Lima, Pucallpa is served by several **bus companies**—all of whom go via HUANUCO (roughly the halfway point at twelve hours). The full journey is approximated at 24 hours but can take a fair bit longer. Companies include *Tepsa* and *Leon de Huanuco*. In the mid- to late 1980s a new jungle road was opened between **La Merced** and Pucallpa via **Puerto Bermudez**—the *Hostel Tania* here is good—making it possible to travel overland to Pucallpa without going through the drug-trafficking zone

around Huanuco and Tingo María (see p.196). Unfortunately, it can't be guaranteed that even this new road (10 hours minimum through some incredible edge-of-the-rainforest scenery from La Merced to Puerto Bermudez and another day's travel on to Pucallpa from there) will be completely safe from drugrunners, politicos, or bandits since the cocaine problem is, at the time of going to print, still spreading on the margins of the rainforest. So far there have been no reports of theft or violence on this road, but it's worth noting that only trucks are able to complete the journey at the moment.

Both *AeroPeru* and *Faucett* operate regular **flights** connecting Pucallpa with Lima and Iquitos; on Thursday *Faucett* also flies here from Tarapoto.

Sleeping, Eating, and Drinking

Pucallpa is full of **hotels**, old and new, and most of the better ones are grouped around the last few blocks of Jiron Tacna and Jiron Ucayali—near the Parque San Martin. At the upper end of the scale the *Gran Hotel Mercedes* (Raymondi 610; ☎6190) costs around $10 a night but has the added attraction of a swimming pool, while the *Hostel Confort* (Coronel Portillo 381; ☎6091) is another good upscale choice; slightly cheaper is the *Hotel Amazonas* (Coronel Portillo 729; ☎6080), and considerably more so the basic *Hotel Europa* and *Hostel Los Angeles* (both on Ucayali).

Restaurants too are plentiful, including a number of excellent *chifa* places—*Chifa Mang Keong* (in the Hotel Mercedes) and *Chifa Pucallpa* (on the corner of Tacna/San Martin) are two of the best among them. For international cuisine it's hard to beat the restaurant in the *Hostel Inambu* (Federico Basadre 271). Slightly cheaper and very good for fish dishes is the *Hotel Mercedes* restaurant. Opposite the *Mercedes*, *Café Don Jose* is an excellent place for breakfasts, snacks, and juices. *El Rinconcito Loretano* (on block 8 of Tacna) is good for local dishes like the delicious *sarapatera* (soup in a turtle shell), and Pucallpa is also famous for producing Peru's first canned **beer**—*San Juan*.

Lake Yarinacocha

Some 9km from Pucallpa and easily reached by bus, **Lago Yarinacocha** is without doubt a more attractive place to stay than the city itself. A contrast to the southern jungle lakes, its 22km-long waters are excellent for swimming and there is considerable settlement around its banks. River channels lead off towards small villages of *Shipibo* Indians, and there's an artists' community called Nueva Eden (led by the charismatic wood sculptor Augustino Rivas), three luxury tourist lodges, and the slightly bizarre *Summer Institute of Linguistics*. The latter is the headquarters of an extremely well equipped, U.S.-funded missionary organization, their aim being to bring God to the natives by translating the New Testament into all Indian languages. At present they're working on some 43, "each as different from each other as Chinese is from Greek."

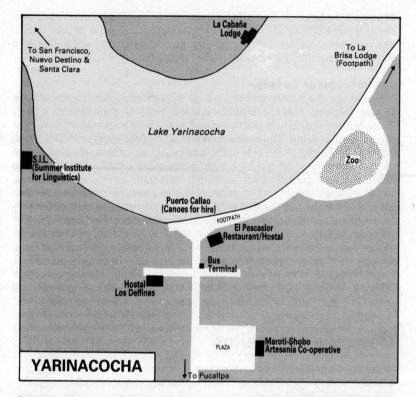

To San Francisco,
Nuevo Destino &
Santa Clara

La Cabaña
Lodge

To La
Brisa Lodge
(Footpath)

Lake Yarinacocha

S.I.L.
(Summer Institute
for Linguistics)

Zoo

Puerto Callao
(Canoes for hire)

FOOTPATH

El Pescaslor
Restaurant/Hostal

Bus
Terminal

Hostal
Los Delfines

Maroti-Shobo
Artesania Co-operative

PLAZA

YARINACOCHA

To Pucallpa

Callao

The main center, though, and the place where most travelers stay, is the lake's port of **CALLAO**, a town known locally as the "Shangri-la de la Selva," its bars and wooden shacks animated by an almost continuous blast of *chicha* music. Towards the lake are most of the liveliest **bars** (try *El Grande Paraiso*), **restaurants** (best is *El Pescador*), and **hotels** (*Hostel Los Delphines* and *El Pescador* are good deals). Keeping a look out for thieves, you can also **camp** anywhere along the lake. It's probably a good idea not to camp too near the **zoo**, however, a small, cheap and sad place beside the waterfront.

The settlement's most recent achievement, the **Moroti-Shobo Crafts Co-operative**—a project organized by the British charity Oxfam but now operated by the local *Shipibo* and *Conibo* Indians—can be found on the main plaza. Beautifully molded ceramics, carved wood, and dyed textiles are always on display here, most of them very reasonably priced.

Trips to see **wildlife**, visit **Indian villages**, or just to **cross the lake** are hawked all along the waterfront. The standard day excursion goes to the Shipibo village of **San Francisco**, sometimes continuing to the slightly more remote settlements of **Nuevo Destino** and **Santa Clara**. San Francisco is now almost completely geared towards tourism, so for a more adventurous trip you'll do better to hire a *peque-peque* canoe and boatman on your own (from around $20 a day); these canoes can take up to eight or nine people and you can share costs, though if you want to go farther afield (say on a three-day excursion) expect prices to be up to $50 a day.

Tourist Lodges on the Lake

If you've got the money and are fed up with camping out, try the **tourist lodges** that surround the lake: they're ten times as expensive as a basic hotel, but are wonderfully positioned and, at the very least, make a good spot for an evening **drink**. The easiest to reach is *La Brisa*, along a walkway leading around the right-hand side of the lake as you face it from the port. Set up in the early 1980s and run by a friendly American couple—the Nixons (no relation)—it's a palatial structure though built more or less on native lines, raised high off the ground on stilts. A double room here will set you back some $25 a night, but the food (and drink) is excellent and quite reasonably priced at around $2. Another lodge, German-run and over on the other side of the lake, is *La Cabaña*—quite possibly the first jungle lodge built in Peru. Prices and accommodation (in bungalows) are similar to those at La Brisa, though it's a smaller place with a different, perhaps more intimate, atmosphere. It can be reached only by boat. Other lodges include *La Perla*, virtually next door to *La Cabaña*, and the new *Ucayali Lodge*; all of them run organized trips, again on a fairly costly basis.

Downriver to Iquitos

Traveling from Pucallpa to Iquitos on a boat sounds more agreeable than it actually is. Very few Peruvians, except of course rivermen, would ever dream of it—over 1000km of water separates these two large jungle towns, with very little in between but the endless undulations of the river, and verdant forest hemming you in on either side. But if you're going to Iquitos anyway, you might as well relax in a hammock for a few days and arrive in the style the rubber barons were accustomed to.

Large **riverboats** generally leave Pucallpa from LA HOYADA port while the smaller **launches and canoes** tend to embark from PUERTO ITALIA. The cheapest and by far the most effective way of finding a boat is to go down to one of these ports and simply ask around. Try to fix a price and a departure date with a reputable-looking captain—the normal cost seems to be around $25 per person, including all food for the trip. It can cost more if you want a cabin but you'll probably be more comfortable, and certainly cooler, with a hammock strung under some mosquito netting. It's quite usual for passengers to string up their hammocks on the boat several days before departure—which can mean great saving in hotel costs and less risk of the boat leaving without you. If the captain asks for money up front don't give the whole bundle to him; you may never see the man or his boat again. Additionally, even when everything looks ready for departure, don't be surprised if there is a delay of a day or two—boats leave frequently but unpredictably. Food on board can be very unappetizing at times so it may be worth your while to take along some extra luxuries like a few cans of fish, a packet or two of cookies, and several bottles of drink. Depending on how big the boat is and how many stops it makes (something that should be checked with the captain beforehand), the journey normally takes between four and six days. Before you leave there's a certain amount of paperwork to go through since this is a commercial port and one of the main illicit cocaine trails. You'll have to show your documents to the port police (PIP) and get permission from the naval office—your captain should help with all of this.

En route to Iquitos the boats often stop at the two main settlements of CONTAMANA (10 hr.; about $1 if this is as far as you're going) and REQUENA (another two to four days). In theory it's possible to use these as pit-stops—hopping off one boat for a couple of days while waiting for another— but you may end up stuck for longer than you bargained for. Contamana, on the right bank of the Ucayali, can be reached fairly easily in a day from Pucallpa. There isn't much here but it's okay to camp and food can be bought without any problem.

REQUENA, a larger settlement, is a genuine jungle town developed during the rubber boom on an isolated stretch of the Río Ucayali, and within a day's journey from Iquitos. There are a couple of basic **hostels**, and you can also camp on the outskirts of town. For those going downstream, Requena is a better stopping point than Contamana since boats leave regularly for Iquitos for around $10 per person. A few hours north of Requena, just a few huge bends away, the Río Marañon merges with the Ucayali to form the mighty Amazon.

IQUITOS AND THE AMAZON

There can be few sights as magnificent as the **Amazon River**, seen from the island city of Iquitos. Surrounded in all directions by brilliant green forest and hemmed in by a maze of rivers, streams, and lagoons, it's not difficult to imagine the awe that Francisco Orellana, the first white man to see it, must have felt only 450 years ago. The Amazon tributaries start well up in the Andes, and when they join together at Iquitos the river is already several kilometers wide; though a mere 116m above sea level, by the time the Amazon runs into the Atlantic, some 4000km downstream, it is powerful enough to produce an estuary over 200km wide from north to south.

Connected to the rest of the world only by river and air, **Iquitos** is the kind of place that lives up to all your expectations of a jungle town, with elegant reminders of the rubber boom years and the atmospheric shanty-town suburb of **Puerto Belen**—one of Werner Herzog's main locations for his film, *Fitzcarraldo*—where you can buy almost anything—gas, ice cream, even sex—while floating in a taxi-dugout canoe. Around the town there are some great island and lagoon beaches, a range of cheap and easy excursions into the rainforest, and the possibility of continuing up the Amazon into **Colombia** or **Brazil**.

Iquitos

By far the largest and most exciting of Peru's jungle towns, **IQUITOS** began life in 1739 as a small Jesuit mission—a particularly daunting one, for the missionaries here faced the task of converting the fierce *Yagua* Indians, renowned as marksmen with their long poison-dart blowpipes. Its strategic position on the Amazon, which makes it accessible by large ocean-going ships from the distant Atlantic, ensured its importance.

The town itself was only founded in 1864, yet by the end of the nineteenth century it was, along with Manaus in Brazil, one of *the* great rubber towns. From that era of grandeur a number of structures survive, but during this century Iquitos has vacillated between prosperity and the depths of depression. At present, buoyed by the export of timber, petroleum, tobacco, and Brazil nuts, and dabbling heavily in the trade of wild animals, tropical fish, and birds, as well as an insecticide called *barbasco*, long used by natives as a fish poison, it is in a period of quite wealthy expansion. The riverfront now stretches all the way from the old port and market of Belen over to a new floating harbor some 3km downriver.

Like most of the jungle towns, much of Iquitos's appeal lies in the possible excursions into the surrounding rainforest—which are detailed in the following section. It is, though, an interesting old city in its own right, many of its turn-of-the-century buildings decorated with Portuguese *azulejo* tiles, some brilliantly extravagant in their Moorish inspiration. The majestic **Iron House** in the Plaza de Armas was created by Eiffel for the 1898 Paris exhibition and shipped out by one of the rubber barons, while outside it, in the shadow of the Mamey trees, lurks an unexpected statue by **Rodin**. There's an **aquarium**, too, on Ramirez Hurtado (off the plaza), a small **zoo** (on Ricardo Palma), and an interesting little **Amazonian Museum** (corner of Fitzcarraldo/Tavara; open 9am–1pm and 4–7pm) devoted to the region's natural history and tribal culture.

Most memorable, however, is **Puerto Belen**, which looms out from the main town at a point where the Amazon joins the Río Itaya inlet. Consisting almost entirely of wooden huts raised above the water on stilts or floating on rafts, it has earned fame among travelers as "The Venice of the Peruvian Jungle"! Actually more Far Eastern than Italian in appearance, it can have changed little over its hundred years or so of life, remaining a poor shanty settlement and continuing to trade in basics like bananas, yucca, fish, turtle, and crocodile meat. Filming *Fitzcarraldo* here, Herzog merely had to make sure that no motorized canoes appeared on screen: virtually everything else, including the style of the *barriada* dwellings, looks to be out of an authentic slum town of the last century.

While you're here it might be useful to know a few local jungle **words**: *pakucho* (the local form of gringo), *shushupero* ("drunk"; from the deadly *shushupe* snake), *La Aguajina* (refreshing palm fruit drink), and *Siete Raices* (a strong drink mixed from seven jungle plants and *aguardiente*).

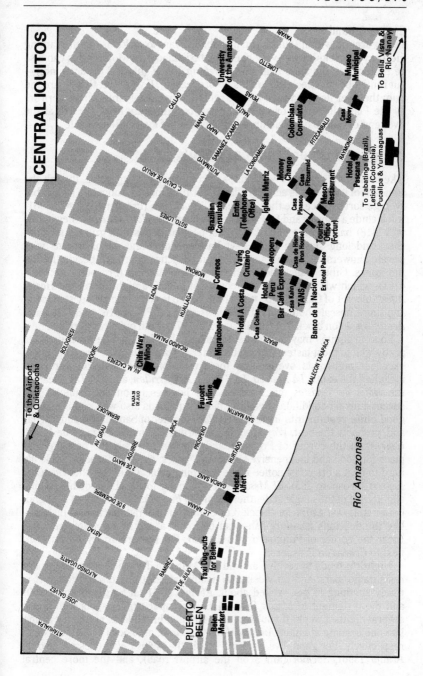

CENTRAL IQUITOS

University of the Amazon
Museo Municipal
Colombian Consulate
Casa Morey
To Bella Vista & Rio Nanay
Hotel Pescana
Meson Restaurant
Money Change
Casa Fitzcarrald
Casa Pinasco
To Tabatinga (Brazil), Leticia (Colombia), Pucallpa & Yurimaguas
Brazilian Consulate
Entel (Telephones Office)
Iglesia Matriz
Tourist Office (Fortur)
Casa de Hierro (Iron House)
Correos
Varig Cruzeiro
Aeroperu
Hotel Peru
Bar Café Express
TANS
Banco de la Nacion
Ex Hotel Palace
Casa Kahn
Chifa Way Ming
Migraciones
Hotel A Costa
Casa Cohen
To the Airport & Quistacocha
Faucett Airline
Hostal Alfert
Rio Amazonas
Taxi Dug-outs for Belen
PUERTO BELEN
Belen Market

Getting Around

To get around within Iquitos you'll probably want to make use of the rattling **motorcycle rickshaws**—very cheap by taxi standards. Motorcycles can also be rented—try the shop near the *Ferreteria Union* (block 2 of Raymondi)—but remember to check the brakes before leaving. If you want to look around from the river itself, **canoes** can be rented very cheaply from the waterfront by the Plaza de Armas or much cheaper **taxi-dugouts** from *Venecia* at the river end of Calle 9 de Diciembre in the market of Puerto Belen itself.

Hotels and Other Practical Details

Like every other jungle town Iquitos is comparatively expensive, though the standard of its **hotels** is actually a lot better than most. A room in a stylish but average sort of place like the very central *Hotel Peru* (Prospero 318; ☎23-4961) will include a shower and fan. Over recent years the *Hotel Pascana* (Pevas 133; ☎23-1418) has become one of the most popular hotels with gringos for both short and long stays in Iquitos—it has individual and double rooms with private showers set around a modern but attractive courtyard beside the Río Amazonas. Other central hotels include *Maria Antonia* (Prospero 616; ☎23-4761), which will cost you just a couple of dollars a night more; the *Hostal Alfert* (block 1 of Garcia Sanz; ☎23-4105), which is one of the cheapest in town; and more upscale hotels like the *Ambassador* (at Pevas 616; ☎23-3110) and *Acosta No. 1* (on block 3 of Huallaga; ☎23-35974), both quite comfortable.

Food in Iquitos may not be haute cuisine, but for a jungle town it caters pretty well to most tastes. Among its better **restaurants** there are a couple of excellent nightspots overlooking the river along the Malecon Tarapaca, including the exotic *La Maloca*, *La Teraca*, *El Barrillon*, and *Tip Top*. Nearby, the *Hotel de Turistas* offers drinks and lunches in one of Iquitos's few successfully air-conditioned environments. Iquitos is also well endowed with good **chifa restaurants** including *Al Paso* (corner of San Martin and Tacna) and, probably the best, *Way Ming* (San Martin 462, on the Plaza 28 de Julio). *Cohens*, on the corner of Prospero and Morona, is easily the best daytime place for good and inexpensive set menus, juices, meals, or snacks, while it's hard to beat a breakfast coffee while watching cable TV in the little *Bar Café Express* (Prospero 285). *El Mesón* is very popular for local fish dishes, while, slightly out of the jungle style, there is also a *Pizza Parlor* (Prospero 338) and, better still, *Don Carmelos* (block 3 of Condamine). Traditional local dishes—like the delicious *tucunare* fish—can be found at the *Restaurante Exclusivo*, (near the corner of Putumayo with Tacna). For **ice cream** try *La Favorita* next to *Cohens* on Prospero.

Nightlife tends to revolve around the Malecón Tarapaca where there are restaurants, bars, and on weekends usually at least one disco, though it is rarely anything to get excited about. *Ebony's 2001* (at Sargento Lores 700) and the restaurant *El Mesón* (Napo 116) are popular night spots with music several nights a week. If you're at all interested in the local scene, try eating late one evening at either *Amauta 1* or *Amauta 2*, on blocks 4 and 2 of Nauta respectively. For good, live Peruvian music the *peñas Colpa* (Cesar Calvo de Aranjo 1396), *Sachun* (km 3 on the airport road), and the more central

Villanueva (Ramirez Hurtado 672) are highly recommended. The **local drink**, incidentally, is *Chuchuasi*, made from a tree bark soaked in rum and reputedly an aphrodisiac.

Information and Onward Travel

The new **post office** is on the corner of Morona and Arica (Mon.–Sat. 8am–6pm; Sun. 8am–noon). The **tourist office** is on the first block of Raymondi fronting the Plaza de Armas. They have a list of local handicraft producers for anyone seriously interested in buying. Entelperu's **telephone offices** are at Arica 276. The *inmigracion* office for all **passport and visa** paperwork is at Arica 477 (☎23-5371). The **Brazilian Consulate** is at Morona 238 (☎23-2081) and the **Colombian Consulate** on the Malecon Tarapaca (☎23-1461).

For **flights** to Lima and Pucallpa, *AeroPeru* has an office at Prospero 246–50 (☎23-1454) and *Faucett* at Prospero 630 (☎23-9195). The office of the Peruvian Air Force, *Grupo Ocho*, which takes civilians on sporadic flights to Leticia in Colombia (by the border with Peru and Brazil), is on Loreto 243. *Cruzeira do Sol/Varig* (Arica 273; ☎23-4381), *TANS* (Sargento Lores 127; ☎23-3512), and other smaller companies also fly within Peru and to Leticia and Brazil; contact travel agents for prices and schedules.

Companies worth checking out for **river transportation**—either to Pucallpa or Yurimaguas, or down the Amazon into Brazil—include: the *Captain of the Port* (Coronel Portillo s/n, block 6; ☎23-2491); *Comercial Bellavista* (Malecon Tarapaca 594–596; ☎23-1311); *Linea Amazonica* (Sargento Lores 258; ☎23-2455); *Negocios Amazonica Peruanos* (Coronel Portillo 464; ☎23-1432); and *Naviera Amazonica Peruanos* (Sagento Lores 415; ☎23-3871).

Trips Around Iquitos

Expeditions **around Iquitos** are probably the most touristically developed in the Peruvian jungle—they're fun but, once again, anything involving over-night stays in the jungle is going to be quite expensive. However, the region immediately around Iquitos offers an unusually wide—and often surprising—range of attractions.

Some 5km from the center of Iquitos, just fifteen minutes by bus, is the suburb of **BELLA VISTA** where bars and restaurants overlook the Río Nanay and canoes can be rented for short boat trips at around $5 an hour. On the western edge of town an affluent of the Nanay forms a long lake called MORONA COCHA, a popular resort for swimming and waterskiing; while farther out (just before the airport) another lake, RUMOCOCHA, has facilities for fishing and hunting. Beyond this, still on the Río Nanay, is the popular weekend beach of SANTA CLARA and, 16km on, the village of SANTO TOMAS. This is a worthwhile trip, well connected by local bus. A center for agriculture and fishing, the village is renowned for its jungle *artesanía*—and has another beach where you can swim and canoe. If you get the chance, try to coincide with Santo Tomas's fiesta (Sept. 23–25), a huge party of dancing and *chicha* music.

Another place you can get to quite easily—by canoe from Belen or the main waterfront—is PADRE ISLA, an island actually in the midst of the Amazon, opposite the town. Over 14km long, it has beautiful beaches during the dry season.

Last, but not least important by any means, there is the **QUISTOCOCHA LAGOON**, a couple of hours' walk (half an hour by bus or *colectivo* from Avenida Jose Galvez in Belen) along the airport road—turn left at the last fork in the road before the airport. Now taken over by the Ministry of Fishing for the breeding of giant *paiche*, it has an interesting zoo and a small site museum of jungle natural history.

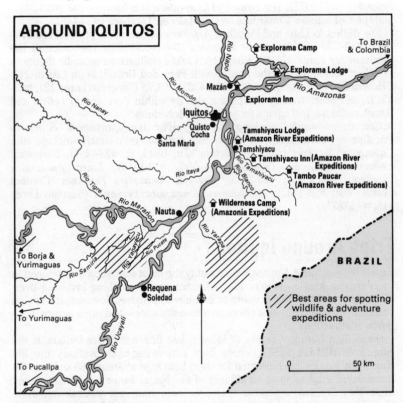

AROUND IQUITOS

Explorama Camp

To Brazil & Colombia

Rio Napo

Explorama Lodge

Rio Momón

Mazán

Rio Amazonas

Explorama Inn

Rio Nanay

Iquitos

Quisto Cocha

Tamshiyacu Lodge (Amazon River Expeditions)

Santa Maria

Tamshiyacu

Tamshiyacu Inn (Amazon River Expeditions)

Rio Itaya

Rio Tamshiyacu

Rio Blanco

Tambo Paucar (Amazon River Expeditions)

Rio Tigre

Rio Marañon

Wilderness Camp (Amazonia Expeditions)

Nauta

Rio Yarapa

To Borja & Yurimaguas

Rio Samiria

Rio Yanayacu

Rio Pucate

BRAZIL

To Yurimaguas

Rio Ucayali

Best areas for spotting wildlife & adventure expeditions

Requena

Soledad

To Pucallpa

BRAZIL

0   50 km

Jungle Expeditions

If you're planning on a trip beyond the limited network of roads around Iquitos you'll have to arrange an expedition through one of the agencies or local guides, or with the boatmen at Belen or those on the main waterfront (you'll find the latter either at Malecón Tarapaca or at the port by *Casa Morey*, near the corner of Raymondi and Loreto).

Organized trips through agencies and tour companies have a pretty well worked-out itinerary and set of prices. It is very hard to break the oligopolistic tactics of the larger local entrepreneurs, and even the few guides who remain more or less freelance and independent are hard to bargain with since so much of their work comes through the larger agents.

You used to be able to rent a boat for around $50 a day (for up to about ten people); nowadays you'd be lucky to get even a day trip for much less than $40 or $50 per person. One or two of the smaller camps sometimes offer deals from as little as $15 to $30 (try *Amazon Camp* and *Anaconda*) but make sure they're providing all the facilities you require before leaving on the cheapest ones. Before approaching the agents or guides it's a good idea to know more or less what you want from the trip in terms of actual time in the forest, total costs, personal needs and comforts, and things you expect to see when in the "real" jungle. On the last point. it's probably worth mentioning that if your jungle trip really doesn't match what the agency led you to believe when selling you the tickets, it would help future visitors if you report this to the **tourist police** (Piquete del Aeropuerto; ☎23-7067)—some people have actually regained some of their money this way.

A general rule of thumb to consider when booking a jungle trip is that any expedition of fewer than about five days is unlikely to offer more wildlife than a few birds, some monkeys, and maybe a crocodile if you're lucky. Any serious attempt to visit virgin forest and see wildlife in its natural habitat really requires a week or more outside of Iquitos. That said, if Iquitos is your main contact with the Amazon and you're unlikely to return here in the near future, then $50 for a conventional day or two in the forest probably isn't too excessive.

Guided Tours

For **guided tours** (i.e., short visits to nearby jungle lodges) one of the best operators is *Amazon River Lodge* (Putumayo 184; ☎23-3976), which offers one-day outings at around $35 per person (sometimes possible to agree on a discount)—including transportation to the lodge, lunch, a walk in the forest to meet some local Indians, and a canoe ride back to Iquitos. Obviously, the lodge (the *Tamshiyacu Lodge*) is so close to civilization that the chances of spotting wildlife are pretty remote and the Indians are a rather sorry sight, now completely dependent on tourism and reduced by the industry to begging cigarettes and coins off gringos. *Amazon River Lodge* also operate two-day (one-night) trips for around $70 per person and three-day (two-night) expeditions for $100 combining a visit to the *Tamishiyacu Lodge* with a trip deeper into the forest, as far as the *Tamishiyacu Inn* on a creek of the same name. *Amazon Camp* (Prospero 151; ☎23-3931/4007) also runs conventional tours at similar prices to their lodge on the Río Momon, less than three hours away by boat. Also worth checking out are *Amazon Safari* and *Hada Tours* (both in the first block of Putumayo) and *Wongs Amazon Tours* (Jr. Lima 577).

The highly reputable *Explorama Tours* (Putumayo 150, or Box 446, Iquitos) was originally set up in 1964 by North American anthropologists and naturalists. These days, running three different sites for interested tourists, they can offer everything from a comfortable *Explorama Inn* just 40km out of Iquitos to virgin jungle around their *Explornapo Camp* over 160km away. Their original *Explorama Lodge* (80km away)—still operational—offers something in between the conventional and the adventure trips. The one major drawback of *Explorama* for budget travelers is the cost, generally somewhere between $100 and $400 per person per day, depending on size of group, length of trip, and the camp or combination of camps visited.

Amazonia Expeditions (Putumayo 124, in Iquitos; ☎23-6374; Jr. Rufino Torrico 837, Oficina 302 in Lima; ☎24-5980), run by Carlos Grandes, is one of the better **adventure tour** and expedition operators in Iquitos, and generally less expensive than *Explorama*. Running standard four-day expeditions to the Yarapa river, more in-depth seven-day trips to the Samiria/Pacaya reserve, and exciting ten-day trips by river and foot into the Yarapa and Tahuayo region, *Amazonia Expeditions* can fulfill the jungle ambitions of most naturalists and photographers. They can also arrange custom-designed expeditions to even more remote regions. If the tour uses a *colectivo* boat rather than its own speed boat to reach the Yarapa river (160km), the trip should cost less since you lose a day each way on travel.

Main agents and agencies apart, there are three characters in the Iquitos travel business who are willing and able to help you secure the right kind of trip. Firstly, there's Jaime Acevedo, who created the *Amazon Explorers Club* and has an office in the airport (and at Morona 121, ☎23-7453; postal address Box 696, Iquitos). Jaime speaks excellent English and German and works primarily to find trips and tours to suit individual needs and expectations. More guide than agent, Juan Nicholas Maldonado (reachable through Jaime Acevedo or the *Hotel Peru*) is a reliable and charming contact who will either arrange for, or undertake himself, anything from a city tour to a jungle survival expedition. And if you're after a long educational trip to virgin forest with a real expert, there's none with a better reputation than Don Moises Torres Viena (contact at either Soledad 718 or Jiron Brasil 217, or through Jaime Acevedo).

Across the Three-Way Frontier: Peru–Brazil–Colombia

Leaving Peru **via the Amazon River** (or, for that matter, arriving this way), is often an intriguing adventure on its own. The Peruvian/Colombian/Brazilian frontier is two or three days downstream from Iquitos and boats run fairly regularly from the waterfront by the corner of Raymondi and Loreto near to the *Sombrillas* bar. Boats also run from here upstream to Pucallpa (6 days) and Yurimaguas (4 days). Check with the commercial river transporters and keep an eye out for the highly recommended river boats *Jhuiliana* (used by Herzog in his epic film) and *Oro Negro*, which costs $25 to the border, including food but not drink. It is usually possible to sling a hammock up and sleep free of charge on the larger boats in the days leading up to the unpredictable departure. Take a good book and plenty of extra food

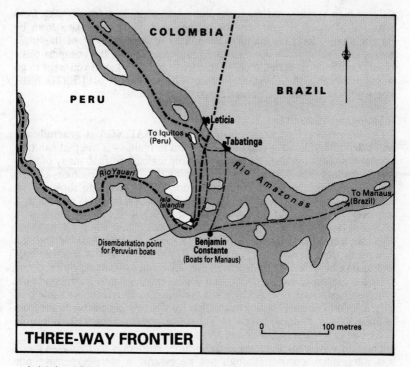

COLOMBIA

PERU

BRAZIL

To Iquitos (Peru)

Leticia

Tabatinga

Rio Yaueri

Rio Amazonas

Isla Islandia

To Manaus (Brazil)

Disembarkation point for Peruvian boats

Benjamin Constante (Boats for Manaus)

0   100 metres

THREE-WAY FRONTIER

and drink with you, along with the hammock and a sweater and one or two blankets. It is also advisable to secure your baggage with a chain as theft is a quite common occurrence on this trip. Before leaving, it's advisable to complete Peruvian **passport formalities** at the *Oficina de Inmigracion* at Arica 447. Theoretically this is also possible at **RAMON CASTILLA**, the last settlement in Peru, but it takes more time and trouble there than it's worth.

On the Peruvian side of the border at **ISLANDIA** (in the middle of the river) you'll find that there are no hotels. To enter Brazil or Colombia you have to take the ferry to Tabatinga or Leticia just across the river. Offering little more than a few places to sleep (try the *Hotel Paje*), the Brazilian Federal Police offices for an entry visa, and a handful of restaurants, TABATINGA is not the most exciting place in South America. Many people stuck here waiting for a boat or plane to Manaus or Iquitos will prefer to hop over the border to **Leticia** for the duration of their stay, even if they don't plan on going any farther into Colombia.

Leticia

Growing rich on tourism and contraband (mostly cocaine), **LETICIA** has more than a touch of the Wild West about it. There are no official *tramites* like paper stamping here, though you should carry your passport at all times. If you intend to go on into Colombia from here you'll need to have picked up a Colombian tourist card from the consulate at Iquitos (or, coming from Brazil, at Manuas). If you stay, be warned that it's an expensive town by Peruvian (and, for that matter, Colombian) standards. Best of the basic **hotels** are *Residencia Monserrate* and *Residencia Leticia*; the cheapest place to eat, and the most varied food, is at the riverside market. If you want to go on into Colombia the cheapest way is to take a canoe to PUERTO ASIS, where you can plug into the **bus** transportation system.

Tabatinga and into Brazil

A few kilometers downstream from Leticia, **TABATINGA** is generally the best place to find boats going back upstream to Iquitos—a trip that can take as many as six to ten days if the boat is badly maintained (and many of them are). Tabatinga has little excitement, but it's the place for customs checks and entry *tramites*: if you're entering Brazil you'll be asked to show an exit ticket or $500. A much smaller place than Leticia, Tabatinga is essentially a stop-over for continuing on downstream into Brazil. **Boats to Manaus**, a four- to seven-day journey that is often very crowded, cost about $30 and tend to leave from BENJAMIN CONSTANTE on the other side of the Río Amazonas from Leticia and Tabatinga. If you arrive at the frontier from Iquitos on a boat that is continuing all the way down to Manaus, it's important to let the captain know whether or not you intend to go into Tabatinga to get your visa business done quickly (use a taxi!) and want to meet the same boat at Benjamin Constante. Bear in mind that it's virtually impossible to get from Islandia to the Federal Police in Tabatinga and then back to Benjamin Constante in less than an hour and a half.

The only other way of crossing these three borders is by **flying**—a much less interesting approach though not necessarily a more expensive one (airport departure tax of $2 is now obligatory). Flights from Iquitos to Leticia are operated by the Peruvian Air Force (*Grupo Ocho*), and *Cruzeira do Sol/Varig* flies to Manaus via Tabatinga twice a week. A number of private small companies fly to the frontier from around $50 upwards.

travel details

To Puerto Maldonado *By truck* from Cuzco (fairly regular; 2–3 days). *By truck* from Cuzco to Shintuya Mission (Mon., Wed., and Fri.; 20–24 hr.) and from there to Boca Manu and Puerto Maldonado. *By boat* (5–6 days). *By air* from Cuzco (daily flights; 1 hr.)

To Iquitos *By air* from Lima and Iquitos (daily; 1 hr.). *By boat* from Pucallpa (as above). Also *boats and flights* to/from Leticia (Colombia) and Tabatinga (Brazil): see above section for details.

To Quillabamba *By train* from Cuzco/Machu Picchu (2 daily; 6½ hr./2½ hr.). *By truck* via Ollantaytambo (12 hr.) or via Calca/Lares (24 hr.)

To Pucallpa By bus from Lima (daily; 24 hr: via Huanuco, 12 hr.). **By truck** from La Merced via Puerto Bermudez (24 hr.). **By air** from Lima and Iquitos (more or less daily flights; 1 hr.). **By boat** from Iquitos (fairly regular; 4–6 days journey but allow at least 10 days to include organization, documentation, mechanical failures, etc.)

PART THREE

THE
CONTEXTS

THE HISTORICAL FRAMEWORK

BEGINNINGS AND PREHISTORY

The first people to set foot in Peru were descendants of nomadic tribes who had crossed into the Americas during the last Ice Age (40,000–15,000 B.C.) when a combination of ice packs and low sea levels exposed a neck of solid "land" to span what's now the Bering Strait. Following herds of game animals from Siberia into what must have been a relative paradise of fertile coast, wild forest, mountain, and savannah, successive generations continued south through Central America. Some made their way down along the Andes, into the Amazon, and out onto the more fertile areas of the Peruvian and Ecuadorian coast, while others found their niches en route.

In a number of tribes there seem to be cultural memories of these long migrations, encapsulated in their traditional mythologies—though these aren't really transcribable into written histories. There is, however, archeological evidence of human occupation in Peru dating back to around 20,000 B.C., concentrated in the **Ayacucho Valley**, where these early Peruvians lived in caves or out in the open. Around 12,000 B.C., slightly to the north

in the **Chillon Valley** (just above modern Lima), comes the first evidence of significant craft skills—stone blades and knives for hunting. At this time there were probably similar groups of hunter tribes in the mountains and jungle too, but the climatic conditions of these zones make it unlikely that any significant remains will ever be found.

The difficulties of traversing the rugged terrain between the highlands and coast evidently proved little problem for the early Peruvians. From 8000 to 2000 B.C., **migratory bands** of hunters and gatherers alternated between camps in the lowlands during the harsh mountain winters and highland summer "resorts", their actual movements well synchronized with those of wild animal herds. One important mountain encampment from this **Incipient Era** has been discovered at **Lauricocha**, near Huanuco, at an altitude of over 4000m. Here the art of working stone—eventually producing very fine blades and arrow points—seems to have been sophisticated, while at the same time a growing cultural imagination found expression in cave paintings depicting animals, hunting scenes, and even dances. Down on the coast at this time other groups were living on the greener *lomas* belts of the desert in places like **Chilca** to the south, and in the mangrove swamps around **Tumbes** to the north.

An awareness of the potential uses of plants began to emerge around **5000 B.C.** with the **cultivation** of seeds and tubers (the potato was one of the most important "discoveries," later taken to Europe); to be followed over the next two millennia by the introduction, presumably from the Amazon, of gourds, Lima beans, then squashes, peanuts, and eventually cotton. Toward the end of this period a climatic shift turned the coast into a much more arid belt and forced those living there to try their hand at **agriculture** in the fertile river beds, a process to some extent paralleled in the mountains.

With a stable agricultural base, permanent settlements sprung up all along the coast, notably at **Chicama**, **Asia**, and **Paracas**, and in the sierra at **Kotosh**. The population began to mushroom, and with it came a new consciousness, perhaps influenced by cultural developments within the Amazon Basin to the east: **Cultism**—the burial of dead in mummy form, the capturing of trophy heads, and the building of grand religious structures—made its first appearance. At the same time there were also overwhelming technological advances in the spheres of weaving, tool-making, and ornamental design.

THE CHAVIN CULT

From around 1200 B.C. to A.D. 200—the **Formative Era**—agriculture and village life became established. Ceramics were invented, and a slow disintegration of regional isolation began. This last factor was due mainly to the widespread dispersal of a religious movement, the **Chavin Cult**. Remarkable in that it seems to have spread without the use of military force, the cult was based on a conceptualization of nature spirits, and an all-powerful feline creator god. This widespread feline image rapidly exerted its influence over the northern half of Peru and initiated a period of interrelations between fertile basins in the Andes and some of the coastal valleys. How—and where—the cult originated is uncertain, though it seems probable that it began in the eastern jungles, possibly spreading to the Andes (and eventually the coast) along the upper Marañon river.

The Chavin Cult was responsible for excellent progress in the work of **stone carving** and **metallurgy** (copper, gold, and silver) and, significantly, for a ubiquity of temples and pyramids which grew up as cultural centers where the gods could be worshiped. The most important known center was the temple complex at **Chavin de Huantar** in Ancash, though a similar center was built at **Kotosh** near Huanuco; its influence seems to have spread over the northern highlands and coast from Chiclayo down as far as the Paracas Peninsula (where it had a particularly strong impact). There were immense local variations in the expressions of the Chavin Cult: elaborate metallurgy in the far north; adobe buildings on stone platforms in the river valleys; excellent ceramics from **Chicama**, and the extravagant stone engravings from Chavin itself. In the mountains life must have been very hard, based on subsistence agriculture and pilgrimages to the sacred shrines—most of which probably originated around ideas formulated by an emergent caste of powerful priest-chiefs. On the coast there was an extra resource—seafood—to augment the meager agricultural yields.

Towards the **end of the Chavin phase**, an experimental period saw new centers attempting to establish themselves as independent powers with their own personalities. This gave birth to **Gallinazo** settlements in the Viru valley; the incredible **Paracas culture** on the south coast (with its excessively beautiful and very advanced textile technology based around a cult of the dead); and the early years of **Tiahuanaco** development in the Lake Titicaca region. These three cultural upsurges laid the necessary foundations for the flourishing civilizations of the subsequent Classical Era.

THE CLASSICAL ERA

A diverse period—and one marked by intense development in almost every field—the **Classical Era (A.D. 200–1100)** saw the emergence of numerous distinct cultures, both on the coast and in the sierra. The best documented, though not necessarily the most powerful, are the **Mochica** and **Nazca** cultures (both probably descendents of the coastal Paracas culture) and the **Tiahuanuco**, all forebears of the better known Incas.

The **Mochica culture** has left the fullest evidence of its social and domestic life, all aspects of which, including its work and religion, are vividly represented in highly realistic pottery. The first real urban culture in Peru, its members maintained a firm hierarchy, an elite group combining both secular and sacred power. Ordinary people cultivated land around clusters of dwelling sites, dominated by sacred pyramids—man-made *huacas* dedicated to the gods. The key to the elite's position was presumably their organization of large irrigation projects, essential to the survival of these relatively large population centers in the arid desert of the north coast. In the Mohica's region, nature and the world of the ancestors seem the dominant elements; occasional human sacrifices were offered and trophy heads were captured in battle. The peak of their influence came around 500 to 600, with cultural and military control of the coast from Piura in the north to the Nepena valley in the south.

More or less contemporaneous with the Mochica, the **Nazca culture** bloomed for several hundred years on the south coast. The Nazca are thought to be responsible for the astonishing lines and drawings etched into the

Pampa de San José, though little is known for certain about their society or general way of life. The Nazca did, however, build an impressive temple complex in the desert at **Cahuachi**, and their burial sites have turned up thousands of beautiful ceramics whose abstract designs can be compared only to the quality and content of earlier Paracas textiles.

Named after its sacred center on the shore of Lake Titicaca, the **Tiahuancuco culture** developed at much the same time as the Mochica—with which, initially at least, it peacefully coexisted. Tiahuanuco textiles and pottery spread along the desert, modifying both Mochica and Nazca styles and bending them into more sophisticated shapes and abstract patterns. The main emphasis in Tiahuanuco pottery and stonework was on symbolic elements featuring condors, pumas, and snakes—more than likely the culture's main gods, representing their respective spheres of the sky, earth, and underworld. In this there seem obvious echoes of the deified natural phenomena of the earlier Chavin cult.

Although initially peaceable, the Tiahuanuco influence is associated in its decadent phase with **militarism**. Originating either at Huari, in the sierra near Ayacucho, or on the central coast, this forceful tendency extended from A.D. 650 to 1100 and was dominated by what today is called the **Huari-Tiahuanuco culture**. The ruins at Huari cover some eight square km and include high-walled enclosures of field stones laid and plastered with mud, decorated only by a few stone statues along Tiahuanuco lines. Whether or not this was the actual inspirational center, by around A.D. 1000 Huari-Tiahuanuco features were dominant in the art forms over virtually all of Peru.

An increasing prevalence of **intertribal warfare** characterized the ultimate centuries of this era, culminating in the erection of defensive forts, a multiplication of ceremonial sites (including over sixty large pyramids in the Lima area), and, eventually, the uprooting of Huari-Tiahuanuco influence on the coast by the emergence of three youthful mini-empires—the **Chimu**, the **Cuismancu**, and the **Chincha**. In the mountains its influence mysteriously disappeared to pave the way for the separate growth of relatively large tribal units such as the **Colla** (around Titicaca), the **Inca** (around Cuzco), and the **Chanca** (near Ayacucho).

Partly for defensive reasons, this period of isolated development sparked off a city-building urge which became almost compulsive by the Imperial Era in the twelfth century. The most spectacular urban complex was **Chan Chan** (near modern Trujillo) built by the **Chimu** on the side of the river opposite to earlier Mochica temples but indicating a much greater sophistication in social control, the internal structure of the culture's clan-based society reflected in the complex's intricate layout. By now, with a working knowledge of bronze manufacture, the Chimu flung the arms of an empire from Chan Chan to Tumbes in the north and Paramonga in the south—dominating nearly half the Peruvian coastline. To the south they were bounded by the **Cuismancu**, less powerful, though capable of building similar citadels (such as Cajamarquilla near Lima) and of comparable attainments in craft industries. Farther down the coastline the **Chincha**—known also as the **Ica culture**—produced fine monuments and administrative centers in the Chincha and Pisco valleys too. The lower rainfall on the southern coast, however, didn't permit the Chincha State—nor (to an extent) the Cuismancu—to create urban complexes anything near the size of Chan Chan.

THE INCAS

With the **Inca Empire** (1200–1532) came the culmination of this city-building phase, and the beginnings of a kind of Peruvian unity, the Incas gradually taking over each of the separate coastal empires. One of the last to go—almost bloodlessly, and just sixty years before the Spanish conquest—were the Chimu, who for much of this "Imperial Period" were a viable and powerful rival.

Based in the valleys around Cuzco, the Incas were for the first two centuries of their existence much like any other of the larger mountain tribes. Fiercely protective of their independence, they maintained a somewhat feudal society, tightly controlled by rigid religious tenets, though often disrupted by intertribal conflict. The founder of the dynasty—sometime around 1200—was **Manco Capac**, who passed into Inca mythology as a culture hero. Historically, however, little definite is known about Inca developments or achievements until the accession in 1438 of Pachacuti, and the onset of their great era of expansion.

THE INCA EMPERORS

MANCO CAPAC (Culture hero ca. 1200)	VIRACOCHA INCA
SINCHI ROCA	PACHACUTI (1438–71)
LLOQUE YUPANQUI	TOPAC YUPANQUI (1471–93)
MAYTA CAPAC	HUAYNA CAPAC (1493–1525)
CAPAC YUPANQUI	HUASCAR (1525–32)
INCA ROCA	ATAHUALPA (1532–33)
YAHUAR HUACA	

Pachacuti, most innovative of all the Inca emperors, was the first to expand their traditional tribal territory. The beginnings of this were not in fact of his making but the response to a threatened invasion by the powerful, neighboring Chanca Indians during the reign of his father, Viracocha. Viracocha, feeling the odds to be overwhelming, left Cuzco in Pachacuti's control, withdrawing to the refuge of Calca along the Urubamba river. Pachacuti, however, won a legendary victory—Inca chronicles record that the very stones of the battlefield rose up in his defense—and, having vanquished the most powerful force in the region, shortly took the Inca crown for himself.

Within three decades Pachacuti had consolidated this power over the entire sierra region from Cajamarca to Titicaca, defeating in the process all main imperial rivals except for the Chimu. At the same time the capital at **Cuzco** was spectacularly developed, with the evacuation and destruction of all villages within a 10km radius, a massive program of agricultural terracing (watched over by a skyline of agro-calendrical towers), and the construction of unrivaled palaces and temples. Shrewdly, Pachacuti turned his forcible evacuation of the Cuzco villages into a positive plan, relocating the Incas in newly colonized areas. He extended this practice too, towards his subjugated allies, conscripting them into the Inca armies while their chiefs remained as hostages and honored guests at Cuzco.

Inca territory expanded north into Ecuador, almost reaching Quito, under the next Emperor—**Topac Yupanqui**—who also took his troops down the coast, overwhelming the Chimu and capturing the holy shrine of Pachacamac. Not surprisingly the coastal cultures influenced the Incas perhaps as much as the Incas influenced them—particularly in

the sphere of craft industries. With Pachacuti before him, Topac Yupanqui was nevertheless an outstandingly imaginative and able ruler. During the 22 years of his reign (1471–93) he pushed Inca control southwards as far as the Río Maule in Chile; instigated the first proper census of the empire and set up the decimal-based administrative system; introduced the division of labor and land between the state, the gods, and the local *allyus*; invented the concept of Chosen Women (*Mamaconas*); and inaugurated a new class of respected individuals—the Yanaconas. An empire had been unified not just physically but also administratively and ideologically.

At the end of the fifteenth century the Inca Empire was thriving, probably as much as any civilization this planet has ever witnessed. Its politico-religious authority was finely tuned, and could extract what it needed from its millions of subjects and give what was necessary to maintain the status quo—be it brute force, protection, or food. The only obvious problem inherent in the Inca system of unification and domination was one of overextension. When **Huayna Capac** continued Topac Yupanqui's expansion to the north he created a new Inca city at **Quito**, one which he personally preferred to Cuzco and which laid the seed for a division of loyalties within Inca society.

This came to a head even before his death. Ruling the empire from Quito, along with his favorite son **Atahualpa**, Huayna Capac had installed another son, **Huascar**, at Cuzco. In the last year of his life he tried to formalize the division—ensuring an inheritance at Quito for Atahualpa—but this was totally resisted by Huascar, legitimate heir to the Lord Inca and the empire, and by many of the influential Cuzco priests and nobles. In 1527, with Huayna Capac's death, civil war broke out. Atahualpa, backed by his father's army, was by far the stronger and immediately won a major victory at the Río Bamba—a battle which, it was said, left the plain littered with human bones for over a hundred years. A still bloodier battle, however, took place along the Apurimac River at Cotabamba in 1532. This was the decisive victory for Atahualpa, and with his army he retired to relax at the hot baths near Cajamarca. Here, informed of a strange-looking, alien band, successors of the bearded adventurers whose presence had been noted during the reign of Huayna Capac, they waited.

THE SPANISH CONQUEST

Francisco Pizarro, along with two dozen soldiers, stumbled upon and named the Pacific Ocean in 1513 while on an exploratory expedition in Panama. From that moment his determination, fired by native tales of a fabulously rich land to the south, was set. Within eleven years he had found himself financial sponsors and set sail down the Pacific coast with the priest Hernando de Luque and Diego Almagro.

With remarkable determination, having survived several disastrous attempts, the three explorers eventually landed at **Tumbes** in 1532. A few months later a small band of Spaniards, totaling less than 170 men, arrived at the Inca city of **Cajamarca** to meet the leader of what they were rapidly realizing was a mighty empire. En route to Cajamarca, Pizarro had learned of the Inca civil wars and of Atahualpa's recent victory over his brother Huascar. This rift within the empire provided the key to success that Pizarro was looking for.

The day after their arrival, in what at first appeared to be a lunatic endeavor, Pizarro and his men massacred thousands of Inca warriors and captured Atahualpa. Although ridiculously outnumbered, the Spaniards had the advantages of surprise, steel, cannons, and, above all, mounted cavalry. The **decisive battle** was over in a matter of hours: with Atahualpa prisoner, Pizarro was effectively in control of the Inca empire. Atahualpa was promised his freedom if he could fill the famous ransom room at Cajamarca with gold. Caravans overladen with the precious metal arrived from all over the land and within six months the room was filled: a treasure, worth over one-and-a-half million *pesos*, which was already enough to make

each of the conquerors extremely wealthy. Pizarro, however, chose to keep the Inca leader as a hostage in case of Indian revolt, amid growing suspicions that Atahualpa was inciting his generals to attack the Spanish. Atahualpa almost certainly did send messages to his chiefs in Cuzco, including orders to execute his brother Huascar who was already in captivity there. Under pressure from his worried captains, Pizarro brought Atahualpa to trial in July 1533, a mockery of justice in which he was given a free choice: to be burned alive as a pagan or strangled as a Christian. They baptized him and then killed him.

With nothing left to keep him in Cajamarca, Pizarro made his way through the Andes to Cuzco where he crowned a puppet emperor, **Manco Inca**, of royal Indian blood. After all the practice that the Spaniards had had in imposing their culture on both the Moors in Spain and the Aztecs in Mexico, it took them only a few years to replace the Inca empire with a working colonial mechanism. Now that the Inca civil wars were over, the natives seemed happy to retire quietly into the hills and get back to the land. However, more than wars were responsible for the almost total lack of initial reaction to the new conquerors. The **native population** had dropped from some 32 million in 1520 to only 5 million by 1548—a decline due mainly to new European diseases such as smallpox, measles, bubonic plague, whooping cough, and influenza.

COLONIAL PERU

Queen Isabella of Spain indirectly laid the original foundations for the political administration of Peru in 1503 when she authorized the initiation of an **encomienda system**, which meant that successful Spanish conquerors could extract tribute for the crown and personal service in return for converting the natives to Christianity. They were not, however, given title to the land itself. As Governor of Peru, Pizarro used the *encomienda* system to grant large groups of Indians to his favorite soldier-companions. In this way the basic colonial land-tenure structure was created in everything but name. "Personal service" rapidly came to mean subservient serfdom for the native population, many of whom were now expected to raise animals introduced from the Old World (cattle, hens, etc.) on behalf of their new overlords.

Many Inca cities were rebuilt as Spanish towns, although some, like Cuzco, retained native masonry for their foundations and even walls. Other Inca sites, like Huanuco Viejo, were abandoned in favor of cities in more hospitable lower altitudes. The Spanish were drawn to the coast for strategic as well as climatic reasons—above all to maintain constant oceanic links with the homeland via Panama.

The **foundation of Lima** in 1535 began a multilayered process of satellite dependency which continues even today. The fat of the land (originally mostly gold and other treasures) was sucked in from regions all over Peru, processed in Lima, and sent on from there to Spain. Lima survived on the backs of Peru's municipal capitals which, in turn, extracted tribute from the scattered *encomenderos*. The *encomenderos* depended on local chieftains (*curacas*) to rake in service and goods from even the most remote villages and hamlets. At the lowest level there was little difference between Inca imperial exploitation and the economic network of Spanish colonialism. Where they really varied was that under the Incas the surplus produce circulated among the elite within the country, while the Spaniards sent much of it to a distant monarch on the other side of the world.

In 1541 Pizarro was assassinated by a disgruntled faction among the Conquistadors who looked to Diego Almagro as their leader, and for the next seven years the nascent colonial society was rent by civil war. In response, the first **Viceroy**—Blasco Nuñez de Vela—was sent from Spain in 1544. His task was to act as Royal Commissioner and to secure the colony's loyalty to Spain; his fate was to be killed by Gonzalo Pizarro, brother of Francisco. But Royalist forces, now under Pedro de la Gasca, eventually prevailed—Gonzalo was captured and executed and crown control firmly established.

COLONIAL SOCIETY

Meanwhile **Peruvian society** was being transformed by the growth of new generations: *Creoles*, descendants of Spaniards born in Peru, and *mestizos*, of mixed Spanish and native blood, created a new class structure. In the coastal valleys where populations had been decimated by European diseases, slaves were imported from Africa. There were over 1500 black slaves in Lima alone by 1554. At the

same time, as a result of the civil wars and periodic Indian revolts, over a third of the original conquerors had lost their lives by 1550. Nevertheless effective power remained in the hands of the independent *encomenderos*.

In an attempt to dilute the influence of the *encomienda* system, the Royalists divided the existing 20 or so municipalities into **corregi-mentos**, smaller units headed by a *corregidor*, or royal administrator. They were given the power to control the activities of the *encomenderos* and exact tribute for the crown—soon becoming the vital links in provincial government. The pattern of constant friction between *encomenderos* and *corregidores* was to continue for centuries, with only the priests to act as local mediators.

Despite the evangelistic zeal of the Spanish, **religion** changed little for the majority of the native population. Although Inca ceremonies, pilgrimages, and public rituals were outlawed, their mystical and magical base endured. Each region quickly reverted to the pre-Inca cults which were deep-rooted in their culture and cosmology. Over the centuries the people learned to absorb symbolic elements of the Catholic faith into their beliefs and rituals—allowing them, once again, to worship relatively freely. Magic, herbalism, and divination have continued strongly at the village level and have successfully pervaded modern Peruvian thought, language, and practice. (The Peruvian World Cup soccer squad in 1982 enlisted in vain the magical aid of a *curandero*). At the elite level, the Spanish continued their fervent attempts to convert the entire population to their own ritualistic religion. They were, however, more successful with the rapidly growing *mestizo* population who shared the same cultural aspirations.

Miraculous occurrences became a conspicuous feature in the popular Peruvian Catholic Church, the greatest example being Our Lord of Miracles, a cult which originated among the black population of colonial Lima. In the devastating earthquake of 1665, an anonymous mural of the Crucifixion on the wall of a chapel in the poorest quarter was supposedly the only structure left standing. This direct sign from God took hold among the local population, and Our Lord of Miracles remains the most revered image in Peru. Thousands of devotees process through the streets of Lima and other Peruvian towns every October, and even today many women dress in purple throughout the month to honor Our Lord of Miracles.

In return for the salvation of their souls the native population was expected to surrender their bodies to the Spanish. Some forms of service (*mita*) were simply continuations of Inca tradition—from keeping the streets clean to working in textile mills. But the most feared was a new introduction, the *mita de minas*—**forced work in the mines**. With the discovery of the "mountain of silver" at Potosí (now Bolivia) in 1545 and of mercury deposits at Huancavelica in 1563, it reached new heights. Forced off their small holdings, few Indians who left to work in the mines ever returned. Indeed the mercury mines at Huancavelica were so dangerous that the quality of their toxic ore could be measured by the number of weekly deaths. Those who were taken to Potosí had to be chained together to stop them from escaping: if they were injured, their bodies were cut from the shackles by sword to save precious time. Some 3 million Indians worked in Potosí and Huancavelica alone; some of them had to walk over 1000km from Cuzco to Potosí for the privilege of working themselves to death.

In 1569, **Francisco Toledo** arrived in Peru to become viceroy. His aim was to reform the colonial system so as to increase royal revenue while at the same time improving the lot of the native population. Before he could get on with that, however, he had to quash a rapidly developing threat to the colony—the appearance of a **neo-Inca State**. After an unsuccessful uprising in 1536, Manco Inca, Pizarro's puppet emperor, had disappeared with a few thousand loyal subjects into the remote mountainous regions of **Vilcabamba**, northwest of Cuzco. With the full regalia of high priests, virgins of the sun, and the golden idol *punchau*, he maintained a rebel Inca state and built himself impressive new palaces and fortresses between Vitcos and Espíritu Pampa—well beyond the reach of colonial power. Although not a substantial threat to the colony, Manco's forces repeatedly raided nearby settlements and robbed travelers on the roads between Cuzco and Lima.

Manco himself died at the hands of a Spanish outlaw, a guest at Vilcabamba who hoped to win himself a pardon from the crown.

But the neo-Inca State continued under the leadership of Manco's son, Sairi Tupac, who assumed the imperial fringe at the age of ten. Tempted out of Vilcabamba in 1557, Sairi Tupac was offered a palace and a wealthy life in return for giving up his refuge and subversive aims. He died a young man, only three years after turning to Christianity and laying aside his father's cause. Meanwhile Titu Cusi, one of Manco's illegitimate sons, declared himself emperor and took control in Vilcabamba.

Eventually, Titu Cusi began to open his doors. First he allowed two Spanish friars to enter his camp, and then, in 1571, negotiations were opened for a return to Cuzco when an emissary arrived from Viceroy Toledo. The talks broke down before the year was out and Toledo decided to send an army into Vilcabamba to rout the Incas. They arrived to find that Titu Cusi was already dead and his brother, **Tupac Amaru**, was the new emperor. After fierce fighting and a near escape, Tupac Amaru was captured and brought to trial in Cuzco. Accused of plotting to overthrow the Spanish and of inciting his followers to raid towns, Tupac Amaru was beheaded as soon as possible—an act by Toledo which was disavowed by the Spanish crown and which caused much distress in Peru.

Toledo's next task was to establish firmly the viceregal position—something that outlasted him by some two centuries. He toured highland Peru searching for ways to improve crown control, starting with an attempt to curb the excesses of the *encomenderos* and their tax-collecting *curacas* (hereditary native leaders) by implementing a program of **reducciones**—the physical resettlement of Indians in new towns and villages. Hundreds of thousands of peasants, perhaps millions, were forced to move from remote hamlets into large conglomerations or *reducciones* in convenient locations. Priests, or *corregidores*, were placed in charge of them, undercutting the power of the *encomenderos*. Toledo also established a new elected position—the local mayor (or *varayoc*)—in an attempt to displace the *curacas* (hereditary native leaders). The *varayoc*, however, was not necessarily a good colonial tool in that, even more than the *curacas*, his interests were rooted firmly in the *allyu* and in his own neighbors, rather than in the wealth of some distant kingdom.

REBELLION

When the Hapsburg monarchy gave way to the Bourbon kings in Spain at the beginning of the eighteenth century, shivers of protest seemed to reverberate deep in the Peruvian hinterland. There were a number of serious **native rebellions** against colonial rule during the next hundred years. One of the most important, though least known, was that led by **Juan Santos Atahualpa**, a *mestizo* from Cuzco. Juan Santos had traveled to Spain, Africa, and, some say, to England as a young man in the service of a wealthy Jesuit priest. Returning to Peru in 1740 he was imbued with revolutionary fervor and moved into the high jungle region between Tarma and the Ucayali River where he roused the forest Indians to rebellion. Throwing out the whites, he established a millenarian cult and, with an Indian army recruited from several tribes, successfully repelled all attacks by the authorities. Although never extending his powers beyond Tarma, he lived a free man until his death in 1756.

Twenty years later there were further violent native protests throughout the country against the enforcement of *repartiementos*. Under this new system the peasants were obliged to buy most of their essential goods from the *corregidor*, who, as monopoly suppliers, sold poor quality produce at grossly inflated prices.

In 1780, another *mestizo*, José Gabriel Condorcanqui, led a rebellion, calling himself **Tupac Amaru II**. Whipping up the already inflamed peasant opinion around Cuzco into a revolutionary frenzy, he imprisoned a local *corregidor* before going on to massacre a troop of nearly 600 Royalist soldiers. Within a year Tupac Amaru II had been captured and executed but his rebellion had demonstrated both a definite weakness in colonial control and a high degree of popular unrest. Over the next decade several administrative reforms were to alter the situation, at least superficially: the *repartimiento* and the *corregimento* systems were abolished. In 1784, Charles III appointed a French nobleman—Teodoro de Croix—as the new viceroy to Peru and divided the country into seven *intendencias* containing some 52 provinces. This created tighter direct royal control, but also unwittingly provided the pattern for the Republican state of federated *departmentos*.

The end of the eighteenth century saw profound changes throughout the world. The North American colonies had gained their independence from Britain; France had been rocked by a people's revolution; and liberal ideas were spreading everywhere. Inflammatory newspapers and periodicals began to appear on the streets of Lima, and discontent was expressed at all levels of society. A strong sense of **Peruvian nationalism** emerged in the pages of *Mercurio Peruano* (first printed in the 1790s), a concept which was vital to the coming changes. Even the architecture of Lima had changed in the mid-eighteenth century, as if to welcome the new era. Wide avenues suddenly appeared, public parks were opened, and palatial salons became the focus for the discourse of gentlemen. The philosophy of the enlightenment was slowly but surely pervading attitudes even in remote Peru.

When, in 1808, Napoleon took control of Spain, the authorities and elites in all the Spanish colonies found themselves in a new and unprecedented position. Was their loyalty to Spain or to its rightful king? Who *was* the rightful king now?

Initially there were a few unsuccessful, locally based protests in response both to this ambiguous situation and to the age-old agrarian problem, but it was only with the intervention of outside forces that independence was to become a serious issue in Peru. The American War of Independence, the French Revolution, and Napoleon's invasion of Spain all pointed towards the opportunity of throwing off the shackles of colonialism, and by the time Ferdinand returned to the Spanish throne in 1814, Royalist troops were struggling to maintain order throughout South America. Venezuela and Argentina had already declared their independence, and in 1817 San Martin liberated Chile by force. It was only a matter of time before one of the great Liberators—**San Martin** in the south or **Bolivar** in the north—reached Peru.

San Martin was the first to do so. Having already liberated Argentina and Chile, he contracted an English naval officer, Lord Cochrane, to attack Lima. By September 1819 the first rebel invaders had landed at Paracas. Ica, Huanuco, and then the north of Peru soon opted for independence, and the Royalists, cut off in Lima, retreated into the mountains

Entering the capital without a struggle, San Martin proclaimed Peruvian **independence** on July 28, 1821.

THE REPUBLIC

San Martin immediately assumed political control of the fledgling nation. Under the title "Protector of Peru" he set about attempting to devise a workable **constitution** for the new nation—at one point even considering importing European royalty to establish a new monarchy. A libertarian as well as a liberator, San Martin declared freedom for slaves' children, abolished Indian service, and even outlawed the term "Indian." But in practice, with Royalist troops still controlling large sectors of the sierra, his approach did more to frighten the establishment than it did to help the slaves and peasants whose problems remain, even now, deeply rooted in their social and territorial inheritance.

The development of a relatively stable political system took virtually the rest of the nineteenth century, although Spanish resistance to independence was finally extinguished at the Battles of Junin and Ayacucho in 1824. By this time San Martin had given up the political power game, handing it over to **Simon Bolivar**, a man of enormous force with definite tendencies towards megalomania. Between them, Bolivar and his right-hand man, Sucre, divided Peru in half, with Sucre first president of the upper sector, renamed Bolivia. Bolivar himself remained dictator of a vast Andean Confederation—encompassing Colombia, Venezuela, Ecuador, Peru, and Bolivia—until 1826. Within a year of his withdrawal, however, the Peruvians had torn up his controversial constitution and voted the liberal **General La Mar** as president.

On La Mar's heels raced a generation of *caudillos*, military men, often *mestizos* of middle-class origins who had achieved recognition (on either side) in the battles for independence. The history of the early Republic consists almost entirely of internal disputes between the *Creole* aristocracy and dictatorial *caudillos*. Peru plunged deep into a period of domestic and foreign plot and counterplot, while the economy and some of the nation's finest natural resources withered away.

Generals **Santa Cruz** and **Gamarra** stand out as two of the most ruthless players in this high stakes power game; overthrowing La Mar in 1829, Santa Cruz became President of Bolivia and Gamarra of Peru. Four years later the liberal *Creoles* fought back with the election of General Orbegoso to the presidency. Gamarra, attempting to oust Orbegoso in a quiet palace coup, was overwhelmed and exiled. But the liberal Constitution of 1834, despite its severe limitations on presidential power, still proved too much for the army—Orbegoso was overthrown within six months.

Unable to sit on the side lines and watch the increasing pandemonium of Peruvian politics, Santa Cruz invaded Peru from Bolivia and installed himself as "Protector" in 1837. Very few South Americans were happy with this situation, least of all Gamarra, who joined with other exiles in Chile to plot revenge. After fierce fighting, Gamarra defeated Santa Cruz at Yungay, restored himself as President of Peru for two years, then died in 1841. During the next four years Peru had six more presidents, none of any notable ability.

Ramon Castilla was the first president to bring any real strength to his office. On his assumption of power in 1845 the country began to develop more positively on the rising wave of a booming export in *guano* (birdshit) fertilizer. In 1856 a new moderate constitution was approved and Castilla began his second term of office in an atmosphere of growth and hope—there were railroads to be built and the Amazon waterways to be opened up. Sugar and cotton became important exports from coastal plantations and the *guano* deposits alone yielded a revenue of $15 million in 1860. Castilla abolished Indian tribute and managed to emancipate slaves without social-economic disruption by buying them from their "owners"; *guano* income proved useful for this compensation.

His successors fared less happily. **President Balta** (1868–72) oversaw the construction of most of the railroads, but overspent so freely on these and a variety of other public and engineering works that he left the country on the brink of economic collapse. In the 1872 elections an attempted military coup was spontaneously crushed by a civilian mob, and Peru's first civilian president—the *laissez-faire* capitalist **Manuel Pardo**—assumed power.

THE WAR OF THE PACIFIC

By the late nineteenth century Peru's foreign debt, particularly to England, had grown out of all proportion. Even though interest could be paid in *guano,* there simply wasn't enough. To make matters considerably worse, Peru went to war with Chile in 1879.

Lasting over four years, this **"War of the Pacific"** was basically a battle for the rich nitrate deposits located in Bolivian territory. Peru had pressured its ally Bolivia into imposing an export tax on nitrates mined by the Chilean-British corporation. Chile's answer was to occupy the area and declare war on Peru and Bolivia. Victorious on land and at sea, Chilean forces had occupied Lima by the beginning of 1881 and the Peruvian president had fled to Europe. By 1883 Peru "lay helpless under the boots of its conquerors," and only a diplomatic rescue seemed possible. The **Treaty of Anco**, possibly Peru's greatest national humiliation, brought the war to a close in October 1883.

Peru was forced to accept the cloistering of an independent Bolivia high up in the Andes, with no land link to the Pacific, and the even harder loss of the nitrate fields to Chile. The country seemed in ruins: the *guano* virtually exhausted and the nitrates lost to Chile, the nation's coffers were empty and a new generation of *caudillos* prepared to resume the power struggle all over again.

THE TWENTIETH CENTURY

Modern Peru is generally considered to have been born in 1895 with the forced resignation of General Caceres. But in fairness the seeds of industrial development had been laid under his rule, albeit by foreigners. In 1890 an international plan was formulated to bail Peru out of its bankruptcy. The **Peruvian Corporation** was formed in London and assumed the $50 million national debt in return for "control of the national economy." Foreign companies took over the railroads, navigation of Lake Titicaca, vast quantities of *guano,* and were given free use of seven Peruvian ports for 66 years as well as the opportunity to start exploiting the rubber resources of the Amazon Basin. Under Nicolas de Pierola, some sort of stability had begun to return by the end of the nineteenth century.

In the early years of the twentieth century, Peru was run by an oligarchical clan of big businessmen and great landowners. Fortunes were made in a wide range of exploitative enterprises, above all sugar along the coast, minerals from the mountains, and rubber from the jungle. Meanwhile, the lot of the ordinary peasant worsened dramatically.

One of the most powerful oligarchs, **Augusto Leguia** rose to power through his possession of franchises for the New York Insurance Company and the British Sugar Company. He became a prominent figure, representing the rising bourgeoisie in the early 1900s, and in 1908 he was the first of their kind to be elected president. Under his rule the influence of foreign investment increased rapidly, with North American money taking ascendency over British. It was with this capital that Lima was modernized—parks, plazas, the Avenida Arequipa, and the Presidential Palace all date from this period. But for the majority of Peruvians, Leguia did nothing. The lives of the mountain peasants became more difficult, and the jungle Indians lived as near slaves on the rubber plantations. Not surprisingly, Leguia's time in power coincided with a large number of Indian rebellions, general discontent, and the rise of the first labor movement in Peru. Elected for a second term, Leguia became still more dictatorial, changing the constitution so that he could be reelected on another two occasions. A year after the beginning of his fourth term, in 1930, he was ousted by a military coup—more as a result of the Stock Market crash and Peru's close links with U.S. finance than as a consequence of his other political failings.

During Leguia's long dictatorship, the **labor movement** began to flex its muscles. A general strike in 1919 had established an eight-hour day, and ten years later the unions formed the first National Labor Center. The worldwide Depression of the early 1930s hit Peru particularly badly; demand for its main exports (oil, silver, sugar, cotton, and coffee) fell off drastically. Finally, in 1932, the Trujillo middle class led a violent uprising against the sugar barons and the primitive conditions of work on the plantations. Suppressed by the army, nearly 5000 lives are thought to have been lost, many of the rebels being taken out in trucks and shot among the ruins of Chan Chan.

The rise of **APRA**—the American Popular Revolutionary Alliance—which had instigated the Trujillo uprising, and the growing popularity of its leader, **Haya de la Torre**, kept the nation occupied during World War II. Allowed to participate for the first time in the 1945 elections, APRA chose a neutral candidate—**Dr. Bustamante**—in place of Haya de la Torre whose fervent radicalism was considered a vote loser. Bustamante won the elections, with APRA controlling 18 out of 29 seats in the Senate and 53 out of 84 in the Chamber of Deputies.

Postwar euphoria was short-lived however. Inflation was totally out of hand and apparently unaffected by Bustamante's exchange controls; during the 1940s the cost of living in Peru rose by 262 percent. With anti-APRA feeling on the rise, the president leaned more and more heavily on support from the army, until General Odria led a coup d'état from Arequipa in 1948 and formed a military junta. By the time Odria left office, in 1956, a new political element threatened oligarchical control—the young **Fernando Belaunde** and his **National Youth Front** (later *Acción Popular*) demanding "radical" reform. Even with the support of APRA and the army, Manuel Prado barely defeated Belaunde in the next elections: the unholy alliance between the monied establishment and APRA has been known as the "marriage of convenience" ever since.

The economy remained in dire straits. Domestic prices continued to soar and in 1952 alone there were some 200 strikes and several serious riots. Meanwhile much more radical feeling was aroused in the provinces by **Hugo Blanco**, a charismatic *mestizo* from Cuzco who had joined a Trotskyist group—the Workers Revolutionary Party—which was later to merge with the FIR—the Revolutionary Left's Front. In La Convencion, within the Department of Cuzco, Blanco created nearly 150 syndicates, whose peasant members began to work their own individual plots while refusing to work for the *hacienda* owners. Many landowners went bankrupt or opted to bribe workers back with offers of cash wages. The second phase of Blanco's "reform" was physically to take over the *haciendas*, mostly in areas so isolated that the authorities were powerless to intervene. Blanco was finally arrested in 1963 but the effects of his peasant revolt outlived him: in future Peruvian governments were to take agrarian reform far more seriously.

Back in Lima, the elections of 1962 had resulted in an interesting deadlock, with Haya de la Torre getting 33 percent of the votes, Belaunde 32 percent, and Odria 28.5 percent. Almost inevitably, the army took control, annulled the elections, and denied Haya de la Torre and Belaunde the opportunity of power for another year. By 1963, though, neither *Accion Popular* or APRA were sufficiently radical to pose a serious threat to the establishment. Elected president for the first time, Belaunde quickly got to work on a severely diluted program of agrarian reform, a compromise never forgiven by his left-wing supporters. More successfully, though, he began to draw in quantities of foreign capital. President de Gaulle of France visited Peru in 1964 and the first British foreign secretary ever to set foot in South America arrived in Lima two years later. Foreign investors were clamoring to get in on Belaunde's ambitious development plans and obtain a rake-off from Peru's oil fields. But by 1965 domestic inflation had so severely damaged the balance of payments that confidence was beginning to slip away from Belaunde's international stance.

LAND REFORM AND THE MILITARY REGIME

By now, many intellectuals and government officials saw the agrarian situation as an urgent economic problem as well as a matter of social justice. Even the army believed that **land reform** was a prerequisite for the development of a larger market, without which any genuine industrial development would prove impossible. On October 3, 1968, tanks smashed through the gates into the courtyard of the Presidential Palace. General Velasco and the army seized power, deporting Belaunde and ensuring that Haya de la Torre could not even participate in the forthcoming elections.

The new government, revolutionary for a **military regime**, gave the land back to the workers in 1969. The great plantations were turned virtually overnight into producer's cooperatives, in an attempt to create a genuinely self-determining peasant class. At the same time guerrilla leaders were brought to trial, political activity was banned in the universities, indigenous banks were controlled, foreign banks nationalized, and diplomatic relations established with East European countries. By the end of military rule, in 1980, the land reform program had done much to abolish the large capitalist landholding system.

Even now, though, a shortage of good land in the sierra and the lack of decent irrigation on the coast mean that less than 20 percent of the landless workers have been integrated into the cooperative system—the majority remain in seasonal work and/or the small farm sector. One of the major problems for the military regime, and one which still plagues the economy, was the **fishing crisis** in the 1970s. An overestimation of the fishing potential led to the build up of a highly capital-intensive fish-canning and fish-meal industry, in its time one of the world's most modern. Unfortunately, the fish began to disappear because of a combination of ecological changes and overfishing—leaving vast quantities of capital equipment inactive and thousands of people unemployed.

Although undeniably an important step forward, the 1968 military coup was always an essentially bourgeois revolution, imposed from above to speed up the transformation from a land-based oligarchy to a capitalist society. Paternalistic, even dictatorial, it did little to satisfy the demands of the more extreme peasant reformers, and the military leaders eventually handed back power voluntarily in democratic elections.

CONTEMPORARY PERU

After twelve years of military government the 1980 elections resulted in a center-right alliance between *Accion Popular* and the Popular Christian Party. **Belaunde** resumed the presidency having become an established celebrity during his years of exile and having built up, too, an impressive array of international contacts. The policy of his government was to increase the pace of development still further, and in particular to emulate the Brazilian success in opening up the Amazon—building new roads and exploiting the untold wealth in oil, minerals, lumber, and agriculture. But inflation continued as an apparently insuperable problem, and Belaunde fared little better in coming to terms with either the parliamentary Marxists of the United Left or the escalating guerrilla movement led by *Sendero Luminoso*.

Sendero Luminoso (the Shining Path), founded in 1970, have persistently discounted the possibility of change through the ballot box. In 1976 they adopted armed struggle as the only means to achieve their "anti-feudal, anti-imperial" revolution in Peru. Following the line of the Chinese Gang of Four, *Sendero* is led by Abimael Guzman (aka **Comrade Gonzalo**) whose ideas they claim to be in the direct lineage of Marx, Lenin, and Chairman Mao. Originally a brilliant philosophy lecturer from Ayacucho (specializing in the Kantian theory of space), Gonzalo now lives underground, rarely seen even by *Senderistas* themselves.

Sendero remains very active, however, and is thought to have some 10,000 secret members. They reject Belaunde's style of technological development as imperialist and the United Left as "parliamentary cretins." They have carried out attacks on business interests, local officials, police posts, and anything regarded as outside interference with the self-determination of the peasantry. On the whole members are recruited from the poorest areas of the country and from the Quechua-speaking population, coming together only for their paramilitary operations and melting back afterwards into the obscurity of their communities.

Although strategic points in Lima have been attacked—police stations, petrochemical plants, and power lines—*Sendero*'s main center of activity is in the sierra around **Ayacucho** and **Huanta**, more recently spreading into the remote regions around **Vilcabamba**: site of the last Inca resistance, a traditional hide-out for rebels, and the center of Hugo Blanco's activities in the 1960s. By remaining small and unpredictable, *Sendero* has managed to wage its war on the Peruvian establishment with the minimum of risk of major confrontations with government forces.

Belaunde's response was to tie up enormous amounts of manpower in counterinsurgency operations whose main effect seemed to be to increase popular sympathy for the guerrillas. In 1984 more than 6000 troops, marines, and antiterrorist police were deployed against *Sendero*, and at least 3000 people, mostly peasants, are said to have been killed. "Disappearances," especially around Ayacucho, are still an everyday occurrence, and most people blame the security forces for the bulk of them.

In August 1984 even the chief of command of the counterinsurgency forces joined the criticism of the government's failure to provide promised development aid to Ayacucho. He was promptly dismissed for his claims that the problems were "the harvest of 160 years of neglect" and that the solution was "not a military one."

THE SITUATION WORSENS

By 1985, new urban-based terrorist groups like the *Movimiento Revolutionario Tupac Amaru* (**MRTA**) had begun to make their presence felt in the shanty towns around Lima. Belaunde lost office in the April **1985 elections**, with APRA taking power for the first time and the United Left also getting a large percentage of the votes.

Led by a young, highly popular new president, **Alan Garcia**, the APRA government took office riding a massive wave of hope. *Sendero Luminoso*, however, has stepped up its tactics of antidemocratic terrorism at the Andean grass roots, and the isolation of Lima and the coast from much of the sierra and jungle regions has become a very real threat. With *Sendero* proclaiming their revolution by "teaching" and terrorizing peasant communities on the one hand, and the military evidently liquidating the inhabitants of villages suspected of "collaboration" on the other, the 1980s have been a sad and bloody time for a large number of Peruvians.

Sendero's usual tactics are for an armed group to arrive at a peasant community and call a meeting. During the meeting it is not uncommon for them to publicly execute an "appropriate" local official—like a Ministry of Agriculture official or, in some cases, foreign aid workers—as a statement of persuasive terror. In May 1989 a British traveler found himself caught in the middle of this conflict and was executed (shot in the head) after a mock trial by *Senderistas* in the plaza of Olleros, a community near Huaraz in Ancash, which had offered him a bed for the night in its municipal building. Before leaving a village, *Sendero* always selects and leaves "intelligence officers," to liaise with the terrorists, and "production officers," to ensure that there is no trade between the village and the outside world—particularly with Lima and the international market economy.

Most of *Sendero*'s funding these days comes from the **cocaine trade**. Vast quantities of coca leaves are grown and partially processed all along the margins of the Peruvian jungle. Much of this is flown clandestinely into Colombia where the processing is completed and the finished product exported to North America and Europe for consumption. The thousands of peasants who have come down from the Andes to make a new life in the tropical forest over the last ten years have found that coca is by far the most lucrative cash crop. The cocaine barons pay peasants more than they could earn elsewhere and at the same time buy protection from *Sendero* (some say at a rate of up to $10,000 per clandestine plane load).

So much of the jungle has been destroyed to make way for coca production that that the **environmental** aspects of the situation have become at least as critical as the associated law-and-order problems. To make matters worse, the United States government is working hard to persuade the Peruvian authorities to spray herbicides over the coca growing valleys from helicopters. It might work, but at disastrous cost to human populations and local flora and fauna. Much of Peru's nonmilitary U.S. aid depends ultimately on their performance in the war on cocaine. Such a war is not only expensive but it is also unlikely to succeed in dissuading the many thousands of coca-growing peasants and the drug syndicates that they should give up what is undoubtedly Peru's most lucrative earner. The fact that the drug network is better funded, better equipped, and geographically better protected than the Peruvian authorities also serves to discourage any major anti-cocaine initiative.

The **1980s**, then, have seen the growth of two major attacks on the political and moral backbone of the nation—one through terrorism, the other through cocaine. With these two forces working hand in hand the problems facing Garcia have proved insurmountable. To make things worse, a right-wing death squad—the **Rodrigo Franco Commando**—appeared on the scene in 1988, evidently made up of disaffected police officers, army personnel, and even one or two *Apristas*. Their most prominent victim so far has been Saul Cantoral, General Secretary of the Mineworkers' Federation. RFC has also been sending death threats to a wide range of left-wing militants, union leaders, women's group coordinators, and even the press.

The appointment of **Agustin Mantilla** as Minister of the Interior in May 1989 suggests that there is knowledge and approval of RFC at the very highest level. Mantilla has been widely condemned as the man behind the emergence of the death squads and their supply of arms. He is known to want to take back by force large areas of the central Andes simply by supplying anti-*Senderista* peasants with machine guns. Opposition to the arming of the peasantry is one topic on which the military and human rights organizations seem to agree. Many of the arms would probably go straight to *Sendero*, and such action could easily set in motion a spiral of bloody civil war beyond anyone's control.

Sendero's power, and even its popular appeal, seem still to be advancing as the 80s come to a close. While they try to cut off Lima and the coast from the rest of Peru, the right wing are pushing for a war of extermination or a purge of the extreme left. In terms of territorial influence *Sendero* has spread its wings over most of central Peru. It has made persistent attacks in Puno to the very south—destroying the *Instituto de Educacíon Rural* in Ayaveri, for example, an organization popular for its support work with local peasants—and appears to have begun attacking tourists and tourist facilities around Huaraz to the northwest of Lima. In the Alto Huallaga region *Sendero* has built up mass support by giving local coca growers protection from the police, the army and, to a certain extent, from the drug mafias. In areas like Huanuco and San Martin, *Sendero* is now the effective government, administering justice, raising taxes, and possessing the firepower to maintain control.

The **MRTA** have had less success, having lost several of their leaders to Lima's prison cells. Their military confidence and capacity were also devastated when a contingent of some 62 MRTA militants was caught in an army ambush in April 1988; only eight survived from among two truckloads.

THE 1990s

Presidential elections are next due in March 1990. Perhaps the most bizarre development in Peruvian politics as they approach was the attempt of the internationally renowned author, **Mario Vargas Llosa**, in his mid-fifties, to build the foundations of a right-wing coalition. Though he enjoyed the backing of the main TV companies, his biggest problem was convincing the majority of people that the overblown state infrastructure (which he wants to dismantle) is in fact their problem. Most people are aware only of day-to-day issues like the price of bread and fuel, outrageous inflation, enormous foreign debts, foreign control of the economy, terrorism, underdevelopment, and overcentralization. As leader, at least in name, of the *Fredemo* coalition of the two traditional right wing parties (*Acción Popular* and *Partido Popular Cristiano*), Vargas Llosa faced major problems: firstly trying to win over party members upset at the loss of their individual party idenities, and more fundamentally having to convince many of them of the value of his "Reaganite" policies. Few industrialists relish the idea of losing the subsidies which currently keep them afloat, or a reduction of the tariffs which keep Peruvian firms just able to compete in the international market.

In typically flamboyant style, Vargas Llosa bowed out of the electoral challenge on June 21, 1989, accusing his fellow leaders within *Fredemo* of making it impossible for him to carry on as a candidate. Some suspect he will be back, but for the moment this has opened the possibility of Belaunde achieving his goal of being the first Peruvian to be President three times this century.

All this aside, the **United Left**, despite an untimely split, is much more likely to succeed Alan Garcia than Llosa or even Belaunde. Garcia, unable to please any section of the electorate during the turbulent and violent years of his presidency, is given no chance. He lost face several times over his apparent lack of control of the army—failing to prevent attacks on peasant communities or the massacre of between 200 and 300 *Senderistas* in Lima's prisons—and made himself equally unpopular with a different section of the electorate when he nationalized many of the banks early in his term of office and when he refused to repay the interest on foreign debts.

The important question which seems to remain before the election is whether the United Left can be reunited. The split first appeared in January 1989 at the UL Congress in Huampari, when a group known as *Acuerdo*

Socialista (Socialist Accord) walked out. They believe that the presence of the radical left would be unacceptable to the military, and that a United Left electoral victory as things stand would be an invitation for a coup. The far left on the other hand refuse to drop the notion of an armed struggle. *Acuerdo Socialista*'s main strength lies in having **Alfonso Barrantes**— easily the most popular leader on the left—in their camp. Without him, the United Left are unlikely to win, which gives *Acuerdo Socialista* a strong hand in internal disputes.

CHRONOLOGY

20,000–10,000 B.C.	First evidence of **human settlement** in Peru.	Cave dwellings in the **Ayacucho Valley**; stone artifacts in the **Chillon Valley**.
8000–5000 BC	**Nomadic tribes**, and more permanent settlement in fertile coastal areas.	Cave Paintings and fine stone tools.
5000-2000 B.C.	Introduction of **cultivation** and stable settlements.	Early agricultural sites include **Huaca Prieta** in the Chicama Valley, Paracas, and Kotosh.
1200 B.C.–200 A.D.	Formative Era and emergence of the **Chavin Cult**, with great progress in ceramics and metallurgy.	Temple complex at **Chavin de Huantar**, important sites too at **Kotosh** and **Sechin**.
300 A.D.	Technological advances marked above all in the Viru Valley—the **Gallinazo Culture**—and at Paracas.	Sites in the **Viru Valley**, at Paracas, and the growth of Tiahuanuco culture around **Lake Titicaca**.
200–1100 A.D.	**Classical Cultures** emergent throughout the land.	**Mochica** culture and Temples of the Sun and Moon near Trujillo; further **Tiahuanuco** development; **Nazca lines** and **Cahuachi** complex on the coast; **Wilkawain** temple; **Huari** complex; and **Tantamayo** ruins.
1200	The age of the great city builders.	Well-preserved adobe settlements survive at **Chan Chan** (near Trujillo) and **Cajamarquilla** (Lima).
1438–1532	Expansion of the **Inca Empire** from its base around Cuzco, north into Ecuador and south into Chile.	Inca sites survive throughout Peru, but the greatest are still around **Cuzco**—**Sacsayhuaman** and **Machu Picchu** above all. **Inca Highway** constructed from Colombia to Chile; parts still in existence.
1532	**Pizarro** lands at Tumbes, captures Atahualpa.	
1533	**Atahualpa executed**, Pizarro reaches Cuzco.	
1535	**Foundation of Lima.**	**Colonial architecture** draws heavily on Spanish influences, though native craftsmen also leave their mark. Church building above all—at **Arequipa** (Santa Catalina Convent) and around Cuzco. The Spanish city of **Cuzco** incorporates much Inca stonework. Meanwhile, the rebel Incas build new cities around **Vilcabamba**.
1536	**Manco Inca** rebels.	
1545	Silver deposits of **Potosi** discovered.	
1572	Spanish invade final Inca refuge at Vilcabamba; **Tupac Amaru executed**.	

1742	Juan Santos Atahualpa leads first **peasant revolt**.	Throughout colonial rule building follows European fashions, especially into **Baroque**: churches, mansions, and a few public buildings.
1780–81	**Rebellion** under Tupac Amaru II.	
1819	San Martin's forces land at Paracas.	
1821	Peru declares **Independence**.	
1823	**Simon Bolivar** arrives; Peru and Bolivia divided.	University of Trujillo founded by Bolivar.
1824	Final defeat of the Royalists at Junin and Ayacucho.	
1870s	Construction of the railways and other engineering projects. First exploitation of Amazonian rubber.	High-altitude **railways** are remarkable engineering feats.
1879–83	**War of the Pacific** bankrupts the country: Chilean troops occupy Lima.	
1890–1930	Peru effectively under control of foreign capital.	Much modernization in **Lima** (Presidential Palace etc.), grandiose public buildings elsewhere.
1932	Violent **APRA uprising** in Trujillo—APRA outlawed.	Massive **urban growth** in Lima from the 1930s onwards.
1945	APRA candidate **Bustamante** wins presidential election.	
1948	**Military coup**.	
1956	APRA-army alliance wins elections.	
1963	*Accion Popular* leader **Belaunde elected**.	**Barriadas**—organized shanty towns—begin to grow around Lima.
1968–80	**Military rule**—Belaunde exiled—extensive agrarian reform.	
1980	**Return to democracy**. Belaunde re-elected.	**Development of the jungle**—lumber trade, oil companies, and settlers threaten traditional tribal life and ecology; construction of "Marginal Highway" into central Amazon resumed.
1985	New presidential elections won by **Alan Garcia** for APRA. *Sendero Luminoso* and other terrorist groups increasingly disrupt national life.	

INCA LIFE AND ACHIEVEMENT

In less than a century, the Incas developed and knitted together a vast empire peopled by something like 20 million Indians. They established an imperial religion which didn't drastically clash with those of their subject tribes; erected monolithic fortresses, salubrious palaces, and temples; and, astonishingly, evolved a viable economy—strong enough to maintain a top-heavy elite in almost godlike grandeur. To understand these achievements and get some idea of what they must have meant in Peru 500 or 600 years ago, you really have to see for yourself their surviving heritage: the stones of Inca ruins and roads; the cultural objects in the museums of Lima and Cuzco; and their living descendants who still till the soil and speak Quechua—the language used by the Incas to unify their empire. What follows is but the briefest of introductions to their history, society and achievements.

INCA SOCIETY

The Inca Empire rapidly developed a **hierarchical structure**. At the highest level it was governed by the **Sapa Inca**, son of the sun and direct descendant of the god Viracocha. Under him were the priest-nobles—the royal **allyu** or kin-group which filled most of the important administrative and religious posts—and, working for them, regional *allyu* chiefs, **curacas** or *orejones*, responsible for controlling tribute from the peasant base. One-third of the land belonged to the emperor and the state; another to the high priests, gods, and the sun; the last was for the *allyu* themselves. Work on the land, then, was devoted to maintaining the Empire rather than mere subsistence, though in times of famine storehouses were evidently opened to feed the commoners.

Life for **the elite** wasn't, perhaps, quite as easy as it may appear; their fringe benefits were matched by the strain and worry of governing an empire, sending armies everywhere, and keeping the gods happy. The Inca nobles were nevertheless fond of relaxing in thermal baths, of hunting holidays, and of conspicuous eating and drinking whenever the religious calendar permitted. *Allyu* chiefs were often unrelated to the royal Inca lineage, but their position was normally hereditary. As lesser nobles (*curacas*) they were allowed to wear earplugs and special ornate headbands; their task was both to protect and exploit the commoners, and they themselves were free of labor service.

The hierarchical network swept down the ranks from important chiefs in a decimalized system. One of the *curacas* might be responsible for 10,000 men; under him two lower chiefs were each responsible for 5000, and so on until in the smallest hamlets there was one man responsible for ten others. Women weren't counted in the census. For the Incas, a household was represented by the man and only he was obliged to fulfil tribute duties on behalf of the *allyu*. Within the family the woman's role was dependent on her relationship with the dominant man—be he father, brother, husband, or eldest son.

In their conquests the Incas absorbed **craftsmen** from every corner of the empire. Goldsmiths, potters, carpenters, sculptors, masons, and *quipumayocs* (accountants) were frequently removed from their homes to work directly for the emperor in Cuzco. These skilled men lost no time in developing into a new and entirely separate class of citizens. The work of even the lowest servant in the palace was highly regulated by a rigid division of labor. If a man was employed to be a woodcutter he wouldn't be expected to gather wood from the forests; that was the task of another employee.

Throughout the empire young girls, usually about 9 or 10 years old, were constantly selected for their beauty and serene intelligence. Those deemed perfect enough were taken to an *acclahuasi*—a special sanctuary for the **"chosen women"**—where they were trained in specific tasks, including the spinning and weaving of fine cloth, and the higher culinary arts. Most chosen women were destined ultimately to become *mamaconas* (Virgins of the Sun) or the concubines of either nobles or the Sapa Inca himself. Occasionally some of them were sacrificed by strangulation in order to appease the gods.

For most Inca **women** the allotted role was simply that of peasant/domestic work and rearing children. After giving birth a mother would wash her baby in a nearby stream to cleanse and purify it and return virtually immediately to normal daily activities, carrying the child in a cradle tied on her back with a shawl. As they still are today, most babies were breast-fed for years before leaving their mothers to take the place in the domestic life-cycle. As adults their particular role in society was dependent first on sex, then on hierarchical status.

Special regulations affected both the **old** and **disabled**. Around the age of 50, a man was likely to pass into the category of "old." He was no longer capable of undertaking a normal workload, he wasn't expected to pay taxes, and he could always depend on support from the official storehouses. Nevertheless, the community still made small demands by using him to collect firewood and other such tasks; in the much the same way the kids were expected to help out around the house and in the fields. In fact children and old people often worked together, the young learning directly from the old. Disabled people were obliged to work within their potential—the blind, for instance, might de-husk maize or clean cotton. Although they were always maintained fairly from official stocks, Inca law bound the deformed or disabled to marry people with similar disadvantages: dwarfs to dwarfs, blind to blind, legless to legless.

The **Inca diet** was essentially vegetarian, based on the staple potato but encompassing a range of other foods like quinoa, beans, squash, sweet potatoes, avocados, tomatoes, and manioc. In the highlands emphasis was on root crops like potatoes which have been known to survive down to 5°F at over 5000m. On the valley floors and lower slopes of the Andes maize cultivation predominated.

The importance of **maize** both as a food crop and for making chicha increased dramatically under the Incas; previously it had been grown for ceremony and ritual exchange, as a status crop rather than a staple. The use of **coca** was restricted to the priests amd Inca elite. Coca is a mild narcotic stimulant which effectively dulls the body against cold, hunger, and tiredness when the leaves are chewed in the mouth with a catalyst such as lime or calcium. Its leaves possessed magical proper-

ties for the Incas; they could be cast to divine future events, offered as a gift to the wind, the earth, or the mountain apu, and they could be used in witchcraft. Today it's difficult to imagine the Incas having great success in restricting coca-growing and use; even with helicopters and machine guns the present-day authorities are unable to control its production. But the original Inca system of control was frighteningly effective.

EXPANSION AND CONTROL

In Inca eyes the known world was their empire and **expansion** therefore limitless. They divided their territories into four basic regions, or **suyos**, each radiating from the central plaza in Cuzco: Chincha Suyo (northwest), Anit Suyo (northeast), Cunti Suyo (southwest) and Colla Suyo (southeast). Each suyo naturally had its own particular problems and characteristics but all were approached in the same way—initially being demoralized or forced into submission by the Inca army, later absorbed as allies for further conquests. In this way the Incas never seemed to overextend their lines to the fighting front.

The most impressive feature of an **Inca army** must in fact have been its sheer numbers—a relatively minor force would have included 5000 men. Their armor usually consisted of quilted cotton shirts and a small shield painted with designs or decorated with magnificent plumes. The common warriors—using slingshots, spears, axes, and maces—were often supported by archers drafted from the "savages" living in the eastern forests. When the Spanish arrived on horseback the Incas were quick to invent new weapons: large two-handed hardwood swords and bolas (wooden balls connected by a string) good for tangling up the horses' legs. The only prisoners of war traditionally taken by a conquering Inca army were chieftains, who lived comfortably in Cuzco as hostages against the good behavior of their respective tribes. Along with the chiefs, the most important portable idols and huacas of conquered peoples were held in Cuzco as sacred hostages. Often the children of the ruling chieftains were also taken to Cuzco to be indoctrinated in Inca ways.

This very pragmatic approach toward their subjects is exemplified again in the Inca policy of **forced resettlement**. Whole villages were sometimes sent into entirely new regions, ostensibly to increase the crop yield of plants like coca or corn and to vary their diet by importing manioc and chilis—though it was often criminals and rebellious citizens who ended up in the hottest, most humid regions. Large groups of people might also be sent from relatively suspect tribes into areas where mostly loyal subjects lived, or into the newly colonized outer fringes of the empire; many trustworthy subjects were also moved into zones where restlessness might have been expected. It seems likely that the whole colonization project was as much a political maneuver as a device to diversify the Inca economic or dietary base. As new regions came under imperial influence, the threat from rebellious elements was minimized by their geographical dispersion.

ECONOMY, AGRICULTURE, AND BUILDING

The main **resources** available to the Inca Empire were agricultural land and labor, mines (producing precious and prestigious metals such as gold, silver, or copper), and fresh water, abundant everywhere except along the desert coast. With careful manipulation of these resources, the Incas managed to keep things moving the way they wanted. Tribute in the form of **service** (*mita*) played a crucial role in maintaining the empire and pressurising its subjects into ambitious building and irrigation projects. Some of these projects were so grand that they would have been impossible without the demanding whip of a totalitarian state.

Although a certain degree of local barter was allowed, the state regulated the distribution of every important product. The astonishing Inca **highways** were one of the chief keys to this economic success. Some of the tracks were nearly 8km wide and at the time of the Spanish Conquest the main Royal Highway ran some 5000km, from the Ancasmayo River in Colombia down the backbone of the Andes to the coast at a point south of the present-day Santiago in Chile. The Incas never used the wheel, but gigantic llama caravans were a common sight tramping along the roads, each animal carrying up to fifty kilos of cargo.

Every corner of the Inca domain was easily accessible via branch roads, all designed or taken over and unified with one intention—to dominate and administer an enormous empire. **Runners** were posted at *chasqui* stations and *tambo* rest-houses which punctuated the road at intervals of between 2 and 15km. Fresh fish was relayed on foot from the coast and messages were sent with runners from Quito to Cuzco (2000km) in less than six days. The more difficult mountain canyons were crossed on bridges suspended from cables braided out of jungle *lianas* (creeping vines) and high passes were—and still are—frequently reached by incredible stairways cut into solid rock cliffs.

The primary sector in the economy was inevitably **agriculture** and in this the Incas made two major advances: large terracing projects created the opportunity for agricultural specialists to experiment with new crops and methods of cultivation, and the transportation system allowed a revolution in distribution. Massive agricultural **terracing projects** were going on continuously in Inca-dominated mountain regions. The best examples of these are in the Cuzco area at Tipón, Moray, Ollantaytambo, Pisac, and Cusichaca. Beyond the aesthetic beauty of Inca stone terraces, they have distinct practical advantages. Stepping hillsides minimizes erosion from landslides, and by using well-engineered stone channels gives complete control over irrigation. Natural springs emerging on the hillsides became the focus of an intricate network of canals and aqueducts extending over the surrounding slopes which had themselves been converted into elegant stone terraces. An extra incentive to the Inca mind must surely have been their reverence of water, one of the major earthly spirits. The Inca terraces are often so elaborately designed around springs that they seem to be worshiping as much as utilizing water.

Today, however, it is Inca construction which forms their lasting heritage; vast **building projects** masterminded by high-ranking nobles and architects, and supervised by expert masons with an almost limitless pool of peasant labor. Without paper, the architects resorted to imposing their imagination onto clay or stone, making miniature models of the more important constructions—good examples of these can be seen in the Cuzco Archeological Museum. More importantly, Inca masonry survives throughout Peru, most spectacularly at the fortress of Sascayhuaman above Cuzco, and on the coast in the Achirana aqueduct, which even today still brings water down to the Ica valley from high up in the Andes. In the mountains, Inca stonework gave a permanence to edifices which would otherwise have needed constant renovation. The damp climate and mold quickly destroy anything but solid rock; Spanish and modern buildings have often collapsed around well-built Inca walls.

ARTS AND CRAFTS

Surprisingly, perhaps, Inca masonry was very rarely carved or adorned in any way. Smaller stone items, however, were frequently elaborate and beautiful. High technical standards were achieved, too, in **pottery**. Around Cuzco especially the art of creating and glazing ceramics was highly developed. They were not so advanced artistically, however; Inca designs generally lack imagination and variety, tending to have been mass-produced from models evolved by previous cultures. The most common pottery object was the *aryballus*, a large jar with a conical base and a wide neck thought to have been used chiefly for storing *chicha*. Its decoration was usually geometric, often associated with the backbone of a fish; the central spine of the pattern was adorned with rows of spikes radiating from either side. Fine plates were made with anthropomorphic-shaped handles, and large numbers of cylindrically tapering goblets—*keros*—were manufactured, though these were often of cedar wood rather than pottery.

The refinements in **metallurgy**, like the ceramics industry, were mostly developed by craftsmen absorbed from different corners of the Empire. The Chimu were particularly respected by the Incas for their superb metalwork. Within the empire, bronze and copper were used for axe-blades and *tumi* knives; gold and silver were restricted to ritual use and for nobles. The Incas smelted their metal ores in cylindrical terra-cotta and adobe furnaces which made good use of prevailing breezes to fire large lumps of charcoal. Molten ores were pulled out from the base of the furnace. Although the majority of surviving metal artifacts—those you see in museums—have been made from beaten sheets, there were plenty of cast or cut solid gold and silver pieces too.

Most of these were melted down by the Conquistadors, who weren't especially interested in precious objects for their artistic merit.

RELIGION

The Inca **religion** was easily capable of incorporating the religious features of most subjugated regions. The setting for beliefs, idols, and oracles, more or less throughout the entire empire, had been preordained over the previous 2000 years: a general recognition of certain creator deities and a whole pantheon of nature-related spirits, minor deities, and demons. The customary form of worship varied a little according to the locality, but everywhere they went the Incas (and later the Spanish) found the creator god among other animistic spirits and concepts of power related to lightning, thunder, and rainbows. The Incas merely superimposed their variety of mystical, yet inherently practical, elements onto those that they came across.

The main religious novelty introduced with Inca domination was their demand to be recognized as direct descendants of the creator-god **Viracocha**. A claim to divine ancestry was, to the Incas, a valid excuse for military and cultural expansion. There was no need to destroy the *huacas* and oracles of subjugated peoples; on the contrary, certain sacred sites were recognized as intrinsically holy, as powerful places for communication with the spirit world. When ancient shrines like Pachacamac, near Lima, were absorbed into the empire they were simply turned over to worship on imperial terms.

The sun is the most obvious symbol of Inca belief, a chief deity and the visible head of the state religion; Viracocha was a less direct, more ethereal, force. The sun's role was overt, as life-giver to an agriculturally based empire, and its cycle was intricately related to agrarian practice and annual ritual patterns. To think of the Inca religion as essentially sun worship though would be far too simplistic. There were distinct layers in **Inca cosmology**: the level of creation, the astral level, and the earthly dimension.

The first, highest level corresponds to Viracocha as the creator-god who brought life to the world and society to mankind. Below this, on the astral level, are the celestial gods—the sun itself, the moon and certain stars (particularly the Pleiades, patrons of fertility). The earthly dimension, although that of man, was no less magical, endowed with important *huacas* and shrines which might take the form of unusual rocks or peaks, caves, tombs, mummies, and natural springs.

The astral level and earthly dimension were widespread bases of worship in Peru before the Incas rose to power. The creator and whomever he favored was the critical factor in their claims to divine right of imperial government, and the hierarchical structure of religious ranking also reflects the division of the religious spheres into those that were around before, during, and after the empire and those that only stayed as long as Inca domination lasted. At the very top of this **religio-social hierarchy** was the *Villac Uma*, the high priest of Cuzco, usually a brother of the Sapa Inca himself. Under him were perhaps hundreds of high priests, all nobles of royal blood who were responsible for ceremony, temples, shrines, divination, curing, and sacrifice within the realm, and below them were the ordinary priests and chosen women. At the base of the hierarchy, and probably the most numerous of all religious personalities, were the **curanderos**, local curers practicing herbal medicine and magic, and making sacrifices to small regional *huacas*.

Most **religious festivals** were calendrically based and marked by processions, sacrifices, and dances. The Incas were aware of lunar time and the solar year, although they generally used the blooming of a special cactus to gauge the correct time to begin planting. Sacrifices to the gods normally consisted of llamas, cuys, or chicha—only occasionally were chosen women and other adults killed. Once every year, however, young children were apparently sacrificed in the most important sacred centers.

Divination was a vital role played by priests and *curanderos* at all levels of the religious hierarchy. Soothsayers were expected to talk with the spirits and often utilized a hallucinogenic snuff from the vilca plant to achieve a trance-like state and communion with the other world. Everything from a crackling fire to the glance of a lizard was seen as a potential omen, and treated as such by making a little offering of coca leaves, coca spittle, or chicha. There were specific problems which divination was considered particularly accurate in solving: retrieving lost things; predicting the outcome of certain events (the oracles were always consulted prior to important military escapades); receiving a vision of contemporaneous yet distant happenings; and the diagnosis of illness.

Mochica ray motif

ANCIENT WIZARDS IN MODERN PERU

Bearing in mind the country's poverty and the fact that almost half the population is still pure Amerindian, it isn't altogether suprising to discover that the ancient shamanic healing arts are still flourishing in Peru. Evidence for this type of magical health therapy stretches back over 3000 years on the Peruvian coast. Today, "*curanderos*" (Spanish for "curers"), can be found in every large community, practicing healing based on knowledge which has been passed down from master to apprentice over millennia.

Curanderos offer an alternative to the expensive, sporadic, and often unreliable service provided by scientific medics in a developing country like Peru. But as well as being a cheaper, more widely available option, *curanderismo* is also closer to the hearts and understanding of the average Peruvian. Even ex-President Belaunde's family use the services of a healing wizard.

With the resurgence of herbalism, aromatherapy, exotic healing massages, and other aspects of New Age "holistic" health, it should be easier for us in the West to understand *curanderismo* than it might have been a decade or so ago. Combine "holistic" health with psycho-therapy, and add an underlying cultural vision of spiritual and magical influences, and you are some way toward getting a clearer picture of how healing wizards operate.

There are two other important characteristics of modern-day Peruvian *curanderismo*. Firstly, the last 400 years of Spanish domination have added a veneer of Catholic imagery and nomenclature. Demons have become saints, ancient mountain spirits and their associated annual festivals continue disguised as Christian ceremonies. Equally important for any real understanding of Peruvian shamanism is the fact that most, if not all, *curanderos* utilize hallucinogens among their power plants. The tribal peoples in the Peruvian Amazon who

have managed, to a large extent, to hang on to their culture in the face of the oncoming industrial civilization, have also maintained their spiritual traditions. In almost every Peruvian tribe these traditions include the regular use of hallucinogenic brews to give a visionary ecstatic experience. Sometimes just the shaman partakes, but more often the shaman and his patients, or entire communities, will trip together, singing traditional spirit-songs which help control the visions. The hallucinogenic experience, like the world of dreams, is the Peruvian forest Indian's way of getting in touch with the **ancestral world** or the world of spirit matter.

THE ORIGINS OF SHAMANISM

The history of healing wizards in Peru matches that of the ritual use of hallucinogens and appears to have emerged alongside the first major temple-building culture—**Chavin** (1200 B.C.–A.D. 200). Agriculture, ceramics, and other technical processes including some metallurgy had already been developed by 1200 B.C., but Chavin demonstrates the first unified and widespread cultural movement in terms of sacred architectural style, and the forms and symbolic imagery used in pottery throughout much of Andean and coastal Peru during this era. Chavin was a religious cult which seems to have spread from the central mountains, quite possibly from the large temple complex at Chavin de Huantar near Huaraz. Taking hold along the coast, the central Chavin deity was woven, molded, and carved onto the finest funerary cloths, ceramics, and stones. Generally represented as a complex and demonic looking feline deity, the Chavin god always has fangs and a stern face. Many of the idols also show serpents radiating from the deity's head.

As far as the central temple at Chavin de Huantar is concerned, it was almost certainly a center of sacred pilgrimage which was built up over a period of centuries into a large ceremonial complex used at appropriate calendrical intervals to focus the spiritual, political, and economic energies of a vast area (at least large enough to include a range of produce for local consumption from tropical forest, high Andean, and desert coast regions). The magnificent stone temple kept growing in size until, by around 300 B.C., it would have been one of the largest religious centers anywhere in the world, with some 3000 local attendants. Among the fascinating finds at Chavin there have been bone snuff-tubes, beads, pendants, needles, ceremonial spondylus shells (imported from Ecuador), and some **quartz crystals** associated with ritual sites. One quartz crystal, covered in red pigment, was found in a grave, placed after death in the mouth of the deceased. Contemporary anthropological evidence shows us that quartz crystals still play an important role in shamanic ceremonies in Peru, the Americas, Australia, and Asia. The well documented Desana Indians of Colombia still see crystals as a "means of communication between the visible and invisible worlds, a crystalization of solar energy, or the Sun Father's semen which can be used in esoteric undertakings."

In one stone relief on the main temple at Chavin the feline deity is depicted holding a large **San Pedro cactus** in his hand. A Chavin ceramic bottle has been discovered with a San Pedro cactus "growing" on it; and, on another pot, a feline sits surrounded by several San Pedros. Similar motifs and designs appear on the later Paracas and Mochica craft work, but there is no real evidence for the ritual use of hallucinogens prior to Chavin. One impressive ceramic from the Mochica culture (A.D. 500) depicts an owl-woman—still symbolic of the female shaman in contemporary Peru—with a slice of San Pedro cactus in her hand. Another ceramic from the later Chimu culture (around A.D. 1100) shows a woman healer holding a San Pedro.

As well as coca, their "divine plant," the **Incas** had their own special hallucinogen: *vilca* (meaning "sacred" in Quechua). The vilca tree (probably *Anadenanthera colubrina*) grows in the cloud-forest zones on the eastern slopes of the Peruvian Andes. The Incas utilized a snuff made from the seeds which was generally blown up the nostrils of the participant by a helper. Evidently the Inca priests used *vilca* to bring on visions and make contact with the gods and spirit world.

SHAMANISM TODAY

Still commonly used by *curanderos* on the coast and in the mountains of Peru, the San Pedro cactus (*Trichocereus panchanoi*) is a potent hallucinogen based on active mescaline. The *curandero* administers the hallucinogenic brew to his or her clients to bring about a period of revelation when questions are asked of the intoxicated person, who might also be asked to choose some object from among a range of magical curios which all have different meanings to the healer. Sometimes a *curandero* might imbibe San Pedro (or one of the many other indigenous hallucinogens) to see into the future, retrieve lost souls, divine cause of illness, or discover the whereabouts of lost objects.

On **the coast**, healing wizards usually live near the sea on the fringes of a settlement. Most have their own San Pedro plant which is said to protect or guard their homes against unwanted intruders by letting out a high-pitched whistle if somebody approaches. The most famous *curandero* of all lives just outside Trujillo on the north coast of Peru. Eduardo Calderon—better known in Peru as **El Tuno**—is a shaman and a healer. An impressive looking man, large but not tall, El Tuno is obviously fit and very agile. His bright beaming eyes give his patients immediate confidence, and his powerful reputation goes before him. His daily work consists of treating sick and worried people who come to him from hundreds of miles around. His job is to create harmony where tensions, fears, jealousies, and sickness exist. Essentially a combination of herbalism, magical divination and a kind of psychic shock therapy involving the use of San Pedro, his shamanic craft has been handed down by word of mouth through endless generations of men and women. El Tuno's knowledge makes him a specialist in healing through inner visions, contact with the "spirit world." He is a master of the unconscious realms and regularly enters non-ordinary reality to combat the evil influences which he visualizes or *sees* as making his patients sick.

Describing the effects of San Pedro, El Tuno said that at first there is "a slight dizziness that one hardly notices. And then a great 'vision,' a clearing of all the faculties of the individual. It produces a light numbness in the body and afterward a tranquility. And then comes a detachment, a type of visual force in the individual inclusive of all the senses, including the sixth sense, the telepathic sense of transmitting oneself across time and matter ... It develops the power of perception ... in the sense that when one wants to see something far away ... he can distinguish powers or problems at great distance." (Quoted in *Wizard of the Four Winds* by Douglas Sharon, The Free Press, 1978.)

El Tuno and many other coastal wizards get their most potent magic and powerful plants from a small zone in the northern Andes. The mountain area around Las Huaringas and **Huancabamba**, to the north of Chiclayo and east of Piura, is where a large number of the "great masters" are believed to live and work. But it is in the **Amazon basin** of Peru that shamanism continues in its least changed form.

Even on the edges of most jungle towns there are *curanderos* healing local people by using a mixture of jungle Indian shamanism and the more Catholicized coastal form. These wizards generally use the most common tropical forest hallucinogen, **ayahuasca** (from the liana *Banisteriopsis caapi*). Away from the towns, among the more remote tribal people, *ayahuasca* is the key to understanding the native consciousness and perception of the world—which for them is the natural world of the elements and the forest plus their own social, economic, and political setup within that dominant environment. It has been argued by some anthropologists, notably Reichmal Dolmatoff from his work among the Desana Indians of the Colombian rainforest (who also use *ayahuasca*), that the shaman controls his community's ecological balance through his use of mythological tales, ceremony, rituals, and a long-established code of avoiding killing and eating certain creatures over complex temporal cycles. Dolmatoff appears to be suggesting that the Desana culture's ritual food taboo cycles are, in fact, a valid system or blueprint for the survival of the tribe and their natural eco-niche—a system worked out and regulated over millennia by the shaman, who listens to the spirits of nature through visions and inner voices.

The Shipibo tribe from the central Peruvian Amazon are famous for their excellent ceramic and weaving designs; extremely complex geometric patterns usually in black on white or beige, though sometimes utilizing reds or yellows too. It's not generally known, however, that these designs were traditionally given to a shaman (male or female) by the spirits while they were under the influence of *ayahuasca*. The shaman imbibes the hallucinogen, whose effect is described as "the spirits coming down." The spirits teach the shaman songs which he sings. The vibration of the songs, better described as chants, helps determine the shaman's visions. The geometric designs used on pots and textiles are his or her material manifestation of the vision. The vision and its material manifestations are in turn highly valued as healing agents in themselves. They make something look beautiful; beauty means health. Traditionally the Shipibo painted their houses and their bodies with geometric designs to maintain health, beauty, and harmony in their communities. Similarly, painting a sick person from head to toe in the designs given, say, by a hummingbird spirit, was seen as an important part of the healing process. If the visual patterns were also repeated as vibrations in the form of the original spirit song, then all the better.

Throughout the Peruvian Amazon **native shaman** are the only real specialists within indigenous tribal life. In terms of their roles within traditional society—as healers, masters of ritual and mythology, interpreters of dreams, visions and omens, controllers of fish, game, and the weather—the forest Indian shaman commands respect from his group. But it is precisely his group and the nonmaterialist, nonaccumulative tendencies of their seminomadic lifestyles (which it is the shaman's role to promote and preserve) which keeps them on an economic par with their fellows. Consequently the tribes have retained their organic anarchy on a political and day-to-day level. The size of communities has generally remained low. There is no cultural impetus for the shaman to turn high priest or king, just as there is no cultural incentive to accumulate surplus material objects or surplus forest produce. The shaman in traditional tribal societies is often a major conservative force—preserving his or her culture and conserving the environment, particularly in the face of encroaching development and consumerism.

It is clearly hard to generalize with any accuracy across the spectrum of healing wizards still found in modern Peru, yet there are definite threads connecting them all. On a practical level even the most isolated jungle shaman may well have trading links with several coastal *curanderos*—there are many magical cures imported via a web of ongoing trans-Andean trading partners to be found on the *curanderos'* street market stalls in Lima, Trujillo, Arequipa, and Chimbote. It has been argued by some of the most eminent Peruvianists that the initial ideas and spark for the Chavin culture came up the Marañon Valley from the Amazon. If it did, then it could well have brought with it—some 3000 years ago—the first shamanic teachings to the rest of ancient Peru, possibly even the use of power

plants and other tropical forest hallucinogens, since these are so critical to understanding even modern day Peruvian Amazon Indian religion. One thing which can be said for sure about ancient healing wizards in modern Peru is that they still question the very foundations of our rational scientific perception of the world. With recent developments in understanding the human mind even the scientific establishment may soon find itself learning about the inner cosmos from some hitherto unknown Peruvian masters of *curanderismo*.

For further information on the shamanic way get in touch with:

The Foundation for Shamanic Studies, Box 670, Belden Station, Norwalk, CT 06852 (☎203/454-2825).

Vantage Tours, Box 5774, Greenville, SC 29606 (☎800/826-8268), organize tour groups to study traditional Peruvian medicine and *curanderismo*.

BOOKS

PERUVIAN WRITERS

Mario Vargas Llosa *Aunt Julia and the Scriptwriter* (Avon, $9.95), *The Time of the Hero* (Farrar, Strauss, Giroux, $9.95), and others. The best known and the most brilliant of contemporary Peruvian writers, Vargas Llosa is essentially a novelist but has also written many books and articles commenting broadly on Peruvian society, has run his own TV current affairs program in Lima, and even made a (rather average) feature film. *Aunt Julia*, the latest of his novels to be translated into English, is a fabulous book, a grand and comic novel spiralling out from the stories and exploits of a Bolivian scriptwriter who arrives in Lima to work on Peruvian radio soap-operas. In part too, it is autobiographical, full of insights into Miraflores society and goings on. Essential reading—and perfect for long Peruvian journeys.

Ciro Alegria *Broad and Alien is the World* (Dufour, $13.95). Another good book to travel with, this is a distinguished 1970s novel about life in the Peruvian highlands.

Manuel Scorza *Drums for Runcas* (Harper & Row, o/p). Radical novel dealing with the miners' struggle in the sierra. Like Llosa, Scorza writes in a style of magical surrealism. Highly recommended.

Julio Ramon Ribeyro Ribeyro is one of Peru's best short story writers. Not yet translated into English, his works are available in Spanish in Lima.

Jose Mario Arguedas *Deep Rivers* and *Yawar Fiesta* (University of Texas Press, $9.95/$8.95) Arguedas is an *indigenista*—writing for and about the native peoples.

Cesar Vallejo *Collected Poems of Cesar Vallejo* (Penguin, UK). Peru's one internationally renowned poet—and deservedly so—but not available in US edition. *Peru: The New Poetry* (Red Dust, $10.95) includes a fairly broad selection of other modern Peruvian poets.

INCA AND ANCIENT HISTORY

John Hemmings *The Conquest of the Incas* (Harcourt Brace, $12.95). The authoritative narrative tale of the Spanish Conquest, very readably brought to life from a mass of original sources.

Ed. Richard Keatinge *Peruvian Prehistory* (Cambridge University Press, $15.95). The very latest reputable book on the ancient civilizations of Peru—a collection of serious academic essays on various cultures and cultural concepts through the millenia prior to the Inca era.

Ed. J. Haas, S. Pozorski and T. Pozorski *The Origins and Development of the Andean State* (Cambridge University Press, $42.50). One of a series "New Directions in Archaeology", detailed and quite academic but nevertheless interesting.

William Prescott *The Conquest of Peru* (o/p). Hemmings's main predecessor—a nineteenth-century classic that remains a good read.

Johan Reinhard *Nazca Lines: A New Perspective on their Origin and Meaning* ($5.50) Original theories about the Lines and ancient mountains gods—available through the *South American Explorers' Club* in Lima or the U.S.

Evan Hadingham *Lines to the Mountain Gods* ($15.95) More interesting stuff on the Nazca Lines, including maps and illustrations—also available through the *South American Explorers' Club* in Peru or the U.S.

John Hyslop *The Inca Road System* ($45) Very detailed report—available from the *South American Explorers' Club* in Peru or the U.S.

J. Alden Mason *Ancient Civilisations of Peru* (Penguin, $7.95). Now somewhat out of date, but nevertheless a good summary of the country's history from the Stone Age through to the Inca Empire.

Ann Kendall *Everyday Life of the Incas* (Putnam, o/p). Accessible, very general description of Peru under Inca domination.

Victor Von Hagen *The Realm of the Incas* (New American Library, o/p). An easy introduction to the history/architecture of the Incas but now considerably outmoded.

Gene Savoy *Antisuyo: The Search For the Lost Cities of the Amazon* (International Community of Christ, $35). Exciting account of Savoy's important explorations, it combines the history of the Incas with Savoy's journeys.

Elizabeth Benson *The Mochica: A Culture of Peru* (Praeger, o/p). Brief sketch of the Mochica civilization through its vast and astonishingly realist ceramic heritage.

Garcilasco de la Vega *The Royal Commentaries of the Incas*, 2 vols. (Burt Franklin, $63). Most good libraries have a copy of this—the most readable and fascinating of contemporary sources, written shortly after the Conquest by a "Spaniard" of essentially Inca blood.

Hiram Bingham *Lost City of the Incas* (Atheneum, $4.95). The classic introduction to Machu Picchu—exploration accounts are interesting but many of his theories are to be taken with a pinch of salt. Widely available in Peru.

Geoffrey Hext Sutherland Bushnell *Peru* (Praeger, o/p). Surveys social and technological change from 2500 B.C. to 1500 A.D.—clear and well illustrated, but dated.

Clements Markham *Incas of Peru* (AMS Press, $28.75). A collection of essays based on fifty years of research by Markham—covers a fascinating variety of subjects, and includes an Inca love story from 1585. Markham also translated *Narratives of the Rites and Laws of the Yncas* (Burt Franklin, $25.50), four Spanish manuscripts dating from 1570 to 1620, giving a rare view of early texts on the Incas.

MODERN HISTORY AND SOCIETY

Luis Martin *The Kingdom of the Sun: A Short History of Peru* (Scribner, o/p). Best available general history, concentrating on the post-Conquest period and bringing events more or less up to the present.

Henry Dobyns and Paul Doughty *Peru: A Cultural History* (Oxford University Press; $9.95). Similar breadth to the above—though a heavier, much more comprehensive tome.

F. Bruce Lamb and Manuel Cordova-Rios *The Wizard of the Upper Amazon* (North Atlantic, $9.95). Masterful reconstruction of the true life story of Manuel Cordoba Rios—"Ino Moxo," the famous herbal healer from Iquitos. A fairly compelling read.

Harold Osborne *Indians of the Andes: Incas, Aymaras, and Quechas* (Gordon Press, $59.95) An interesting, well-traveled study.

Roger Stone *Dreams of Amazonia* (World Wildlife Fund, $6.95) On the future of the Amazon forest.

Peter Lloyd *The "Young Towns" of Lima* (Cambridge University Press, $42.50). Excellent account of the *barriadas* and urbanization in Peru. Quite academic.

Eduardo Calderon, Richard Cowan, Douglas Sharon and F. Kaye Sharon *Eduardo El Curandero: The Words of a Peruvian Healer* ($7.95). Peru's most famous shaman—El Tuno—in his own words. See also *Wizard of the Four Winds* by Douglas Sharon (The Free Press).

TRAVEL

Ronald Wright *Cut Stones and Crossroads: A Journey in the Two Worlds of Peru* (Penguin, $7.95). An enlightened travel book—and probably the best general writing on Peru over the last couple of decades.

Dervla Murphy *Eight Feet in the Andes* (Overlook Press, $9.95). Enjoyable enough account of a rather adventurous journey Dervla Murphy made across the Andes with her young daughter and a mule. Can't compare with her Indian books, though.

George Woodcock *Incas and Other Men* (Faber, 1959, o/p). Still a good introduction to Peru 40 years on—an enjoyable, light-hearted tour, mixing modern and ancient history and travel anecdotes.

Christopher Isherwood *The Condor and the Cows* (Methuen, 1949, o/p). Published in England and difficult to find now here or there, this is a diary of Isherwood's South American trip after the World War II, most of which took place in Peru (the Condor of the title is a symbol of the Andes). Like Theroux (see below) Isherwood eventually arrives in Buenos Aires, to meet Jorge Luis Borges.

Paul Theroux *The Old Patagonian Express* (Washington Square Press, $4.95). Theroux didn't much like Peru, nor Peruvians ("the only way to handle a Peruvian is to agree with his pessimism"), but for all the self-obsessed pique, and Evelyn-Waugh-like disgust for most of humanity, at his best—being sick in trains—he is highly entertaining.

Peter Matthiessen *At Play in the Fields of the Lord* (Random House, $6.95). Celebrated American novel that catches the energy and magic of the Peruvian selva.

SPECIFIC GUIDES

Hilary and George Bradt *Backpacking and Trekking in Peru and Bolivia* (Hunter Publishing Co., $11.95). Detailed and excellent coverage of some of Peru's most rewarding hikes— worth taking if you're remotely interested in the idea, and good anyway for background on wildlife and flora, etc.

Tanis and Martin Jordan *South American River Trips, II* (Bradt Enterprises). Useful practical sections on river trips in general, along with detailed accounts of a number of Peruvian possibilities some no longer entirely advisable. Third edition in preparation.

Peter Frost *Exploring Cuzco* (Bradt Enterprises). A very practical and stimulating site-by-site guide to the whole Cuzco area. Unreservedly recommended if you're spending more than a few days in the region.

Ed. John Brooks *The South American Handbook* (Trade and Travel Publications, 1989; $35). The original and most comprehensive guide to the South American continent— known as the "Bible."

Rob Rachowiecki *Peru: A Travel Survival Kit* (Lonely Planet; 1987). One of the very few complete travel guide books specializing on Peru—plenty of sketch maps and basic travel information.

South American Explorers' Club *PERU PACKET* Up-dated monthly, the SAEC prints this 7 page summary on everything from "how not to get robbed" to "politics and exchange rates."

Jim Bartle *Trails of the Cordillera Blanca and Huayhuash* (Bradt Enterprises). Excellent trail guide for what is probably the best walking country in Peru.

Charles Brod *Apus and Incas: A Cultural Walking and Trekking Guide to Cuzco* (Charles Brod, $9.95). An interesting selection of walks in the Cuzco area. Available locally.

David Mazel *Pure and Perpetual Snow: two climbs in the Andes* (1987). Climbing reports on Ausangate and Alpamayo peaks. Available locally or from the *South American Explorers' Club*.

Lynn Meisch *A Traveller's Guide to El Dorado and the Incan Empire* (Penguin, $14.95). Huge paperback full of fascinating detail—well worth reading before visiting Peru.

Most of these guides are available in Lima through the South American Explorers' Club (Av. Portugal 146), from specialist bookshops in the U.S. (in New York City try The Complete Traveller, 199 Madison Avenue, 10016, or Travellers Bookstore, 22 West 52nd Street, 10019), or by mail through Bradt Enterprises (95 Harvey Street, Cambridge, MA 02140).

WILDLIFE AND ECOLOGY

Peru may well have the most diverse array of wildlife of any country on earth; its varied ecological niches relate to an incredible range of climate and terrain. And although mankind has occupied the area for perhaps as long as 20,000 years, there has been less disturbance there until relatively recently, than in most other parts of our planet. For the sake of organization this piece follows the country's usual regional divisions—coastal desert, Andes mountains, and tropical jungle—though a more accurate picture would be that of a continuous intergradation, encompassing literally dozens of unique habitats. From desert the land climbs rapidly to the tundra of mountain peaks, then down again into tropical rainforest, phasing gradually through a whole series of environments in which many of the species detailed below overlap.

THE COAST

The **COASTAL DESERT** is characterized by an abundant sea life and by the contrasting scarcity of terrestrial plants and animals. The Humboldt Current runs virtually the length of Peru, bringing cold water up from the depths of the Pacific Ocean and causing any moisture to condense out over the sea, depriving the mainland coastal strip and lower western mountain slopes of rainfall. Along with this cold water,

large quantities of nutrients are carried up to the surface, helping to sustain a rich planktonic community able to support vast numbers of fish, preyed upon in their turn by a variety of coastal birds: **gulls**, **terns**, **pelicans**, **boobies**, **cormorants**, and wading birds are always present along the beaches. One beautiful specimen, the **Inca tern**, although usually well camouflaged as it sits high up on inaccessible sea cliffs, is nevertheless very common in the Lima area. The **Humboldt penguin**, with gray rather than black features, is a rarer sight—shyer than its more southerly cousins it is normally found in isolated rocky coves or on off-shore islands. Competing with the birds for fish are schools of **dolphins**, **sea lion** colonies, and the occasional coastal **otter**. Dolphins and sea lions are often spotted off even the most crowded of beaches or scavenging around the fishermen's jetty at CHORRILLOS, near Lima.

One of the most fascinating features of Peruvian bird life is the vast, high-density colonies: although the number of species is quite small, their total population is enormous. Many thousands of birds can be seen nesting on islands like the BALLESTAS off the **Paracas Peninsula** (see p.126) or simply covering the ocean with a flapping, diving carpet of energetic feathers. This huge bird population, and the **Guanay cormorant** in particular, is responsible for depositing mountains of *guano* (bird droppings), which form a traditional and potent source of natural fertilizer.

In contrast to the rich coastal waters **THE DESERT** lies stark and barren. Here you find only a few trees and shrubs; you need endless patient sitting to see wild animals other than birds. The most common animals are feral **goats**, once domesticated but now living wild, and **burros** (or donkeys) introduced by the Spanish. A more exciting sight is the attractively colored **coral snake**—shy but deadly and covered with a black-and-orange hooped skin. Most animals are more active after sunset; when out in the desert you can hear the eerily plaintive call of the *Huerequeque* (or **Peruvian thick-knee** bird), and the barking of the little **desert fox**—alarmingly similar to the sound of car tires screeching to a halt. By day there are several species of small birds, a favorite being the vermillion-headed **Peruvian fly-catcher**. Near water—rivers, estuaries, and lagoons—desert wildlife is at its most populous. In addition to residents such as **flamingos**, **herons**, and **egrets**, many migrant birds pause in these havens between October and March on their journeys south and then back north.

In order to understand the coastal desert you have to bear in mind the phenomenon of **EL NIÑO**, a periodic climatic shift caused by the displacement of the cold Humboldt Current by warmer equatorial waters; it last occurred in 1983. This causes the plankton and fish communities either to disperse to other locations or to collapse entirely. At such a period the shore rapidly becomes littered with carrion since many of the sea mammals and birds are unable to survive in the much tighter environment; scavenging condors and vultures, on the other hand, thrive, as does the desert where rain falls in deluges along the coast, with a consequent bloom of vegetation and rapid growth in animal populations. When the Humboldt Current returns, the desert dries up, its animal populations decline to normal sizes (another temporary feast for the scavengers), and at least ten years usually pass before the cycle is repeated. Generally considered a freak phenomenon, *El Niño* is probably better understood as an integral part of coastal ecology; without it the desert would be a far more barren and static environment, virtually incapable of supporting life.

THE MOUNTAINS

In the **PERUVIAN ANDES** there is an incredible variety of habitats. That this is a mountain area of true extremes is immediately obvious if you fly across, or along, the Andes towards Lima—the land below shifting from high puna to elfin wood, cloud forest to riparian valleys and eucalyptus woods (introduced from Australia in the 1880s). The complexity of the whole makes it incredibly difficult to formulate any overall description that isn't essentially misleading: climate and vegetation vary according to altitude, latitude, and local characteristics. Generally, though, the vegetation is sparse and the climate extreme, allowing relatively few species to adapt to life here permanently.

Much of the Andes has been settled for over 2000 years—and hunter tribes go back another 8000 years before this—so the larger predators are rare, though still present in small numbers in the more remote regions. Among the most exciting you might actually see are the **mountain cats**, especially the **puma**, which lives at most altitudes and in a surprising number of habitats. Other more remote predators include the shaggy-looking **maned wolf** and the likable **spectacled bear**, which inhabits the moister forested areas of the Andes and actually prefers eating vegetation to people.

The most visible animals in the mountains, besides the sheep and cattle, are the *cameloids*—the wild **vicuña** and **guanaco**, and the domesticated **llama** and **alpaca**. Although these species are clearly related, zoologists disagree on whether or not the alpaca and llama are domesticated forms of their wild relatives. Of the two wild cameloids, the vicuña is the smaller and rarer—living only at the highest altitudes (up to 4500m). **Andean deer** are quite common in the higher valley and with luck you might even come across the rare **mountain tapir**. Smaller animals tend to be confined to particular habitats—rabbit-like **viscachas**, for example, to rocky outcrops; **squirrels** to wooded valleys; and **chinchillas** (Peruvian chipmunks) to higher altitudes.

Most birds also tend to restrict themselves to specific habitats. The **Andean goose** and **duck** are quite common in marshy areas, along with many species of waders and migratory waterfowl. A particular favorite is the elegant, very pink, **Andean flamingo**, which can usually be spotted from the road between Arequipa and Puno where they turn Lake Salinas into one great red mass. In addition, many species of *passarines* can be found alongside small streams. Perhaps the most striking of them is the **dipper**, which hunts underwater for larval insects along the stream bed, popping up to a rock every so often for air and a rest. At lower elevations, especially in and around cultivated areas, the **ovenbird** (or *Horneo*) constructs its nest from mud and grasses in the shape of an old-fashioned oven; while in open spaces many birds of prey can be spotted, the comical **caracaras, buzzard-eagles** and the magical **red-backed hawks** among them. The **Andean condor**, the bird most often associated with these mountains, is actually one of the more difficult species to see; although not especially rare they tend to soar at tremendous heights for most of the day, landing only on high, inaccessible cliffs or at carcasses after making sure that no one is around to disturb them. A glimpse of this magnificent bird soaring overhead on its 3m wing span will only come about either by frequent searching with binoculars or by a lucky break as you climb to hilltops in relatively unpopulated areas.

TROPICAL RAINFOREST

Descending the eastern edge of the Andes you pass through a number of distinct habitats including puna, shrub woods, cloud forest, high and then lowland jungle or rainforest. In spite of the rich and luxuriant appearance of the **RAINFOREST** it is in fact extremely fragile. Almost all the nutrients are recycled by rapid decomposition, with the aid of the damp climate and an incredible supply of insect labor, back into the vegetation—thereby creating a nutrient-poor soil that is highly susceptible to large-scale disturbance. When the forest is cleared, for example, usually in an attempt to colonize the area and turn it into viable farmland, there is not only heavy soil erosion to contend with but also a limited amount of nutrients in the earth, only enough for 5 years' of good harvests and 20 years' poorer farming at the most. Natives of the rainforest have evolved cultural mechanisms by which, on the whole, these problems are avoided: they tend to live in small, dispersed groups, move their gardens every few years, and obey sophisticated social controls to limit the chances of overhunting any one zone or any particular species.

The most distinctive attribute of the **AMAZON BASIN** is the overwhelming abundance of plant and animal species. Over 6000 species of plants have been reported from one small 250-acre tract of forest, and there are at least a thousand species of birds and dozens of types of monkeys and bats spread about the Peruvian Amazon. There are several reasons for this marvelous natural diversity of flora and fauna. Most obviously, it is warm, there is abundant sunlight, and large quantities of mineral nutrients are washed down from the Andes—all of which help to produce the ideal conditions for forest growth. Secondly, the rainforest has enormous structural diversity, with layers of vegetation from the forest floor to the canopy 30m above providing an infinity of niches to fill. Thirdly, since there is such a variety of habitat as you descend the Andes, the changes in altitude mean a great diversity of localized ecosystems. And lastly, because the rainforest has been more stable over longer periods of time than temperate areas (there was no Ice Age here, nor any prolonged period of drought), the fauna has had freedom to evolve, and to adapt to often very specialized local conditions.

But if the Amazon Basin is where most of the plant and animal species are, it is also the most difficult place to see them. Movement through the thick vegetation is extremely limited and the only real chance for extensive observation is along the rivers from a boat. The river banks and flood plains are richly diverse areas: here you are likely to see **caymans, macaws, toucans, oropendulas, terns, horned screamers**, and the primitive **hoatzins**—birds whose young are born with claws at the wrist to enable them to climb up from the water into the branches of overhanging trees. You should catch sight, too, of one of a variety of **hawks** and at least two or three species of **monkeys** (perhaps the **spider monkey**, the **howler**, or the **capuchin**). And with a lot of luck and more determined observation you may spot a rare **giant river otter, river dolphin, capybara**, or maybe even one of the **jungle cats**.

In the jungle proper you're more likely to find mammals such as the **pecary** (wild pig), **tapir, tamandua tree sloth**, and the second largest cat in the world, the incredibly powerful **spotted jaguar**. Characteristic of the deeper forest zones too are many species of birds, including **hummingbirds** (more common in the forested Andean foothills), **manakins**, and **trogons**, though the effects of widespread hunting make it difficult to see these around any of the larger settlements. Logging is proving to be another major problem for the forest wildlife since with the valuable trees dispersed among vast areas of mixed tree species in the rainforest, a very large area must be disturbed to yield a relatively small amount of lumber. Deeper into the forest, however, and the farther you are from human habitation, a glimpse of any of these animals is quite possible.

As preparation for all this, **LIMA ZOO**, in the Parque de las Leyerdas, is well worth a visit. It contains a good collection of most of the animals mentioned above, particularly the predators, and since there are no handy field guides (a book based on "Animals of Peru" would be a very neat aid for travelers) this is about the best way to familiarize yourself with what you might see during the rest of your journey. Be prepared, however, to see animals kept in appalling conditions. You might also check out the **Natural History Museum** in Lima and the Ministry of Agriculture's "*Vida Silvestre*" section for publications and off-prints on Peruvian flora and fauna.

Among the few directly relevant books currently in print are:

M. Koepke *The Birds of the Department of Lima* (Harrowood Books, Newtown Square, PA)

South American Birds (Harrowood Books). A photographic aid to identification.

Parker, Parker, and Plengue *A Checklist of the Birds of Peru* (Buteo Books)A useful summary with photos of different habitats.

R. M. de Shounnsee and Phelps *The Birds of Venezuela* (Princeton Univ. Press).

CONFLICTING INTERESTS IN THE JUNGLE

Within the next twenty years Peru's jungle Indians may cease to exist in in the face of persistent and increasing pressure from external colonization. The indigenous people of the Peruvian jungles are being pushed off their land as these words are being written by coca-growing farmers organized by drug-trafficking "mafiosa barons." Daily, at present, their land and culture are being eroded by these invaders of Indian territory who, like the lumber companies, miners, and other cash croppers, are content to destroy one area of forest after another like a plague of locusts.

All along the main rivers and jungle roads, settlers (and missionaries) are flooding into the area—and in their wake, forcing land title agreements to which they have no conceivable right, are the main lumber companies and multinational oil corporations. In large tracts of the jungle the fragile *selva* ecology has already been destroyed; in others the tribes have been more subtly disrupted by becoming dependent on outside consumer goods and trade. But, most importantly, the sustainable Indian economy is being disrupted and becoming obsolete, leaving behind it, after the initial timber and chemical exploitation, nothing but irredeemable waste. Forest land does not respond well to prolonged intensive cultivation.

Since the early 1970s the Indians — and in particular the **Campa Ashaninka communities** from the much threatened Ene river area — have been coordinating opposition. Representatives, working sometimes in conjunction with the Indian aid groups *CIPA* and *Acopeta*, have gone more and more regularly to Lima to get publicity and assert indigenous Indian claims to land titles on the **Ene** and **Tambo**, the only regions left to them after four centuries of "civilizing" influence. In publicity terms they have met with some success. The exploitation of the forests has become a political issue, fueled ironically within Peru (and outside) by the bizarre events surrounding Werner Herzog's filming of *Fitzcarraldo*, a film *about* exploitation of Indians, yet whose arrogant and exploitative director so angered local commmunities that at one stage a whole production camp was burned down. And the Indians, certainly, have undergone a radical growth in political awareness. In real terms, though, they have made no progress. Former President Belaunde, whose promises of human rights in the late 1970s led to many thousands of Campas making their way down to polling stations by raft to vote for him, has merely speeded up the process of colonization. The 1974 *Law of Native Communities*, which specifies indigenous land rights, has been almost totally ignored. And at present in the Ene region alone, the Indians face multinational claims to millions of acres of their territory.

Below, an eloquent witness to the problems, and to the way of life that colonists and corporations are rushing to destroy, is an account by a local **Amarakaeri Indian** from the southeast province of Madre de Dios. This account was originally given as testimony to a human rights movement in Lima. It is reprinted by permission of *Survival International*.

"We Indians were born, work, live, and die in the basin of the Madre de Dios River of Peru. It's our land—the only thing we have, with its plants, animals, and small farms: an environment we understand and use well. We are not like those from outside who want to clear everything away, destroying the richness and leaving the forest ruined forever. We respect the forest; we make it produce for us.

Many people ask why we want so much land. They think we do not work all of it. But we work it differently from them, conserving it so that it will continue to produce for our children and grandchildren. Although some people want to take it from us, they then destroy and abandon it, moving on elsewhere. But we can't do that; we were born in our woodlands. Without them we will die.

In contrast to other parts of the Peruvian jungle, Madre de Dios is still relatively sparsely populated. The woodlands are extensive, the soil's poor, so we work differently from those in other areas with greater population, less woodland, and more fertile soils. Our systems do not work without large expanses of land. The people who come from outside do not know how to make the best of natural resources here. Instead they devote themselves to taking away what nature gives and leave little or nothing behind. They take wood, nuts, and above all gold.

The man from the highlands works all day doing the same thing whether it is washing gold, cutting down trees, or something else. Bored, he chews his coca, eats badly, then gets ill and leaves. The engineers just drink their coffee and watch others working.

We also work these things but so as to allow the woodland to replenish itself. We cultivate our farms, hunt, fish, and gather woodland fruits, so we do not have to bring in supplies from outside. We also make houses, canoes, educate our children, enjoy ourselves. In short we satisfy almost all our needs with our own work, and without destroying the environment.

In the upper Madre de Dios River wood is more important than gold, and the sawmill of Shintuya is one of the most productive in the region. Wood is also worked in other areas to make canoes and boats to sell, and for building houses for the outsiders. In the lower region of the River we gather nuts—another important part of our economy. Much is said about Madre de Dios being the forgotten Department of Peru. Yet we are not forgotten by people from outside nor by some national and foreign companies who try to seize our land and resources. Because of this we have formed the *Federation of Indian Peoples of Madre de Dios* to fight for the defense of our lands and resources.

Since 1974 we have been asking for legal property titles to the land we occupy in accordance with the Law of Indian Communities. The authorities always promise them to us, but so far only one of our communities has a title and that is to barely 5000 hectares.

You may ask why we want titles now if we had not had them before. The answer is that we now have to defend our lands from many people who were not threatening us in the past.

In spite of journeys to Puerto Maldonado to demand guarantees from the authorities, they do not support us by removing the people who invade our land. On the contrary when we defend our land, forcing the invaders to retreat, they accuse us of being wild, fierce, and savage.

Equally serious are invasions by gold mining companies. The Peruvian State considers the issue of mining rights to be separate from that of land rights, and there are supposed to be laws giving priority to Indian communities for mining rights on their lands—but the authorities refuse to enforce them. Many people have illegally obtained rights to mine our lands, then they do not allow us to work there. Others, without rights, have simply installed themselves.

There are numerous examples I could give; yet when my community refused entry to a North American adventurer who wanted to install himself on our land, the Lima *Commercio* accused us of being savages, and of attacking him with arrows. Lies! All we did was defend our land against invaders who didn't even have legal mining rights—without using any weapons, although these men all carried their own guns.

We also suffer from forms of economic aggression. The prices of agricultural products we sell to the truck drivers and other traders in the area have recently been fixed by the authorities. For example, 25lb of yucca used to sell for 800 *soles*. Now we can only get 400 *soles*. Such low prices stop us developing our agriculture further, and we are not able to sell our products outside because we cannot cover our costs and minimal needs. On the other hand, the authorities have fixed the prices of wood and transport so that the amount that we can earn is continually diminishing. And the prices we have to pay for things we need from outside is always rising.

There are also problems with the National Park Police. They no longer allow us to fish with *barbasco* (fish poison) in the waters of our communities, although they are outside the National Park. They say that *barbasco* will destroy the fish. But we have fished this way for so long as we can remember, and the fish have not been destroyed. On the contrary: the fish are destroyed when people come from outside and overfish for commercial sale, especially when they use dynamite.

Our main source of food, after agriculture, is fishing—above all the *boquichico* which we fish with bow and arrow after throwing *barbasco*. We cannot stop eating, and we are not going to let them stop us from fishing with *barbasco* either!

There are so many more problems. If our economic position is bad, our social position is even worse. Traders reach the most remote areas, but medical facilities don't, even now with serious epidemics of malaria, measles, tuberculosis, and intestinal parasites in the whole region. Our children go to primary schools in some communities, but often the schools are shut. And there are no secondary schools.

The commercial centers in the gold zone are areas of permanent drunkenness. Outsiders deceive and insult us and now some of our people no longer want to be known as Indians or speak our languages; they go to the large towns to hide from their origins and culture.

We are not opposed to others living and benefiting from the jungle, nor are we opposed to its development. On the contrary, what we want is that this development should benefit us, and not just the companies and colonists who come from outside. And we want the resources of the jungle to be conserved so that they can serve future generations of both colonists and Indians."

SURVIVAL INTERNATIONAL

If you want to know more about—or keep up to date on—the cause of forest Indians in Peru, the best people to contact are **Survival International**, a charity established to publicize and support worldwide the struggles of tribal people towards self-determination. *Survival* has groups throughout the U.S. and the rest of the world, who support aid projects for tribal land rights, health, and education, publish literature and reports, and provide speakers, bookstalls, and exhibitions. Their main national branches are:

WASHINGTON: 2121 Decatur Place NW, Washington D.C. 20008 (☎202-265 1077).

LONDON: 310 Edgware Road, London W2 1DY (☎01-723-5535).

PARIS: 45 Rue du Faubourg du Temple, 75010 (☎42-41-47-62)

MILAN, ITALY: Via Ludovico di Breme 48, Milan 20156 (☎2-306-202)

MADRID: Apartado de Correos 46.469, Madrid

PERU'S WHITE GOLD

At isolated stations like Ayaviri on the desolate Peruvian altiplano, ragged children clamber daily into the train waving oranges and sweetcorn. Behind them follow their stout mothers thrusting woolen sweaters and socks towards tourists as they shout "Alpaca! Alpaca!" Generally unable to sell anything, most mountain Indians find it virtually impossible to make a living from weaving or agriculture any more.

The only people who make decent money engage in "cooking" **cocaine**. Illegal "kitchens," makeshift coke refineries, have become the main means of livelihood for many ordinary peasant families. Peru's coca industry netted an estimated $3 billion in 1984—20 percent of the country's gross national product. At the end of the 1980s this figure is much higher and the cocaine problem now an issue of global dimensions.

Coca, the plant from which cocaine is derived, has traveled a long way since the Incas distributed this "divine plant" across fourteenth-century Andean Peru. Presented as a gift from the gods, coca was used to exploit slave labor under the Spanish rule: without it the Indians would never have worked in the gruelling conditions of colonial mines such as Potosí.

The isolation of the active ingredient in coca, cocaine, in 1859 began an era of intense medical experimentation. Its numbing effects have been appreciated by dental patients around the world, and even Pope Leo XIII enjoyed a bottle of the coca wine produced by an Italian physician who amassed a great fortune from its sale in the nineteenth century. The literary world, too, was soon stimulated by this white powder: in 1885 Robert Louis Stevenson wrote *"Dr. Jekyll and Mr. Hyde"* during six speedy days and nights while taking this "wonder drug" as a remedy for his tuberculosis, and Sir Arthur Conan Doyle, writing in the 1890s, used the character of Sherlock Holmes to defend the use of cocaine. On a more popular level, coca was one of the essential ingredients in Coca Cola until 1906. Today, cocaine is the most fashionable—and expensive—of drugs.

From its humble origins cocaine has become very big business. Unofficially, it may well be the biggest export for countries like Peru and Bolivia, where coca grows best in the Andes and along the edge of the jungle. While most mountain peasants always cultivated a little for personal use, many have now become dependent on it for obvious economic reasons: coca is easily the most profitable cash crop and is readily bought by middlemen operating for extremely wealthy cocaine barons. A constant flow of semi-refined coca—*pasta*, the basic paste—leaves Peru aboard Amazon river boats or unmarked light aircraft heading for the big-time laboratories in Colombia. From here the pure stuff is shipped or flown out, mostly to the U.S. via Miami or Los Angeles.

Reputed to be a "fun drug," few people care to look beyond the wall of illicit intrigue that surrounds this highly salable contraband. In the same vein as coffee or chocolate, the demand for this product has become another means through which the privileged world directly dictates and controls the lives of Third World peasant farmers. As more Peruvian Indians follow world market trends by turning their hands to the growing and "cooking" of coca, their more staple crops like cereals, tubers, and beans are cultivated less and less.

It's a change brought about partly by circumstance. Agricultural prices are state-controlled, but manufactured goods and transportation costs rise almost weekly, preventing the peasants from earning a decent living from their crops. Moreover, the soil is poor and crops grow unwillingly. Coca, on the other hand, grows readily at the most barren heights and needs little attention. Revered by the Indians for centuries for its stimulant and hunger-suppressing effects, the plant now promises wealth as well.

The kitchens are in cottages or backyards, and the equipment is simple—oil drums, a few chemicals, paraffin, and a fire. Bushels of coca leaves are dissolved in paraffin and hydrochloric acid, heated, and stirred, eventually producing the *pasta*, which is then washed in ether or acetone to yield powdery white cocaine.

For this work the peasant receives the equivalent of $7, better than the average daily wage of about 60¢. He may produce kilograms of cocaine, which goes to the dealer. This man supplies the chemicals, and perhaps some of the leaves, and lives in town. He is well off, selling the cocaine in Peru for about $12 a gram—an enormous profit. Dollars are accepted, but the Peruvian *sole* is not, at least not by the dealers in quantity.

By the time the cocaine reaches New York or Los Angeles, each gram is worth between $80 and $120, even more because of the pure coke's dilution by "cuts" such as lactose or talcum powder.

In the Department of Puno, on the shores of Lake Titicaca, the Capachica peninsula pokes like a crooked finger into the lake. No buses run there, and the dirt road is closed by a chain. Men lounging nearby mutter, "No entry": controlled by the Peruvian underworld, this peninsula is the site of many kitchens. No Civil Guard has visited it for years; the last occasions produced nothing but sniper fire. Since then it is said that the Civil Guards in Puno have become the richest in all Peru. Even the

presence of the PIP, the secret police, merely keeps the kitchens outside the town limits. Transportation is done along back roads at night.

The dealers invest much of their profits in legitimate enterprises, particularly clubs and restaurants, and 90 percent of the cocaine is exported, as few Peruvians have that sort of money to blow on blow. The peasant farmers, on the other hand, have temporarily given their landbase, time, and energy for the benefit of the dealers and hedonistic Westerners. While the coke trade is internationally deplored, the Peruvian peasant digging with his foot plow no doubt dreams of the chance to keep his radio supplied with batteries and maybe one day buy a truck, a more permanent key to wealth in the Andes. Anonymously connected to a fickle world market, the coca grower's lot is to hope that the chain of demand never falls drastically in relation to the supply.

With thanks to Dan Richardson for original research.

PERUVIAN RECIPES

Peruvian cooking—even in small restaurants well away from the big cities—is appealing stuff. The seven recipes below are among the classics, fairly simple to prepare and (with a couple of coastal exceptions) found throughout the country. If you're traveling and camping you'll find all the ingredients listed readily available in local markets; alternatives are suggested for trying them outside Peru. All quantities given are sufficient for four people.

Ceviche

A cool, spicy dish, eaten on the Peruvian coast for at least the past thousand years.

1kg soft white fish (lemon sole and halibut are good, or you can mix half fish, half shellfish)
2 large onions (sliced)
1 or 2 chilis (chopped)
6 limes (can use lemons but not so good)
1 tbsp. olive oil
1 tbsp. fresh coriander or cilantro leaves (chopped parsley is a poor substitute)
salt and pepper to taste

Wash and cut fish into bite-sized pieces. Place in a dish with sliced onions. Add the chopped chili and coriander. Make a marinade using the lime juice, olive oil, salt, and pepper. Pour over fish and place in a cool spot until the fish is "soft cooked" (from 10 to 60 min.). Serve with boiled potatoes (preferably sweet) and corn-on-the-cob.

Papas a la Huancaina

An excellent and ubiquitous snack—cold potatoes covered in a mildly *picante* cheese sauce.

1 kg potatoes (boiled)
1 or 2 chilis (chopped)
2 cloves of garlic (chopped)
200g soft goat's cheese (feta is ideal, cottage cheese all right)
6 saltines or soda crackers
1 hard-boiled egg
1 small can of evaporated milk

Chop very finely (or liquidize) all the above ingredients except for the potatoes. The mixture should be fairly thin but not too runny.

Pour sauce over thickly sliced potatoes. Arrange on a dish and serve garnished with lettuce and black olives. Best served chilled.

Palta Rellena

Stuffed avocados—another very popular snack.

2 avocados (soft but firm)
1 onion (chopped)
2 tomatoes (chopped)
2 hard-boiled eggs (chopped)
200g cooked chicken or tuna fish (cold and either chopped or flaked)
2 tbsp. mayonnaise

Cut avocados in half and remove stones. Scoop out a little of the flesh around hole. Gently combine all other ingredients before piling into the center of each avocado half.

Causa

About the easiest Peruvian dish to reproduce outside the country, though there are no real substitutes for Peruvian tuna and creamy Andean potatoes.

1kg potatoes
200g tuna fish
2 avocados (the riper the better)
4 tomatoes
4 tbsp. mayonnaise
salt and black pepper
1 lemon

Boil potatoes and mash to a firm, smooth consistency. Flake tuna fish and add a little lemon juice. Mash avocados to a pulp, add the rest of lemon juice, some salt and black pepper. Slice tomatoes. Press one quarter of the tuna fish over this, then a quarter of the avocado mixture on top. Add a layer of sliced tomato. Continue the same layering process until you have four layers of each. Cut into rough slices. Serve (ideally chilled) with salad, or on its own as an appetizer.

Locro de Zapallo

A vegetarian standard found on most set menus in the cheaper, working-class restaurants.

1kg pumpkin
1 large potato
2 cloves of garlic
1 tbsp. oregano
½ cup of milk
2 corn-on-the-cob

1 onion
1 chili (chopped)
salt and pepper
200g cheese (mozarella works well)

Fry onion, chili, garlic, and oregano. Add half a cup of water. Mix in the pumpkin as large cut lumps, slices of corn on the cob, and finely chopped potato. Add milk and cheese. Simmer until a soft, smooth consistency, and add a little more water if necessary. Serve with rice or over fish.

Pescado a la Chorillana

Probably the most popular way of cooking fish on the coast.

4 pieces of fish (cod or any other white fish will do)
2 large onions (chopped)
4 large tomatoes (chopped)
1 or 2 chilis (chopped into fairly large pieces)
1 tbsp. oil
½ cup of water

Grill or fry each portion of fish until done. Keep hot. Fry separately the onions, tomatoes, and chili. Add the water to form a sauce. Pile the hot sauce over each portion of fish and serve with rice.

Asado

Roast. An expensive meal for Peruvians, though a big favorite for family gatherings. Only available in fancier restaurants.

1kg or less of lean beef
2 cloves of garlic
200g butter
1 tin of tomato puree
salt and pepper
1 tbsp. soy sauce

2 tomatoes
1 chili (chopped)

Cover the beef with premixed garlic and butter. Mix tomato puree with salt, pepper, and soy sauce. Liquidize tomatoes with chopped chili. Spread both mixtures on the beef and cook slowly in a covered casserole dish—perhaps for 4 or 5 hours. Traditionally the *asado* is served with *pure de papas*, which is simply a runny form of mashed potatoes whipped up with some butter and a lot of garlic. A very tasty combination.

Quinoa Vegetable Soup

Quinoa—known as "mother grain" in the Andes—is "a natural whole grain with remarkable nutritional properties," quite possibly a "supergrain" of the future. It's simple and tasty to add to any soups or stews.

4 cups of water
¼ cup quinoa
½ cup diced carrots
¼ cup diced celery
2 tbsp. finely chopped onions
¼ of a green pepper
2 mashed cloves of garlic
1 tbsp. vegetable oil
½ cup chopped tomatoes
½ cup finely chopped cabbage
1 tbsp. salt
some chopped parsley

Gently fry the quinoa and all the vegetables (except the cabbage) in oil and garlic until browned. The add the water, cabbage and tomatoes before bringing to the boil. Season with salt and garnish with parsley.

Night Sky design from Mochica ceramic

ONWARDS FROM PERU

As illustrated by the incredible expansion of the Inca Empire, Peru is ideally situated to begin (or continue) an extended tour of the South American continent. Its Pacific coastline offers easy access by road north into Ecuador, towards the Gulf of Guayaquil and the fascinating Galapagos Islands, or south into the cooler climates of Chile. The southern sierra leads naturally across the Titicaca Basin into Bolivia; from here it's relatively simple to travel overland to Brazil or Argentina. Flowing down the eastern side of the Peruvian Andes, the Amazon (downriver from Iquitos) connects with Brazil and Colombia, as well as offering an alternative ("scenic") route into Equador via the Río Napo. Whichever way you go onwards from Peru the journey can't fail to cover a variety of startlingly different landscapes, climates, and cultures. By the same token no other South American country offers as broad a range of attractions as Peru, and it's hard to advise you to leave. Perhaps the most popular overland trip is south or east via Bolivia.

BOLIVIA

Twice the size of Spain, **BOLIVIA** sits on top of the Andes, cut off from the Pacific but rolling down its high plains into the southeast corner of the Amazon Basin. Politically very unstable, Bolivia's power games have been complicated by the intrigues of its booming cocaine industry, and although **Sucre** is the legal capital, **La Paz** is in practice the center of government and commerce. Fortunately it's generally safe and easy to travel around the country, whatever might be happening in La Paz. The country is easily entered by **bus or boat train** from **Puno** in Peru, or **by air** from **Lima** and **Cuzco**. Many travelers continue by train across the Andes to Antofagasta on the Chilean coast, although a more popular route is the breathtaking railroad from Santa Cruz via Corumba to São Paulo on the Brazilian Atlantic. **Tourist cards**, usually valid for 90 days, are available for all nationalities except those of Communist countries

(who'll need to approach embassies or consulates). Most of Bolivia's health hazards are similar to those of Peru and the relevant **inoculations** are the same—typhoid, paratyphoid, yellow fever, gamma globulin, and antimalaria pills if you intend to visit the jungle zone.

CHILE

Smaller but longer than Peru, the narrow strip of **CHILE** reaches right down the Pacific coastline to Tierra del Fuego. An extremely beautiful country with deserts in the north and tall pine forests in the south, its controversial and oppressive politics belie the friendliness of the people. Since President Allende's Marxist coalition was violently overthrown by the army in 1973, the country has been dictatorially run by General Pinochet, apparently with a lot of CIA help. Although it's possible to approach Chile by **air** from **Lima**, the **bus trip to Santiago** is a much more rewarding journey (particularly if you break it at **Arequipa, Arica**, and **Antofagasta**). Chile also has rail links with both Bolivia and Argentina. **Tourist cards** for a 90-day period are available from Chilean consulates and many airline offices throughout South America—only African nationals and citizens of Communist countries need visas. Healthwise Chile is generally safer than Peru but typhoid **inoculations** are still recommended.

BRAZIL

BRAZIL is an attractive goal, particularly for anyone into long river journeys or the jazzy rhythms of good live music (in or out of the February fiestas). Virtually the same size as the mainland U.S., Brazil is the fifth largest country in the world. The Amazon Basin's tropical forest takes (or took) up much of the land, though it is bounded in the north by the Guiana Highlands and in the south by the Brazilian mountains. Most of its 120 million people, however, are concentrated on the narrow coastal belt, a mixture these days of heavy industry, trendy beach resorts, and dire poverty.

To approach Brazil from Peru can require some planning. Rio can be reached by **air** from **Lima**, but from **Iquitos** flights rarely go farther than Manaus. **Overland** the easiest route is through Bolivia to Santa Cruz, then by train via **Corumba** to São Paulo. A more adventurous journey takes the most-obvious route—**down the Amazon** from **Pucallpa** and **Iquitos** to Manaus, or even as far as Belem on the Atlantic; some of these can also be routed along the amazing trans-Amazonica highway. There are three more rugged land links between Peru and Brazil. One goes by plane (though it is possible on foot and in canoes) from Pucallpa to **Cruzeiro do Sul**. A more recent link is made these days by the occasional truck from Puerto Maldonado in southeastern Peru to Inapari where the river is the frontier with Brazil at **Assis**. Also from Puerto Maldonado, some people travel downstream on the Madre de Dios, through Bolivian jungle and on into the Brazilian *Rio Madeira*, which eventually makes its way to the Amazon at **Manuas**. **Visas** are necessary for most nationalities including U.S., but not for Western European tourists. All visitors, however, are required to provide evidence of sufficient funds to survive in and eventually get out of the country (standard stamp for 90 days). **Inoculations** recommended for Brazil include typhoid, paratyphoid, cholera, yellow fever, and (for children) poliomyelitis; antimalarial pills and water sterilizing tablets are also a good idea. Bubonic plague, too, has caused increasing devastation in restricted zones over recent years—best to make inquiries about this at Brazilian tourist offices when you arrive.

COLOMBIA

One of the lesser visited but most interesting of South American countries, **COLOMBIA** is an invigorating land with diverse mountain and jungle terrain and with both Pacific and Caribbean coasts. Liberals and conservatives have battled for power since World War II; at present the country has a conservative president. More recently there's been a growth in active terrorism and extremist splinter groups—though this rarely affects conditions for travelers—many of which are linked in with Colombia's largest problem of being the world's primary international cocaine processing and distribution center. Robbery, however, happens a lot: be careful.

From Peru most people approach Colombia **by air** from **Lima** to Bogota, or **overland through Ecuador** (two or three days). From **Iquitos**, however, Colombia's Amazon zone can be entered **by river** at Leticia—a tough river trip to "civilization" at Puerto Asis, but superb for wildlife. Only an onward ticket is needed for Western European passport holders, though U.S. citizens require a **visa** from an embassy or consulate (on provision of two photos and return/onward ticket) or two-week transit visas which are issued on board aircraft. For Australians and New Zealanders a visa is also necessary and it's important to apply in plenty of time. **Inoculations** recommended include: typhoid, paratyphoid, and gamma globulin (antimalaria pills are useful for certain areas).

ECUADOR

ECUADOR, a relatively small country squeezed out towards the Pacific, away from the Amazon, by Colombia and Peru, is dominated by two beautiful highland ranges separated by a central valley. The population is essentially split between the fertile coast and the sierra, with very little settlement in the eastern jungles and extensive rural migration to the two main cities—**Quito** and **Guayaquil**.

A simple overland approach from Peru via **Tumbes** or **La Tina** takes you in a day to Guayaquil. From here there's a magnificent railroad to **Quito** in the mountains. Virtually all nationalities are given a **tourist card** for up to 90 days on arrival, though sometimes travelers are asked to provide evidence of $20 for every day they intend to stay in the country. The usual **inoculations** are recommended: typhoid, paratyphoid, gamma globulin, and yellow fever, along with antimalaria pills for everywhere but the highlands.

USEFUL GUIDEBOOKS

Lastly a few **books** you might find of use outside Peru. For **South America as a whole** the *South American Handbook* (Prentice Hall, $29.95) is the standard—a bible for most overland travelers, and adequate (if not always culturally illuminating) for each of the continent's nations. Along similar lines, and also with its good points, is Geoff Crowther's *South America on a Shoestring* (Lonely Planet, $6.95). Individually, in **Ecuador**, Rob Rachowiecki's *Climbing and Hiking in Ecuador* (Bradt Publications, $8.50) is trusty—and newly researched. For **Mexico** John Fisher's *REAL GUIDE* (Prentice Hall, $11.95) is very good. A *REAL GUIDE* to Brazil is also planned.

LANGUAGE

Although Peru is officially a Spanish-speaking nation, a large proportion of its population, possibly more than half, regard Spanish as their second language. When the Conquistadors arrived, Quechua, the official language of the Inca Empire, was widely spoken everywhere but the jungle. Originally known as *Runasimi* **(from** *runa,* **person, and** *simis,* **mouth) the name Quechua—which means "high Andean valleys"—was coined by the Spanish.**

Quechua was not, however, the only pre-Columbian tongue. There were, and still are, well over thirty Indian languages within the jungle area and, up until the late nineteenth century, *Mochica* had been widely spoken on the north coast for at least 1500 years.

With such a rich linguistic history it is not surprising to find non-European words intruding constantly into any Peruvian conversation. *Cancha,* for instance, the Inca word for court-yard, is still commonly used to refer to most sporting areas—*la cancha de basketball* for example. Other linguistic survivors have even reached the English language: *llama, condor, puma,* and *pampa* among them. Perhaps more interesting is the great wealth of traditional **Creole slang**—utilized with equal vigor at all levels of society. This complex speech, much like London's Cockney rhyming slang, is difficult to catch without almost complete fluency in Spanish, though one phrase you may find useful for directing a taxi driver is *de fresa alfonso*—literally translatable as "of strawberry, Alfonso" but actually meaning "straight on" (*de frente al fondo*).

Once you get into it **Spanish** is the easiest language there is—and in Peru people are eager to understand even the most faltering attempt. You'll be further helped by the fact that South Americans speak relatively slowly (at least compared to Spaniards in Spain) and that there's no need to get your tongue round the difficult lisping pronunciation.

PRONUNCIATION

The rules of **pronunciation** are pretty straight-forward and, once you get to know them, strictly observed. Unless there's an accent, words ending in d, l, r, and z are **stressed** on the last syllable, all others on the second last. All **vowels** are pure and short.

A somewhere between the "A" sound of back and that of father

E as in get

I as in police

O as in hot

U as in rule

C is soft before E and I, hard otherwise: *cerca* is pronounced serka.

G works the same way, a guttural "H" sound (like the *ch* in loch) before E or I, a hard G elsewhere—*gigante* becomes "higante".

H is always silent

J the same sound as a guttural G: *jamon* is pronounced hamon.

LL sounds like an English Y: *tortilla* is pronounced torteeya.

N is as in English unless it has a tilde (accent) over it, when it becomes NY: *mañana* sounds like manyana.

QU is pronounced like an English K.

R is rolled, RR doubly so.

V sounds more like B, *vino* becoming beano.

X is slightly softer than in English—sometimes almost SH—except between vowels in place names where it has an "H" sound—e.g. México (Meh-Hee-Ko) or Oaxaca.

Z is the same as a soft C, so *cerveza* becomes servesa.

Overleaf is a list of a few essential words and phrases, though if you're traveling for any length of time a dictionary or phrase book is obviously a worthwhile investment—some specifically Latin-American ones are available (see over). If you're using a **dictionary**, bear in mind that in Spanish CH, LL, and Ñ count as separate letters and are listed after the Cs, Ls, and Ns respectively.

B A S I C S

Yes, No	*Si, No*	Open, Closed	*Abierto/a, Cerrado/a*
Please, Thank you	*Por favor, Gracias*	With, Without	*Con, Sin*
Where, When	*Donde, Cuando*	Good, Bad	*Buen(o)/a, Mal(o)/a*
What, How much	*Qué, Cuanto*	Big, Small	*Gran(de), Pequeño/a*
Here, There	*Aqui, Alli*	More, Less	*Mas, Menos*
This, That	*Este, Eso*	Today, Tomorrow	*Hoy, Mañana*
Now, Later	*Ahora, Mas tarde*	Yesterday	*Ayer*

G R E E T I N G S A N D R E S P O N S E S

Hello, Goodbye	*Ola, Adios*	I (don't) understand	*(No) Entiendo*
Good morning	*Buenos días*	Do you speak English?	*¿Habla (usted) Ingles?*
Good afternoon/ night	*Buenas tardes/noches*	I don't speak Spanish	*(No) Hablo Castellano*
See you later	*Hasta luego*	My name is . . .	*Me llamo . . .*
Sorry	*Lo siento/disculpeme*	What's your name?	*¿Como se llama usted?*
Excuse me	*Con permiso/perdón*	I am Canadian/	*Soy canadiense/*
How are you?	*¿Como está (usted)?*	American	*estadunidense.*
Not at all/You're welcome	*De nada*	(literally, 'unitedstatesian')	

N E E D S — H O T E L S A N D T R A N S P O R T

I want	*Quiero*	Left, right, straight on	*Izquierda, derecha, derecho*
I'd like	*Querría*		
Do you know . . . ?	*¿Sabe . . . ?*	Where is . . . ?	*¿Donde esta . . . ?*
I don't know	*No se*	. . . the bus station	*. . . la estación de autobuses*
There is (is there) ?	*(¿)Hay (?)*		
Give me . . .	*Deme . . .*	. . . the railway station	*. . . la estación de ferrocarriles*
(one like that)	*(uno asi)*		
Do you have . . . ?	*¿Tiene . . . ?*	. . . the nearest bank	*. . . el banco mas cercano*
. . . the time	*. . . la hora*		
. . . a room	*. . . un cuarto*	. . . the post office	*. . . el correo (la oficina de correos)*
. . . with two beds/ double bed	*. . . con dos camas/ cama matrimonial*		
		. . . the toilet	*. . . el baño/ sanitario*
It's for one person (two people)	*Es para una persona (dos personas)*		
. . . for one night (one week)	*. . . para una noche (una semana)*	Where does the bus to . . . leave from?	*¿De donde sale el camion para . . . ?*
It's fine, how much is it?	*¿Está bien, cuanto es?*	Is this the train for Lima?	*¿Es este el tren para Lima?*
It's too expensive	*Es demasiado caro*		
Don't you have anything cheaper?	*¿No tiene algo más barato?*	I'd like a (return) ticket to . . .	*Querría un boleto (de ida y vuelta) para . . .*
Can one . . . ?	*¿Se puede . . . ?*	What time does it leave (arrive in . . .)?	*¿A qué hora sale (llega en . . .)?*
. . . camp (near) here?	*¿ . . . acampar aqui (cerca)?*	What is there to eat?	*¿Qué hay para comer?*
Is there a hotel nearby?	*¿Hay un hotel aquí cerca?*	What's that?	*¿Qué es eso?*
How do I get to . . . ?	*¿Por donde se va a . . . ?*	What's this called in Spanish?	*¿Como se llama este en Castellano?*

NUMBERS AND DAYS

1	un/uno/una	20	veinte	1989	mil novocientos
2	dos	21	veintiuno		ochenta y nueve
3	tres	30	treinta		
4	cuatro	40	cuarenta	first	primero/a
5	cinco	50	cincuenta	second	segundo/a
6	seis	60	sesenta	third	tercero/a
7	siete	70	setenta		
8	ocho	80	ochenta	Monday	lunes
9	nueve	90	noventa	Tuesday	martes
10	diez	100	cien(to)	Wednesday	miercoles
11	once	101	ciento uno	Thursday	jueves
12	doce	200	doscientos	Friday	viernes
13	trece	201	doscientos uno	Saturday	sabado
14	catorce	500	quinientos	Sunday	domingo.
15	quince	1000	mil		
16	diez y seis	2000	dos mil		

PHRASEBOOKS AND DICTIONARIES

Any good Spanish phrasebook or dictionary should see you through in Peru; but specifically Latin-American ones are a help—*Berlitz Latin-American Spanish for Travelers* (Macmillan $4.95), *Teach Yourself Everyday Spanish* (McKay $6.95), and the University of Chicago *Spanish-English, English-Spanish Dictionary* (Pocket, $3.95) are all worthwhile.

PERUVIAN TERMS: A GLOSSARY

APU mountain god

ALLYU kinship group, or clan

ARRIERO muleteer

BARRIO suburb (sometimes a shanty town)

BURRO donkey

CACIQUE headman

CALLE street

CALLEJÓN corridor, or narrow street

CEJA DE LA SELVA edge of the jungle

CHACRA cultivated garden or plot

CHAQUIRAS pre-Columbian stone or coral beads

CHICHA maize beer

COLECTIVO collective taxi

CORDILLERA mountain range

CURACA chief

CURANDERO healer

EMPRESA company

ENCOMIENDA colonial grant of land and native labor

FARMACIA chemist

FLACO, FLACA skinny (common nickname)

GORDO, GORDA fat(common nickname)

GRINGA, GRINGO European or North American (female/male); a very common term, occasionally replaced by EXTRANJERO (foreigner)

HACIENDA estate

HUACA sacred spot or object

HUACO pre-Columbian artifact; hence **HUAQUERO**, someone who digs or looks for *huacos*

JIRÓN road

LOMAS place where vegetation grows with moisture from the air rather than from rainfall or irrigation

MAMACONA Inca Sun Virgin

PEÑA nightclub with live music

PLATA silver—so slang for "cash"

POBLADO settlement

PUEBLOS JOVENES shantytowns

PUNA barren Andean heights

QUEBRADA stream

SELVA jungle; hence **SELVATICO/A**, jungle dweller

SIERRA mountains; hence **SERRANO**, mountain dweller

SOROCHE altitude sickness

TAMBO Inca Highway rest-house

TIENDA shop

TRAMITES red tape, bureaucracy

UNSU throne, or platform

INDEX